The Economist
BUSINESS
TRAVELLER'S
GUIDES

FRANCE

The Economist
BUSINESS
TRAVELLER'S
GUIDES

FRANCE

The
Economist
PUBLICATIONS

PRENTICE HALL PRESS
NEW YORK

This edition published in the United States and Canada in 1988 by
Prentice Hall Press
A division of Simon & Schuster, Inc.
Gulf + Western Building
One Gulf + Western Plaza
New York, New York 10023

PRENTICE HALL PRESS is a trademark of Simon & Schuster, Inc.

Guidebook information is notoriously subject to being outdated by changes to telephone numbers and opening hours, and by fluctuating hotel and restaurant standards. While every care has been taken in the preparation of this guide, the publishers cannot accept any liability for any consequences arising from the use of information contained herein.

Where opinion is expressed it is that of the author, which does not necessarily coincide with the editorial views of The Economist newspaper.

The publishers welcome corrections and suggestions from business travellers; please write to The Editor, *The Economist Business Traveller's Guides,* 40 Duke Street, London W1A 1DW, United Kingdom.

Series Editor Stephen Brough
Assistant Series Editor Brigid Avison
Editors Derek Barton (*overview*);
Stephen Dobell (*travel*)
Designer Alistair Plumb
Sub-editor Patricia Burgess
Editorial assistants Mary Pickles,
Bettina Whilems
Researchers Stephen Irving,
Holly Joulia
Design assistants Clare Bryan,
Lynn Hector
Indexer Fiona Barr

Maps and diagrams by Oxford Illustrators
Typeset by SB Datagraphics, Colchester, England
Printed in Italy by Arnoldo Mondadori, Verona

Contributors *overview* John Aqrab, John Ardagh, Ian Carson, Roberta Dahdi, Ian Furnivall, Michael Harrison, David Jeffries, Mario Kakabadse, Dinah Louda, Gill O'Meara, Bridie Pritchard, Michael Stone, Michael Sutton, Claire Wilson; *travel* John Ardagh, Susie Boulton, Peter Graham, Vivienne Menkes-Ivry

Consultants Richard Green, Michael Sutton, Derek Wise

Copyright © 1988 The Economist Publications Ltd and Webster's Business Traveller's Guides Ltd
Maps and diagrams copyright © 1988 The Economist Publications Ltd and Webster's Business Traveller's Guides Ltd

Library of Congress Cataloging-in-Publication Data
The Economist business traveller's guides. France.
  Includes index.
  1. France – Description and travel 1975 – Guide-books. 2. Business travel – France – Guide-books.
  3. France – Commerce – Handbooks, manuals, etc.
  I. Economist (London, England)
DC16.E28 1988
914.4'04838—dc1987-35948
ISBN 0-13-227521-X

Contents

Glossary

Agent commercial Self-employed sales representative.

Agent de change Stockbroker or dealer.

Bourse Stock exchange.

CAC index (*Compagnie des Agents de Change*) The most widely used stock indicator in the Paris market.

CAP Common agricultural policy of the EC.

CEA *Commissariat à l'Energie Atomique.*

CGT Communist trade union.

CNPF (*Conseil National du Patronat Français*) Employers' federation.

Commissariat Général au Plan Prestigious central economic planning authority, downgraded by the Chirac government in late 1987.

Commission Bancaire Regulatory body for the banking industry.

DATAR (*Délégation à l'Aménagement du Territoire et à l'Action Régionale*) State body responsible for regional development and the promotion of overseas investment in France, especially for job creation.

Dirigisme State intervention or supervision of economic affairs.

EC European Community, also known as the Common Market. Founded in 1957; by 1987 had 12 members: Belgium, Denmark, Eire, France, Greece, Italy, Luxembourg, the Netherlands, Portugal, Spain, the UK and West Germany.

EDF *Electricité de France.*

EFTA European Free Trade Association: Norway, Sweden, Austria, Iceland, Switzerland and, with associate membership, Finland.

EMS European monetary system, created in 1979 to aid management of the exchange rates between European currencies.

Etatisme State socialism, state control.

GATT General Agreement on Tariffs and Trade. Instituted in 1947 to liberalize trade and prevent discrimination. Over 100 countries are signatories.

GDF *Gaz de France.*

GDP Gross Domestic Product. The best measure of a country's economic performance, GDP is the total value of a country's annual output of goods and services. It is normally valued at market prices; GDP can, however, be calculated at factor cost, by subtracting indirect taxes and adding subsidies. To eliminate the effects of inflation, GDP growth is usually expressed in constant prices.

GIE (*Groupement d'intérêt économique*) Economic interest grouping.

GNP Gross National Product. A country's GDP plus residents' income from investments abroad minus income accruing to nonresidents from investments in the country.

Green Plan Federal schemes for rural regeneration.

IBRD The International Bank for Reconstruction and Development (also known as the World Bank), the largest single source of development aid.

INSEE Central government statistical agency.

NATO North Atlantic Treaty Organization. The alliance for the defence of the West against the Soviet Union. Formed in 1949, it includes the USA and Canada and most West European nations with the notable exception of France which withdrew in 1966.

OPEC Organization of Petroleum-Exporting Countries.

Pieds noirs White settlers or inhabitants of French colonies, particularly in North Africa.

Plan d'Epargne National savings plan.

SA (*Société Anonyme*) Corporation.

SARL (*Société à Responsabilité Limitée*) Limited liability company.

SICAV (*Sociétés d'Investissement à Capital Variable*) Unit investment trust.

SNCF (*Société Nationale des Chemins de Fer Français*) French national railways.

TEE Trans Europ Express

TGV (*Train à Grande Vitesse*) The high-speed train used on main business routes throughout France.

TVA (*Taxe sur la valeur ajoutée*) Value-added tax, a form of indirect taxation borne by the final consumer.

Taux de base bancaire Bank base rate.

Using the guide

The Economist Business Traveller's Guide to France is an encyclopedia of business and travel information. If in doubt about where to look for specific information, consult either the Contents list or the Index.

City guides

Each city guide follows a standard format: information and advice on arriving, getting around, city areas, hotels, restaurants, bars, entertainment, shopping, sightseeing, sports and fitness, and a directory of local business and other facilities such as secretarial and translation agencies, couriers, hospitals with emergency departments, and florists. There is also a map of the city centre locating recommended hotels, restaurants and other important addresses.

For easy reference, all main entries for hotels, restaurants and sights are listed alphabetically.

Abbreviations

Credit and charge cards AE American Express; DC Diners Club; MC MasterCard (Access, Eurocard); V Visa (Carte Bleue).

Figures Millions are abbreviated to m; billions (meaning one thousand million) to bn.

Publisher's note

Although *The Economist Business Traveller's Guide to France* is intended first and foremost to provide practical information for business people travelling *in* France, the general information will also be helpful to anyone doing business with France, wherever and however that business may be conducted.

Price bands

Price bands are denoted by symbols (see below). These correspond approximately to the following actual prices at the time of going to press. (Although the actual prices will inevitably go up, the relative price category is likely to remain the same.)

Hotels (one person occupying a typical room)		*Restaurants* (typical *à la carte* meal, including coffee, service, and half a bottle of modest wine)	
F	up to 250Fr	F	up to 180Fr
$F/$	250–400Fr	$F/$	180–230Fr
$F//$	400–600Fr	$F//$	230–300Fr
$F///$	600–900Fr	$F///$	300–400Fr
$F////$	900–1,200Fr	$F////$	400–500Fr
$F/////$	over 1,200Fr	$F/////$	over 500Fr

INTRODUCTION

France's "economic miracle" of the postwar decades took many people by surprise, not least the French themselves. A nation that between the wars had seemed sluggish and backward suddenly became dynamic and forward-looking – or some key elements of it at least. Many industries were resolutely modernized, technical innovation was given its head, production and exports soared, while a silent revolution on the farms brought the huge agricultural sector into the modern world at last. How did it all happen?

Some explanations seem clear. The shock and humiliation of wartime defeat and occupation gave the impetus for a new start on new lines; many leaders of the economy emerged discredited by their collaborationist role, and they gave way to younger people with fresh ideas. Then the mass exodus from the modernized farms helped to give industry the new labour that it needed for its expansion; and the trade unions, which in France are weak and divided, played a generally docile role even while making a loud noise. But above all – according to a still widely held view – it was the central role of the state as leader, guide and planner that carried the French economy along its brilliant postwar path. The Plan created by Jean Monnet set the guidelines for expansion, while state technocrats provided the dynamism and enthusiasm and state-owned firms such as Renault acted as pacesetters in many industries. After 1958, the creation of the European Community dealt a blow to deep-rooted French protectionism, forcing firms to become more competitive and modern-minded, which they did more successfully than had been expected.

Declining performance

Today the economic picture is less rosy than even ten years ago, and many experts have come to see state omnipotence as more of a liability than a strength. In the 1960s and 1970s France's growth rate had been one of the highest in the West and, by 1980, France had drawn level with Japan as third equal among world exporters. But in 1980–87 its share of world export markets dropped back from 10.2% to 8.2%, and growth in the 1980s has been below the average for major industrial countries. Inflation has been curbed, as in other countries, but unemployment has risen steadily to over 10%, and even such vaunted showpieces of French prowess as the automobile industry piled up huge losses. These diverse ills can be blamed partly on the energy crisis, or even on Socialist policies in 1981–82: but the more relevant fact is that since the mid-1970s French industry has been failing to invest adequately in new equipment.

The end of *étatisme*?

Today the state is being used as a scapegoat for this poorer economic performance. According to this view, state control and assertive state leadership may have been valuable in the years when France was modernizing and industry needed a strong lead; but they have now become a waning asset under new world conditions of open frontiers and multinational groupings where the French economy can prosper only if it becomes more market-oriented, and if state considerations of political kudos and prestige give way to more strictly commercial criteria. Industry should be in private, not state, hands and companies will do better if they learn to be more self-reliant.

This was roughly the view of the right-of-centre Chirac government that took power in March 1986, apparently drawing on many of the ideas put forward by Britain's Margaret Thatcher. Not only did it set about dismantling the preceding Socialist government's nationalizations of key industries and private banks, but its privatization plans extended far more widely, and in 1987 even the main state television network was sold off – a startling break with French tradition. Chirac's programme also included wide-ranging decontrol of prices, cuts in company taxation, a reduction in state subsidies to public and private firms, an easing of the rules limiting the layoff of workers, and a bid to reduce the size and powers of the state bureaucracy. Oddly enough, this broad movement to restrict the role of the state had been started by the Socialist government in 1981–86; despite their nationalizations, they too had taken a hand at price decontrol, while their major reform of local government transferred many powers from Paris to the regional and city councils and other local bodies. Today, *la décentralisation* and *le libéralisme* are much in vogue. But it remains to be seen how effectively the French can adapt to a new system that is alien to their tradition, and possibly also to their temperament. *Etatisme* still has its powerful advocates in high places.

Faith in the future

The French today may be uncertain about the proper role of the state but they remain extremely proud of their postwar technological achievements. France has the world's most advanced and ambitious nuclear power programme, where notably it has pioneered the development of fast-breeder reactors. The new French high-speed passenger train (TGV) is the world's fastest. The telephone service, once an antiquated disgrace, is now one of the most modern, with a videotex "minitel" in over 3m homes. And in aeronautics, satellites and space research, France is Europe's unquestioned leader.

For these and other futuristic projects, the French still show a youthful enthusiasm and faith in a scientific future. And this eagerness and dynamism, this taste for novelty and willingness to take risks, extends through many levels of industry and commerce, even to very small firms, helping to make France a stimulating country in which to do business. But the capital market is still weak, and many firms still fail to match their technical prowess with the right financial skills and resources. As Renault and Peugeot know well, brilliant technical innovation does not always guarantee a healthy balance sheet.

The Economic Scene

Natural resources

Endowed with a temperate climate, a fertile soil and a relatively large cultivable area, France has an agricultural sector that is unusually strong and varied: the high quality and range of its produce is certainly one of the factors behind the nation's pre-eminence in gastronomy. In economic terms, agriculture was held back until recent decades by its archaic peasant structures; but since World War II it has been dynamically modernized, enabling it to realize its rich potential. By contrast, France is relatively short of mineral resources: there is some iron ore but virtually no oil and only small, dwindling reserves of coal and natural gas.

Agriculture

This sector accounts for 5.3% of GNP, more than twice the figure for the UK or USA. France has the largest utilized farm area of the European Community (31m ha/76.6m acres) and is its leading food producer: hence the strong political emphasis that French governments have always placed on defending the EC's Common Agricultural Policy (CAP). But the pattern of farming still varies greatly from region to region, being generally more efficient and prosperous in the north than in the west and southwest, where many farms are too small.

Until about 1968 this mighty farming nation had a net trade deficit in food and drinks. Exports were still mainly the traditional ones of quality wines and some cheeses. By 1986, basic agriculture exports showed a balance over imports of Fr18.7bn, thanks largely to the export of cereals, while processed foods showed a surplus of Fr7.9bn. As well as cereals, France is a heavy net exporter of dairy products, wines and sugar, but still has a trade deficit in live animals, vegetables and fish.

Production Wheat and other cereal crops are grown mainly on the big modern estates of the Paris basin, Picardy and Champagne, where productivity levels are among the world's highest. France is the world's fifth-biggest cereals producer and the EC's biggest by far: thanks to changes in world markets, it has boosted its annual trade surplus in cereals to some Fr30bn.

Livestock is another major sector, providing 38% of the total value of farm produce. High-quality beef is produced in such areas as Normandy and Charolais, but is still hampered by inefficient marketing. Sheepmeat comes mainly from the hilly Massif Central and southwest France, where the mostly small farms have found it hard to compete with British lamb. Similarly pig-breeders, who are numerous in Brittany, have been outdone by the more efficient Dutch and Danes.

Dairy products are a traditional strength in this land of over 300 cheeses. Camembert from Normandy, Brie from east of Paris and Roquefort from ewes' milk in the Massif Central are among the most famous, while high-quality butter comes from both Normandy and the Charente. The sugar-beet industry is big in Picardy and the Nord. Brittany, with its mild, wet climate, has boosted its sales of cauliflower, artichokes and other vegetables; Normandy and Brittany are both renowned for apples, often used for cider or Calvados; and fruit and early vegetables of all kinds, including melons and asparagus, are cultivated on a grand scale in Provence and Languedoc-Roussillon. Languedoc is also the major producer of cheap French table wine (see *Food and drink*).

The farm revolution With the mechanization of farming and the growth of urban industry, over 6m people have moved off the land since 1945, and agriculture's share of the active population has dropped from 35% then to 8% today; it is expected to level off at about 6% by the year 2000. Through sales and mergers, the average farm has increased since 1955 from 14ha/34.6 acres to 32ha/79 acres.

These changes have brought another, just as striking, change in mentalities. The old-style peasant, individualist, ignorant, suspicious of progress, is one of a dying breed. Younger farmers especially now tend to be modern-minded and business-oriented, far readier than the old guard to share know-how or equipment or to group into cooperatives. But the pattern varies regionally. In the poorer parts of the west and southwest there are still too many small, inefficient farms, and far too many people working on the land.

As elsewhere in the EC, technical advance has led to soaring productivity, hence to huge surpluses in some sectors. France in the 1960s was the prime architect of the CAP which was shaped to meet French needs, and French farmers have prospered from it. But now, despite falling incomes in the 1980s, they reluctantly accept the need to limit production. The number of dairy producers has fallen by 30% since milk quotas arrived in 1984; and the French are ready to face lower cereal prices. The real issue is whether further cuts in production will necessitate some land falling into disuse.

Forestry

France has much the largest forested area in the EC: it covers 15m ha/37m acres, a quarter of the country, and 650,000 people are employed in forestry and related industries. Yet France is a net importer of both timber and papers; the wood-pulp industry is backward, and much forest land is still inefficiently parcelled out between small owners. Three-quarters of French forest is in private hands, the rest belonging to the state and local bodies. South of Bordeaux, the flat pine forest of the Landes, which was planted in the 19th century, is France's largest (1.3m ha/3.4m acres). Natural forests cover much of the Massif Central, also Savoie and the Vosges where tree-sickness has begun to take its toll, though less so than in Germany.

Fishing

France today ranks only 20th among the world's fishing nations; the number of full-time fishermen has dropped since 1980 from 22,000 to 18,400, and France now imports three times as much fish as it exports. Increased British and Spanish competition within EC waters, and the loss of more distant fishing grounds under the 200 mile/320km fishing limit, are among the causes of the decline. Boulogne is the main deep-sea fishing port (sole, cod, herring, and suchlike). Shellfish, notably oysters and mussels, are bred intensively on the Atlantic coast to meet the eager demand of French consumers.

Minerals

Iron ore is still mined in Lorraine, and France remains the EC's leading ore producer (14.5m tonnes/16m US tons in 1985). Output has been falling as the mines wear thin, but it still satisfies some 40% of French domestic needs. Apart from this, non-ferrous and non-fuel minerals are scarce. France produces some bauxite (mainly in Provence) and zinc, but no copper or tin. (See also *Energy*.)

Human resources

Helped by immigration and by one of Europe's highest birth rates, France's population has grown steadily since World War II, from 41m to 55m. The birth rate, as elsewhere, is lower than 20 years ago but is still above the EC average. There is plenty of elbow room, for in this sizable country the density is still relatively low, only 101 people per sq km/247 acres. Despite postwar urbanization, Greater Paris (8.7m) is still the only really large conurbation; Lyon, Marseille and Lille are each well below 1.5m.

Shifts of population

France, with its strong rural heritage, was slow to urbanize and in 1945 most Frenchmen were still living on farmsteads, in villages or small towns. Then rapid industrial growth and farm modernization caused a drift to the cities: some, led by Grenoble and Toulouse, have more than tripled in size. But this trend has now largely ended with industrial jobs scarce and city life less attractive to new generations. Nearly all large towns have ceased to grow, though many smaller ones are still doing so.

Declining areas In the past 20 years, and mainly for reasons of climate and environment, shifts of population within France are favouring the sunny south at the expense of older industrial regions of the north, such as the "rust belt," and even Paris itself. But there is also a drift away from the hilly areas of central France and from parts of Lorraine and the Nord where the old coal, steel and textile industries are waning.

Paris losing its appeal Greater Paris grew fast during the 1950s and 1960s; but today for the first time ever, the net migration is away from the capital, at the rate of some 60,000 a year – an historic change. Parisians used to despise provincials and Paris was the sole magnet for all ambition; but today many a young executive will consider it just as "smart" as well as more pleasant to live, say, in Annecy or Avignon rather than in the *seizième*, and thousands are making the move. An age-old snobbery is being stood on its head.

Growth areas The growth areas are in the sunbelt where the new high-tech industries are expanding: Toulouse, Montpellier, the hinterland of Nice, also Grenoble in the Alps and around Lyon. Provence and Languedoc have growing populations, as have the Atlantic coast areas.

The age structure

France was vigorously rejuvenated by the high birth rate of the postwar decades, a major psychological as well as practical factor in its economic renewal. The falling birth rate then levelled off in 1976 and has since risen slightly, so that births are exceeding deaths by 200,000 a year. Moreover, the abnormally low natality of the 1914–18 period has meant that the percentage of over-65s (13.1% in 1986) is actually lower than in 1974 and little more than it was in 1946, despite the fact that people now live much longer. So France has a healthier age pyramid than many countries. But this will change as the World War I generation dies, and France increasingly faces the common problem of how to pay for a growing number of senior citizens.

Minorities and immigrants

France has an honourable tradition of welcome to immigrants, including political refugees who today number some 200,000: mostly these are exiles from communist Europe, Indo-China, the Middle East and extremist Latin-American regimes. But they are few in number compared with other waves of immigrants, notably the 800,000 French citizens repatriated from Algeria at the time of its independence in 1962. These *pieds noirs* easily found new jobs in France during that boom era, and on the whole they have re-integrated easily.

Of the 4.4m foreigners in France in 1986 some 1.9m were from other EC countries, led by 860,000 Portuguese, 425,000 Italians and 380,000 Spanish. Some have been in France two or three generations; nearly all are easily accepted by the French. The 780,000 Algerians, 520,000 Moroccans and 215,000 Tunisians, who by reason of their race, lifestyles and Muslim religion appear so different have been less readily integrated into the community. The North Africans usually live with their families in ghetto-like housing where high birth rates have caused further tensions. Recent governments both of left and right have tried not very successfully to deal with the problem by offering bribes for them to return home, by setting bans on new immigrants and by trying to find and deport the illegal ones.

France has some 650,000 blacks, most of them French citizens from the Caribbean. Many are educated middle-class people and they are much more easily accepted than the North Africans. The Jewish community (700,000) is the largest in Western Europe.

The workforce

The total working population in 1987 was around 23.9m, including 3.3m self-employed, 250,000 conscripts and 2.4m registered unemployed.

Growth in service industries
Over the past ten years the numbers working in agriculture have declined by 25%, and the total employed in manufacturing and building has fallen by 18%. Some traditional industries, such as textiles, steel, shipbuilding and even motor vehicles have become less competitive. New industries such as electronics have developed fast, but these tend to be less capital intensive. Service industries have grown rapidly, by some 17% since 1976, and this trend is likely to persist.

Working women Women account for 41% of the workforce and 75% of them work in the distribution, transport and service sectors. Nearly half (45%) work in only 20 (of a possible 455) job categories. The highest numbers are in education, nursing and healthcare, the secretarial professions and the service industries, particularly retailing. Women do well in the professions, but few hold senior positions in industry. Maternity leave provisions are relatively generous in France and employment legislation has afforded women a high degree of protection. Overall very few women are unionized.

Unemployment Until the early 1970s the unemployment figure remained under 500,000 (2% of the workforce). It then began to rise fast, reaching 1.8m by 1981, but has since levelled off at 2.4m (10.5%) in 1986, which puts France roughly on the EC average. It seems likely that, under changing conditions, full employment in the old sense is no longer attainable.

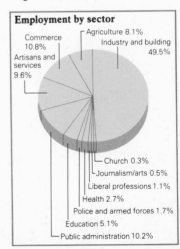

Employment by sector

Commerce 10.8%
Artisans and services 9.6%
Agriculture 8.1%
Industry and building 49.5%
Church 0.3%
Journalism/arts 0.5%
Liberal professions 1.1%
Health 2.7%
Police and armed forces 1.7%
Education 5.1%
Public administration 10.2%

International trade

Since the early 1970s France's trade has displayed a growing dependence on European markets, and its economic fortunes have been increasingly bound up with those of the EC. Flagging international competitiveness has become a major concern of economic policy.

Main trading partners

EC More than half of France's foreign trade is with other EC countries; West Germany remains by far France's most important trading partner. The enlargement of the EC in 1973 led to a considerable increase in Franco–British trade, while the addition of Spain to the Community in 1986 produced another surge of exports.

European challenge Owing to the slow rates of growth in the EC over much of the 1980s, France has been handicapped by its heavy dependence on the EC for export markets; the planned removal of all non-tariff barriers between EC countries by 1992 will represent a major challenge for France. This is especially true in the fields of financial services and of manufactures, where export opportunities have been distorted by restrictive national public procurement procedures; France's buoyant telecommunications sector is likely to benefit.

USA The world's leading economy has become France's single most important market outside the EC. Imports from the USA have always been sizable, while the appreciation of the dollar between 1980 and 1985 boosted France's exports of luxury goods to the USA.

Japan Trade with the world's second-largest economy is relatively limited. The Japanese market has been largely closed to French exporters, while Japanese exports to France have in the past been limited by France's robust reaction to export drives, such as the ceiling on Japanese car sales and the delaying tactic of insisting that all Japanese VCR imports passed through the small inland customs office at Poitiers, though this has now stopped.

Other countries France is not a major exporter of plant and equipment to Comecon countries. It is, however, a major importer of natural gas from the Soviet Union, as well as from Algeria and the Netherlands. Algeria, once part of metropolitan France, is France's foremost trading partner within OPEC, and is even more important as an export market than as a supplier. There are also close trade ties with Iraq, and this has caused tensions in the Middle East. Other important suppliers of petroleum from OPEC are Saudi Arabia and Nigeria. France secured a strong foothold in OPEC markets during the 1970s for contract engineering projects; as a result it suffered in the 1980s, and especially in 1986, as these countries' oil revenues declined markedly.

Export strengths

Apart from such specifically national products as top quality wines and cheeses, perfumes and *haute couture* clothes, France's export strengths are impressively diversified. Like the USA, it has specialized in meeting two of man's oldest needs, those for food and weapons.

Food for thought France is second only to the USA as an exporter of agricultural produce. In the North African and Soviet markets, competition for wheat sales between France and the USA has been particularly fierce. Processed foodstuffs are even more important than basic agricultural products.

Military might Official statistics show military material accounting for no more than 5% of France's visible exports, but this is based on a narrow definition of military equipment. Major customers for French weaponry include Iraq in the Middle East, Morocco in North Africa and Argentina in South America (see *Defence and aerospace*).

High technology The engineering skills that have helped to produce sophisticated military equipment have also been applied to the civilian aerospace industry. Aerospatiale dominates the European Airbus Industrie consortium. France also enjoys a justified reputation for its technically advanced railway equipment, and its pre-eminence in telecommunications technology has allowed France to win a significant share of world sales (see *Telecommunications*).

Slowing down Prior to the downturn of Europe's economies in the second half of the 1970s, France's motor vehicle industry was the leader of much of France's export growth. By the early 1980s, however, the industry had overreached itself and was in a state of deep crisis. The domestic recovery of both sales and profitability in 1986–87 was reinforced by a trade surplus in cars of Fr12bn, though the goods vehicle sector remained flat.

Manufacturing weak Much of the anxiety that surfaced in France in 1985–86 over the declining competitiveness of French industry can be traced to the dramatically weak performance of a few subsectors. Heavy factory machinery, particularly machine tools, is a key area where Germany, Japan, the USA and Italy all enjoy a keen competitive edge over France. A further area of weakness is in electrical consumer durables, where competition, particularly from Japan and Italy, has been acute.

Balance of payments On the current account, a strong surplus on invisibles – notably tourism and contract engineering – has largely offset a deficit on merchandise trade. The 1986 slide in international oil prices swung the current account balance into a comfortable surplus, but by 1987 it was again in deficit.

Currency movements
France's trade competitiveness benefited considerably from the appreciation of the dollar in 1980–85 and suffered from its subsequent descent. However, much of the export trade in agriculture produce is cocooned by the EC's CAP export price subsidies. To boost the flagging manufacturing sector, the franc was devalued within the framework of the EMS exchange rate mechanism in April 1986 and again in January 1987.

Top ten imports, 1985

	Frbn
Crude oil, natural gas & refined petroleum products	200.7
Chemicals	68.6
Office machines & professional electronic material	68.3
Processed foodstuffs	67.3
Heavy machinery & mechanical appliances	59.2
Textiles & clothing	53.9
Basic agricultural products	52.9
Non-ferrous metals & semi-finished manufactures	41.0
Passenger cars	34.5
Paper & packaging	25.6
	69.4% of total

	Frbn
Chemicals	76.8
Processed foodstuffs	76.6
Basic agricultural products	74.7
Heavy machinery & mechanical appliances	68.7
Office machines & professional electronic material	60.4
Passenger cars	47.6
Textiles & clothing	46.1
Pharmaceutical products	38.4
Vehicle spare parts & equipment	38.0
Non-ferrous metals & semi-finished manufactures	35.9
	62.1% of total

Top ten exports, 1985

Source: Tableaux de l'économie française,1986

The nation's finances

There is a long tradition of public enterprise and of state intervention in the economy in France. Its efficiency, in terms of profitability or reduced losses, has improved in recent years. Government expenditure in relation to the size of the economy, however, is not high by European standards (16% of GDP as against an average of 18% for EC countries). Government debt as a proportion of GDP is also low, despite a rapid increase in the first half of the 1980s.

Setting the budget

The fiscal year is the calendar year. The finance minister prepares the budget during the summer, and proposals are normally put before the Council of Ministers for approval in September. The draft budget then goes before Parliament, from which it emerges in December, generally little changed, as the initial Finance Act.

Where the money comes from

Most government revenue is from taxation. The most important tax is the Taxe sur la Valeur Ajoutée (TVA). Personal income tax rates have been reduced in recent years; that on the highest band of personal income stood at 56.8% in 1988. In the same year corporate income tax – payable on retained and distributed profits alike – was 45%, but this is to be reduced to 42% in 1988.

Government revenue	
	1987 (Frbn)
Direct taxes	
Income tax	212.8
Corporation tax	115.3
Payroll tax	27.3
Miscellaneous	92.6
Indirect taxes	
TVA	498.4
Petrol tax	94.1
Non-fiscal receipts	63.1
Special allocations receipts	40.9
Total	1,144.5

Source: *France in Figures*, 1987

Where the money goes

The high-spending ministries include national education, social affairs and employment, defence and health. The servicing of the national debt swallows a substantial portion of government revenue. One of the Chirac government's policy priorities has been to cut government expenditure, and there was a slight fall in the ratio of public spending to GDP in the period 1985–87.

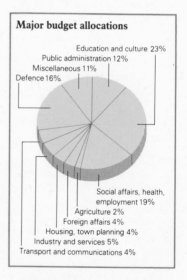

Major budget allocations

Education and culture 23%
Public administration 12%
Miscellaneous 11%
Defence 16%
Social affairs, health, employment 19%
Agriculture 2%
Foreign affairs 4%
Housing, town planning 4%
Industry and services 5%
Transport and communications 4%

The Chirac government's cuts in spending have been spread over most ministries, with defence being the main exception. Reductions in public sector employment, and the lowering of government subsidies to industry, including a cut in the Ministère de l'Industrie's budget of more than 10%, are intended to set the tone of government fiscal restraint for some years to come.

Borrowing

The central government budgeted for a deficit of 3% of GDP and is likely to maintain this relatively low level through 1987 and 1988. This, coupled with the allocation of a large proportion of the receipts of privatization to the repayment of public debt, has eased the government borrowing requirement. The Chirac government has planned to balance the budget – with the exception of servicing the public debt – by 1989.

Social security accounts

In France the social security system is treated separately from the rest of the central government budget, with its own sources of revenue. Total annual social security contributions amount to close to Fr900bn; employers' contributions make up roughly half of this total.

Under pressure Despite the high level of revenue, the social security system has come under a considerable strain in recent years, with an ageing population and burgeoning unemployment promoting massive increases in spending on health care, old age pensions and unemployment benefits.

More increases Successive governments have tried to redress the balance by raising the various types of social security contribution or by imposing special levies, effectively an income tax by another name. Similar stopgap measures were taken in the summer of 1987. A major revision of the system is planned after the 1988 presidential election but further increases in contributions are seen as inevitable.

Public finance control

Rigorous public finance control – at least of the central government budget – has been one of the hallmarks of the Fifth Republic, with the exception of the first years of Socialist government, when there was a misjudged dash for economic growth through fiscal expansion. Remedial measures were soon introduced as part of the Socialist government's economic policy U-turn in 1982–83. In recent years, the general government deficit (the budget deficit plus any social security balance) as a percentage of GDP has remained lower than in other EC countries, with the exception of West Germany, and both the USA and Japan.

Privatization receipts

The privatization programme introduced in 1986 began by generating huge windfall revenue for the government. Early in 1987 they estimated these receipts at Fr30bn, but it was clear by late 1987 that the success of the privatization programme would more than double that conservative estimate. The receipts are "off-budget" and a large proportion is being used for repayment of the national debt. Sizable sums, however, have been channelled into public investment, such as the construction of highways, high-speed railway lines and research and development in the aerospace industry. This has been through the capital funding of public enterprise.

EMS constraints

The French franc has been part of the European Monetary System (EMS) since its inception in 1979. As a result, fiscal policy as an instrument of demand management has been made partly subordinate to exchange rate policy.

A related aspect of France's EMS exchange rate commitment has been a determined effort to bring down the rate of increase in consumer prices to the EC average, or below it. Helped by the slide in international oil prices, the inflation rate in 1986 was down to 2.5%, though there was acceleration in price rises early in 1987.

The Industrial Scene

Industry and investment

The 1980s have been marked by profound industrial change in France. The older manufacturing industries have declined, bringing economic difficulties to many regions, especially in the north, while there has been strong growth in the services sector. Political factors have also affected French industry. Following François Mitterrand's accession to the presidency in 1981, a wave of nationalization substantially restructured some of France's leading industrial groups. Then, four years later, the Chirac government initiated a privatization programme to cut back radically the state's role in France's industrial life.

Altered perceptions

The early 1970s was a time of great confidence. There was even the view that the French economy was potentially the strongest in Europe. The striking pace of modernization since the war, reflected in an annual average real increase of nearly 6% in GDP in the ten years preceding the first oil shock, encouraged this view. Within industry, the growth of such an important sub-sector as motor vehicles promoted hopes that France might rival West Germany as an economic power.

In the 1980s, however, chronically slow growth in Europe and above all in France – coupled with the realization that the main exceptions to the general rule were none other than Italy and Britain – turned French economic confidence on its head. The new axiom was that France was set on a decline; one exaggeration replaced another.

Out with the old

Industrial employment fell by one-sixth between the mid-1970s and mid-1980s. Much of the loss took place in the crisis-ridden steel, textile and ship-building industries.
Steel production has been drastically cut after years of EC cartel management from Brussels, and the slimming down has led to the merging of the once-independent Usinor and Sacilor state-owned steel companies.

Textiles Despite the protection afforded by successive multi-fibre agreements (MFAs: global arrangements restraining developing countries' textile exports) and the EC's bilateral restraint agreements with non-EC Mediterranean countries, many French textile firms have closed. Those remaining have invested heavily and become more capital-intensive.
Shipbuilding France is now left with just one major yard, the Chantiers de l'Atlantique owned by Alsthom at St-Nazaire.

In with the new

New jobs created in the services sector between the mid-1970s and mid-1980s more than offset the net losses in industry. Market-priced services now account for almost half of total gross value-added in the economy and for well over a third of total employment, having overtaken industry in 1980. Such a development is in line with the pattern in all advanced industrial countries. In the early 1980s, the contribution of market services to total gross value-added was higher in France than in any other major EC country, though still less than in either the USA or Japan. There has been fast expansion in the past ten years in health care, long-distance passenger railway transport, computer software services and telecommunications. (See also *Telecommunications*.)

Nationalizations

The first wave The present structure of public enterprise was laid down at the end of World War II; more precisely, by the Provisional Government of September 1944 to December 1946. The general policy was to restrict nationalization to those sectors of the economy whose efficient functioning was deemed indispensable to national recovery. The list was long: it included the fuel power industries, leading commercial banks and insurance companies and transport services of strategic importance, such as those provided by Air France. It also included the firms that had worked directly for the Germans, notably Renault, Berliet and the aircraft engine works that became the present-day Snecma.

1982 – the second wave It was not until the second year of Socialist government under François Mitterrand that there was a further advance in the role of the state. The nationalizations of 1982 included six of the country's leading industrial groups (CGE, Saint-Gobain, Thomson, Rhône-Poulenc, Pechiney and Bull) and all the remaining big private banks, together with their parent financial holding companies, such as the powerful Paribas and Indosuez groups. The underlying aim of this two-pronged nationalization effort was to give the government almost total control over the selection and financing of large-scale industrial development with a view to accelerating the modernization of the economy. This confidence in the power of the state proved misplaced, especially in the depressed European economic climate of the early 1980s. However, the concentration of control in the hands of the state did allow a rationalization of activity between the leading industrial groups. In the sphere of telecommunications, for example, Thomson-CSF relinquished its manufacture of public switching equipment to the Compagnie Générale d'Electricité (CGE), and this partly prepared the way for CGE's takeover of ITT's telecommunications equipment business in early 1987 through the vehicle of Alcatel NV.

Privatizations

The Privatization Act of August 7 1986 passed by the Chirac government not only undid the Nationalization Act of February 1982 but also provided for the selling off of much of the public enterprises resulting from the postwar measures, notably the leading commercial banks and insurance companies and Elf Aquitaine. The privatization programme got off to an excellent start but ran into difficulties after the world stockmarket fall of late 1987 (see *Government and business*).

Question mark over fixed investment

The nationalization of 1982 and the privatizations of 1986 had a common aim. They were intended to promote fixed capital investment, especially in manufacturing, and the modernization and improved competitiveness of the economy. The difference is that the more recent strategy is founded on a faith in the virtues of the free market economy. The quality of senior management and the efficiency of investment resource allocation may well improve as a result of the changes flowing from privatization, but it is a moot point whether the widening of the equity capital market will necessarily lead to a stepping up of investment in plant and machinery in the economy as a whole. The growth of such investment in France has in any case been relatively satisfactory; the rate of growth in France's capital stock in industry and services in 1980–85 was higher than that in West Germany and the USA. The French problem of insufficient investment and faltering competitiveness is a problem affecting certain sectors rather than a disease of the whole economy.

Defence and aerospace

The French military programme rolls forward seemingly irrespective of which government is in power. While some 180 companies are active in the aerospace and defence sector, the lion's share of contracts goes to a small group of largely state-owned manufacturers led by Aérospatiale and Thomson-CSF. In both civilian and defence procurement the French have historically followed policies of a high degree of strategic national planning and bureaucratic control and of spending their money at home. Less than 5% of military purchasing is done abroad. However, the defence ministry is officially committed to opening more contracts to competitive tender. In 1986 the French airforce bought the Boeing AWACS early warning aircraft as a quid pro quo for the US army buying the Rita battlefield communications system.

Defence budget

After a pause in the early 1980s, defence expenditure increased again under the Chirac government as the French strove to meet a number of costly nuclear and aircraft commitments by the mid-1990s. The budget in 1987 was just under Fr170bn and in terms of both total value and as a proportion of GDP is second only to that of Britain in the European context. More significantly for suppliers, the proportion of the budget spent on equipment has begun to exceed the amount spent on service personnel. France's ambitious programme to renew, rather than just update, its fighter aircraft, missile systems, helicopters and nuclear fleet will continue to mean fat contracts for the aircraft manufacturing and electronics sectors, the latter dominated by Thomson-CSF, until the end of the century.

Main military programme

Rafale is an advanced fly-by-wire fighter aircraft for the 1990s being developed by the premier military aircraft manufacturer Dassault-Bréguet. The French decided to go ahead alone with this Fr100bn programme after a spectacular withdrawal from the European Fighter Aircraft (EFA) project. The incident demonstrated the insistence of the French on dominating almost every pan-European project. France now plans to build 350 of the aircraft for both the French airforce and export market where Rafale will compete head on with the EFA.

Missiles The reputation of Aérospatiale's Exocet missile was made during the Falklands conflict and it has since achieved huge export sales. The latest programme includes a short- to medium-range air-to-air missile, the MICA, and the ASMP medium-range air-to-ground nuclear missile fired from Super Etendards and the Mirage 2000N aircraft.

Nuclear weapons France's nuclear programme is exclusively French. Its fleet of six nuclear-armed submarines is now 20 years old. The replacement programme will provide France with four nuclear submarines by the year 2000 with Aérospatiale developing the warheads. In parallel, the Hadès project will provide the French army with a ground-to-ground nuclear weapon system.

Naval The main naval programme is for a new generation of eight nuclear-powered submarines by the year 2000. Two nuclear-powered aircraft carriers are also scheduled to enter service in the mid-1990s. All are being built at state dockyards under the authority of the Direction des Constructions Navales (DCN), the state procurement body.

Main civil programmes

Airbus is a joint venture by France, Britain, West Germany and Spain with a strong Gallic influence: its headquarters are in Toulouse and the French hold a 38% stake through Aérospatiale and the engine builder, Snecma. The latest A330 and A340 medium- and long-range aircraft, due to enter service in the early 1990s, attracted just over Fr18bn in start-up funding of which Fr6bn was guaranteed by the French. Airbus has a total sales target of 2,100 aircraft by the year 2005, worth Fr732bn. For the A330 and A340 programmes, the partners are entirely dependent on a sales levy to recoup the heavy investment, and the consortium faces intense competition from Boeing and McDonnell Douglas. Cut-throat pricing seems certain over the next decade and, quite possibly, some form of eventual collaboration, for which Britain and Germany have pressed. It seems likely that strains within the Airbus consortium will grow, particularly if it fails to meet its private target of breaking even by 1995.

Space programme

France has been the most vigorous of European nations in identifying the money-spinning potential of space, in both military and civil terms. By 1986 the French space budget was Fr6bn, and, although most of the European space effort is channelled through the European Space Agency (ESA), this too is French-dominated. France has a 60% stake in the Ariane space-launcher programme established in 1984. French space contractors such as Aérospatiale, Matra, SEP and Alcatel Espace will continue to enjoy the fruits of the ESA programme until the end of the century with the planned launch of Ariane 5 and Hermès, a space shuttle capable of lifting astronauts into orbit and returning them to earth by landing like a glider. French industry is also assiduously using its domination of the European space industry to develop a burgeoning overseas market. Space exports, negligible in the 1970s, will account for 10% of all French aerospace sales by the end of the decade.

Changing perspectives

The French defence industries have enjoyed a strong sales record in the Middle East with such programmes as the Fr24bn Thomson-CSF Shahine short-range ground-to-air missile contract with Saudi Arabia. Despite this, however, and hopes of a further Fr20bn sale of submarines, doubts over the long-term health of the oil economies have foreshadowed some possible changes in the pattern of French export sales. Thomson-CSF has recently concentrated on the European and the huge US market. The Fr24bn Rita communications contract was a vindication of this strategy, which considerably strengthened the prospect of selling the technology to other export customers.

Principal companies – 1986

Aérospatiale (*sales* Fr25.4bn; *employees* 38,300) Aircraft (principally civil, including Airbus). Military and civil helicopters. Space satellites and launchers. Missiles, including Exocet, and warheads.

Thomson-CSF (*sales* Fr24.5bn; *employees* 31,700) Electronics, weapon systems, radar, flight instrumentation, simulators, missiles, military command systems.

Dassault Bréguet (*sales* Fr15.6bn; *employees* 15,800) Aircraft (principally military including Mirage, Super Etendard and Rafale).

Snecma (*sales* Fr15.4bn; *employees* 25,826) Military and civil engines, including CFM engines produced with General Electric of USA.

Matra (*sales* Fr6bn; *employees* 4,500) Missiles.

Turbomeca (*sales* Fr2bn; *employees* 4,288) Civil and military aircraft engines.

Motor vehicles

Simplicity, comfort, practicality and panache in design and technical innovation have characterized French motor cars. Once a shining example of postwar growth, since the late 1970s the industry has been in a sorry state: French car production fell from a peak of 3.4m a year in 1980 to 2.8m in 1985. Both Peugeot-Citroën and Renault have experienced serious operating and financial trouble from which they only began to emerge in 1985–86. Peugeot was the first to put its house in order. A changing market has seen it take the lead from Renault, with 34% of sales in early 1987, 3.5% ahead of the state-owned company, with the rest of the market accounted for by imports from West Germany, Italy and more recently Japan, though the Japanese still hold less than 6% of the market.

Peugeot-Citroën

Now the largest motor manufacturer in France, Peugeot made profits of Fr543m in 1985 and multiplied that more than sixfold the following year to Fr3.6bn. But these successes followed five years of continuous losses totalling Fr8bn, causing the company to run up debts of Fr30bn, three times its market capitalization. The company emerged in early 1987 as holding the fourth-largest market share in Europe behind Audi Volkswagen, Fiat and Ford Europe, with 11.4% of total sales.

Takeover problems Peugeot's problems started when it took over the ailing Citroën company and then Chrysler France in rapid succession at the end of the 1970s. It was a bad time to be expansionist, just as the Japanese were becoming highly competitive in all the European car markets. Peugeot found itself saddled with too many factories, too many workers and overlapping and demoralized dealer networks.

Slimming down Peugeot has successfully increased employee output and lowered the level of production at which it can break even. It ended 1986 with a workforce of 165,000, and an output of 1.7m cars, the same number that, in 1981, was produced by 218,000 employees.

Towards the 1990s The company aims to become the top European car producer and plans to increase output to 2m cars a year, stepping up annual investment from Fr7bn in 1986 to Fr9bn a year through the late 1980s. Its recent marketing policy has been to seek growth outside France in the other European markets. It has an ambitious policy of one new model a year, alternating between Peugeot and Citroën badges.

Models Much of the Peugeot recovery can be put down to the success of its 205 supermini model and the mid-range 309, with the Citroën BX range also making a sizable contribution. Keeping up the flow of new models as well as modernizing plant will be expensive for a group with such heavy debts. In mid-1987 Peugeot raised Fr2.67bn through an issue of new shares, with the aim of reducing the debt in its balance sheet. The main shareholders in the firm remained the original Peugeot family, with 23%.

Renault's recovery attempt

Nationalized by De Gaulle after World War II, Renault became in some ways a social laboratory for every trendy new theory about industrial organization. The labour unions – particularly the Communist CGT – were very powerful in the early 1980s and defeated management's best efforts to improve the company's productivity.

Turning around In 1982 Renault was Europe's biggest car maker with

14.6% of the market; by mid-1987 it had fallen to number six with 10.7%, two places behind Peugeot. Being state-owned, Renault could always call on sufficient cash to plug the holes caused by mounting losses: between 1981 and 1985 it lost no less that Fr33bn. There was relief when the 1986 results showed the tide turning with production at 1.67m vehicles, losses halved to Fr5.5bn and debt falling from Fr62bn to Fr51bn. Renault has been trading in the black since late 1986, having shed about 25% of its 100,000-strong workforce since 1984. In late 1987 the government agreed to write off Fr12bn of Renault's debt but declined to inject further state funds into the company. However, the level at which the company can break even has been reduced to 1.2m cars a year, which is realistic in the European market where over-capacity of some 2m units a year seems likely to persist.

American dream Renault aggravated its position by an ill-fated attempt to become the only European car maker with a base in the US market. In 1980 it acquired 51% of the troubled American Motors Corporation (AMC) and then poured Fr1bn into the venture without establishing any real hold in the US market. Eventually, Renault was forced to sell to the revived Chrysler Corporation in early 1987.

Commercial vehicles and industrial machinery (about 20% of sales) have also been a drain on Renault, with sales stagnant in the early 1980s. Renault Véhicules Industriels (RVI), the trucks subsidiary, lost Fr983m in 1986. Under a recovery plan initiated in 1984 the break-even level of truck production was reduced from 80,000 units to 37,000. Output has risen again and RVI is hoping to make annual profits of Fr1bn from 1987.

Privatization When the Mitterrand government in 1981 was planning the nationalization of a handful of major private companies, Renault was still hailed as the model of good state management. In fact, the newly nationalized firms prospered as Renault declined; recently there has been a growing wish in France for the state-owned company to be privatized at any price. The first tough boss put in to take on the unions, Georges Besse, was murdered in 1986, and the task of seeing through Renault's recovery now rests with Raymond Levy.

The European context

Neither Renault nor Peugeot wants to merge with another European firm. Instead both are likely to increase the number of international collaborative deals with other producers as the best way to lower the costs. France looks like continuing with two major car groups, though the betting is that both will be in the private sector by the mid-1990s.

European car makers' sales in France (1986)

Company	Units sold (000s)	Market share (%)
Peugeot-Citroën	612,979	32.1
Renault	602,910	31.5
Fiat group	133,283	7.0
Ford	131,077	6.9
Audi/VW group	114,773	6.0

European car makers' sales in Europe (1986)

Company	Units sold (m)	Market share (%)
Audi/VW	1.47	13.1
Fiat group	1.43	12.8
Ford	1.33	11.9
Peugeot-Citroën	1.29	11.6
GM	1.24	11.1
Renault	1.18	10.6

Source: The Society of Motor Manufacturers and Traders, 1987

Energy

In common with the rest of the industrialized world, France has attempted to secure economic growth while cutting overall energy consumption, especially since the second round of oil price rises in 1979. What is striking is the success of French government policy since the mid-1970s in reducing the country's dependence on imported energy (mostly oil) and in rapidly expanding its nuclear power generation programme. The share of oil in total primary energy consumption fell from 59.8% in 1970 to 44.3% in 1985 and the underlying trend in consumption has been flat since 1980.

The nuclear surge

The development of a large, efficient nuclear power industry is, along with aerospace and telecommunications, the shining example of the effectiveness of the (now largely abandoned) *dirigiste*-style of economic planning in France. By the end of 1986 France had 43 working pressurized water reactors (PWRs) and two fast-breeder stations, with 13 more PWRs planned for completion by the mid-1990s. This makes France second only to the USA in total nuclear power generation and world leader in proportional terms.

The nuclear power brokers The development of nuclear power in France has depended on three organizations: the state-owned electricity utility Electricité de France (EDF), the Commissariat à l'Energie Atomique (CEA) and the power-station builders, Framatome. Financed by heavy borrowing on the international capital markets, EDF began ordering two stations a year in the mid-1960s. Under CEA guidance the decision was taken to use American PWR reactors under licence from the US firm Westinghouse which was for a time a 45% shareholder in Framatome, alongside the French engineering group Creusot-Loire. In recent years Westinghouse has sold out and Creusot-Loire relinquished its shareholding when it got into financial difficulties. The shareholders of Framatome are now CEA (with 35%), the recently privatized electrical engineering group Compagnie Générale d'Electricité (40%) with EDF and the construction company Dumez holding the rest of the shares.

Exporting the technology
Framatome has captured a quarter of the international export business in nuclear power station construction and recently won a contract (of which its own share, after subcontracting out work, will be Fr5.3bn) to build two nuclear stations for China. Another indication of the industrial effect of France's nuclear energy policy has been the dominance of CEA's Cogema subsidiary in enriching and reprocessing nuclear fuel at its two main plants in Normandy and on the Rhône. Cogema alone has a fifth of the world market in uranium enrichment.

Power to spare By going for a big rolling programme based on the uniform PWR technology, France has become the most efficient producer of nuclear energy in the world, largely because the capital cost of each station is relatively low because of economies of scale in design and plant engineering. But the pro-nuclear policy of the government is now being affected by pro-conservation policy: with electricity demand levelling out, the power station building programme has been cut to one a year. Even that will leave a surplus of between six and ten stations by the early 1990s, before some of the older stations have to be taken out of service. There are two ways in which the French aim to tackle the surplus of their early nuclear zeal: exports of electricity and inward investment of manufactures. France already exports a significant proportion of its electricity: in 1985 from a total of 329twh (tera-watt hours) produced, 29twh was exported, mainly to Switzerland, Italy and Britain. Revenues have been running at Fr3.5bn a year. But France has the lowest industrial electricity prices in Europe, excluding Scandanavia, and hopes this will convince a growing number of energy-intensive industries, such as chemicals, ceramics and glass, to locate new capacity in France. At 20.8 mills per kwh ($.001), France also has the lowest nuclear power generation costs. This is less than half the cost in the USA (43.8 mills per kwh).

The future

Even the Socialist government of the early 1980s quickly abandoned any attempts to stop the rundown of France's coalmining industry: output of 15m tonnes/15.24m US tons a year is barely a quarter of what it was in the 1950s. Coal has been allotted only 16% of the total of primary energy which the government wants to produce in France. The remainder of French energy production breaks down as: oil 3% (reserves of the sole Aquitaine oil field run out before the end of this century), gas 2% (only seven years' reserves left), hydropower 13%, nuclear 55% and renewable energy (which includes biomass synfuels, geothermal energy, solar power and marine power schemes such as the tidal barrage at Rance on the Normandy/Brittany border) 11%. Since 1982 the Agence Française pour la Maîtrise de l'Energie (AFME) has been established, whose role is oil substitution, energy conservation and increasing the production of renewable energy. It operates by providing low-interest loans, grants

and tax breaks for deserving projects. The Chirac government, however, laid rather less emphasis on conservation and AFME had its budget cut to Fr700m in 1987.

There is another possible change in policy in the further deregulation of the energy sector. There have been suggestions that, as part of the deregulation process, EDF's monopoly on electricity distribution should be brought to an end. Privatization in the sector has been deemed impossible, with the exception of Elf Acquitaine, but the state monopolies on gas and coal imports are likely to be lifted.

Non-nuclear challenge Some of the gilt has begun to rub off France's nuclear power programme. The Chernobyl disaster has awakened French fears about nuclear power. One serious accident in a French PWR could shut down two-thirds of the country's generating capacity. And there have been recurring problems with the fast-breeder nuclear power station at Creys-Malville in the Rhône valley; production there is still costing twice that of PWR electricity and there have been coolant leaks that caused serious alarm. The really interesting question is to what extent the passing of the nuclear energy boom will see France taking an equally pioneering role in other forms of renewable energy production.

Top six primary nuclear energy producers in Europe (in twh)				
	Nuclear	Hydro	Thermal	Total
France	252.4	63.7	42.1	358.4
W. Germany	121.1	18.1	264.9	404.3
Sweden	70.2	60.2	71.0	137.5
UK	59.5	6.9	235.5	302.0
Belgium	39.9	1.3	17.6	58.6
Spain	36.0	26.8	59.8	122.6

Source: *Power Europe, 1987*

Chemicals

All the major chemical companies are state-owned, though Rhône-Poulenc is scheduled for privatization in the late 1980s or early 1990s. Extensive programmes of takeovers, staff reductions and plant closures have yet to make the industry competitive with its more successful European rivals. Agrochemical, petrochemical and bulk plastic sectors continue to be weak, and salvation is being sought, through R&D and acquisition, in high-price, low-volume specialty chemicals such as food additives.

Good sales, poor profits

Total sales in 1986 were Fr282bn of which Fr108bn was exported. Imports were Fr86bn, making France a net exporter, second only to West Germany as a chemical producer but lagging behind in profitability.

The big three

The three largest companies, the bulk chemical concerns CdF Chimie and Atochem (a subsidiary of Elf Aquitaine – see *Top ten companies*) and the specialty-orientated Rhône-Poulenc, owe their present shape to the nationalization programme of the early 1980s.

CdF Chimie lost Fr2.6bn on sales of Fr20.5bn in 1986. A "last chance" government cash injection of Fr3.1bn is designed to help it back into the black by the end of the decade. Since agrochemicals and petrochemicals have proved loss-makers, the company hopes to move into more specialties. The upturn in the world petrochemical market suggests further investment, perhaps with a US or European partner.

Atochem has been making modest profits (Fr300m in 1986 on sales of Fr15.3bn) since its foundation in 1983. Plant closures and tie-ups with Arco, ICI and BP Chemicals have improved the bulk chemical position, but the PVC business still needs help.

Rhône-Poulenc continues to wrestle with overcapacity and dumping in its traditional sectors such as synthetic fibres, while investing heavily in high-tech operations in biotechnology and agrochemicals. The 1986 purchase of Union Carbide's agrochemical sector has made it the world's third-largest pesticides producer. Profits in 1986 were Fr2bn on sales of Fr52.7bn.

Agrochemicals

France's agrochemical industry has a steady market in the EC where heavy subsidies keep land under agriculture. Environmentalist pressures make little impact in France. The biggest cloud on the export horizon is the fall in demand in the USA, the world's largest pesticide market. Rice pesticides may find Far Eastern markets, and Rhône-Poulenc and others are dealing with the USSR.

Biotechnology is hailed as the saviour of the agrochemical industry. Multinationals have been buying seed companies against the day when genetically-engineered crops with high yield and disease resistance are commonplace. Rhône-Poulenc is active in this field, as are Sanofi, Sandoz, Shell and Oisan.

Growing problems Stagnating demand, overproduction, and dumping by East European producers have hit France's fertilizer companies hard. CdF Chimie lost Fr600m in 1986, resulting in plant closures and divestments to concentrate on nitrogen fertilizers.

Solid gases

France's Air Liquide leads the world with 20% of the $11.5bn industrial gases market. Gross profits were Fr2.5bn in 1986, when Air Liquide boosted its US market position with the $1bn takeover of Big Three, the Texan industrial gases manufacturer.

Pharmaceuticals

The French take a lot of drugs; theirs is the fourth-largest ethical drug market in the world and they have the third-largest per capita consumption in Europe, after the West Germans and the Swiss.

A healthy market

The value of the domestic market has been growing steadily. The industry's turnover was Fr53bn in 1986, up 9.5% on the previous year, with the domestic market accounting for Fr42.6bn, a rise of 10.5%. The increase is due in part to the ageing population and in part to the introduction of new, more costly drugs. Cardiovascular, anti-ulcer and central nervous system drugs account for more than half the market; anti-infective and respiratory drugs are also important, and there is a large homoeopathic sector.

Major companies

Of the companies operating in the French market, only Rhône-Poulenc is of sufficient size to become a major multinational. Sanofi, Roussel-Uclaf and Servier are in the second rank. Others are all subsidiaries of multinationals such as Merck, Sharp and Dohme, Sandoz, Ciba-Geigy, and Hoffman La Roche.

Health-care funding comes from the social security system through payments made by employers and employees. Patients pay for their drugs, then claim "reimbursement" from the national fund. This varies between 40% and 100% depending on the nature of the drug and the illness it is used to treat. Ethical drugs, or those prescribed by doctors, account for 83% of total sales; over-the-counter medicines take a 7% slice, while off-patent (generic) drugs are relatively unimportant.

Drug pricing is a key element in the government's control of health-care spending; the manufacturer is obliged to negotiate with the government before introducing a new product to the market and it is at this stage that the level of "reimbursement" is set.

Manufacturers attempt to stress the therapeutic advantages offered by new drugs since the level of reimbursement is higher for such drugs. The price-fixing process takes a minimum of seven months. After 2–3 years on the government's list of approved drugs, each product is compared with others available; if no extra therapeutic benefits can be demonstrated a drug may only remain on the list by virtue of being cheaper than comparable products. Prices are reviewed twice a year. There are no price controls on over-the-counter medicines.

Research gap

Drug price rises have lagged behind inflation for years; on average drugs cost 25% less than they do elsewhere in the EC. Research spending is also low, and French companies are falling behind in key areas like biotechnology. Around Fr6bn was spent on research and development in 1985, 12% of all pharmaceutical sales. Only a tiny 0.5% of drug R&D is state-funded, in contrast to 19.5% for the rest of French industry.

Patents and testing Under the European Patent Convention French drug patents last twenty years; patents are usually filed soon after the drug is developed, but before it can be marketed it must undergo several years of testing on animals followed by stringent clinical trials. Most French firms conduct some of this research outside France. After successful testing, final government approval must be obtained before marketing. This takes at least seven months from the date of submission. When testing, approval and pricing procedures are complete, a manufacturer may have as little as six or seven years of patent cover in which to recoup development costs.

Retailing

Deteriorating economic conditions made the first half of the 1980s a difficult period for French retailers. A drop in purchasing power created more cost-conscious consumers and forced retailers to intensify competition. This led to a polarization within retailing. On the one hand there has been an increase in hypermarkets and supermarkets, the only sector experiencing real volume growth. On the other, smaller specialized shops, especially franchises, have achieved some success.

Going for growth

In a stagnant market French retailers have shown some resourcefulness and several common elements have emerged in their growth strategies.

"Supercentrales" In an attempt to keep prices down without squeezing their margins, the supermarket chains got together to create these central purchasing organizations to strengthen their bargaining position and force concessions from suppliers.

Freedom fighters Retailers have attempted to remove restrictions on what they can sell. Centres Leclerc, for example, has run vigorous campaigns, with limited success, to win the right to sell products traditionally stocked by pharmacists.

Technology The use of modern technology such as bar codes, scanning and electronic payment systems has been rapid and widespread.

Big is beautiful

Hypermarkets Since Marcel Fournier opened the first Carrefour hypermarket in 1963 more than 600 similar stores have been built and in 1987 they accounted for 17% of retail trade. Despite restrictions on the size of outlets, the average French hypermarket remains larger than that of many other European countries. There is a growing tendency for hypermarkets to emphasize their non-food ranges, particularly textiles and household appliances.

Specialization

The problems affecting traditional retailers are shown by the declining numbers and market share of *les*
grands magasins (department stores) and *les magasins populaires* (variety stores) such as Monoprix and Prisunic. They have faced competition from both hypermarkets and the specialist chains.

Non-food chain stores have been relatively slow to develop in France. The exception has been footwear, where groups such as André, Bally and Eram have flourished. Two of the most successful chains are FNAC (audio, video and books), and Darty (household appliances). Foreign chains operating in France include Habitat, C&A and Jaeger and the Swedish furniture firm IKEA.

Franchising The physical structure of the French market has encouraged a full development of franchising arrangements. There are many medium-size towns but few large conurbations outside Paris.

Direct marketing

Mail order The French mail order market is the third largest in Europe after West Germany and the UK. The market leaders, La Redoute and Les Trois Suisses, compete on stable catalogue prices and high-quality merchandise.

Teleshopping The introduction of Minitel to connect homes to a catalogue database, with credit card payment systems, is in its infancy but is expected to grow rapidly; 300,000 households in the Paris area already have a terminal.

Factory discount centres French consumers are more than ever before willing to accept discount pricing. In some centres savings vary between 30% and 70%.

Tourism

France is the third-largest earner of tourist receipts in Europe after Spain and Italy. It received some 37m visitors in 1985, the figure having grown annually from 30m in 1980. The net balance of payments surplus on travel rose from Fr9.4bn in 1980 to Fr30.4bn in 1985. The French take more main holidays at home (84%) than either the Germans (40%) or the British (65%). Of Fr343bn spent on "interior tourist consumption" in 1984, Fr66bn came from nonresidents.

La Belle France

Although primarily known as a cultural or seaside destination – the Paris galleries or the growing number of music festivals, and the beaches of the Côte d'Azur, for example – France has something to offer a diverse range of visitors. It has seven mountain ranges, including the French Alps which provide the largest fully-equipped skiing area in Europe. The Atlantic and Mediterranean coasts cater for beach holidays and France has huge tracts of unspoilt countryside.

Independent travellers

Eighty-five per cent of tourists visiting France arrive by surface transport, 60% by road, 13% by sea and 12% by rail, while only 15% arrive by air. Some 75% of all arrivals organized the trip without using the services of the retail travel industry and this reflects the dominance of the private car as the mode of travel to and within France.

Somewhere to stay

Capacity in all forms of commercial accommodation – hotels, gîtes, chambres d'hôtes and family holiday homes – was 3.4m in 1975. This grew in less than a decade by more than 1m to 4.5m in 1984. Over half this capacity is in camping and caravan sites, nearly 40% in hotels and 10% in other forms of accommodation.

Government policy

In 1986 the government replaced several agencies with one *Groupement d'Interêt Economique* called *Maison de la France* to oversee development of the range and quality of the tourist services at home and promote France abroad.

Government assistance for specific developments can be impressive; the preparations for the Winter Olympics of 1992 include a major hotel and roadbuilding programme that will benefit not just the main centre at Albertville but surrounding areas in the Savoie.

Problems

In common with most other countries with a big tourist trade, seasonality is a major problem and the biggest threat to profitability. *Visas* have recently presented another difficulty. Both 1986 and 1987 were poor years for tourist receipts in France. This resulted from a combination of factors. In late 1986 the French introduced a visa requirement for all non-EC nationals in response to a terrorist bombing campaign in Paris during 1986. This campaign, combined with the falling dollar, caused many Americans to stay away.

Prices At the same time price deregulation caused a rise in hotel and café prices. The cost-conscious have tended to favour Spain whose net receipts in 1986 were more than three times those of France.

Prospects

A number of major events are planned for the next few years; the French tourist calendar includes the bicentenary of the French Revolution in 1989, the Winter Olympics and the opening of Euro-Disneyland northeast of Paris in 1992.

Telecommunications

The telecommunications industry has been one of France's most successful sectors in recent years. After suffering from one of the worst telephone services in Europe 20 years ago, France has transformed the system and made it one of the most modern in the world with 70% of local circuits and 56% of inter-city lines digitalized. More than 50% of telephones lines are now linked to a fully electronic exchange. It also makes an important contribution of around Fr20bn to the state budget. Telecommunications, which boasts a very high *valeur ajoutée* (added value) of over Fr80bn, represents almost 1.7% of French GDP and is likely to remain a high priority area within the French economy.

Regulation

In late 1987 control of the telecommunications network in France was still almost entirely in state hands despite a plan to open up some of the services to competition. A new "independent" regulatory authority, the Commission Nationale de la Communication et des Libertés (CNCL), was set up in 1986 to coordinate policy and regulate the sector as well as the broadcasting services, but the body that controls almost all telephone services is the Direction Générale des Télécommunications (DGT). Operating under the Ministère des Postes et Télécommunications (PTT), DGT is preparing for a programme of deregulation. However, the market in France is less regulated than in many countries. Private companies have been operating for some time on a completely open market for the installation of telephones. The number of lines tripled in the 1970s and, with 24m subscribers, the French telecommunications market is the third largest in the world. There are also plans to open up to competition services for telephone booths, mobile telephones and highly profitable value-added-networks (VANs).

Developing services

Digital switching Aware of increasingly competitive markets, the DGT has been investing heavily in new equipment since 1985. In 1986 its Fr32.4bn investment was second only to Electricité de France (EDF) in public sector investment. A large proportion of this is now being directed away from the domestic phone service and into *télématiques* (integrated digital services) such as Réseau Numérique à Intégration des Services (RNIS) and video communications.

Minitel is the most visible success in recent years. Launched as a public service in May 1985, this simplified computer can be linked to any telephone and is supplied free of charge in many areas. It provides the subscriber with a nationwide phone directory service at minimal cost but also offers some 6,000 other services from information providers. There were 3.4m subscribers to the service at the end of 1987, a figure expected to reach 8m by the 1990s.

Satellites The French are keen to exploit the success of DGT's Telecom 1 business satellites. A second satellite has permitted the development of digital, telecommunications and video communication links. A third was due for launch in early 1988.

The direct broadcasting satellite (TDF1), due for launch in 1988, will have four visual channels and 16 sound channels. The project, after much opposition, is government funded at a cost of Fr2bn.

"Plan cable" Fibre optics is also a high priority area. In 1987 the government signed an agreement to cable 52 French towns (5.5m homes). This represented an initial investment of roughly Fr25bn and is expected to be complete by 1995.

High-tech industries

Until 1986 the development of telecommunications and computers was under the control of the PTT. This administrative burden was deemed too great for one ministry and responsibility for the development of computers and data processing (*informatique*) and office automation systems (*bureautique*) was transferred to the Ministère de l'Industrie. Since then the emphasis has shifted away from government-sponsored research programmes to joint-company ventures.

Crowded market

There are more than 500 companies in the fast-growing computer market. The largest is IBM France with sales of almost Fr38bn (1986). The state-owned Machines Bull ranks second but has only half the turnover. Of the top 15 companies more than a third are multinationals, including Burroughs (4th), Hewlett Packard (5th), and Digital (6th).

Software growth

French companies have been remarkably successful in the software sector and are among the biggest in Europe. The best-known example is the European leader in computer services, Cap Gemini Sogeti. Cap Gemini moved quickly from a highly successful debut on the *second marché* to a full listing on the Bourse. Other software companies to have gone public in recent years include CEGID, a young Lyon-based group, the Compagnie Générale d'Informatique, the French leader in multiuser software packages for industry.

Filière électronique Many of the French software groups owe their initial growth to government-financed technology programmes. The Chirac government, perhaps surprisingly, made few changes in the Socialist government's *filière électronique*, a wide-ranging programme launched in 1982 to give impetus to the electronics sector. Under Chirac there was also a new policy of redirecting resources towards small companies. Software producers themselves have also been helped by a protection law introduced in July 1985 and the lifting of price controls.

Self-reliance

Companies are now being forced to become less reliant on government aid, and joint ventures with overseas firms are more common. For example, SESA (one-third owned by Cap Gemini) which developed TRANSPAC, the nationwide packet-switching system, now derives most of its sales from building turnkey systems such as the communications network for the French air force. This has led to healthy export sales.

ESPRIT

French companies have been at the forefront of this EC technology programme since its launch in 1984.

Three of France's largest groups, Thomson, CGE and Bull, were among the 12 European groups chosen to form the Directive Committee which established the work plans for this innovative programme of industrial cooperation in R&D. While these three take the lion's share, a number of smaller, often recently created, service companies are also involved.

Smart cards

Bull is expecting to expand rapidly after investing over Fr300m in the "smart card." Similar in size to a credit card, the smart card has a microchip memory which will enable the user to pay shopping bills and accounts, as well as make telephone calls. It can also access financial information and may be used in a range of other applications.

Food and drink

The reputation of the French as a nation of gourmets is based on the excellence of their chefs, the worldwide proliferation of French cooking and restaurants, and their pre-eminence as wine producers. However, the traditions of painstaking home cooking and prodigious eating and drinking are both in decline, affected by changes in attitudes to health, in the population structure and in attitudes towards processed convenience foods. The industry is dominated by medium and small-sized companies which, on the one hand, have the flexibility to respond well to new challenges but on the other are vulnerable to multinational takeover.

Steady growth

Food sales have risen by a steady 1.6% per year in real terms for more than twenty years. This rate is expected to decrease to around 0.6% as a result of a saturated market and a decline in population growth.

A healthier outlook France is following the general European trend towards a greater awareness of the nutritional values of food. This is expressed as an avoidance of "harmful" foods rather than embracing "health food" alternatives on a large scale. Products in relative decline include bread, sugar, pasta products, butter and other fats and foods with additives. Low-fat and low-sugar products are increasingly popular, as are high-fibre products; breakfast cereal, formerly a tiny sector, has been growing at 20% per annum, with muesli products leading the market. In the drinks sector there is a pronounced swing towards fruit juices and carbonated drinks using artificial sweeteners rather than sugar. The consumption of bottled mineral water is high – at 56 litres per head per year it is by far the highest in Europe – and is likely to remain so. New ranges of products such as flavoured mineral water are being released to meet the demand for healthier drinks.

Small is profitable The responsibility for the cooking and preparation of food is inexorably shifting from the housewife to the manufacturer. Lunch times are shorter, more women are working, and eating has become less of a family occasion and more a matter of personal taste and individual choice. This "destructuralization" of mealtimes has been compounded by a trend towards smaller households. There are 11.5m households of one or two people and their number is increasing twice as fast as households in general. The main effect for the food industry has been an increased emphasis on the production of small packs, and the introduction of one-person portions, both of processed foods and of pre-packed meats, fruit and vegetables.

Eating out Every category of restaurant has benefited from the changes in French eating habits. Even fast-food hamburger restaurants, once anathema to the French with their reputation for preferring traditional cooking, have been gaining ground, especially among the young. Around 15% of meals are now taken outside the home, and the commercial catering market is worth Fr107.5bn (1986). A quarter of this is accounted for by fast food chain restaurants and cafés such as France Quick and its closest rival McDonalds. There are over 1,000 fast food restaurants, 40% of them in and around Paris.

A matter of convenience

Changes in the size of households and in eating habits have gradually eroded resistance to convenience foods. Product growth areas include semi-prepared foods and frozen foods. Frozen foods met with particular resistance in France, as canned foods had many years earlier. Even today, canned foods such as vegetables and complete meals are only really popular when quality is emphasized; instant or canned soups are not popular. Now frozen foods are a buoyant sector, but again quality is the important factor. France is a net importer of frozen foods, and though home output is increasing by as much as 20% per year the gap is widening. Prepared meals, at around 5%, are the smallest subsector but the fastest-growing, aided by the increasing ownership of freezers and microwave ovens.

Industry strategies Faced with a more or less stable home market in terms of volume, manufacturers are seeking to strengthen their domestic position through more research and innovation and quality improvements.

Export growth

France has for the past few years been a net exporter of foods; indeed the industry is now one of the country's biggest foreign exchange earners. In 1985 total exports of processed foods were worth Fr77bn against imports of Fr67bn. The only sectors in which France is a net importer are fruit, fish, shellfish, biscuits, chocolate products, soft drinks and fruit juices.

Aggressive export drives provide opportunities for growth not available in the domestic market. France's leading food and drinks group, BSN, has built up a position as leader in the world yogurt market through Gervais Danone, breaking out from a strong home base to Europe, but also to Latin America, the USA and even the notoriously milk-resistant Japan.

Consolidation Ironically, the very success of French food exporters has made them more susceptible to takeover by multinationals. With sales of Fr35bn, BSN is the only company large enough to feel

relatively secure. The second company in sales terms, Source Perrier, producers of soft drinks and cheeses, has sales of just Fr11bn. Takeovers within the country and protective shareholdings are seen as the best defence against takeovers from abroad; in 1986 BSN consolidated its position with the takeover of Générale Biscuit.

Wine and spirits

The world's finest wines are still acknowledged to come from France, though quality is by no means even throughout the industry. The last ten years have seen a striking improvement in *vins de table* from cooperatives who have equipped themselves with modern technology and trained personnel with the help of French and EC grants and loans. Cooperatives also benefit from favourable tax treatment.

There has been a marked drop in the volume of wine drunk in France, however, particularly of the low-quality wines drunk by the ageing rural population. Nevertheless, consumption still runs at 80 litres per head per year, and wine is still the older generation's favourite drink. The top-quality wines, those designated Appellation d'Origine Contrôlée (AOC), are holding their own, and even increasing sales. As quality becomes more important, so more wines are produced that meet the requirements of the AOC regulations. Wine exports were worth Fr17bn in 1985, more than three-quarters of that AOC wines. The UK, West Germany and the USA are the largest markets for French wines, though US consumption has been declining for the past two years. In world markets France now faces increasing competition from the table wines of reliable quality produced in California and Australia.

A large proportion of the wine grapes grown in France go to make brandies, which added Fr5.9bn of exports in 1985.

France's leading companies

The impact of the privatization programme and distortions caused by the turbulent markets of late 1987 made company rankings subject to frequent change.

Elf Aquitaine

Elf ranks number 11 in the worldwide oil and gas sector. It is 56% state-owned, but the government's stake is gradually being reduced; 11% of the shares were sold off to the public in 1986. Elf has major interests in chemicals, plastics and – through its 61% stake in Sanofi – in pharmaceuticals, bio-industries, perfumes and cosmetics. Most of its production comes from declining gasfields at Lacq in France and Frigg in the North Sea, and a stake in an oilfield at Ekofisk (North Sea). The stock market has long since recognized Elf's problems. *1986 sales* Fr115bn; *profits* Fr4.3bn.

Air Liquide

Air Liquide is the world's biggest producer of industrial gases with 67% of its sales derived from industrial gas; the remainder comes from chemicals (17.9%), welding materials (10.6%) and engineering/construction (4.5%). *1986 sales*: Fr20.6bn; *profits* Fr1.2bn.

Thomson-CSF

A 55.3% subsidiary of state-owned Thomson SA, Thomson-CSF is a world leader in electronic defence systems (68% of sales). The group is also involved in electronic components (14% of sales) and engineering and industrial products (5%). Thomson-CSF's success has been achieved through a sweeping reorganization; it shed its civil telecommunications business, and in 1987 it sold its loss-making medical equipment business. *1986 sales* Fr35.6bn; *profits* Fr2.2bn.

Peugeot

The Peugeot group, embracing the Peugeot and Citroën marques, is the fourth-largest car manufacturer in Europe and the largest in France. It has two broad operating areas: the automobile division (96% of sales), and the mechanical engineering and services division. (See also *Motor vehicles*.) *1986 sales* Fr104.9bn; *profits* Fr3.6bn.

LVMH

Created as a holding company in July 1987, LVMH groups together Louis Vuitton and Moët-Hennessy. The holding company has three main sub-divisions: the Louis Vuitton branch owns Veuve Cliquot champagne and a stake in Guerlain perfumes, as well as making luggage and leather goods; the Moët-Hennessy branch makes champagne and other wines (42% of sales), cognac and spirits (30% of sales) and a number of other products, and Christian Dior, the third branch, which was formerly a subsidiary of Moët, is France's second-largest manufacturer of perfumes and beauty products. The new group is a powerful player in the luxury goods sector. *1986 sales* Fr9.8bn; *profits* Fr1.1bn.

BSN

Formerly BSN Gervais Danone, BSN is France's largest food company: its six divisions take in biscuits, beer, general grocery products, champagne and mineral water, and containers. Among the more famous brands, it produces Danone yogurts and Kronenbourg beer. Since acquiring the Générale Biscuit group in 1986, it has expanded aggressively. It is now the second-biggest pasta manufacturer in the world, controlling Italian producers Panzani, Agnesi, Ponte and others. The management of BSN was worried about its vulnerability to a hostile bidder and in 1987 it took the precaution of placing shares with friendly institutions, virtually guaranteeing its independence. *1986 sales* Fr33.6bn; *profits* Fr1.1bn.

Michelin

Michelin is the world's second-largest producer of tyres after Goodyear. It also makes tubes, wheels, steel cables, and has a separate division producing maps and travel guides. The group exports to 150 countries, and has manufacturing plants in the USA, Latin America and Africa, as well as 80 factories in Europe. In 1987, it announced a tie-up with the tyre-maker Wuon Poong in Korea, aimed at increasing its penetration of Far Eastern markets. *1986 sales* Fr46.3bn; *profits* Fr1.9bn.

Saint-Gobain

Europe's top producer of flat glass and bottles, Saint-Gobain is also a leader in many other sectors – insulation materials, refractories, fibre-cement and fibre reinforcements. Through its merger in 1970 with Pont-à-Mousson, it became the world leader for cast-iron pipes, and it is also an important producer of paper and packaging. Saint-Gobain's track record has been chequered in recent years. Nationalized in 1982, four years later it became the first industrial company to be privatized under M. Chirac's programme. From a loss of Fr478m in 1982, it recovered to become one of France's best growth companies in 1986; profits rose by 130%, with sales up 12.6%. While much remains to be done, the company holds a dominant position in all its markets and huge potential for further cost-saving and productivity gains make it a favourite for long-term earnings growth. *1986 sales* Fr77.7bn; *profits* Fr1.3bn.

L'Oréal

L'Oréal is the biggest cosmetics company in the world. Its sales are made up of hairdressing and consumer products (50.6% of sales), perfumes and beauty aids (30.55%) and pharmaceuticals (15.07%). It owns a 55% stake in Synthélabo, the fourth-largest French pharmaceutical company with sales of Fr2.6bn. Under the L'Oréal brand name it makes a variety of shampoo and haircare products, and it has numerous well-known brands of perfume such as Cacharel, Anaïs and Lancôme. L'Oréal sells 60% of its products outside France; its biggest market is the USA. In 1986 it had a good year, with sales up 11%. *1986 sales* Fr18.1bn; *profits* Fr930m.

Lafarge-Coppée

The world's largest cement-producer, ranking number one both in France and the USA. The group is also active in construction, and has diversified into plaster, refractories, sanitary ware, aluminous cement and biotechnology. In 1982, Lafarge reorganized its North American operations and introduced a new holding company, Lafarge Corporation, to the New York stock exchange. The group now has a higher proportion of sales in North America (43%) than in France (39%). Further expansion in the USA is on the way. Trends are buoyant for cement, concrete and aggregates in France, where a number of major civil engineering projects are in progress. *1986 sales* Fr16.9bn; *profits* Fr1.1bn.

Générale des Eaux

The group Générale des Eaux is the leader in France for provision of water services to local and municipal authorities. Although originally its function was uniquely the distribution of water, it has diversified into other areas such as waste treatment, production and distribution of thermal energy, building and public works. It has recently become a major player in the media and broadcasting business. It holds a 21% stake in France's TV pay channel, Canal Plus, and leads in the development of cable TV networks. *1986 sales* Fr48bn; *profits* Fr765m.

The Political Scene

The government of the nation

Since 1870 France has had a republican form of government, with a president, a prime minister and two houses of parliament. The constitution of the present Fifth Republic was devised by de Gaulle in 1958, partly to suit his own style of paternalistic rule. It greatly increased the powers of the president, but it has left ambiguous the exact share-out of power between the president and the lower house of parliament, the Assemblée Nationale. As both are directly elected by the people, they are both sovereign, and the prime minister is responsible to both – a *cohabitation* that has sometimes proved uneasy.

The constitution

France's rulers are bound by a written constitution of some 8,000 words, divided into 92 articles. This stipulates the powers and duties of president, government and parliament, as well as the conditions of election and the ways in which the constitution can be amended and is to be implemented and safeguarded.
Amendments The constitution can be amended on the initiative either of the president or of parliament, but any amendments must be approved by parliament and under some circumstances they must also be submitted to popular referendum.
Safeguards The Conseil Constitutionnel, a nine-member supreme court, exists to interpret the constitution and to make sure that all elections are fair and proper and that all acts of parliament, all actions of government or president, are fully constitutional. On the whole, this court works well and impartially; although its members are politically selected (three by the president, three each by the heads of the two houses of parliament), it has set itself above the maelstrom of party feuding, as the supreme arbiter.

The president

The president, who is both head of state and executive head of government, is elected every seven years on a direct popular vote, with a two-round ballot, and can be re-elected for a second term. If he dies while in office or resigns, a new election is called.

The president's powers under the constitution are considerable. He is commander-in-chief of the armed forces and he negotiates and ratifies treaties. He appoints the prime minister, on whose proposal he also then appoints the other ministers; and every Wednesday he presides over a regular meeting of the Conseil des Ministres at the Elysée Palace. He signs the council's decrees, makes the senior civil and military appointments, and he has the right to dissolve the Assemblée Nationale and call for new elections, as both de Gaulle and Mitterrand have done. He normally cannot block the legislation of parliament, but he can in some circumstances bypass it by appealing over its head directly to the nation via referendum. In the event of a grave national crisis, Article 16 allows the president to take special powers and rule dictatorially as de Gaulle did in 1961, in face of an army revolt in Algeria.

Parliament

Parliament also has considerable powers; but, being by its nature less single-minded than the president, it does not so easily make full use of them; indeed it, generally, plays a lesser role than it does in many countries. It meets for only 120 days a year, in two sessions. There are two houses, the directly-elected Assemblée Nationale (lower house), and the indirectly-elected Sénat (upper house). New legislation is passed between them, for two or more readings by each. Bills can be presented either by the government or by individuals, but matters of importance are rarely covered by private members' bills.

L'Assemblée Nationale This consists of 577 deputies who sit in the Palais Bourbon in a semicircular chamber with the parties ranged from far left to far right as viewed from the rostrum that faces them. The Assemblée's president, usually a leading figure of the main party in office, chairs the debates, which tend to be rhetorical in the Latin manner, with long speeches from the rostrum and only brief interventions from the benches. Much preparatory work is done by the Assemblée's various committees. Though deputies are well paid (Fr348,000 a year in 1987), many have other part-time jobs too. Far fewer than in former days are from a legal background (only 33), while 140 are teachers by profession; 33 are women. If a deputy is appointed minister, he or she must give up his or her seat to a previously nominated substitute – a sensible system that frees a minister from constituency chores.

Elections to the Assemblée take place every five years at the maximum. The centre-right won a whole series of them in 1958–81, then the left won in 1981, then the centre-right again in 1986. The electoral system has varied over the years. The Socialists introduced proportional representation for 1986 with constituencies grouped by *département*; the right then arranged to return to the previous single-member system. But they have retained the French tradition of a double ballot, whereby the first round eliminates all but the two best-placed candidates, who then face a run-off a week later.

Le Sénat is indirectly elected by a college of some 130,000 local councillors: hence it is weighted towards rural areas and its make-up tends to be to the right of the Assemblée. It consists of 318 senators, mostly local politicians, each with a nine-year mandate. The Sénat can amend or try to throw out bills passed to it by the Assemblée but if the two reach stalemate, the latter has the final decision. The Sénat's influence is thus limited.

Local government

This is based on a three-tier structure: the 22 regions, each with its own elected assembly and executive; the 96 *départements*, each with an elected council; the 36,500 *communes*, each with its council and mayor, varying in size from large cities to tiny villages. Until recently the system was highly centralized: each *département* was tightly supervised by a Paris-appointed *préfet* and local bodies had little autonomy.

Devolutionary changes Under growing regionalist pressure, the Socialist government in 1982–86 carried through wide-ranging devolutionary reforms. The *préfet* has lost much of his power and his role is now mainly one of coordination, arbitration and security, while the regions for the first time have directly elected assemblies, and all local bodies have increased budgets and financial autonomy. Briefly, *communes* are in charge of their own town-planning, building and environment, *départements* look after welfare and social services, and regions deal with adult education and some aspects of culture, tourism and industrial development, but the state retains control of education, justice and the health service.

Local government influences national government through personal factors, for it is a strong French tradition that senior politicians need to seek a local base, maybe as mayor of a large town or, conversely, that a local potentate will develop national ambitions.

The reins of power

At national level, all works relatively smoothly so long as the president is backed by an Assemblée of the same political colour as himself. He can then appoint a prime minister and government of that same colour and can effectively rule the roost, but with the result that the Assemblée can be reduced to something of a rubber stamp, approving the designs of president and premier. This was roughly the situation from 1958 to 1986. But de Gaulle, with little concern for *l'après-moi*, had bequeathed a constitution that gives the president a mandate of seven years and the Assemblée one of five: it was thus inevitable that one day, with the ordinary swing of the pendulum, the voters would elect an Assemblée hostile to the ruling president. When this happens, as it did for the first time in 1986, the reins of power become severely tangled. For the constitution states that it is the government, not the president, that decides and conducts national policy; and the government is above all answerable to the Assemblée.

The perils of cohabitation

Even before 1986, there were some policy or personality clashes between an ambitious prime minister and the president, notably in 1974–76 when Jacques Chirac, the forceful neo-Gaullist, duelled with President Giscard d'Estaing. But the president was usually able to win by changing his prime minister (as Giscard did then). However, when the right regained the Assemblée from the Socialists in the March 1986 elections, a lonely Mitterrand in the Elysée had little option but to appoint a right-wing prime minister (Chirac again got the job) and to let him form a government of his own choice. The ensuing *cohabitation* worked rather better than had been expected, for two reasons. First, it was popular with a French public that favoured consensus and a truce in the old left–right dogfights. The two leaders were therefore condemned to go along with it. Second, they and their parties mainly saw eye-to-eye on the two key issues of defence and foreign affairs, areas where constitutionally and by precedent the president has a strong direct voice. But, in the whole field of domestic and economic matters, Mitterrand was obliged to let the government push ahead with

policies which he disliked, such as privatization. He could have refused to sign laws and decrees but this would have jeopardized his own position. So he was forced into a more negative role, and tensions grew. The system may have the virtues of balance, but many French people now believe that it will have to be amended, possibly by reducing the president's mandate to five years in line with the Assemblée.

The ministries

The prime minister has a staff of advisers and specialists whose main role is to coordinate the work of the various ministries. Until March 1986 the Elysée itself directly supervised many ministries, but under *cohabitation* its influence was largely limited to defence and foreign affairs. The Conseil de Ministres, usually about 15–20 strong, is made up of the heads of the main ministries. **The Ministère de l'Economie, des Finances et de la Privatisation** is somewhat dreaded by the other ministries, whose annual budgets it allocates. It also decides the totals of public spending and manages interest rates. One of this huge ministry's dependent sub-ministries looks after the budget, a second is in charge of the privatization programme, a third of foreign trade; one key department, the Direction des Rélations Economiques Extérieures (la DREE), is in charge of foreign trade promotion and has offices in many overseas embassies.

The Ministère des Affaires Etrangères (Foreign Ministry), usually known as *le Quai d'Orsay*, runs foreign policy and supervises the embassies. Though it leaves commercial matters to the DREE, it deals with financial relations and is also in charge of official French cultural activity abroad. (The EC's economic policy is coordinated by a special body: the Secrétariat-Général du Comité Interministériel.)

The Ministère de la Défense supervises all the armed forces and the *gendarmerie*. It is the biggest single purchaser from French industry.

The Ministère de l'Intérieur plays a powerful and varied role. It operates the *préfectures* throughout the provinces; it is in charge of prisons and much of the police; and it deals with immigration, crime and the fight against terrorism.

The Ministère de l'Industrie, des Postes et Télécommunications et du Tourisme coordinates industrial policy, including the granting of subsidies. Telecommunications and tourism are under its umbrella.

The Ministère de l'Equipement, du Logement, de l'Aménagement du Territoire et des Transports has as wide-ranging a brief as its title suggests. It deals with public works such as the Channel Tunnel; one of its sub-ministries looks after civil aviation and other transport matters.

The Ministère de la Culture et de la Communication and **the Ministère de l'Agriculture** are both especially important in France.

Other ministries Other major ministries and sub-ministries are those of Justice, Education, and Social Affairs and Labour. There are also a number of special state

agencies: most notably, the Délégation à l'Aménagement du Territoire et à l'Action Régionale (DATAR) which supervises regional development; and the Commissariat Général au Plan (*le Plan*) which still prepares its five-year economic plans but has much less influence than in the immediate postwar years.

The civil service

French civil servants have helped to provide continuity and stability during periods of rapidly shifting governments like that of the Fourth Republic. When there is a sharp change of power between left and right, as happened in 1981 and 1986, certain heads roll but not too many: those in top positions in the main state services are replaced, and so is the *cabinet ministériel* (private office) that accompanies each minister, but the permanent staff of each ministry stays in place, ready to serve a new master.

Staff belong either to the ordinary ranks or to the elitist stream of the upper civil service that wields so much of the true power in France and is a crucial and unique phenomenon. This elite tends to be recruited from ENA and the Grandes Ecoles (see *Education*) and many of the best go into the Grands Corps, such as the Cour des Comptes which verifies public accounts, and the Conseil d'Etat which advises on legal disputes between state and citizen. As well as performing such humdrum routine duties, these exclusive club-like bodies act as reservoirs of top talent, and their privileged members are often seconded to serve the state in various fields. Some will join a minister's personal cabinet, the small decision-making power unit within each ministry. More ordinary civil servants, without the right diplomas and Grands Corps privileges, struggle along in the ministry's routine departments. This elitist system is a cause of controversy, but even the Socialists made little attempt to reform it.

Party politics

In France, with its revolutionary tradition, the conflict between left and right has long been sharper than in most countries, and until recently the political scene was polarized into warring blocs – Socialists-plus-Communists versus an anti-left coalition. Since the mid-1980s, however, as the Socialists have moved towards the centre and broken with their troublesome partners, so the prospect appears of some centre-focused coalition, or of a normal alternation of power between moderate groups. This portends a striking change towards consensus in French politics, and one which seems to find favour with the public. The recent *cohabitation*, which was on the whole quite a success, would have been unthinkable even ten years ago.

The parties

About 1m people belong to a political party, but the respective memberships give little guide to the sharp fluctuations in the voters' loyalties. Nor are parties divided on a clear class basis. For example, Gaullism has always had a sizable following in the working class, while a large number of the bourgeoisie vote for the Socialists.

Under the Fourth Republic there were many splinter parties, but today only five or six are represented in the Assemblée Nationale. In the March 1986 elections, the Front National (extreme right-wing) won 35 seats, the neo-Gaullist RPR (Rassemblement pour la République) 155, the right-of-centre UDF group of parties (Union pour la Démocratie Française) 131, the Socialists and allies 212, the Communists 35.

Rassemblement pour la République

The RPR is the present-day incarnation of de Gaulle's party and many of its older members still loyally seek to apply the General's ideals. But since his death, the party has shifted to a vaguer kind of neo-Gaullism, centring round a new leader, Jacques Chirac. It is a popular mass movement with no very clear philosophy, attracting a political spectrum ranging from the hard law-and-order right to liberal progressives. The party is less nationalistic and wary of NATO and "Europeanism" than it used to be. It has also modified its old Gaullist belief in a strong centralized state, and since returning to power in 1986 it has actively pursued the new politics of encouraging privatization, relaxed control of prices, permitted greater freedom of labour, and cut taxation and public spending. It has generally enjoyed good relations with the world of business and industry.

Union pour la Démocratie Française

The RPR's main coalition partner is itself a loose grouping of diverse elements, bound together historically by a distaste for Gaullism. An even greater dislike of the left has led them into alliance with the RPR.

The major formation within the UDF is the Parti Républicain (PR), founded by Giscard d'Estaing and which loyally supported him during his presidency, 1974–81. Giscard is still a leading member, but the party machine has now been taken over by a much younger group of very dynamic and ambitious men led by François Léotard and Alain Madelin (*la bande à Leo*, as it is called) who fervently preach ultra-liberal economic ideas and want the power of the state to wane much further. The smaller Centre des Démocrates Sociaux (CDS), led by Jean Lecanuet and Pierre Méhaignerie, is closer to the centre ground: it has committed "social" ideas and is strongly pro-European and pro-Atlantic. Outside both these parties is the enigmatic Raymond Barre, who has no clear power base but is widely regarded by the UDF as a presidential front-runner.

Parti Socialiste

In sharp contrast to the rigid and hermetic Communists, the Parti Socialiste is open and easy-going. When Mitterrand became its leader in 1971, the party was at a low ebb with only 16% of the vote. He restored its morale and strength, so that it soon grew much larger than its Communist rival, and with 36% of the vote was the dominant partner when the left won power in 1981.

Mitterrand's government started out in a doctrinaire spirit with a wave of nationalizations, plus a neo-Keynesian package of reflation, high public spending and costly social measures. In economic terms this swiftly spelt disaster, and in 1982–83 the Socialists faced the unpleasant facts, learned market realism, broke with dogma and moved over to austerity. This restored the economy but the voters nonetheless threw the Socialists out in 1986. During their five years in power they made some valuable reforms of local government and labour relations.

Mitterrand's great achievement was in reforming the party without losing its unity. He drew the party towards social democracy, neutralizing its Marxist wing which had helped shape the earlier dogmas. Today the party still has its factions and disputes but basically is now in favour of a market economy and has tacitly dropped plans to renationalize. It is pro-Europe and pro-NATO, and its relations with the business world, though still wary, have much improved.

Extremist and fringe parties

Parti Communiste (PCF) From a postwar peak of 28% of the vote, the PCF has declined, and recently very fast, to 9.7% in 1986, and is likely to fall much lower in future elections.

Though its four cabinet ministers under Mitterrand gave a good showing, this failed to convince its own voters who grew increasingly weary of the mediocre, ghetto-like and secretive leadership of Georges Marchais and his clique. The PCF may not in reality be as closely subservient to the Soviet Union as it appears, but it is still Stalinist in its make-up, and it has consistently expelled all those who try to modernize it. Most intellectuals have deserted a party that is a waning force in French politics by splitting the left vote. However, it is still making it hard for the Socialists to regain power.

Front National (FN) The recent ascent of this racist extreme-right party can be explained by popular fears that coloured immigrants, mainly Arab, are responsible for a rise in crime and are fuelling unemployment. Its rousingly demagogic leader, Jean-Marie Le Pen, has shorn the FN of some of its more violent elements, and is trying to make it seem respectable; but its main platform is still to "turn back the tide of immigration" by sending the foreigners home, and to crack down hard on all crime and disorder. The FN's support, mostly lower middle-class and urban, is especially strong among former French settlers in Algeria. Many working-class defectors from the Parti Communiste have also sided with the FN.

Fringe groups The extreme-left *groupuscules*, Maoist, Trotskyist and other, that played so vocal and virulent a role in the post-1968 period have now largely withered away, even in student circles. The very radical Parti Socialiste Unifié has also greatly declined. Les Verts, the green party, is still vocal but has never made much impact in France. Two tiny fringe royalist movements still exist. And there are small separatist parties in regions such as Corsica and Brittany. None of these groups has any seats in the Assemblée Nationale.

National security

In matters of defence, France is the leading nuclear power in Western Europe, and also has the largest armed forces after West Germany.

The armed forces

The total number of men under arms (excluding the *gendarmerie* and joint service personnel) is about 513,000, of whom just half are conscripts serving a 12-month period. About two-thirds of all young males perform this compulsory service (the rest are exempt on such grounds as health, family obligations and studies), though conscription is increasingly unpopular, and is even being questioned by the authorities.

Defence spending is 15% of the state budget and 3.8% of GDP; this puts France below the UK but ahead of West Germany and the USA in its defence effort.

Of the three services, the army is the largest and most prestigious. The air force is much more high-tech oriented, and very efficient. The navy, based mainly at Toulon and Brest, is the smallest of the three and has the least proud record. Rivalry persists, mostly over budget allocation.

The intelligence services

There are three main services. First, the Direction Générale de la Securité Extérieure (DGSE) which belongs to the Ministry of Defence, is staffed mainly by army officers, and runs France's foreign intelligence operations; some of its agents are military attachés in embassies abroad. The DGSE possesses trained commando units which can carry out clandestine combat missions. But to run an intelligence service on rigid army lines is not always successful, and the DGSE has a reputation for amateurishness and bungling – as witness the Greenpeace affair in 1985, when one commando unit was caught red-handed in Auckland harbour attempting to destroy a Greenpeace vessel involved in protests against French nuclear tests in the Pacific. The DGSE has also long been riddled with political intrigues started by extreme-right elements. Since 1985 it has been reorganized in a bid to purge it of these activists and make it more efficient.

By contrast, the Direction de la Surveillance du Territoire (DST), which looks after internal security and counter-espionage, is a police force run by the Ministry of the Interior and is a great deal more effective. And it cooperates closely with other Western security services, whereas the DGSE is more isolated and nationalistic. The third service is the Renseignements Généraux, a police branch that provides the government with political, economic, and social information about what is going on in France at the local level.

The police

Like the intelligence services, the police forces in France are divided up between the ministries of Defence and the Interior, and inevitably there are rivalries. The 87,000-strong Gendarmerie Nationale is part of the army. A highly armed force that patrols in rural areas, in practice it deals mainly with traffic accidents, crimes and other disturbances. The Ministère de l'Intérieur's police, some 120,000 strong, includes, as well as the two intelligence branches mentioned above, four other forces: a vice squad, the judiciary police, a general police force operating in towns, and the famous Compagnies Républicaines de Sécurité (CRS) which are used for riot and crowd control. The French police used to have a reputation for rudeness and rough-handling of suspects. Recently they have been at pains, with some success, to behave more gently and to improve their image.

International alignments

France's highly competitive and assertive stance on the world stage leads her to favour intense economic cooperation within the EC, balanced by a rigorously independent role in defence matters within the general framework of the Western Alliance.

Defence commitments

De Gaulle took France out of the military structure of NATO in 1966 because he disliked US hegemony and felt that France could protect French interests better. France has never returned to the fold, even though defence politics have shifted since de Gaulle's day. There are still no French forces under NATO's integrated command. However, France has always remained an active member of the civil side of the Alliance, participating in its debates and financing, even signing agreements that enable participation in some joint manoeuvres. It has also played a participatory role in the production and standardization of weapons.

Other options, other tasks The Chirac government tried to revive the somewhat moribund seven-nation Western European Union, and it seems likely that France might favour the creation of a new integrated European defence force. The Chirac government also expressed anxieties about the US–Soviet missile deal that was agreed in 1987, believing that this might weaken the West. Moreover, while there is no formal treaty, France has assured West Germany that its nuclear forces might well come to Germany's aid if it were attacked. France maintains a substantial army just inside West Germany and, like the other wartime Allies, it has a token force in Berlin.

Outside Europe, France keeps small detachments in dependent territories in the Caribbean and Far East. But the main French overseas effort is in Africa, where France has treaties with 17 nations, mostly former colonies.

Economic relationships

The European Community

France was one of the six founder members of the EC in 1957, and still sets enormous store by it. Despite West Germany's superior economic strength, France manages to remain in many respects the de facto leader and pacesetter of the EC; it tends to identify Community interests with French national ones; or, put another way, tries to exploit the Community for its own ends – and often succeeds. Given the size of its farm sector, it is not surprising that France puts a huge emphasis on a Common Agricultural Policy which has mainly benefited French farmers, and for many years resisted attempts to weaken or dismantle it. France also played the major role in setting up the European Monetary System. In short, the French see themselves as the champions of European cooperation.

The world scene France is an active member of the International Monetary Fund (IMF) and the World Bank (IBRD), where it has argued consistently – but without much success – for tighter control of money markets. France's latent anti-Americanism in world affairs was shown also by its refusal to follow the US lead and pull out of UNESCO, whose headquarters are in Paris.

Aid increase France's aid to the dependent overseas territories, the so-called DOM-TOMs, stands at about 0.22% of GNP. Aid to other Third World countries was only 0.3% of GNP in 1980, but it rose under the Socialists to 0.54% by 1986. France has a number of bilateral aid agreements with African countries of the franc zone, and many thousands of young *coopérants* go to work there each year on aid schemes.

The Business Scene

Government and business

The Chirac government made the reduction of state intervention in industry a priority when it took office in March 1986. Later, the policy was to progress towards a greater degree of free-market economic liberalism, abolishing many of the bureaucratic controls associated with the old-style French *dirigisme*. The privatization programme was to form a major part of this, de-nationalizing virtually the entire financial sector and several industrial groups. Progress was rapid and largely successful until the volatile state of the stock markets of late 1987 forced a series of postponements. The dividing line between the private and public sectors in France is, however, still blurred by the power of government-controlled investment. The government controls two of the biggest investors in French industry, the Caisse des Dépôts which specializes in infrastructure loans, and the Crédit Agricole which plays a major role in agricultural and rural development. From the foreigner's point of view, investment in France is still dominated by the government's power within the EC context to authorize or refuse entry to overseas competitors.

State-owned industry

In theory, there is only one area of French industry that is dominated by government manufacturers, that of arms and weaponry. In fact there are several small private-sector arms companies and the Dassault family still has a significant share in Dassault-Bréguet. However, many other areas are also effectively state monopolies including the whole tobacco industry (through SEITA which manufactures the famous French brands of Gitanes and Gauloises), rail transport (Société Nationale des Chemins de Fer Français or SNCF), the distribution of electrical power and gas (Electricité de France and Gaz de France), and several others. Nonetheless France has a long and unusual tradition of certain private sector utilities, for example, in water distribution. Private companies have gradually replaced local authorities for water distribution and they now have some 70% of the market. Elsewhere in French industry, the trend towards privatization will need to continue for many years if France wants to catch up with her European neighbours. In other areas, traditional state ownership is being replaced by private sector capital. The Socialist government of the early 1980s took France back to the outmoded belief in radical government ownership which most countries had discarded by the mid-1970s. Starting from a base of heavy state ownership, Chirac or his successor will have an uphill struggle to achieve an all-encompassing private enterprise economy.

Directing investment

Like many other countries, postwar France has had the problem of avoiding a concentration of industry and commerce around its capital and encouraging development in other parts of France.

As part of an attempt to address this problem, Président de Gaulle set up in 1963 an institution to manage the geographical growth of industry and encourage firms through grants and other incentives to set up in the regions. Known as the Délégation a l'Aménagement du Territoire et à l'Action Régionale (DATAR), its purpose was to "balance the hexagon." DATAR was charged with the dual tasks of encouraging regional economic development and at the same time planning infrastructure and environmental developments across the country.

Today DATAR has come under fire for its outdated and bureaucratic approach. It costs almost Fr2bn a year and employs 550 staff. The Chirac government's 1987 budget stripped DATAR of a large part of its funding: the spirit of economic liberalism, moreover, has meant that DATAR's role has become principally that of advising rather than implementing policy. It seems likely that DATAR will undergo changes in the future though it was given a reprieve from abolition in the run up to the 1988 elections.

Incentives
At the same time as DATAR's role has been cut back, new funds have been allocated to the Ministère de l'Agriculture to develop rural and mountain areas and there have been other changes in the incentive systems. In July 1987 the government announced a list of zones in which subsidies of up to Fr50,000 per employee are available to firms investing in certain chosen regions. The first three Enterprise Zones, in areas of high unemployment following the closure of dockyards, are at Dunkerque in the Nord and at La Ciotat and La Seyne on the Mediterranean coast. Companies setting up in these areas will not be required to pay corporation tax for 10 years and may receive partial or total exemption from the business licence tax.

The privatization programme
The list below shows the progress the Chirac government made in privatizing French companies. Until

October 1987 the programme was widely hailed as a success. An estimated 6.5m investors had taken up the government's offer to buy shares and the government raised over Fr60bn during the year. The later turbulence of financial markets left several of the major quoted stocks like Paribas, CGE and Société Générale well below the original offer prices. The government was forced to postpone the sale of other state-owned companies.

Hard-core holdings Chirac's administration came in for criticism of the way in which it placed a tranche of the shares in privatized companies with a so-called *noyau dur* (hardcore) of investing institutions. The object was perhaps partly simply to insure stable ownership but was also to protect the newly privatized companies from predators, particularly the acquisitive multinationals from outside France. Criticisms of the way in which these *noyau dur* shares were allocated were voiced by both opposition and members of the parliamentary majority, though the allegations of "cronyism" were stoutly defended.

Privatizations to end 1987
Saint-Gobain (industrial) December 1986; *Paribas* (banking, financial and holding company) February 1987; *Sogénal* (banking), *Banque du BTP* (banking), *BIMP* (banking) April 1987; *Crédit Commercial de France* (banking) May 1987; *TF1* (television), *Agence Havas* (advertising), *CGE* (industrial) June 1987; *Société Générale* (banking) July 1987; *Suez* (banking, financial and holding company) October 1987.

On the list for privatization
Banque National de Paris (banking); *Crédit Lyonnais* (banking); *Union d'Assurances de Paris* (UAP), *Assurances Générale de France* (AGF), *Groupe des Assurances Nationales* (GAN) (insurance); *Rhône-Poulenc* (chemicals); *Pechiney* (non-ferrous metals); *Matra* (telecommunications).

Power in business

Powerful groups within the French business community have always been evident. They fall into six main categories. First there are the big business families. French business is no longer family dominated and in many cases their importance has been eclipsed by multinationalism and the need for wider share ownership. But there are still many firms which remain firmly under the control of their founding families. Then there are the financiers, most of whom lost control of their empires in the nationalizations of 1982, only to reappear as influential bankers in the new climate of economic liberalism of the mid-1980s. The third powerful group comprises the chiefs of the holding companies which invest across a broad range of industries and some of these are themselves the vehicles for family fortunes. A growing slice of the power in French business is now passing to a fourth group, the new breed of aggressive entrepreneurs, some of whom are in the sunrise sectors while others are in the more traditional areas of manufacturing and retailing. Fifth, there are the foreigners who may be financiers or entrepreneurs. Finally, there are the "technocrats," those graduates of the Grands Ecoles who, as civil servants or employees in the private sector, exert considerable influence over the dealings of the business community and whose importance should not be underestimated.

France's business families

The fortunes of France's biggest business families have varied widely. Some have sold out to conglomerates, like the Thèves family, which in 1986 sold its last remaining shares in Générale Biscuit to the food conglomerate BSN. Most commonly, families have sought protection by merging with other family-controlled businesses. Thus Moët et Chandon merged with Hennessy in 1971, and with Louis Vuitton in 1987 to form LVMH. The original founding families now control almost half the shares in the new group, and the board still includes Jean-Remy Chandon-Moët and Kilian Hennessy. The Pernod Ricard group was formed for similar considerations. Other family businesses have remained fiercely independent: L'Oréal is still controlled by the Bettencourt family which founded it, Perrier by the Leven family, and Moulinex by Jean Mantelet. The Dassault family still maintains a large stake in Avions Marcel Dassault, now government-controlled.

The financiers

The first two years of postwar socialism in France (1981–82) were calamitous for the country's powerful private bankers. Most have re-emerged and again hold powerful positions within French business. Undoubtedly the most influential, the Rothschild family, shifted its attention to two holding companies, Paris Orléans and Francarep. David de Rothschild promptly established a new bank, originally called PO Bank, later re-christened Rothschild et Associés Banque. In 1986 he also formed an investment company called Saint-Honoré Matignon, to take stakes in privatized companies. Similarly, Jean-Marc Vernes, whose Banque Vernes was nationalized and eventually merged into the Suez group, acquired a new merchant bank called Banque Industrielle et Commerciale du Marais (BICM). Another of France's elite bankers, Nicolas Clive-Worms, who lost control of the Banque Worms, became director of the independent Banque Démachy.

The power of the holding companies

Holding companies exercise control over a large slice of French industry. Paribas and Suez both have the important roles of holding equity in companies as well as being bankers. One of the biggest of the pure holding companies is Compagnie du Midi, whose chairman Bernard Pagezy astonished the financial community in 1987 by buying the UK life assurance company Equity and Law, and a fortnight later purchased France's largest stockbroker Meeschaert-Rousselle. Several of the holding companies are controlled by well-known patriarchs of French industry: Chargeurs by Jérôme Seydoux, and CGIP by the Wendel family. Many of France's small- and medium-sized companies have sought the backing of the holding companies, seeking to enlist their help to fend off unwelcome bids from foreign predators.

The entrepreneurs

The postwar entrepreneurs of French industry come from a different social background from that of the traditional aristocrats of the business arena. They range from the high-flying and comparatively young businessmen like Bernard Tapie, who made a fortune rejuvenating companies in the manufacturing and retail sectors, to the star of the French construction industry, Francis Bouygues. Bouygues started out in 1951 with Fr12,000 borrowed from an uncle. He now controls the world's largest construction and civil engineering company, with interests in television (TF1), property, retailing and utilities. Other entrepreneurs include Serge Kampf of the software company Cap Gemini Sogeti, and Jean-Jacques Poutrel of Ingénico, which has developed the technology of electronic payment systems.

The foreigners

France has traditionally been protective of its business environment, and the breakthrough by foreigners is a recent phenomenon. The major Italian groups are now building up a significant presence. Since 1981 the Ferruzzi group has controlled France's leading sugar producer, Béghin-Say, and Ferruzzi's chief executive Raul Gardini intends to diversify from this base. Others have entered the fray more recently. Fiat's Giovanni Agnelli bought a 6% stake in the BSN food group, whilst Carlo De Benedetti, the head of the Olivetti group, has through his Paris-quoted holding company Cerus built up large stakes in French industry. These include a 25% stake in Yves St Laurent and majority control of the car parts manufacturer Valéo.

The Anglo-French financier Sir James Goldsmith held several important stakes in French industry before selling out in 1987. The Belgian conglomerate Groupe Bruxelles Lambert has also bought positions in French banking and in the advertising and media sectors. Some foreigners are clearly making new inroads into French business, but the corporate raiders from the USA, Australia and the UK have yet to make any headway.

The technocrats

The other group with significant power in French business is that group of elite technocrats, mainly civil servants, known as the Grands Corps de l'Etat. Graduates of the Grands Ecoles (usually Ecole Polytechnique or the Ecole Nationale d'Administration), they move between the senior levels of the civil service and positions in private industry in a way that would be impossible in many countries. This process is perhaps most noticeable in the financial sector. The movement of senior officials from the Ministère des Finances, the *Inspecteurs des Finances*, into positions of power within private industry is legendary (see *The reins of power*).

The business framework

The French business arena has two dominant influences. The first is the state; nationalized industries still account for over 40% of sales of larger companies (those employing more than 2,000 people) in spite of the privatizations of 1986–87. The state exerts influence in other ways too. A history of periodic price controls, protectionist policies and direct intervention is now being reversed, but the old *dirigisme* still survives in many areas. The second influence, which is far less tangible, is the dynastic structure of ownership in the private sector. Many of France's best known companies are still controlled by their founding families. The web of control is more complex than it appears. Since many manufacturing companies are controlled through holding companies or investment banks, there exists a plethora of unofficial allegiances, sometimes supported by cross-holdings of equity stakes and by reciprocal board memberships. This structure makes the largest French companies almost invulnerable to hostile bids.

Nevertheless, France goes to great lengths to encourage small companies and sole traders (the *petites et moyennes entreprises* or PMEs, and *entreprises individuelles*). Foreign entrants are also encouraged, and many leading industrial and service companies have had successful subsidiaries in France for many years.

Corporate France

At the top of France's business league are the 196 companies quoted on the monthly settlement stock exchange. Two of the top ten are state-controlled, with only a minority of shares being held by institutional and private investors. Of the remaining eight, three are family controlled, and a further three have a nucleus of "friendly" shareholders which insures that they will not be taken over.

The holding companies have sizable stakes in quoted companies too. Some have made a handsome living from buying ailing companies cheap and revitalizing them with new management and capital. One of France's biggest pure holding companies is Compagnie du Midi, which owns an insurance company, a bank, several property companies and has industrial interests ranging from a 16% stake in the second largest cement producer, to a 54% stake in a company which produces seeds and runs garden centres.

Further down the scale are the companies quoted on the Paris cash market and *second marché*. Here too, the majority have a protected share ownership, either by family control or by big backers. Many of the non-voting shares of the nationalized industries are also quoted on the cash market.

But quoted companies account for a much smaller proportion of GDP in France (22% at the end of 1986) than in countries such as the UK or the USA. This is partly because of the vast number of small and medium-sized firms, which makes French industry as a whole very fragmented, and partly because of the protected share ownership structures, which makes expansion by acquisition very difficult. Thus Carrefour, France's largest retailer, is about one-quarter of the size of Britain's largest (Marks & Spencer), and an eighth of the size of Sears, Roebuck of the USA. In a different sector, UAP is France's largest insurance company, but it ranks only number 40 in the world. There are some exceptions: in the construction and public works industry, Bouygues has a justifiable claim to be among the world leaders, while in the luxury goods and cosmetics areas, France has a traditional pre-eminence, and companies such as LVMH and L'Oréal are among the biggest.

Business structures

The last major company law to define the legal vehicles for doing business was passed in July 1966. French law specifies seven basic types of business entity:

• *Société Anonyme* or SA (corporation)
• *Société à Responsabilité Limitée* or SARL (limited liability company)
• *Société en Nom Collectif* or SNC (there are several variations)
• *Société Civile* (civil company)
• *Groupement d'intérêt économique* or GIE (economic interest grouping)
• *Succursale* (branch) for foreign companies
• *Entreprise Individuelle* (sole trader)

In addition, there are special purpose companies which are subject to specific legal, tax, and other regulations. These include *Sociétés d'Investissement à Capital Variable* (SICAV), the most common type of investment trust, several types of property investment company, of which the most common are the *Sociétés d'Investissement Immobilières* (SII), as well as certain others such as regional development companies or those involved in the financing of R&D and exploration in the field of oil and gas.

Société Anonyme The SA has to have at least seven shareholders. There are two possible management structures. It may have a board of between three and twelve directors (*conseil d'administration*), headed by the *président-directeur général* (P-DG). Alternatively, it may have a supervisory board (*conseil de surveillance*) and an executive committee (*directoire*) under it. The ownership of the shares of an SA is registered by an entry on the company's share transfer register,

unless the shares are bearer, in which case ownership of the share certificate is proof of a holding. The majority of quoted companies still have bearer shares.

Société à Responsabilité Limitée
The SARL is for smaller businesses. It must have at least two and not more than 50 shareholders. There is no board of directors; instead, the company has one or more managers (*gérants*). Shareholders' resolutions can be in writing, and do not require approval at a general meeting, except for the accounts: these have to be approved by simple majority at an ordinary general meeting, not more than six months after the year-end. The capital requirements are far less stringent for a SARL. Minimum capital is only Fr50,000, compared to Fr250,000 for an SA. A SARL cannot be quoted on the stock market, and it cannot offer its shares to the public. Any transfer of shares must be by written deed. This gives rise to a registration fee of 4.8% of the price paid.

Partnerships A partnership can assume one of four forms:
Société en nom collectif The SNC is the most common form of partnership, where each partner trades under the name of the SNC, and all partners are jointly and severally liable for the debts and obligations of the partnership. The partnership can choose the partner's name by which it wishes to be known followed by "and company" (such as Rousseau et Cie). There are no requirements for public disclosure of the records of the partnership, however the law of 1986 stipulates that the accounts must be filed with the local Register Commercial.
Société en participation The SP is a silent partnership, and its existence needs to be disclosed only to the tax authorities. However, a modification to the company law in 1978 allowed for the existence of an SP which disclosed its status to the outside world too. The managing partner (*gérant*) concludes any contract with

third parties, and it is he who is liable to the third party for any debt or obligation. If the SP is disclosed, however, all the partners are jointly liable.

Société en Commandité Simple and *Société en Commandité par Actions*
These limited partnerships can now be quoted on the stock market. In both types, the managing partner has unlimited liability. The difference between the two is that in the first case, shares transferable are only with the consent of all the partners.

Setting up

The procedures to be followed are laid down in the 1966 Company Act. A company exists for legal purposes once it has been given a registration number, which takes between two and three months. The first step is the drafting of the (*statut*) articles of association, after which the capital must be deposited with a bank. Once the shareholders have signed the articles, the board and chairman are elected, and the constitution of the company must be publicized in one of the legal journals such as the *Bulletin d'Annonces Legal Officielle.* The shareholders and board of the company must then file a declaration with the clerk of a commercial court, and submit an application for entry in the Commercial Register. Once the clerk has issued a certificate of entry, the capital may be withdrawn and used for the business. The notifications must then be sent to the fiscal and social security authorities, and registration taxes paid.

Foreign investment

For a foreigner, setting up business is an even longer process. No special authorization is needed by EC investors, but the Treasury has the right to demand proof of residence in the EC. Non-EC investors have to make a formal declaration to the Treasury for any investment and must apply for authorization before starting operations. The Treasury may approve, postpone or decline the application.

Foreign investments likely to create jobs will be encouraged. The Chirac government declared itself in favour of foreign investment but there are still some sensitive areas such as defence.

Competition law

In January 1987 France adopted comprehensive competition (antitrust) laws based on Treaty of Rome provisions. While bringing France closer to EC rules the legislation preserved some existing French antitrust measures. Mergers and acquisitions, discriminatory pricing, restrictions on competition and abuses of dominant positions are strictly regulated in France. There are defences, such as "contributing to economic progress," providing those affected with a share of the benefits, not eliminating competition in relation to a substantial segment of the products affected, and not imposing undue restrictions. Some practices are banned outright: refusal to supply, discriminatory pricing, resale price maintenance and loss-leading. Concentrations – where one or more companies have more than a given percentage of the market – are subject to controls. Investigative powers are vested in the Commission de la Concurrence and the Ministère de l'Economie, des Finances et de Privatisation and improved rules on investigations are intended to offer companies better safeguards. The Commission can impose financial penalties and issue injunctions. Fines of up to 5% of annual company turnover can be imposed and there are heavy fines (up to Fr10m) on individuals, though personal liability will only be incurred if individuals can be shown to have participated actively in a violation. Where previously violations had been part of the criminal law, they are now part of the civil law. Decisions by the Commission may be appealed against through the courts.

Mergers and acquisitions

Takeovers and mergers have until recently been relatively rare in France because most quoted companies are protected either by majority family stake, or by safe distribution of a blocking minority among friendly institutions. In 1987, however, there were a number of acquisitions: the biggest was Chargeurs' acquisition of a minority holding in the textile company Prouvost. Normally, takeovers tend to be agreed offers rather than predatory raids. The latter, however, are not unknown: in 1986 there was an acrimonious battle between Axa and Compagnie du Midi for control of the Providence insurance company, which Axa eventually won.

Regulations concerning takeovers have been issued by the Commission des Opérations en Bourse (COB) and the Chambre Syndicale des Agents de Change (CSAC). A bid must take the form of a cash offer (*offre publique d'achât* or *OPA*) or a share exchange (*offre publique d'échange* or *OPE*).

The bidder's first step is to obtain the approval of the CSAC and the Treasury, which keep the request secret until the offer is publicized. A bid is open for one month, but the period can be extended if a counter-bid is received. Documents containing all the relevant bid information must be submitted to the COB and made available to the public. An increased offer must be made within ten days of the expiry of the first bid, and it must be at least 5% above the first offer.

On acquiring a business, the purchaser is required to take on all the employees in the absence of an agreement to the contrary with them and the vendor. Various taxes are payable: on the intangible assets transferred; a fixed duty on patents; and TVA (which is recoverable) on the stock. Reduced duty is paid on a transfer of shares and is only payable if the transfer is in writing. The sale of a business has to be publicized formally to give creditors and the tax authorities due notice.

Tax

The biggest source of tax revenue in France is TVA, which accounts for almost 45% of the state's total tax receipts. The rest is made up of corporation tax (9%), personal tax (20%) and other taxes (26%).

The Chirac government set out to cut direct taxation both on personal income and on corporate profits. Tax rates were lowered in the first two budgets. Rates of TVA on certain consumer durables and products were due to be reduced in 1988, the cuts amounting to some Fr7bn. There was also a planned reduction of some Fr2bn in the unpopular *taxe professionnelle*, a local staff and asset-based tax.

Corporation tax All companies, whether SAs or SARLs, are treated identically for tax purposes, as are limited liability partnerships and branches of foreign corporations.

The standard rate of tax for businesses is 42% for the fiscal year 1988 (having been reduced from 50% to 45% in the first budget of the Chirac government, and then to 42% in the 1987 budget).

"Territoriality" A number of important differences exist between the French method of computation of tax liabilites and that of other countries. The basic principle of "territoriality" determines whether a company's profits are liable for tax: profits earned abroad are only taxable after they have been repatriated to France and made available for distribution to shareholders. With a few specific exceptions, all business expenses incurred for the production, sale and supply of services or goods in connection with the business are tax deductible. Depreciation is allowed on a straight line, declining-balance, or on a special accelerated basis for certain types of fixed assets. Deferred depreciation is also allowed for loss-making businesses. Provisions must be set up for a specific purpose and concern a specific loss or expense item.

Capital gains tax Short-term capital gains are considered to be those made on assets held for less than two years. They are treated as profits on operations, and tax is levied at the standard 42%.

Long-term capital gains, including gains on shares, are currently taxed at 15%; standard 42% corporation tax applies if the gains are distributed as part of the company's dividend. Capital losses may be offset against gains, or carried forward for a period of up to ten years. They may not, however, be offset against profits on operations.

Personal tax Liability to *impôt sur le revenu* (personal tax) is dependent upon domicile. An individual who is nonresident pays tax only on revenue earned in France.

The rates of tax vary from 5% at the lowest band of income to 58% at the top. One of the steps taken by the government in the budgets of 1986 and 1987 was to reduce the personal tax levy by a total of Fr27.1bn.

The tax rates on the lowest and lower middle brackets of earnings are lower than in most European countries. However, the separate social security contributions, which directly finance health and state welfare benefits, are much higher. In contrast with the reductions in tax, social security contributions are rising rapidly, mainly because of the burgeoning health service deficit.

TVA (*Taxe sur la valeur ajoutée*) is levied on all services, sales and imports. Exports are exempt, and goods purchased in France for export may be eligible for a reimbursement of the TVA paid.

The standard rate is 18.6%, and there are rates of 7% and 5.5%. Luxury goods, however, are subject to a higher rate of 33.3%, but in September 1987, the rate on cars and motorcycles was reduced to 28% (from 33.3%). Certain other reductions have also been made recently, including the rate on records, cassettes and compact discs.

Going public

A company going public may apply to have its shares quoted on the *cote officielle* (official list, which comprises both cash and forward settlement markets), the *second marché* (second market), or the *hors cote* (over-the-counter market).

Companies quoted on the official list must offer at least 25% of their stock and a minimum of 80,000 shares. There are strict reporting requirements: the reports of the general shareholder meetings must be made available to the general public, information on activities must be published biannually in the press, and comparable historical data must also be published.

Authorization for a listing has to be obtained from the Chambre Syndicale des Agents de Change (CSAC) and from the Commission des Operations en Bourse (COB), which issues the official decision.

For foreign companies, further authorization must be obtained from the Treasury in respect of exchange controls. All of the official documents and press communiques must be translated into French. The COB requires foreign companies to issue shares on the French market over a three-year period, equal at least to Fr10m. The procedure for listing takes between three and six months.

Requirements for a second market are less stringent. Only 10% of the capital needs to be offered for sale, and reporting requirements are easier. Unlike companies applying for a listing on the full market, there is no requirement for three years of profitable trading.

The over-the-counter market is quite different: there is no "market" as such, but brokers either match buying and selling orders, or act as principals. The market is therefore very illiquid and is suitable only for small companies. Nevertheless, COB approval must be sought, and disclosure requirements are the same as for the official list.

Employment

While employment regulation – some might say overregulation – remains extensive in France some of the rigidities in both the labour market and wage negotiations are finally in the process of being dismantled. One of the Chirac government's first, and highly symbolic, measures in December 1986 was to drop the requirement to obtain prior administrative approval for redundancies.

Like its Socialist predecessor, the Chirac government attempted to promote job creation by encouraging flexibility, relaxing controls on part-time, fixed-term and temporary contracts, and introducing variable working hours. It also tried to promote collective bargaining at plant level and these local contracts now cover about one-third of the workforce, compared with one quarter in 1981. Under legislation introduced by the Socialists in 1982, individual companies are required to negotiate with their employees every year on wages and working hours.

Labour unions

Union power has weakened dramatically since the late 1970s. Indeed, French unions are having to rethink their role, and some are finding it hard to shed confrontational traditions, replacing them with discussion and negotiation. *Falling membership* As in other industrialized countries, recent trends in the composition of the workforce (more part-time workers, more women) have meant a fall in union membership over and above that caused by unemployment. And, as elsewhere, this has been compounded by the decline in the unions' traditional industrial bases. *Union delegates* Since 1968 unions have had the right to organize through representatives on a company's premises. Union delegates have ironclad protection against dismissal. Indeed, all employee representatives are protected by rules that make it difficult for an employer to dismiss them in the absence of "gross misconduct."

Employees' rights and representation

Employees in companies with more than ten workers are entitled to personnel representatives who monitor rights under the law; the employer must meet representatives on a monthly basis.

Companies employing more than 50 workers must have works councils. Members are elected by employees and have the right to sit in on board meetings as observers; in addition, employers must consult the works council on all decisions concerning working conditions, though they need not act on its opinion on most matters.

Industrial action With some exceptions in the public sector, the French constitution gives every citizen the right to strike regardless of contracts signed by the unions. Unions are therefore reluctant to sign away their right to strike, whether or not a contract is in force. Striking workers are seen as having suspended their employment contract, but not to have breached it. They cannot be dismissed for having taken part in industrial action. But use of strikes as a weapon is in decline. Days lost through strikes, which numbered over 3.6m in 1977–79, dropped to 1.3m in 1984 and 885,000 in 1985, a postwar low.

Flexible working hours Unions consistently opposed legislation on flexible working hours for many years. However, new measures were adopted in 1987 which enable companies to negotiate working weeks up to 44 hours without overtime pay as long as the average week worked over a year does not exceed the legal norm of 39 hours.

The new legislation confirms practices already in operation in many firms and although the unions are uniformly hostile to the changes they have, in practice, accepted the new flexibility.

Dismissal An employer who wishes to dismiss one or more employees must follow specific procedures. Except in cases of serious wrongdoing dismissal gives rise to severance payments. The courts may require an employer to rehire an employee who was dismissed without "real and serious cause" but in practice they rarely do so. A period of notice must be observed in case of termination by an employer and by the employee in case of resignation. The firm is required to make a termination payment based on length of service. The rules for "economic dismissals" were relaxed by the Chirac government so that no prior administrative approval is required. However, employees are able to sue in the labour courts to challenge employers' motives; the court may award damages if it finds the "economic dismissal" unjustified.

Health and safety Responsibility for enforcing the wide range of laws governing working conditions in factories, offices and shops rests with the Ministère des Affaires Sociales et de l'Emploi. A 1982 law strengthened the role and powers of company level committees on hygiene and safety procedures. Companies can be fined for flouting the law, and a company head can be sued for manslaughter in cases of injury resulting in death. The rules are not always applied.

Discrimination Despite the Equal Pay Act of 1972 and the 1983 law on "professional equality," female earnings are still only around 75% of those of male workers. This reflects the fact that women work in lower-pay industries and hold lower-pay

positions within those industries.

Three-quarters of the female workforce earn the minimum wage but the automatic rise in the minimum in recent years, which has risen more than average wages, has had a positive influence on female wage levels.

Women have been particularly well protected by employment legislation in France – to such an extent that it has been seen as a disincentive to hiring them. The current trend is to preserve the main legislative arrangements while introducing greater flexibility in work practices.

Wages and taxes
For many years France had a fully indexed wage-fixing system for the public sector. The Socialist government abandoned the system in 1982, providing the Chirac government with an opportunity to introduce more far-reaching reforms.

Wage increases fell to 3.5% in 1986, though this figure was still a point above the inflation rate. Public sector wages were contained roughly within the target rate of 3% in 1987 while the private sector averaged slightly higher at 3.5%.

Personal taxes are lower than the EC average. The Chirac government made a 6% reduction in taxes in 1987–88.

Collective agreements Three-quarters of the wages paid in France are subject to collective bargaining and three-quarters of all collective agreements involve pay issues. Two-thirds of all wage bargaining now takes place at industry level. Outside the (diminishing) state-owned sector, negotiations take place at regional or industry level or can involve both. Covering nearly all industrial and professional sectors, the resulting agreements are binding on all companies in the region or industry. However, the wages specified are frequently only minimum thresholds and are exceeded by most major companies.

Companies have also been relying

increasingly on individual and collective merit-related and productivity-linked bonuses. The government has tried to link wages to productivity by encouraging profit-sharing plans through tax concessions.

Profit-sharing

Ever since de Gaulle introduced "participation" in 1967 as a means of giving workers a direct stake in the running of their companies, profit-sharing has been a feature of French corporate life.

Until a further change in the law in 1986, however, few firms took up an earlier de Gaulle initiative, the "loi sur l'interessement," aimed at encouraging firms to set up their own voluntary profit-sharing schemes. The new law simplified the introduction of such schemes and made the tax benefits more attractive. Companies have found that profit-sharing can be an important motivational tool and the number of voluntary schemes is expected to rise sharply in the next few years.

Executive salaries

The salaries of the French *cadres dirigeants* (top executives) have risen faster than the retail price index during the 1980s, especially since the sharp rise in profitability since 1983.

A 1986 survey by *L'Expansion* showed that average earnings of a *president-directeurs general* (PDG), *directeur general* (managing director) and of a *directeur financier* (finance director) were Fr890,000, Fr745,000 and Fr550,000.

Bonuses and perks French executives receive an ever-increasing proportion of their salaries in bonuses. Chief executives receive around 20% in bonuses, as do sales staff, while finance directors receive around 11%. Stock option plans are also becoming more widespread, particularly for top managers.

Fringe benefits in France are extensive, although such perks as free company cars are less widespread

than in other countries. Additional health, education and pension plans have developed rapidly since the late 1970s. In 1986 companies spent an average of 2.25% of wages on training, while for some larger companies the amount was as much as 10%.

Many French firms pay administrative personnel a bonus equivalent to a month's salary at the end of the year; in Paris this is almost universal, and some even pay another month's salary before the annual vacation. Although subsidiaries of international firms sometimes try to restrict fringe benefits, some French firms far exceed the legal requirements.

"L'économie souterrain"

Figures for participation in the "black economy" are difficult to estimate but one study put the loss to tax revenue at Fr30bn a year, with up to 1m people involved. The main areas of abuse are the construction, textile and service industries.

Employing foreign nationals Work permits are required for all foreign nationals except those from other EC countries. Permits are usually granted without difficulty but the authorities may limit the number of foreigners a single enterprise may employ. There are periodic bans on granting permits to non-EC nationals due to France's high unemployment levels but these do not affect managers who earn more than Fr18,000 a month. Moreover, DATAR, the French regional development organization, or local officials can help to obtain permits for non-EC executives needed for investment projects likely to create new jobs.

All foreigners must obtain a *carte de séjour temporaire* (temporary residence permit) or a 10-year *carte de résident* (residence permit) from the police, which carries with it the right to work. Non-EC nationals who wish to work as company managers need a *carte de commerçant étranger*.

Banks and other sources of finance

French banks have changed dramatically in the 1980s. Until 1986, the industry was almost entirely nationalized; it was short of capital, low on profits, and chronically over-staffed. Now it is emerging as one of the fastest improving sectors in France. This is partly because of privatization. However the improvement stems mainly from a change of government thinking on the whole financial sector: credit ceilings have been abolished, new markets in options and financial futures have been opened, and once forbidden products like commercial paper have been introduced. Old *dirigiste* tactics have been replaced by a free market liberalism. All banks have started to prune staff levels, although there is still plenty of scope to reduce the branch networks. As elsewhere, France has chosen to break down the barriers between the securities and banking industries, but the pace of change will be relatively much slower; the banks will not be able fully to own *agents de change* (stockbrokers) until 1990.

Control and regulation

The mechanism of control of the banking system was substantially revised by the 1984 Banking Reform Act. There are four separate authorities which have different spheres of control: the Commission Bancaire, which makes sure that the banking rules are complied with and carries out periodic inspections of the banks; the Comité de Règlementation Bancaire, which is the main rule-making body; the Comité des Etablissements de Crédit, which issues banking licences and authorizes mergers, acquisitions and transfers of ownership in the sector; the Conseil National de Crédit, which acts as a consultative body.

In addition to these, there is a professional association called the Association Française de Banque, to which all mainstream banks belong.

Clearing banks

The "big three" clearing banks – Banque Nationale de Paris, Crédit Lyonnais and Société Générale – have a dominant position in the sector. Collectively, they control 45% of all lending in France and have almost 7,000 branches.

Until June 1987, all three were government controlled. Société Générale was the first to be privatized, with the other two due to rejoin the private sector when the market permits.

Although their core business is domestic retail banking, all three are becoming highly diversified within the financial services sector. All have subsidiaries in consumer credit, leasing, factoring, venture capital and merchant banking. More recently, the net has been spread wider to take in life assurance. All of them have a significant presence overseas, and each is involved in world corporate banking. Since the Big Bang deregulation in the UK, all three have taken stakes in British stockbrokers – the BNP in a new venture called Ark Securities, Société Générale in Strauss Turnbull and Crédit Lyonnais in Alexanders Laing and Cruickshank.

With a conservative management style, the big three have a very high level of provision against Third World debt. Their main problem is to control costs in France, and at the same time cope with the massive volume of cheques their customers issue. Attempts to charge for processing cheques have so far been thwarted.

Smaller banks squeezed Some of the smaller clearing banks are in trouble. Squeezed by their big competitors, market shares are declining. Crédit Commercial de France, privatized in 1987, has successfully found its market niche, but others, such as the Paribas subsidiary Crédit du Nord, have much to do to catch up. Crédit du Nord was losing money in 1987 and undergoing a painful restructuring imposed by its parent company.

Green pastures The commercial banks are turning their attention to the lucrative securities industries, as their margins on corporate business have come under competitive pressure. But profits are increasing: Banque Indosuez made Fr793m in 1986, up 52%, while Banque Paribas made Fr346m, up 14.5%.

The Crédit Agricole

France's biggest bank is not strictly a bank at all. Crédit Agricole is a federation which controls 3,084 local banks. It was founded in 1894 when mutual credit organizations were first permitted under the banking laws. The head of the federation is the Caisse Nationale de Crédit Agricole, which acts as the centralized treasury for the whole organization. Originally, Crédit Agricole existed solely for farmers and rural communities. Since 1982, it has been allowed to operate as a normal retail bank and lend to companies in any sector, provided that they employ fewer than 500 staff and are located in towns with less than 65,000 inhabitants. Although much of its business is still derived from the agricultural sector, it now markets aggressively to all sectors. The huge branch network of 10,100 offices is somewhat unwieldy.

Corporate banks

These are the banks which have shunned labour-intensive retail banking and concentrated on the corporate sector. They include Banque Paribas, a subsidiary of Compagnie Financière de Paribas, and Banque Indosuez, controlled by holding company Compagnie

Financière de Suez. In both cases the holding companies have much wider interests than banking; they control stakes in a variety of industries and also have insurance and property interests. The two have much in common: both were nationalized by the Socialist government in 1982, and both were privatized when the right regained control. The two banks have big overseas networks, and they both concentrate on the same mix of corporate banking, capital markets products and investment. The smaller, but more domestically orientated CIC Group has a Paris-based commercial bank and ten regional subsidiaries as well as branches in 38 countries overseas.

Foreign banks

The foreign banks have only a small market share in France. Hamstrung by decades of protectionist policies and restrictive credit growth ceilings, few of the foreign banks have posed a threat to the giant domestic retail banks. They control 14.5% of customer lending in France, and 9.7% of deposits.

Despite this small share, there are 142 foreign banks in France – more than in any European country apart from the UK. The banks have mostly chosen a "niche marketing" strategy, concentrating resources on small areas of expertise. One exception, though, is Barclays Bank of the UK, which has a network of 38 branches and offers the full range of retail services. Others, such as Citicorp of the USA, have expanded aggressively by acquisition. In 1984 it bought France's third largest (at the time) consumer credit company, Famicrédit.

Liberalization of the financial sector has brought increased opportunities in France, and even stronger competitive pressure. In an environment which is over-banked and heading towards saturation, some foreign banks will certainly pull out. Potential new entrants are already deciding to cover their French marketing from a European head office based in London.

The savings banks

The savings bank system, known as L'Ecureuil (the squirrel), consists of a network of 421 banks controlling around 6,000 branches. They are non-profit-making, and pay neither dividends to their "members" nor taxes to the government. The main products are tax-spared savings accounts for householders.

Until 1983, they paid all their deposits to a centralized treasury, the Caisse Dépôts et Consignations. Now they have greater flexibility, with the treasury organized on a regional basis.

In recent years, they have increased their share of retail deposits faster than any of the mainstream clearing banks. The main reason is the tax perk which only they can offer. The product range, however, is rather more limited than that of the banks.

The top ten banks

	Assets (Frbn)	Domestic branches
Crédit Agricole	996.7	10,100
Banque Nationale de Paris	915.7	2,010
Crédit Lyonnais	852.5	2,448
Société Générale	748.8	2,200
Caisses d'Epargne	730.0	6,000
Banque Paribas*	263.1	62
CIC Group	266.7	1,412
Banque Indosuez	260.6	13
Crédit Commercial de France	206.8	225
Crédit du Nord	97.9	600

* Includes Crédit du Nord and Compagnie Bancaire.

Other credit institutions

Apart from the mainstream banks, France has an extensive array of specialized credit institutions which offer a range of products geared to specific sectors of industry.

The Banque Populaire, a cooperative mutual bank, similar in structure to the Crédit Agricole, specializing in small and medium-sized industries, craftsmen and professionals.

Crédit National, which provides financing for capital goods through long-term loans or by re-discounting medium-term credit granted by other banks.

Caisse Centrale de Crédit Hôtelier, Commercial et Industriel, which offers long-term credit for capital investment by smaller businesses.

Crédit Foncier de France, the main source of mortgages in France for both private residential and commercial purchasers. It also organizes and distributes state subsidies on housing loans.

Caisse National des Marchés de l'Etat, acts as guarantor for companies awarded public works contracts and provides financing for small and medium-sized companies.

Banque Française du Commerce Extérieur Particularly useful for overseas trading activities, BFCE is one of two institutions that specialize in providing import and export financing.

Compagnie Française d'Assurance pour le Commerce Extérieur The other overseas specialist (COFACE), offers a comprehensive system of export insurance, rather like ECGD in the UK or Eximbank in the USA.

Government aid

France offers a number of state development grants and regional incentives to manufacturing industries setting up in the country. Grants are administered by the Délégation à l'Aménagement du Territoire et à l'Action Régionale (DATAR), which has offices in London, New York, Chicago and Los Angeles, Tokyo, Frankfurt and other financial centres. The French chamber of commerce can also advise on schemes currently available.

The financial markets

Paris has big ambitions as a money market. The Chirac government set out to make it a major centre for financial services, second only to London in Europe. Outsiders, however, are sceptical. The finance minister in the Chirac government, M. Balladur, refused to introduce a sweeping reform programme but he did continue to chip away at the old *dirigiste* controls as his Socialist predecessor had done. In 1987 he added an options market to the financial futures market which had been set up a year earlier. However, in the equity markets, illiquidity and archaic practices forced more and more international investors to buy and sell their French shares through market-makers in London.

The stock market

The French stock market is the third largest in Europe after London and Frankfurt. The market peaked in March 1987. At the end of August it had a capitalization of Fr1,185bn (US$190bn) but was already in decline before the crash of October which wiped more than 30% off values. Paris has the lion's share of business – around 95% – with the regional Bourses in Lyon, Lille, Bordeaux, Nantes, Nancy and Marseille accounting for the rest.

There are four markets on each of the exchanges: the *règlement mensuel* (forward market), where all the big companies are quoted, and where settlement is made on the basis of a four-week account; the *marché à comptant* (cash market); the *second marché*, originally modelled on the London unlisted securities market (USM); and the *hors cote* (over-the-counter market).

Many of the procedures for buying shares are antiquated. The full session of the Bourse lasts for only two hours, between 12.30 and 2.30, although in 1986 a morning session was introduced for a limited number of shares. Now there is also continuous trading for a growing proportion of shares quoted on the forward market.

Until the summer of 1987, brokers transacted business by standing around a ring (called *la corbeille*) and shouting out bids. The ring has been replaced by a notoriously unreliable computer.

Owning shares in French companies

The Chirac government's privatization programme has made share ownership much more widespread. Overseas investment in French equities has greatly increased, too. Institutions drawn to the market between 1985 and 1986 saw their investments rise by over 45% in each of those years and the volume of transactions has increased by 160%.

There are no restrictions on the purchase of French equities by non-residents. Indeed, the government's policy was actively to encourage foreign investment, including direct equity investment. There is a 30% withholding tax on dividends, but investors from countries which have a double taxation agreement can offset this against their domestic tax liability.

Private investors can instruct a bank in France where they have an account, or indeed deal with a French stockbroker direct. Most, however, prefer to invest in one of the many investment trusts, called *sociétés d'investissement à capital variable* or SICAVs.

Institutional investors have a vast choice of French brokers or banks, or they can go through a financial intermediary in any of the main financial centres.

The stockbrokers

There are 45 *agents de change* (stockbroking firms) in Paris and 15 in the provinces. The profession has been a protected monopoly dating from Napoleon's day. The monopoly remains in force but this will change in 1992, possibly earlier. Research is generally far more limited and publications similar to those produced by USA or UK brokers are less common. Almost all deal with private clients as well as institutions. Of the bigger brokers:

Courcoux-Bouvet is best known for large-scale block trading; it publishes a useful quarterly guide in English covering 30 leading stocks.

Meeschaert Rousselle covers the widest range of French stocks, and publishes some research in English.

Chevreux de Virieu has a first-class reputation for its brief but accurate research and market commentary, published weekly.

De Cholet Dupont produces good research, particularly on the financial and retailing sectors.

However, the structure of French stockbrokers is changing rapidly: apart from those which have already aligned with banks, many others are expected to do so in the near future. Only one, Tuffier Ravier, has said that it intends to remain independent. Many overseas investors prefer to do their French securities business in London, rather than Paris. Seven UK brokers act as market-makers in France, and many others produce excellent research on French companies. The best are Warburg Securities, Savory Milln, James Capel, and Phillips and Drew.

Big Bang French style

Instead of a single sweeping reform as took place in the UK, the French have adopted a gradual programme of deregulation, whereby the banks are being permitted to buy into an *agent de change* over three years, building up to 100% control by 1990. But the monopoly enjoyed by the brokers will be completely protected until 1991. There is no plan yet to introduce negotiated commissions, nor any firm commitment to allow London-style market-making.

Most of the banks have now announced their intention to team up with brokers: the BNP with du Bouzet, a small house for which the BNP no doubt has big plans; Société Générale with Delahaye Ripault; Crédit Lyonnais with de Cholet Dupont; and Banque Paribas with Courcoux-Bouvet.

The bond market

Fixed rate government bonds, called *obligations assimilables du trésor* (OATs), form the biggest part of the French bond market. Around half of the new issues in 1986 were OATs, the rest being mainly public sector – state-owned agencies and local authorities. Only 15% of new issues came from corporate borrowers.

The volume of trading in the market has increased dramatically over the last five years: it increased tenfold between 1983 and 1986.

Overseas investors can invest in French bonds through any bank in Paris or through a stockbroker. There are important differences in the tax liability on differently dated bonds – those issued before 1984 suffer a 15% withholding tax for government instruments or 25% for others. However, there is no capital gains tax on profits realized by nonresidents.

Financial futures

A futures market called the *marché à terme des instruments financiers* (MATIF) was opened in February 1986. Its existence was designed to help institutional holders of cash to hedge against adverse interest rate fluctuations, rather than to allow wholesale currency trading. Hence at present only one type of contract is traded, in a notional 7–10 year treasury bond with 10% coupon and a nominal value of Fr500,000.

So far the market has been a success, with trading volume topping 10,000 contracts a day.

The law

France has a civil law system, based on Roman law and codified (set out as statements of general principle) into five Napoleonic codes. This contrasts with common law systems such as those of the USA and UK where the law has evolved through court cases and statute. Although court decisions do not constitute binding precedent in France, they do in practice have persuasive effect. Legal commentary by academics and others carries much greater weight and can be more influential on court decisions than in common law countries.

One benefit of a codified system is that commercial agreements tend to be short since clauses can be incorporated by reference to the code rather than spelt out in full. The inclusion of one type of term will automatically import other, similar terms as the parties will be deemed to have intended those to be included as well. Great emphasis is placed on the spirit of the agreement.

The courts

There are two types of court. Judicial courts adjudicate disputes involving private parties. The administrative courts adjudicate disputes involving state or administrative bodies. There are lower administrative tribunals and the Conseil d'Etat, the highest administrative court. Conflicts between the jurisdictions are resolved by the Tribunal des Conflits.
Litigation There is a misconception in common law countries that litigation in France is inquisitorial (a judge establishing the facts by questioning the parties) and not adversarial (the facts emerging from the parties' arguments and counter-arguments). In fact, the procedure in civil disputes is largely adversarial, the course of the case depending on the parties' pleadings and evidence, but there is a greater emphasis on written briefs and evidence and the judge plays a more active role in the trial's progress.
Costs Usually, court and bailiffs' costs are paid by the losing party and lawyers' fees are normally borne by each party separately. However, the courts have discretion to require either party to contribute. In practice, awards tend not to be a full indemnity although the courts are sympathetic to foreign creditors trying to recover debts.

The profession

There are two types of lawyer: *avocats*, who can plead in court, and *conseils juridiques*, who cannot except in certain commercial proceedings and arbitrations and before administrative bodies. In addition there are *notaires* – public officers who draw up, certify and authenticate instruments, particularly in relation to land and succession – and court officers who effect procedural acts (*avoués*) but only in the court of appeal, process-servers (*huissiers*) and registrars or clerks of the court (*greffiers*).

There are about 16,000 *avocats* in France (6,500 in Paris), between 3,000 and 4,000 *conseils juridiques* (1,200 in Paris), and 7,000 *notaires*.
Avocats All *avocats* can appear before the lower courts and the courts of appeal but only a few, of higher status, are allowed to appear before the Cour de Cassation and the Conseil d'Etat. *Avocats* are bound by written rules of ethics. The Ordre des Avocats (there is one for each court of appeal) has disciplinary authority and sanctions range from written warnings to bans from practising.
Conseils juridiques have regional and national commissions which represent them before public authorities, encourage training and education and defend their interests.

Status and rewards Lawyers have the same status in society as their counterparts in common law countries. Most practise alone or in loose partnerships sharing costs but not clients. Those earning the most practise business, commercial and financial law in Paris. They charge for their time by the hour. A client of one of these firms can expect to pay Fr500 for a junior assistant, Fr900 for a senior assistant and Fr1,500 for a partner. Foreign firms in Paris may charge more. For instance, a US firm might charge $160–180 for a senior associate and $200–250 for a partner.

Using a lawyer

Business in France is less lawyer-intensive than in, say, the USA partly because the codified law is superficially simpler and partly because there is a strong tradition in the middle class of studying law whether or not you intend to qualify. The top executives in companies and banks are often *énarques* (graduates of ENA, the Ecole Nationale d'Administration, which teaches economics, finance and law) or the highly regarded Ecole Polytechnique. They will often draw up their own contracts without reference to in-house legal departments.

Traditional roles This has meant that the legal profession has traditionally been one of the *avocats*, practising alone and specializing in court work. Over the last 20 years firms have sprung up either in the form of partnerships (*associations*) or professional corporations (*sociétés civiles professionelles*). Some firms, however, are little more than arrangements between sole practitioners to share overheads but neither clients nor fees. Firms are usually much smaller than their equivalents in the UK and USA, and smaller than firms in Germany and the Netherlands. They range in size from under five to over 20 lawyers. Only a few firms are larger than that. A factor in the formation of firms has been the need to specialize in order to meet the demands of overseas clients. In Paris there are about 50 such firms, employing 500 lawyers between them and 70 firms of *avocats* with 200 lawyers between them. Many firms of *avocats* do not work regularly for overseas clients, and only about 50 *avocats* outside Paris do so.

Looking ahead Change is likely, in line with the creation of an internal European market by 1992. Proposals are under consideration to allow *conseils juridiques* and *avocats* to merge and even to allow them to enter into partnership with accountants. At the moment, *avocats* are not allowed to be employees and can only practise in partnership with other *avocats*. Prohibitions against *avocats* opening a second office outside the jurisdiction of the court of appeal to which they belong have only recently been challenged and overturned in the courts. Only a few firms have offices overseas. But French lawyers are not parochial. Paris is a centre for commercial arbitration (under the auspices of the International Chamber of Commerce) and for business with francophone Africa.

Aspects of business law

Contracts can be administrative (subject to administrative law and courts) or private contracts (civil or commercial, both subject to the judicial courts). Commercial contracts are those made between merchants. They can be oral but some – bills of exchange, promissory notes, contracts between or for the sale of a business (*fonds de commerce*), for example – can only be proved in court by written evidence. Only a few, such as mortgages or contracts affecting land, have to be by formal, notarial deed or instrument. Some require registration with the tax authorities and payment of duty within a month of signature. These include transfers of land and certain movable property, certain leases and agreements relating to companies or partnerships.

Except for certain contracts (such as employment), the parties to a contract are free to choose which country's law governs it. If no law is specified, the French courts will determine the proper law by weighing factors such as the form, purpose, place of performance and any clause stipulating which courts are to have jurisdiction. In disputes involving parties from EC countries, however, there are complicated rules determining which country has jurisdiction in the absence of a jurisdiction clause in the contract.

Product liability A supplier can be liable for hidden defects (*vices cachés*) under specific product liability or under general principles of tort and contract. *Vice caché* applies where the product is defective, the defect was not apparent at the time of sale and the defect is sufficiently material to make the product unfit for use or to substantially reduce its value. The plaintiff is required to bring an action promptly after discovery of the defect. How promptly depends on the circumstances of the particular case, but the courts have allowed actions to be brought several years after the sale and after the guarantee's expiry, if the defect was not previously apparent. A successful plaintiff can rescind the contract, recover the cost of the product or obtain a discount. In addition, the plaintiff can obtain damages where the supplier – especially if professional – knew or should have known of the defect. Similarly, a professional buyer cannot complain of a defect which a professional ought to have been aware of. The courts have also struck out clauses limiting liability where the supplier has tried to invoke them against a consumer.

Copyright, trademarks and patents The copyright laws of March 11 1957 and July 3 1985 protect (among others) brochures, designs, architectural and scientific drawings and plans and software where these involve an *oeuvre d'esprit* (creative work). Trademarks can be registered for services and goods but enforcement is a matter of suing infringers in court. Registration is with the Institut National de la Propriété Industrielle (INPI) or the *greffe* (clerk's office) of the local commercial court or the local Tribunal de Grande Instance. There is no formal examination of originality or prior registration. To be eligible, foreigners must have French domicile. However, trademarks and patents registered in another country are protected in France if French-registered trademarks and patents receive protection in that country. Registration is for 10 years from application, extendible indefinitely for sucessive periods of 10 years. Patents are obtained by application to INPI on the basis of novelty, inventive activity and industrial use. A patent gives the holder a 20-year monopoly (six years only for medicines) for which an annual fee is payable.

Choosing a lawyer

Start with Martindale Hubbell or a similar international law firm directory. Ask your home law firm for recommendations or contacts. Consult colleagues in companies which do business in France. Once you have a list, write to each firm asking for details of: number of lawyers, specializations, foreign law degrees/qualifications held, languages, use of wordprocessors, telex, fax, and fee scales. Short-list about four, then visit them: French law firms are becoming used to the beauty parade (law firm selection by interview). Most of the international firms work to US/UK standards of turn-around of work but that depends in part on their size.

Top firms of avocats *Gide Loyrette Nouel* (founded in 1920) is the largest and best known firm of *avocats*, with over 20 partners and 70 lawyers in total. It has an international reputation for banking, finance, corporate, commercial and arbitration work. *Jeantet L'Eleu* (1925), half Gide's size, and *Siméon, Moquet, Borde* (1974) both have a reputation for general corporate and trade work, as well as tax (Jeantet) and oil licensing (Siméon Moquet). Two firms with outstanding reputations in finance – especially in the Euromarkets – are *Giroux Buhagiar* (1973) and *Monahan & Duhot* (1962). Monahan & Duhot is not alone in deliberately restricting its growth and recruiting only lawyers who have overseas experience or qualifications. *Berlioz & Co* (1978) is known for general corporate, trade and finance work, especially project finance. *Baudel Salès Vincent & Georges* (1977) has a reputation for expertise in direct investment, exchange controls and tax. *Tandeau de Marsac, Serrero, Papineau & Associés* (1971) is known for its general commercial practice. Also well known is *Brosselet Ader*.

Top conseils juridiques *S.G. Archibald* (founded in 1907) has over 30 lawyers – half of them American – and offices in Brussels (practising EC and Belgian law) and New York. It has lawyers admitted in the USA, UK, Germany and Switzerland, and has a broad commercial, finance, banking, tax and arbitration practice. Two firms, *Phillips & Giraud* and *Salans, Hertzfeld, Heilbronn, Beardsley & Van Riel*, were formed in 1977 as splits from the firm of S. Pisar. Phillips & Giraud has a strong Japanese client base while Salans Hertzfeld specializes in East-West trade and arbitration. Another well-regarded firm is Chambaz Suermondt.

Other firms Two interesting firms are *Bureau Francis Lefebvre* and *Fidal*. Lefebvre began in 1925 and now has over 80 lawyers. It has drawn up codes for African countries and has an extensive German trade practice. Fidal, founded in 1925, has over 1,000 lawyers and 100 offices throughout France and an international law practice. Firms worth noting for their particular

overseas links include *Lette & Lette* (Canada) and *Klein & Associates* (Africa).

Small firms and sole practitioners are also well worth investigating, and academics are often consulted by parties on difficult points arising in litigation. Individuals/small firms include *Charles-Henri de Pardieu, J.C. Goldsmith, Anthony Van Hagen, Alain Boituzat, Dominique Perrine, Marc Allez* and *Antoine Vacher-Desvernais*, to name a few among many. Personal recommendation is the best way of seeking out individual lawyers. Also, be on the look-out for new firms (like *Bernard, Gaillot, Tessler & Carton*) formed by lawyers who trained with established international firms.

Paris offices of foreign firms The largest representation of foreign lawyers is from the USA and UK, the USA in response to domestic companies coming to Europe after the war, and the UK more recently in the expectation that Paris would become the natural capital of the European Community. Top City of London firms include *Slaughter and May* (highly regarded by French lawyers), *Freshfields* (commercial and finance practice and has French lawyers), *Clifford Chance* (founded in 1962 by association with an existing Paris firm), *Linklaters & Paines* (Eurobonds), *Herbert Smith* (international litigation and arbitration) and *Theodore Goddard*. The top US firms in Paris include *Shearman & Sterling* (highly regarded, especially for finance), *Cleary, Gottlieb, Steen & Hamilton* (opened in 1949 to work on the Marshall Plan), *Coudert Frères* (in Paris since 1879), *Rogers & Wells, Davis Polk & Wardwell, White & Case, Sullivan & Cromwell* – all with extensive banking, finance and commercial practices – *Wilkie Farr & Gallagher* and *Jones, Day, Reavis & Pogue* (formerly *Surrey & Morse*, with a strong African practice). The international law firm *Baker McKenzie* also has a Paris office.

Accountancy

Since the mid-1960s the accountancy profession in France has been undergoing dramatic change. The codification of company law in 1966 marked the turning point for a profession still in its infancy compared with the UK, the Netherlands or Scandinavia. The influx of the Big Eight to service the needs of the French subsidiaries of multinational clients has been a potent force behind the profession's drive towards larger firms, a greater variety of services and higher standards.

Independence

Statutory audits are required for Société Anonyme (SA) (corporations) and for Société à Responsibilité Limitée (SARL) (limited liability companies) over a certain size. Auditors are appointed for six years, usually in an individual's name. Listed companies and banks require two legal auditors, and it has been common practice for most companies to have two joint auditors.

The rule of *incompatibilité* – aimed at ensuring the independence of the auditor – means that audit firms are prohibited from receiving fees for any other services from an audit client. The rule has resulted in a complicated picture for the accounting profession in France. Firms tend to offer either audit services or accounting services. The two do not consider themselves in direct competition, but in order to provide a comprehensive and competitive service all sorts of networks have been formed to fill geographic or service gaps. Most of the large audit firms have international links, very few accounting firms do.

Nationalism vs internationalism

Another complicating factor in the French accountancy profession is the perceived differences between what are considered "Franco-French" firms and "International-French" firms. When the Big Eight firms followed their multinational clients to France, the only competition at the time was from very small firms unable to service the needs of larger clients. The Big Eight-linked firms

were consequently able to dominate the audit market. A strong nationalist movement emerged in the Franco-French firms which led to the creation of the Association Française pour le Développement de l'Audit (AFDA) in 1982, which sought to raise standards. The international firms have worked hard to present more of a French image, with a majority of French nationals as partners. Antagonism between the two groups is now reducing to a level of healthy competition.

Advertising

Advertising and cold calling are banned. This position was due to be reviewed by the professional bodies in 1988 but short-term changes are unlikely. The profession is dominated by small practitioners who fear the spending power of the big firms. However, the regulations are likely to be relaxed eventually.

Accounting principles

Financial statements for accounting periods after January 1 1987 for all businesses (except banks and insurance companies) must follow the Plan Comptable Général (general chart of accounts) which implements the EC 4th and 7th Company Law Directives. The presentation of a company's annual accounts follows a prescriptive format, often on pre-printed forms. A statutory auditor's report to the shareholders must state that the financial statements are *reguliers et sincères* and give an *image fidèle* of the financial position of the business. This is a similar concept to the UK's "true and fair." If the auditor is unable to do this, a reason must be given.

Regulatory bodies

Professional There are two, to which 80% of accountants belong: *Compagnie Nationale des Commissaires aux Comptes* (CNCC), the professional body which regulates auditors; and *Ordre des Experts Comptables* (OEC), the professional body which regulates accountants, issues recommendations on accounting, auditing and disclosure, and links France with international accounting bodies.

Other *Conseil National de la Comptabilité* (CNC) An official government body attached to the Ministère de l'Economie, des Finances et de la Privatisation.

Commission des Opérations de Bourse (COB) Supervises the issuance and trading of securities, similar to the SEC in the USA. Plays an important role in improving financial reporting practices.

Association Française pour le Développement de l'Audit Association of firms which aims at raising auditing standards and has a supervisory council with representatives from the COB, CNC and OEC.

Training

Accountants in France qualify by obtaining a Diplôme des Experts Comptables, which involves passing 16 examinations. Students may be granted exemptions for up to 12 of these if they have passed approved exams at university or a Grande Ecole. This is then followed by three years of study to complete the exams.

The big firms

Fiduciaire de France Large loose association of small accounting firms formerly linked with KMG, now part of the merged KPMG. A fee income in excess of Fr1.1bn is four times greater than its nearest rival; 200 offices.

Groupe Sofinarex No international association. Aims to beat Fiduciaire

at its own game and top the tables. Performs bookkeeping and related functions, supplies EDP packages to mostly small, French clients. Reputedly very efficient.

Helios, Streco, Durando/Arthur Young One of the first examples of a Big Eight firm merging with a strong national firm. Well rated in audit.

Groupe Petiteau Scacchi/Price Waterhouse Climbed up the table following the merger of PW's two firms in France – Petiteau Scacchi and Blanchard Chauveau. A low-profile, non-aggressive firm.

Guy Barbier/Arthur Andersen Aggressive and high-profile firm set up by AA. Came top in an independent survey of firms offering all services. No non-French partners.

De Bois, Dieterle et Associés/Touche Ross Another firm to merge early with a good French firm. Aggressive and has small business clients as well as multinationals. Good reputation in audit.

ACL Audit/Coopers & Lybrand Not yet merged with significant local firm. Good recent growth. Has more provincial offices (11) than any other Big Eight firm.

Eurex No international association. Works more like a federation than a firm. Takes on small clients.

Befec/BDO Strong portfolio of audits. Possibly a target for a Big Eight firm as the BDO international network is smaller. Linked with the Lefebvre (tax specialist) law firm.

Finault Fiduciaire Previously associated with Fiduciaire de France, but now has an agreement with Arthur Andersen. One of the top audit firms.

Compagnie Générale Fiduciaire 47 offices in France; no international association.

Castel Jacquet et Associés/Ernst & Whinney Close links over a number of years. Good information reporting.

Bernard Montagne, Parex/Deloitte, Haskins & Sells Firms not merged. Non-aggressive, low-profile; but Montagne has a high-calibre clientele.

Advertising and PR

Over the past decade, the French advertising industry has seen steady growth, adding new services and sharpening existing ones. It dropped its image of being strictly a "creative" pursuit and developed as a business run by executives who are the first generation of managers to be graduates in marketing from the country's top business schools such as the Ecole des Hautes Etudes Commerciales (HEC). Advertising professionals are now working to meet the needs of equally sophisticated managers who are well-versed in sales and marketing strategy and who demand a return for advertising investment. Marketing has also developed as a discipline in France, though more slowly than in other countries. French advertising has responded by tightening up standards and maximizing profits without sacrificing quality or its emphasis on stylish imagery.

New spheres of activity

In recent years advertising has finally begun to look beyond the ranks of packaged goods manufacturers to new sources of revenue and a new competitive spirit emerged under the Chirac government. Banks, insurance companies and financial services, as well as political parties, started to advertise for the first time. The campaigns for share offerings in the privatization programme promised to be lucrative but the slump in stockmarket prices of late 1987 threatened major changes and delay.

Public relations continues to be the least developed sector of French communications, due in part to the lack of commitment by specialized international firms whose professional approach and positive results could change PR's negative image. In France, public relations has been eclipsed by sponsorship, which has boomed in less than a decade. Major French companies such as Bic, La Vie Claire, Coca-Cola, and Bull, now sponsor sporting events such as the Tour de France or cultural events, exhibitions or concert seasons. Through tax deregulation and other incentives, the government encourages corporate sponsorship of the arts and conservation.

Direct marketing is the most successful new tool and enjoys an annual growth rate of about 25%.

Toll-free telephone numbers are popular after a slow start; direct response telephone numbers were permitted on television for the first time in 1987. The lack of effective databases hampers the success of direct marketing in France, but is improving.

Expansion

The Fr6bn Havas communications giant controls roughly 38% of the media in France, comprising media brokering, billboard companies, cable television and a 42% stake in Eurocom, the market leader in French advertising. When Havas was privatized in 1987 the government handpicked the new shareholders and retained a "golden share," as a five-year government guarantee against hostile takeover. Havas's abortive bid for one of the new commercial television stations led the Association des Agences-Conseils en Publicité (Advertising Agency Association) to appeal to the government to introduce specific antitrust legislation. Eurocom management claims that Havas's privatization will not change the business fundamentally. With roughly 25% of the market in France, Eurocom's agencies will continue their acquisition policy and the expansion of French agencies such as the Belier group. It will also continue the trend toward joint ventures. Eurocom is a 51% partner in the HDM international network with the US agency Young and Rubicam and the Japanese agency, Dentsu. Two Belier agencies are partners with UK agencies: Belier's Alice division is a partner with UK-based Collett Dickinson Pearce in a European network, CDP International; and Belier Conseil is a partner with Wight, Collins, Rutherford, Scott.

Internationalization

Eurocom's expansion is only one facet of the movement in the advertising industry in France. US firms are trying hard to acquire the few, good independents left, while major French agencies are expanding abroad. The giant Publicis developed an international presence, while smaller shops such as Boulet, Dru, Dupey, Petit and Feldman, Calleux et Associés are carefully moving into other European markets. Third-ranked Roux, Séguéla, Cayzac et Goudard was the first major French agency to open an office in New York.

Recent expansion has shown two major features: the new prosperity of French agencies which has enabled them to invest abroad, and the ability of the French to market themselves internationally.

The stock exchange

The biggest agencies like Publicis are quoted on the Paris Bourse and others are now listed including the billboard advertising groups Dauphin, Avenir and Giraudy. Saatchi and Saatchi are also listed. But the French "Top Ten" have always been dominated by local agencies rather than multinationals. Large agencies have, as elsewhere, lost staff through the process of ambitious younger members setting up a number of small, creative "hot shops." But their independence is often short-lived.

Controls

After years of frustrated demand for television time, the advertising industry has been quick to pick up on the limited new media opportunities available to it. The CNCL, formed in January 1987, liberalized television advertising, opening it up to previously banned product categories such as brewers and travel companies.

Advertising on TV

The *audiovisuel* sector in France has seen substantial changes in the mid-1980s. Successive governments gradually ended the state broadcasting monopoly that existed until 1981. In 1985 a plan to introduce private TV channels saw the inception of Canal Plus, now Europe's only pay-TV channel which was successfully launched on the *second marché* in late 1987. An independent channel, La Cinq, was introduced in 1985 to compete with the three state-owned channels TF1, Antenne 2 and FR3, the regional network.

Since then TF1, the main state channel, has itself been privatized (in 1987), going to a consortium led by Francis Bouygues and the UK publisher Robert Maxwell.

Anyone expecting a bonanza in TV advertising revenue from the changes made was likely to be disappointed, however. TF1 and La Cinq now appear locked in a battle for the middle ground offering lacklustre programmes and monotonous format. Advertising revenues seem to be becoming stretched to support the number of stations. The state-run channels still take advertising (as they always have done) but are not permitted to raise more than 25% of total revenue from this source; the deregulation is far from complete.

The future

The French advertising industry is hoping to achieve dramatic growth over the next decade, and will continue to experiment in the alternative communications areas such as PR, direct marketing and sales promotion.

Importing, exporting and distribution

The French market is now more approachable than ever before. The days of "hidden" protectionism when Japanese video recorders were sent to the wilds of Poitiers for "clearance" testing are over. Imports now account for 23% of GDP, and the removal of all intra-EC trade barriers and the opening of the Channel Tunnel in the 1990s should make the French market even more accessible.

Tariffs and taxes

No import duties are levied on goods originating within the EC or having already incurred duty upon importation into an EC country. The rest of the world is divided into four zones and duty of 7% and 13% is levied according to product category, as defined under the new EC Harmonized Commodity Description and Coding System.

TVA Taxe sur la Valeur Ajoutée (value-added tax) is levied on all goods as they clear customs. Companies can add TVA to the products marketed in France providing they have a French-based fiscal representative to file returns, a service offered by some banks and agents. In practice the French importer usually pays the TVA upon clearance of goods. Exports from France and research for non-resident principals are zero-rated.

Controls

Quotas Import quotas are determined by the EC authorities. Quota licences are issued for pre-defined periods and can be exchanged between member states. Special EC agreements regarding textile importation, known as multi-fibre agreements, have been made with Asian and developing countries and the USA. Quotas are reviewable every six months and duty of between 7% and 13% is levied.

Passing the test There is a long list of products for which approval is necessary before the goods can be sold in France. In most cases, approval is given only if the product meets the standards laid down by the relevant testing authority. It may be necessary to conform to the directives of several different ministries.

Self-regulation For most foods, textiles, construction materials and chemicals, the exporter is only required to complete an official declaration certifying that products conform to standards and labelling requirements. Ministries decide whether products need certification or testing. Your embassy should have up-to-date information.

Customs

Since January 1 1988, French tariffs and clearance procedures conform to the new Brussels directives for the EC. The Single Administrative Document (SAD) has replaced previous documents.

Customs clearance centres exist all over France and are not confined to ports and airports. Items may only be cleared through French customs by either an appointed customs clearing agent or by a French TVA registered importer. An information service is operated by the Direction Générale des Douanes in Paris ☎ 42 60 35 90.

The essential freight-forwarder There is, however, no replacement for a reputable freight-forwarder, who can complete SAD forms and arrange door-to-door delivery and insurance.

Invoices An original invoice or a carbon copy (officially it must be in French and *not* a photocopy) should be submitted to French customs for clearance of goods. It should carry a full description of each item, marks, numbers and weights of the packages, terms of sale, total value of the goods in a specified currency, the name and address of both buyer and seller, and a declaration of origin.

Exchange controls in France have been relaxed but banks may still need sight of an invoice and an SAD to effect payment.

Identifying opportunities

The main areas of potential growth in France have been identified as office and telecommunications equipment, scientific and pharmaceutical products, textiles, sports and gardening goods and quality foods. France is also a good market for luxury items; French consumers lay emphasis on quality at the right price (*rapport qualité-prix*). They are contrary in the fashions they adopt; McDonalds hamburgers set a trend in the land of *haute cuisine*.

Groundwork There is no substitute for a visit, but your own embassy or government department concerned with overseas trade are good starting points in evaluating your potential. Other avenues are the many trade federations in France, which publish statistics and membership rolls. Local chambers of commerce, to which all French companies must belong, can also be very useful. Many countries have chambers of commerce in Paris. They usually have good libraries and can help with finding legal and fiscal experts. Further assistance can be gained from exhibitor guides to the numerous French and international trade fairs, which are a useful source of potential partners as well as competitors.

Adapting to the market

The French have their own approach to advertising, promotion and doing business. Visual impact is a prime consideration. Whether you should retain your foreign identity will largely depend upon your product's reputation in France. Burberry's use of a British aristocrat, Lord Lichfield, in their advertising has established theirs as the raincoat to wear in France.

Advertising in France typically relies more on the three Rs: *rire* (laughter), *risque* (bravado) and *rêve* (dream). In common with many countries, the French consumer responds to pictures of happy, healthy families intent on enjoying themselves. He (and she) is also motivated by the image of sexual self-confidence, whether the product be clothes or cat food.

"New" is often not good news The French are conservative and view innovation with suspicion. Only established companies and brands are trusted to introduce "new" products.

Sales literature High-quality visual presentation will inspire admiration; the French want a clear image of the people with whom they will (or might) be dealing. Documentation must be in French, but a straight translation may be unacceptable. It is very important to get your texts checked by a local expert in your business before going to print.

Selling to the trade Targeting is crucial in your decision whether to sell direct, employ an agent or set up a branch office.

Direct selling You will need persistence to overcome the suspicion which you will encounter and you must speak French. Once trust is established, long-term relationships follow. An advantage is that you remain in control and gain first-hand knowledge of the market.

Branch offices There is much to be said for employing French nationals who understand the people and the market. However, social security overheads can almost double salary costs and the legislation that protects employees is a considerable deterrent. The alternative is to relocate your own staff.

Franchising is a fast-growing means of overcoming the problems of a fragmented marketplace. A highly visible example of success, with shops throughout the country, is Yves Rocher.

Licensing can be a means of overcoming opposition to foreign manufacturing and gaining access to an experienced sales force.

Agents

A good local agent who knows the market offers decided advantages over costly payroll staff and hit-and-miss direct selling.

Is one enough? A Paris agent will probably be both unwilling and unable to cover the whole country, and a team of regional agents may be necessary.

Finding agents At the end of the day, you have to decide who, of the many people you have met and interviewed, will best do the job you want them to do. Sources of help include all those listed in *Identifying opportunities.* It can also make sense to ask the customers you hope to serve.

Mistakes are costly Agents *commerciaux* (VRP) and, to some degree, distributors, are protected by law against unfair termination of contract, with compensation of up to the equivalent of two years' commission. Legal advice is essential, even if using standard French contracts.

Distribution

Road is the dominant method of transporting goods in France. While figures for rail and waterways have slumped by 22% and 35% respectively over a ten-year period, road haulage has increased by nearly 20%, moving over 105bn tonnes/116bn US tons per km per year. Retail distribution is still mainly in the hands of independents who hold 65% of general trade and 60% of food. Wholesalers, and particularly wholesale cooperatives, distribute producers' products to small retailers.

Road transportation France has a network of toll autoroutes spanning the country and crossing the borders to Belgium, West Germany, Switzerland, Italy and Spain. Consignments large and small move quickly and cheaply under groupage. Transfer from international to domestic haulier tends to take place

in the Paris area, although freight forwarders are prolific throughout the country.

Rail The French railway, SNCF, has difficulty competing in today's freight market and is competing aggressively with airlines for the movement of people. Freight represents half of SNCF activity. Hopes are high for increased trade from the Channel Tunnel.

Air Paris has two international airports. Other main airports include Lyon, Marseille, Nice, Strasbourg, Bordeaux and Lille. Only a small fraction of import and export tonnage travels by air.

Sea Some 200m tonnes/220m US tons of goods move in and out of France by sea annually. Marseille is still France's first port, having considerable traffic with the ex-colonies of Africa. Calais is second with the heaviest passenger traffic. Third is Dunkerque which boasts a major coal port, able to accommodate vessels up to 350,000 tonnes/385,000 US tons. Other ports include Le Verdon, a major container terminal near Bordeaux.

Inland waterways An extensive river and canal system has been developed to European dimensions, moving some 9bn tonnes/10.6bn US tons per km per year within France and to and from Britain, the Iberian Peninsula, Scandinavia and the Mediterranean countries.

Retail distribution French distribution networks are so diverse that they have been called "an assault course" even by French nationals. *Représentants de commerce* (travelling sales representatives) are still to be found throughout France selling direct to the independent retailer, who may also buy from wholesalers.

Warehousing Storing goods, either in bond or customs cleared, may be necessary to meet the tight delivery deadlines. Some warehousing services also offer distribution of goods. Garonor just outside Paris is one of the best known companies.

Business Awareness

The French are a stimulating but challenging people with whom to do business. Whether negotiating a deal, entertaining, or writing letters, they have their own ways of going about things that a foreigner may at first find strange. They are tough and competitive in business matters. They also have strict office hierarchies and elite systems of management, but their old social formality is giving way among younger people to an easier approach.

Business hours and attitudes

Most French *cadres* (executives) are committed hard workers who find their jobs absorbing and love to talk about them. Even allowing for the often lengthy lunch break, they readily work long hours; the pattern varies, but Parisian executives may be in the office by 8.30 or 9 and not leave till 7 or 8. Often they will claim that the early evening, when the telephone rings less, is the best time for getting serious paperwork done. But it has also become a kind of status symbol to stay late: those who leave at 6 cannot have important work to do, and are less likely to be promoted.

There are regional variations. In Paris, lunch usually starts at 1, while in the provinces it is more often noon or 12.30. And in the more easy-going south, senior staff are less likely than in Paris to work late, especially on a hot summer day. In Paris and elsewhere, some younger executives have been turning against the French tradition of the heavy lunch and the two-hour lunch-break. This is partly for health reasons; also the spread of suburbs and the growth of commuter living means that far fewer people go home to lunch than in the past. If they do not have a business lunch, they may take a quick light meal in the office canteen, if there is one, and then leave a little earlier at night.

Weekends and holidays

After so much hard work, French executives feel that they need and deserve their weekends and holidays, and they regard them as sacrosanct. Senior people will perhaps take home a briefcase of papers, or may sometimes feel obliged to return to the office on a Saturday. But generally the weekend is to be spent with family, undisturbed, possibly in the rural second home that many successful executives possess.

Holidays are long; four or five weeks in summer is usual, plus a two-week winter break, often spent skiing. The long summer break means that the business world partly closes down from mid-July to early September. This is a period to avoid for a visit, unless you are sure that the people you wish to see will be there. In addition there are various public holidays (see **Planning and Reference**), and when one of these falls on a Tuesday or Thursday, many people will take the Monday or Friday off too, to secure an extended four-day weekend.

Business dealings

The French have a reputation for being somewhat legalistic in business matters and to an extent this is justified; any serious business deal must be drawn up in meticulous legal detail. But once this contract is signed, the French tend to treat it somewhat ambivalently. They will use it as a constant point of reference but will also keep trying to find ways of getting round it. Thus in France there are two sets of rules, the written ones and the real ones. You need to learn how to spot the difference, and how far a French negotiator will go, in a given situation, in bending the written rules. This way of behaving works well in practice and is not far in spirit from the notorious *"Système D"* (the art of bending the rules in such a way as not to break them).

It is best to come to a meeting fully briefed and primed, and to take careful notes if possible. The French allow their enthusiasm to show and value commitment and precision in business dealings. But regional patterns can differ. Southerners, in typical Mediterranean style, may make eager smiling promises which they do not always fulfil; northerners are more cautious – Normans proverbially so.

The "demandeur" approach The French sometimes adopt an unusual tactic if they want something from you; they are especially skilled at manoeuvring you into seeming to be the *demandeur* (petitioner), even if you are responding to an overture of theirs. This is a bid to put you into the weaker position by playing hard to get. They are experts at this form of brinkmanship in discussions and they like to keep their options open and, if necessary, wait for you to call their bluff.

Office hierarchies

The style and structure of French firms vary considerably. Some are very modern, even Americanized; but the traditional old-style firms remain numerous especially in older industries, and most are still small and family-owned. These usually have a keen sense of hierarchy, with strong central control within each firm and little delegation of power or decision-making: this reflects the French centralized tradition.

The head of the firm At the head of each firm is the *président-directeur général* (P-DG) who combines the functions of chairman/chief executive and managing director. He – and it is nearly always a man – may be the family owner, or be salaried or a

shareholder, but often he is a virtual dictator, taking all the key decisions. Below him is a strict hierarchy of executives, from *cadres supérieurs* via the *cadres moyens* down to the clerks, each with a clearly defined position and duties. This structure, in which the boss has full rein to divide and rule, makes interdepartmental liaison difficult. Moreover, relations between seniors and juniors are rarely easy-going, and chains of command tend to be rigid. Thus executives will seldom delegate any of their own responsibility to juniors; and the latter, when faced with a problem outside their immediate sphere, will simply hand it over to a superior, rather than consult.

The strategy for dealing with a French firm of this kind is simple: initially at least, aim at the top of the hierarchy. Write directly to the P-DG at the outset and seek a meeting with him, to which you should send the most senior person possible from your own firm. High-level personal contacts are crucial in France. Later, when it comes to working on more routine matters at a lower level, you should not expect anyone to be much help outside his or her precise sphere of duty. Structures are often so rigid that it may be hard for one executive to communicate with another, and there is seldom any great sense of team responsibility. It is thus important to find out early on exactly who deals with what at each level.

Old habits, new style It is not certain how far these rigid patterns are changing with a new generation. Today's younger executives may be more informal in their social manner and readier than their elders to use first names on initial acquaintance; but they are often just as timidly bound by the hierarchy.

However, in some newer and larger firms the upper ranks have been trying to set a more flexible pattern. Since the 1950s many able and ambitious people have been going to the USA on business courses, or have had close contact with US companies. And some of them, now in senior positions, have been trying to introduce a more flexible approach and to marry French habits and psychology with the best of American methods. Some big French firms have been reorganized by US management consultants. As a result, new notions of group responsibility and decentralized decision-making have been permeating some firms.

Types of manager

It is possible to identify several main types of French manager or senior executive. First, there is the older style of routine-minded family boss. Second, there are the younger, more modern-minded products of the business schools. The third is a small, heterogeneous group of more-or-less self-made men, who, without any elite training, have built up small firms to achieve dazzling results. Some have inherited tiny family concerns and built them into empires; others have started from nothing, or from the shop floor. The French postwar economic success owes much to these *fonceurs* (whiz kids) who have dramatically disproved the notion that in France you get nowhere without the right connections and diplomas. Such men include Edouard Leclerc, who created the discount supermarket chain that bears his name; Paul Ricard, the man whose *pastis* is a household name; and the showman entrepreneur Bernard Tapie, current darling of the media.

The elite Last but far from least, there are the alumni of the elitist *grandes écoles* (see *Education*), such as the Ecoles Polytechnique and Centrale, and of the influential civil service postgraduate college, Ecole National d'Administration (ENA). These privileged, self-confident meritocrats are well aware of their own value. Mostly they go into public service, including the state technical agencies; but you will find *polytechniciens* in the upper ranks of

many larger industrial firms, state or private, while some *énarques* (ENA alumni) and others are in the big banks now being privatized, and many businesses hire graduates of the Ecole des Hautes Etudes Commerciales (HEC).

Many firms have members of these elites on their staff and the "old boy" connections can be extremely useful, for example in cutting civil service red tape. It is worthwhile knowing when you are dealing with one of them both from the point of view of personal communication and to assess their possible influence. In particular, those who have combined a classic *grande école* training with some time spent in the USA can be formidably effective.

These *grandes écoles* networks are still powerful in the financial world, and in the engineering or electronics milieux where *polytechniciens* are thick on the ground; but they are less strong in consumer and service industries, where there is some prejudice against them. In general, their influence is on the wane, now that France is turning against centralized state control and towards greater private initiative. And many modern firms are now making greater efforts to hire or promote people on their true merits, rather than for the elite diplomas they hold. Such firms are aware that the vaunted alumni are not always so very able and, if they have hitherto been in the civil service, they may lack sparkle and initiative.

Women in business

The role of women in French business life has increased considerably in recent years, especially now that so many are taking top places in the passing-out exams of the elite colleges. There are women presidents of some banks and insurance companies, and nearly everywhere women do well in middle and upper-middle management. They hold many senior positions in the media, advertising and retailing.

In industry there is still some prejudice against women, notably in southern France; but in the more modern firms they are making progress in personnel, sales and financial departments.

The French male tends to treat a business woman with gallantry rather than condescension, even with a touch of Gallic flirtatiousness. He appreciates it when she dresses well (which she usually does) and he keeps her fully aware of her femininity. French women are not noted feminists, and they like it that way. "Vive la petite différence!" is a sentiment shared by both men and women involved in business in France.

Secretaries

Many French executives fail to take their secretaries into their confidence or give them any responsibility, but treat them as mere typists. Some quite senior people still open their own mail and do not even show it to their secretaries; hence letters arriving during an executive's absence may not be acknowledged. Also, it can be difficult to make appointments, for secretaries do not always have access to (let alone charge of) their bosses' diaries. So, French secretaries may often seem less helpful to a visitor than they mean to be. But they are important allies who should be won over to your side, for in France a stranger is a potential enemy until proved a friend. In the more modern firms, it is true, executives are now making more intelligent use of their secretaries, many of whom now have the rank of "personal assistant." It is in the media and in government offices that secretaries are given the credit they deserve.

Doing business in France

Senior people, especially those in Paris, have very full diaries and can be hard to pin down for appointments. It is best to contact them well in advance and not expect quick success: in Paris, some top executives and officials think that it increases their prestige if they avoid committing themselves until the last moment – that is, unless they really want something from you. In the provinces, people are gentler and more accessible. On the other hand, in Paris and the north punctuality is aimed at (if not always achieved), whereas in the more relaxed Midi there can be some vagueness about time-keeping.

Office meetings Initial contacts and more complex discussions nearly always take place in a firm's offices, with experts or advisers present. It is not the custom as in many countries to serve coffee or other refreshments during these talks, and only a few senior executives keep a drinks cabinet in their office. But outside entertaining is frequent and generous.

Business entertaining

Business breakfasts These have now become à la mode, like many an American import when it first arrives in France. Le power breakfast, in current jargon, is held in a smart hotel or a firm's executive dining room (or even in a café), and the buffet spread will generally be more substantial than the usual coffee and croissants. The French enjoy the novelty, but may soon tire of it.

Business lunches The heavy lunch is an old and serious tradition. Hospitality forms an important element in the business dealings of the French, whose love of fine food is accompanied by a liking for ceremony. The visitor may not often be invited to a French executive's home – at least not in Paris – but will certainly be taken to lavish lunches in restaurants, lasting up to three hours. The time spent should not be grudged, for it is all part of the deal. General social chat may last till the coffee stage, or it may give place much earlier to discussion of the business topic; the guest need not feel shy about initiating this move.

Whoever issues the invitation to lunch or dinner generally pays.

If you are not invited to lunch on a first meeting, you need not feel that you are being spurned: it may be pure chance. Nor is there any harm in the visitor being the first to issue an invitation. But the choice of restaurant is always very important in France and you should make sure it is a place known for its distinguished cooking. Good food matters more than good decor, though the two often go together.

French executives now place less emphasis on long, heavy business lunches as a matter of daily routine – for reasons of both health and time – and may try to avoid them. The French have always been health-conscious and are now more so than ever. The sumptuous blow-out is reserved for a special occasion – to mark an initial meeting, to clinch or celebrate a deal, or to effect a key introduction. Once the introduction is made your partner may suggest that you eat together simply at a brasserie. Many larger firms have their own dining rooms, where the meal will still be quite lavish but will take less time than in a restaurant. The office working lunch with sandwiches is still rare, and so is the single-status canteen (at least in French-owned firms).

After hours As the French stay late in their offices, the habit of early evening business drinks is not common, except for larger formal receptions. But the business dinner, though less common than lunch, is perfectly in order and here the conventions are much as for lunches. There is no special significance in being invited for dinner rather than lunch; it may simply be a matter of mutual convenience and availability, and it is much more common in the provinces than in Paris where work ends so late. An executive playing host will sometimes bring his or her spouse; but if you are host, do not suggest this unless you have already met the spouse socially.

Social hospitality

In general, executives keep their business and private lives more separate than in many countries. In Paris, their working lives are so hectic that they do not often entertain other than relatives and close friends at home. Outside Paris, however, you are much more likely to be asked home for dinner, and here the French belie the false myth that they are not a hospitable people. But there are some niceties to be observed: in a private home, do not talk shop over dinner before the coffee and brandy; and do not smoke before the cheese. The little courtesies count, too. Bring flowers for your hostess, or good chocolates, or maybe a malt whisky or cognac – but not a bottle of wine, which in France is such a routine object that it is like bringing a cauliflower. A thank-you note afterwards is always appreciated, though the French themselves are not always good at reciprocating.

Conversation The French are mostly good conversationalists; they set high store by wit, intelligence and original opinions and they will mark up those who seem cultured and well informed. They do not suffer fools or dullards gladly (at least not in Paris) and they are selfish to the point of expecting their business social encounters to be amusing. Those who want to succeed in dealings with the French would be advised to take an informed interest in current French politics and economic life, as well as in Gallic culture and history. To appear ignorant of France, or uninterested in it, will upset French susceptibilities. You will also rise in local esteem if you appear to enjoy good living and can show knowledge and appreciation of French cooking and wines. You will clinch it if you speak good, if not fluent, French.

Other invitations Those who pass these tests will find the French extremely generous with their social time, and they may end up as real personal friends once the social reserve has melted. Executives will sometimes invite their more cherished visitors to the opera, or to a festival concert, or to one of the smarter Paris race-meetings. In the Midi, depending on mutual interests, the invitation could well be to a rugby match or even a bullfight. The real token of friendly approval is when you are invited away for the weekend, to your host's country villa or château, or perhaps to a yacht on the Côte. These are invitations you do not refuse.

Etiquette

Although today younger people are more informal in their social manners than their elders, the French still set great store by formal courtesies, titles and the right dress and forms of address. They put high value on doing things with style. To an outsider they may often seem stiff and formal in a social context, but this should not be mistaken for coldness; courtesy may be stylized among older people, yet it can be a channel for expressing warmth. The habitual "Cher Monsieur" is not quite the same as "Dear Sir." An older Frenchman will often call his oldest or closest friend just that, and it can be rather cordial, like "Mon vieux." However, younger people have more easy-going styles.

First names and "tu" The use of first names, once restricted to relatives and close friends, has now become widespread among the under-40s. But many older executives remain shy of using this informality with colleagues: equals working in the same office will often remain on surname terms without thereby being unfriendly. Similarly, the use of the familiar *tu* has been increasing at the expense of the more formal *vous*. *Tutoiement* (the use of *tu*) also used to be confined to family circles, close friends and the male camaraderie of army and student life. Today it is almost universal among teenagers and is spreading fast in business life. In some offices, there is an unwritten code that all executives call each other *tu*; in others, they stick to *vous* unless they know each other well. *Tu* is still used far less widely than first names, and many business acquaintances will call each other "Jacques" or "Henri" while sticking to *vous* though, for obvious reasons, colleagues of the opposite sex call each other *tu* in public far less often than those of the same sex. In your contacts with a French firm, you may find yourself remaining on "Monsieur" or "Madame" terms for the first few meetings. Your French colleague may then venture into first names; but it could be years, if ever, before you are called "tu." These differences are largely a matter of generation. The best advice is to let the French set the pace, remembering that the use of first names in business is still relatively novel in France.

Titles Older French people in particular like being called by their titles, in both letters and speech. The head of a firm will expect to be called "Monsieur (or Madame) le Président": in fact, almost any distinguished-looking older person can safely be addressed in this way, for once a president you retain the courtesy title for ever – even if you were no more than head of your local golf club. If someone has several titles, you should find out which he or she regards as the most flattering: thus, a former governor of the Bank of France who is now president of some firm might still prefer to be called "Monsieur le Gouverneur."

Shaking hands The French shake hands on meeting and parting. Not to do so may give offence. When entering a crowded room, you should do your best to shake hands with all in turn, starting with the most senior. These formalities are less observed by younger people.

Dress It is best to dress smartly for business, and to err on the side of conservatism. Men should always wear a neat suit and tie; women are allowed some colour, but should be well groomed. The French notice the way people dress, and this is one factor that goes to form their overall judgment of them. But the quality and cut of the clothes matter as much as their correctness. On the other hand, ostentation should be avoided. Women should also follow a conservative line but there is now much more of an acceptance of "informal" stylish clothes so long as they are smart as well as comfortable.

In the winter, especially in Paris, men should wear a darkish suit. In summer, or in the south, suits of a lighter colour and weight are acceptable. Always wear a tie. On a hot day in an office, your French partner may well remove his jacket and maybe his tie too, and you can follow; it is best to let him make the move, unless you know him well. In the south in summer, open necks and shirt-sleeves all day are common, even for meals, and women can wear light dresses; again, let your French friends set the pace.

Letters The French are nowhere so formal as in the style of their letter writing, often disconcertingly so. Let us say you have parted from your French business acquaintances on the warmest of terms; they have told you, sincerely, what fun it has been and how they look forward to keeping up the contact. Do not be surprised if a week later they send you an impersonal letter on some point of business, making no reference to your jolly meetings, starting stiffly, *Monsieur*, or *Madame*, and ending with the usual stylized formality. Do not think you are being snubbed or that something has gone wrong. Even between friendly colleagues, the French habitually write in this vein. It is a convention, or they may fear that too cordial a tone might be compromising if on the record.

It is best to reply in more or less similar vein, loosening up a little but not too much. If you write in French, get the conclusion right. The French for "Yours sincerely" is *"Veuillez*

agréer, cher Monsieur, l'assurance de mes sentiments les meilleurs," and for "Yours faithfully," *"Veuillez ... sentiments les plus distingués."* But there are many other subtle variations. To those you do not know well, you should start *"Cher Monsieur"* or *"Chère Madame"* (a mature woman is always *"Madame,"* even if unmarried; today only single women under about 25 are *"Mademoiselle"*).

The French are often bad at replying to letters. Yours may lie unanswered on their desk, unless they really want something from you, in which case they are most likely to telephone or telex. So, if you get no reply to some crucial letter, sink your pride and do what they would do: chase them up by phone.

The need to speak French Few other nations, if any, are as fanatically proud as the French are of their language, once the *lingua franca* of culture and diplomacy. Although many executives now have a good command of English (or other languages), they may often prefer not to use it, for reasons either of national pride or fear of looking foolish by speaking a foreign tongue incorrectly, or simply for reasons of strategy. As a result, if your business letters are to be written in French (which ideally they should), it is important that they should also be without mistakes; the French hate to read or hear their language used incorrectly. And while the person you are writing to may understand English, your letter may be passed to subordinates who do not.

English, particularly, is spoken far more widely than even 15 years ago. Foreign language classes are now compulsory in schools and universities, and 83% of students make English their first choice. The executives you deal with are today quite likely to speak English. But, inside France, you will still get on *far* better with them if at least one of your negotiating team speaks French really well.

The business media

The French weekly press and the regional daily press are varied and flourishing. The weak point is the Paris dailies whose sales have been slipping steadily; provincial papers account for over two-thirds of dailies' total circulation. France has virtually no national daily press.

Paris daily newspapers

Le Monde Published in the early afternoon, *Le Monde* is still regarded as one of the world's great newspapers despite recent ups and downs. It is moderate, left-of-centre in tone. Its format is austere, with no photographs, and its coverage is very serious and thorough, making it essential reading for the educated elite. Economics and business are featured in a Friday pull-out section, *Le Monde des Affaires*. Circulation is high for a paper of its kind, and it is the only Paris daily to have much of a sale in the provinces, where it usually arrives the morning after publication. The staff own many of the shares and elect the editor.

Libération This lively and radical new challenger to *Le Monde* is critical of the establishment and has an influence far greater than its modest sales might suggest. It is well written, but its coverage is somewhat haphazard, stronger on general economic than strictly business matters.

Le Figaro The flagship of the press empire of the right-wing tycoon, Robert Hersant. It used to be the favoured morning reading of the Paris *bourgeoisie*, but has lost some credibility since its political tone has grown more strident. General coverage is uninspired, but company news is reported fully and fairly in the pink economic pages, notably in the Monday pull-out supplement.

Les Echos This is the leading Paris economic daily, though curiously its coverage is mainly regional. Angled at the provincial businessman, it is full of terse factual local reports that seldom have much insight.

International Herald Tribune Published in Paris, Amsterdam and elsewhere in Europe and the world. This English-language daily has good European news coverage and a business section; it carries many articles syndicated from the USA. (The London *Financial Times*, incidentally, has a sizable sale in Paris, where many French executives prefer it to any of their own daily papers.)

Le Tribune de l'Economie is a business and economic daily dealing with the Bourse and other financial matters.

Other Paris dailies Paris has no big popular mass-selling paper; the nearest to it is Hersant's evening *France-Soir*, with a news coverage that is strong on showbiz. Other dailies are a varied bunch: *L'Equipe*, good on sport; *La Croix*, a Catholic paper with long, useful articles on general as well as Church matters; *Les Côtes Défossés*, a Bourse afternoon broadsheet with stock price listings; and its natural enemy *L'Humanité*, the Communist Party's ailing organ. *Le Quotidien* is a conservative voice.

Regional dailies

Ouest-France, published in Rennes and catering to all the northwest, is by far the biggest-selling French daily, with almost twice the circulation of any in Paris! Other major regional dailies, many with a local near-monopoly, are *La Voix du Nord* (Lille), *Le Dauphinée Libéré* (Grenoble), *Sud-Ouest* (Bordeaux), *Le Progrès* (Lyon) and *La Dépêche du Midi* (Toulouse). (See **City by City**.)

Paris weeklies and monthlies

The leading magazines of business interest are the fortnightly *L'Expansion* and the weekly *Le Nouvel Economiste*. The former is the better and weightier of the two. It contains in-depth company profiles and expert macroeconomic analyses, and is much read and admired by senior executives. *Le Nouvel Economiste*, more newsy and middlebrow, is stronger on general economic than company matters.

Paris has no Sunday newspapers, except for the forgettable *Journal du Dimanche*. Their place is taken by the news magazines, which do very well and can be quite serious despite their glossy format and punchy style. The best-known are *L'Express* and *Le Point*, both right-of-centre but not strongly politicized; and *Le Nouvel Observateur* which is more wordy, intellectual and pro-Socialist. The big-selling *Paris Match* has excellent photo features. *Le Figaro Magazine* is the mouthpiece of the intellectual far right, and also has illustrated features. The famous *Canard Enchaîné* plays a unique role, combining radical satire (hard for an outsider to follow) with frequent scoops of political and business scandals and alleged misdeeds. Its exposures have on occasion caused governments to fall.

Other economic weeklies are *La Vie Française* and *Investir*, devoted to the Bourse.

Television

Television Française 1 (TF1)
Formerly the main state channel, privatized in 1987, and now funded largely by advertising. Its current affairs programmes are being remodelled.

Antenne 2 The main rival to TF1
remains in state hands, but depends on advertising as well as public funding. Its approach has generally been more lively and enterprising than TF1's, especially in news and documentary. The two put out rival 8pm news programmes.

France Régions 3 (FR3) A state-
owned channel with studios in the regions that put out networked as well as local material. FR3 has experimented with the nearest thing on French TV to a regular "business programme" – *Espace Trois*, where companies or individuals buy screen time to put their message across.

Other channels *Canal Plus* is a pay-TV channel whose subscribers get a mixed diet of sport and old films; *Channels 5* and *6* are purely commercial, hitherto lowbrow though their new owners since 1987 may have better ideas.

Radio
The main channel of the state-owned Radio France is *France-Inter* which includes business items in its extensive news coverage. It has smaller audiences than the lively non-state networks, *Europe* and *Radio Luxembourg* (RTL), both now fully privatized and both offering good news coverage. Business interviews are part of RTL's feature programmes.

Background reading
For statistical information on a huge range of subjects, INSEE's *Annuaire Statistique de la France* is invaluable, and so is its shorter digest, *Tableaux de l'Economie Française*. La Documentation Française, a government department, publishes ad hoc brochures on a variety of topics, including the economy. The annual *Who's Who in France* is useful. **Official publications** Most useful are the Ministère des Finances's weekly report, *Les Notes Bleues*, and the *Informations Rapides*, published by INSEE on a weekly or even more frequent basis. *Le Journal Officiel* gives texts of bills and other government documents.

Cultural Awareness

A historical perspective

A strong centralization, dating from the early Middle Ages, has welded the very diverse peoples of France – Celts, Vikings, Franks, Latins and others – into a single nation with an unusually keen sense of national pride and identity. This process has been helped by the natural borders of sea, river and high mountain and by a series of powerful autocratic leaders, from Louis IX via Louis XI and Louis XIV and on to Napoleon and de Gaulle, who pursued ideals of national glory and prestige.

30,000–15,000BC Cro-Magnon man, whose cave paintings still exist in the southwest, peoples a France laid bare by the Ice Age.

600BC Greek traders found Massilia, later to be called Marseille.

59–50BC Julius Caesar conquers France.

AD987 Hugh Capet, first of the Capetian monarchs, elected king of France.

1207–29 King Philip Augustus brutally suppresses the Cathar (Albigensian) heresy.

1226–70 Louis IX (St Louis), greatest of the Capetian kings, founds Sorbonne (1253) and wages 7th and 8th Crusades.

1309–77 Transferred from Rome, the papacy rules in Avignon.

1337–1453 The Hundred Years' War, marked by English victories at Crécy and Agincourt, Joan of Arc's campaigns and martyrdom (1431) and the final defeat and withdrawal of the English.

1515–47 Reign of François I under whom the Renaissance flourishes in France.

1562–98 The Wars of Religion between Catholics and Protestants (Huguenots), ending with the Edict of Nantes under which Protestantism is officially recognized.

1643–1715 Reign of Louis XIV, whose revocation of the Edict of Nantes (1685) leads to mass Huguenot exodus.

1715–74 Reign of Louis XV, who was much influenced by his leading mistress, Madame de Pompadour.

1789 The sacking of the Bastille on 14 July marks the start of the French Revolution, leading to the execution of Louis XVI (1793) and then of the revolutionary leaders themselves, notably Robespierre (1794).

1799 Napoleon Bonaparte appointed first consul and then crowned emperor (1804).

1805 French fleet defeated by Nelson at Trafalgar.

1812 Napoleon's empire reaches its zenith with the capture of Moscow, but he is then forced into a humiliating retreat from Russia.

1814-15 Napoleon is forced to abdicate and is exiled to the island of Elba. He escapes, raises a new army, but is defeated at Waterloo. He dies in exile on St Helena (1821).

1814–30 Bourbon monarchy restored, under Louis XVIII, then Charles X.

1830 Revolution in Paris: Charles X replaced by Louis-Philippe.

1830–48 Conquest of Algeria.

1848 Another Paris revolution. Napoleon's nephew Louis-Napoleon elected president, then becomes emperor (Second Empire, 1852–70).

1870–71 The Franco-Prussian War: France is defeated at Sedan, then cedes Alsace and Lorraine to the victors.

1871 In Paris, the revolutionary government of the "commune" is bloodily suppressed.

1875–87 French vineyards ravaged by phylloxera epidemic.

1894–99 The Dreyfus affair: Jewish officer falsely convicted of treason.

1909 Louis Blériot is first to fly a non-balloon aircraft across the Channel.

1914–18 World War I, leading to Treaty of Versailles (1919) and the return of Alsace and Lorraine to France.

1936 "Popular Front" left-wing government under socialist Léon Blum. The railways, some factories and the Banque de France nationalized.

1939 Outbreak of World War II, leading to German invasion and fall of Paris (1940): a collaborationist government is set up at Vichy, in the unoccupied zone, under Marshal Pétain.

1944 Allies liberate France and de Gaulle forms a provisional government. Sweeping nationalizations begin.

1946 Fourth Republic formed.

1954 Fall of Dien Bien Phu leads to French exodus from Indo-China.

1957 Treaty of Rome is signed, setting up European Community.

1958 De Gaulle returns to power: Fifth Republic is created.

1962 France grants independence to Algeria, after an eight-year war.

1968 Student uprising and general strike. De Gaulle resigns (1969).

1974–81 Presidency of Valéry Giscard d'Estaing.

1981–86 Socialist-led government, with François Mitterrand as President. More nationalizations.

1986 Chirac government elected and a period of "cohabitation" begins.

The Capetians create France The kings of the Capetian dynasty in the 11th–13th centuries established the principle of a central monarchy and extended their rule over most of what is now France.

The reign of the Sun King Louis XIV, known as "le Roi Soleil," was on the throne for 72 years, 1643–1715, and this period marked the apogee of French autocratic monarchy and the zenith of France's power and prestige in Europe. He built the Palace of Versailles. But his lavish spending and costly foreign wars antagonized many

of his poor and suffering citizens.

The French Revolution As the despotic monarchy continued during the 18th century, new democratic ideas began to circulate, notably those of Voltaire and Jean-Jacques Rousseau, while France was also influenced by the triumph of these principles in the United States after the War of Independence. These trends led in 1789 to the Revolution, a key event in world history. When the dust had settled, it was the property-owning bourgeoisie that triumphed. Napoleon Bonaparte, as emperor, then introduced modern forms of strong state administration.

A century of growth After Napoleon's defeat in 1815 France enjoyed a period of sustained economic progress and modernization, despite political turbulence, three mini-revolutions, and periods of restored monarchy. During this period France began to acquire a major world empire, mainly in North and West Africa and in the Far East and the Pacific. After 1875 France definitively became a republic and this was followed by a number of reforms. Universal primary school education was introduced in 1881-82.

La belle époque After the turn of the century there followed a golden age of business expansion, social progress, artistic vitality and general optimism – the apogee of "gay Paree." But this idyll was cut short by World War I. The 1920s was marked by industrialization and modernization and this continued into the 1930s.

Postwar renewal After 1940–44, as after 1815 and 1871, defeat in war provided the French with the shock and impetus for renewal. The economic changes were dramatic. A nation formerly based on agriculture became an urban and industrial one; a colonial empire was shed (albeit painfully in Indo-China and Algeria); and the creation of the EC spelt the end of protectionism and opened France's frontiers more than ever before.

Beliefs, attitudes and values

The French today remain assertively proud of a culture and way of life that they take for granted to be the world's most brilliant and civilized, and they expect others to share that verdict. But while traditional attitudes to French individualism, nationalism, rigid social structures and the persuasive influences of Church and family are becoming more relaxed, the underlying conservatism of the French ensures that the process of change is slow.

Patriotism

Pride in French achievements and a liking for the French way of life remain strong among the French, but old-style patriotism has receded. De Gaulle's ideals of *"la gloire"* and *"la grandeur française,"* with their military overtones, have largely vanished with the General himself, except among some older or extreme right-wing people. When the bugles sound and the flags wave on the *quatorze juillet*, the nation may still stand solemnly to attention out of habit, but these rituals are losing their meaning and a younger generation is sceptical. A recent international Gallup survey that put the question, "Do you feel proud to be ... (American, Italian, and so on)?", found only 33% of French answering "yes," far fewer than Americans or British, and not so many more than Japanese (30%) or West Germans (21%).

Yet, paradoxically, the French remain highly competitive on the world stage: in foreign affairs, in business and technology, in sport and culture. French achievements, from Ariane rockets to ocean yachting victories, from Minitel to the new museums and public buildings in Paris, are lauded in the media and stressed by politicians. The French today are not at all insular; they were the driving force behind the creation of the European Community; they continually compare themselves with other nations and try to score points off them, which if you like is a kind of chauvinism, but is very different from insularity. This is apparent in attitudes to Europe. For the most part, the French see the EC as a useful forum for their national ambitions (according to the latest survey, 61% think membership "good" for their country and only 5% think it "bad"), but this leads them to think of themselves very much in a European rather than a purely French context. This goes for ordinary people, as well as for political and business leaders. At the same time, the crude anti-US feeling of the 1950s and 1960s has declined, except sometimes in the cultural field, and individual Americans are accepted quite warmly. The French have also paid Americans and Britons the dubious compliment of distorting many English words into the hybrid newspeak of *Franglais*, such as *un tennisman, le marketing,* or *grand standing* (classy, luxurious), which so angers the purists.

Immigrants and racism

Before the war, nearly all foreigners, white or coloured, were eyed with some suspicion by the average Frenchman. But today the large Italian, Portuguese, Polish and other European minorities are fully accepted and integrated. Instead, a much greater hostility has developed towards non-European immigrants, mainly the Muslims from North Africa. "Generalized xenophobia," as one Frenchman put it, "has now narrowed down to racism – are we to call that progress?"

Of the 1.5m Muslims from Algeria, Morocco and Tunisia, former French possessions, most have their families with them and many have been living in France for decades; many others are now French citizens. Until the 1970s there were few problems. But a sharp rise in unemployment seems to be the main factor that has inspired a recent wave of racist feeling. Muslims are thought to be taking jobs from the French; or they are disliked for their alien religion and customs, or they are believed to be distorting school populations in some areas with large numbers of Muslim children. The backlash of Iran-backed fundamentalism has not made matters any easier. The Muslims tend to live in closed communities in high-rise blocks or in the poorer tenement zones of inner cities. Tensions are worst with the French working-class and lower bourgeoisie. Gangs of French youths have sporadically beaten up Arabs and there has been some worse violence and shootings. Of course many French people are liberal and wish to protect the Muslims, but this has not prevented a growing resentment of the immigrants and the rise of Le Pen's Front National party.

France's 650,000 blacks, mostly from the French Carribbean, are much better received; the French find them more friendly and open, with a more acceptable attitude to women. But they too have begun to suffer from some growing prejudices. The other sizable minority, France's 700,000 Jews, are today far more easily welcomed and integrated than in the past, when right up to the Liberation there had been a sorry history of anti-Semitism. The older-established Jewish residents in France are Ashkenazim from Central and Eastern Europe: since the 1960s their ranks have been swelled by Sephardic emigrés from North Africa who are far more assertive and flamboyant. This has provoked some new anti-Semitic rumbles.

Law and order
Crime has increased considerably in recent years, much of it in the form of muggings, housebreaking, and late-night violence on the Paris

Métro. Rightly or wrongly it is often ascribed to young Muslims. Calls for stronger law-and-order measures are popular with public opinion.

Social classes
Class divisions remain marked in France and depend more on background than on wealth, though the two may go together. The distinctions are taken for granted and seldom discussed publicly except in purely political terms: "*la bourgeoisie*" versus "*la classe ouvrière*." It is true that since World War II a greater social fluidity has emerged and the distinctions between the classes have tended to become blurred, especially among younger people; with prosperity, workers have picked up bourgeois styles of dress and leisure habits, and it has become easier for someone of humble origins to rise to a senior position. However, while accents in France are more a matter of region than of class, working-class origins may still be revealed by vocabulary and social manners. Although children of all classes attend the same state junior and secondary schools, the bourgeoisie has managed to maintain its dominance of the upper rungs of the educational ladder and a near-monopoly of the positions of power. Only 13% of university and college students are from working-class homes. The following are the rough class divisions.

Aristocracy Without a monarchy to give them a focus and *raison d'être*, France's titled families have lost much of their central role in French society and their titles are no longer recognized under the law. They still cling together in their own social circles, giving exclusive parties in their country châteaux or Paris flats. The rest of France ignores them and scarcely resents them.

Upper bourgeoisie This class holds much of the real power in France. Its strength used to be based on family property; but as the family firm has given way to the managerial corporation, so the *haute bourgeoisie* now derives its income from elite salaried positions in industry, finance, the professions or the upper civil service, and it retains its grasp over many of these jobs. Together with the nobility it forms the social milieu today known as "BCBG" (*bon chic, bon genre*) – a class that works hard and has impeccable formal manners and discreet good taste. Just below it is the *bonne bourgeoisie* of doctors, lawyers, teachers and other professional groups.

Middle and lower bourgeoisie
Economic expansion has thrown up a new parvenu class of sales and advertising executives, successful shop-owners, skilled technicians and others. Their lack of pedigree or inherited property may mark them off from the ranks above, but in terms of affluence they are far better placed than the older *petite bourgeoisie* of minor public servants, small traders, and impoverished elderly people living on fixed incomes.

Peasantry Small farmers, *les paysans*, used to be a separate class, living in a world apart. But with farm mechanization and modernization they have begun to pick up the attitudes and lifestyles of the business community and have virtually merged into the middle bourgeoisie; the traditional farm labourer has largely disappeared. This is the biggest class change in postwar France.

Workers Rehousing and industrial change have undermined much of the old solidarity and community sense of the working class. A new, well-paid proletarian elite of skilled workers has emerged in the modern industries, clearly distinct from workers in declining sectors who have been hardest hit by unemployment and still tend to feel alienated from French life. For many, the Parti Communiste and its trade union the CGT, though on the wane, remain the best rallying-point.

Inequalities of wealth Wage differentials, roughly 7.3 between managing director and unskilled worker, are among the highest in the West; the well-to-do also benefit from relatively low taxes on property and income, and in some cases from the old French sport of tax evasion. The Socialist government of the early 1980s did something to improve the lot of the lowest paid, by raising the minimum legal wage, but extra taxes on the rich did not have much affect on the real inequalities. The Chirac government set the pendulum swinging back again.

Families, sex and morality
Family ties and loyalties remain strong in this Latin country. The emphasis, however, has been shifting from the clan-like "extended" family to the smaller "nuclear" one of parents and young children. The big family reunion of cousins and aunts has become rarer, and an elderly widowed parent is now less likely to live with his or her offspring. But relations between parents and adolescent children have been growing closer again after a difficult period. Around 1968 French teenagers rebelled sharply and decisively against traditional parental authority; but now that they have asserted their independence, teenagers have felt able to return to closer emotional ties, on a basis of greater equality. So the family today is united less by constraint or convention and more by genuine need and affection – and the insecurities of high unemployment have strengthened this trend. A boy or girl of 19 or 20 may live away from home, but is likely to keep in close touch with parents. Very small children are indulged in the Latin manner; but baby-breeding is less of a prestige cult than it was in the postwar days of a high birth-rate, and many young professional couples prefer not to have children, at least for some years.

Marriage and divorce The rigid codes of France's Catholic heritage have been loosening. Divorce has been made easier and no longer carries any stigma. One marriage in four now ends in divorce and many couples do not get married in the first place, preferring simply to live together. The annual number of marriages has been declining sharply. In fact the state now recognizes the formal status of *le concubinage*, or common-law marriage, which carries some tax advantages; and an unmarried mother bears the respectable title of *mère célibataire*. Of those couples who do marry, it is reckoned that about half have cohabited before marriage – but this does not mean that the French have become very promiscuous. A teenager may sleep around a good deal, for experience's sake, but then quite early will settle down with a regular partner. The wave of promiscuity in the 1970s had died down even before the advent of AIDS, which has now made the French even more *sérieux*.

Women's equality It was not until 1945 that women won the vote, and not until the late 1970s that new laws removed the last inequalities over property, divorce and employment rights. Couples are now more equal, and the man will often help with the chores. But this does not mean that French women are feminists. They still prize femininity above all, and they still want to be wooed and serenaded with gallantry and romanticism. "Equal to men, but different" is their motto, and domineering, aggressive women are treated with disdain.

Sexual morality Sophisticated Parisians have always been highly tolerant on sexual matters. The provinces have been more strict: but with a certain hypocrisy the bourgeoisie has usually turned a blind eye to discreet affairs (for some, a husband's taking a mistress is simply an honoured French tradition, though for a wife to take a lover is often less acceptable). Homosexuals are easily accepted so long as they do not flaunt their behaviour. But the strong Catholic lobby fought so

tough a rearguard battle that not until 1967 was birth-control fully legalized, and abortion not until 1975. The recent change in public codes of sexual decency has been noticeable especially on state television, which for long was prim and prudish but now parades full nudity almost as freely as the French cinema has always done.

Religion

France is still overwhelmingly a Christian country despite sizable groups belonging to other religions. Of France's Christians some 3% are Protestant and the rest Catholic. The position of the Catholic Church has changed considerably. On the one hand, the old bitter feuding between clericals and anti-clericals has died down (except sometimes on the issue of state aid for Church schools) and the two sides now live quite amicably; on the other, the Church has lost its central role, as in many other countries. Most people still get married, baptized and buried by the Church, but regular weekly attendance at Mass is down to 14% (10% in Paris), the parish priest has lost much influence even in rural areas, and there is a serious shortage of young recruits for the priesthood. But those laymen who still believe and practise their religion now do so with more fervour and sincerity; so the Church, from being a central pillar of society, has become more like a dynamic minority pressure group – or rather, a series of pressure groups, for there are many rival tendencies. Rejecting formal churchgoing, some Catholics have formed private "charismatic" groups or other informal fellowships that meet for prayer and discussion in family homes. Others have moved into radical social action, and here the leftish militant worker-priest movement is still in operation; partly in reaction against this, other Catholics have turned to right-wing "integrism," in a bid to retain the old liturgical purities.

Lifestyles and leisure

Lifestyles and leisure habits in France have been changing, as the French move closer to other nations' habits in some respects. For example, they are now showing a greater concern for home comforts and for health, and are putting less daily stress on elaborate cooking. But these changes are relative, and many typically French pastimes remain unchanged. Though in love with innovation and gadgetry, the French are also a very conservative people in their attachment to old routines and ways of thinking. For example, although the "new franc" (100 old francs) was introduced back in 1959, today many educated people, including young ones, still prefer to calculate large sums in old francs.

Home life

The French are no longer so shockingly badly housed as they were 30 years ago: between the 1954 and 1984 censuses the percentage of homes without bath or shower fell from 90% to 12%, and of homes without indoor flushing lavatories from 73% to 10.7%. A vast programme of building and improvement has finally brought French housing into the modern age, as people have become more concerned for comfort and more willing to spend money on it. In all classes, nearly all urban families live in apartments rather than houses; but new villas have been spreading in the suburbs as more and more Frenchmen realize their dream of a separate house with a garden. Owner-occupation has been growing too, and now accounts for 51% of all homes.

Home equipment The middle and upper classes tend to furnish their homes either with striking modern decor or else in the classic tradition, with heavy reproduction furniture or with genuine antiques, formal settees and spindly Louis XV chairs. None of these styles is exactly comfortable, but the French are less interested in furniture than in modern consumer durables. Their love of new gadgetry has put them in the lead in Europe, ahead even of the Germans. Since 1954, the percentage of homes owning consumer durables has increased dramatically. In 1986 97% owned a refrigerator, 83% a washing machine and 69% a TV set. In the same period the percentage of families owning a car increased from 21% to 73%, while 22% of families have more than one car.

Kitchen and other household appliances have to a large extent replaced servants, for while 498,000 families still have some daily help, hardly any have live-in maids.

Food In all social classes, workers included, the French still eat more than any other people in the West. They talk and think about food a lot, and the housewife will take great care over selecting quality foodstuffs and will buy fresh rather than frozen where possible: hence, despite the rise of the supermarkets, the continued popularity of the long-established street and covered markets where the produce comes straight from the farm. Even so, home eating habits have been changing. The emphasis now is on lighter meals; and whereas elaborate cooking used to be a matter of daily routine, today it is more often reserved for special occasions (see *Food and drink*).

Drinking Although the French remain the world's heaviest consumers of alcohol after the Luxembourgeois, the amount drunk per capita has been slowly falling, by over 20% since 1954. Wine on the table at both lunch and dinner, though still the norm, is no longer universal in middle-class families. With rising prosperity the quality of the *vins de table* has much improved;

the old acid plonk, so bad for health, is now much less evident. Sales of mineral waters and fruit juices have increased hugely: as the latter costs twice as much as cheap wine, this gives it a certain cachet especially among young people. Beer and *pastis* are very popular; and champagne and malt whisky are more then ever the smart drinks among the affluent.

At the lower end of the social scale, alcoholism remains a scourge, causing 17,000 deaths a year. This is a phenomenon of social backwardness in rural and slum areas, where the cause is nearly always cheap red wine rather than hard spirits.

Health The French have recently become fashionably fussy about their health, purchasing increasing quantities of medicines. "We've become a nation of hypochondriacs," was the view of one doctor. While smoking has declined and is now a minority habit the French are still the heaviest smokers in Europe and still produce a considerable quantity of their own state-subsidized tobacco. Fitness and health centres, for gym, massage, saunas and swimming, have mushroomed. *"Le jogging"* is in vogue, too.

Leisure

The French set less store on evening leisure, and more on weekends and lengthy holidays, than many nations. In the provinces, particularly in the Midi, the two-hour lunch break is still common, when banks, shops and offices close from noon till 2 and many people go home for a leisurely lunch.

This pattern has been changing in Paris and other big towns, where the break is now shorter and staggered, so that shops may remain open: but many professional people prefer to stick to the long lunch. Hence work either starts early or ends late (see *Business Awareness*), and people are too tired for much evening leisure activity. They eagerly await the weekend break, which sometimes extends into Monday.

Evening amusements The café used to be the main local centre of social life and gossip. But thousands of smaller cafés have closed in recent years, for the French are now less keen to spend their evenings there. The change has been due to better housing, less drinking, and the lure of TV. The middle classes tend to watch relatively little TV because of its low quality; in working-class homes the set is often in the dining room, to accompany long leisurely dinners that seldom start before 7.30 or 8. Chat and half-an-eye viewing go on together.

Socializing is mainly reserved for the weekend. But close friends or relatives may drop round for an informal meal during the week, and in wealthier circles, mainly in Paris, the very formal dinner or cocktail party is not infrequent. The French are not great club-joiners, but some people will spend evenings at Rotary or veteran meetings (the men without their wives) or at special-interest arts or sports clubs. The young set go to bars and discos.

Culture Along with sport and eating, cultural pursuits are the main leisure interest of the educated classes. The past 20 years have seen a remarkable renaissance of music. In this hitherto not very musical nation many people now go eagerly to concerts of all sorts, or to the countless new summer music festivals that now take place all over France, and they install high-quality sound equipment in their homes. The 14 full-time opera companies around France play to packed houses.

The postwar theatre revival came earlier and it continues, with diversified audiences for boulevard comedies, classical revivals and modern experimental plays. Over 400 theatre companies receive state subsidies; many of the best use the huge Maisons de la Culture built since the 1960s. The cinema remains a highly respected art form among intellectuals, and audiences for both "serious" and "commercial" films have resisted the impact of TV far better than in most countries. Museum-going too has become *à la mode*, and special art exhibitions draw huge attendances.

Sport In line with the new accent on fitness and longer holidays, interest in sport has increased substantially. But the individualistic French put the stress less on team games than energetic solo ones. Sailing is a sport where the French excel, and the number of private yachts and sailing boats has risen since 1960 from 20,000 to over 650,000. Some 4m people, many of them working class, go on skiing holidays each year, mainly to the French Alps. Tennis and riding, once minority sports of the rich, are widely popular; and many new golf-courses have been built, much patronized by business people.

The traditional democratic sports remain football, cycling, hunting and *boules*. Amateur soccer clubs' membership totals 1.7m while rugby is played eagerly in the Midi. *La chasse*, generally conducted with a rifle, not horse and hounds, was once the preserve of peasants and gentry, but so many clumsy urban amateurs have taken to the woods at weekends, with accidents ensuing, that the gun licensing laws have had to be tightened. *Boules* or *pétanque*, a rough kind of bowls, is still much played by groups of older men, and some young ones too, in dusty squares in the Midi and even in northern towns. The major spectator sports, watched outdoors or on TV, are soccer and the annual Tour de France cycle race; bullfighting is confined to Languedoc and the Basque country. Horse-racing is popular mainly as an outlet for betting (much of which takes place in cafés) and is tightly organized by a semi-state body, the Pari Mutuel Urbain (PMU).

Weekends The Sunday outing and the lavish family Sunday lunch have long been major French rituals and they remain so. But the fact that the French have had to borrow the

English term *"le weekend,"* and have no word of their own, indicates that the full weekend off is a fairly recent vogue in France. Until the 1960s most offices and factories worked till Saturday noon, and this is still true of *lycées* (high schools). But most Frenchmen now value their weekend highly and pack into it most of the week's leisure activity. Shops stay open till 7pm on Saturday but many then stay closed on Mondays.

Especially among well-to-do city dwellers, the weekend departure for the *résidence secondaire* has become a new ritual. It may be a modern villa, or a converted farmhouse, or in some cases a château. The French have the highest rate of second home ownership in the world (one for every nine families) and there are three main reasons why there are so many: the postwar farm exodus left much rural property vacant, and therefore cheap to buy; many urban French still have rural roots, and they cherish them; and many people want an escape from the tensions of their congested cities, Paris above all.

Holidays The strains of city life may also explain why holidays too are now such a passion with the French; the legal minimum annual paid holiday, conceded under public and union pressure, is five weeks. The trend among the younger middle classes is for holidays that are active and sporty, that have some gregarious and euphoric community basis, and are in exotic foreign locations – hence the success of that peculiarly French invention, the Club Méditerranée. But the more individual and adventurous holiday is also popular, and an eager minority will go trekking in the Andes or looking for Thai temples. Foreign leisure travel has increased greatly. Those who want to just lie on a beach or go camping in the mountains will probably stay inside France, whose wide open spaces and long coastline offers plenty of scope. But the French still perversely refuse to stagger their holidays outside July and August.

Education

Under the centralized, tightly controlled French school system, the vast majority of children, rich and poor alike, attend the same kind of state day schools. The academically able go on to study for the *baccalauréat*, which is the essential passport for entry to university. But it is the *grandes écoles* rather than the universities that are the route to the top. These elite specialist colleges, each with its own fiercely competitive entrance exam, carry high prestige and wield much influence.

Schools

Before the age of six many children attend *écoles maternelles* (nursery schools), which are run privately or municipally. Education is compulsory from six to sixteen and is free in state schools. The curriculum is laid down centrally by the Ministère de l'Education. Some 83% of children are in state education; the remainder go to private schools, nearly all of which are run by the Catholic Church. These are heavily subsidized by the government and thus charge minimal fees. But the powerful anti-clerical lobby has long fought to remove these privileges and in 1984 the Socialist government produced a Bill for progressively integrating the Catholic schools into the state system. This caused an outcry, not only from practising Catholics but from many others who saw it as an attack on freedom of choice. The Bill was dropped. Since then the Catholic schools have continued to grow in popularity, for many middle-class parents, and not only churchgoers, see them as offering a sounder education.

School life By tradition, education is strongly academic, with the accent on encyclopedic knowledge and learning by heart. Since the 1950s this burden has been steadily lightened, to the point where fears have grown that standards have dropped too far and that many children are not being properly taught the basics of spelling, French history and so on. Since 1984 there has been some renewed emphasis on academic work.

Discipline in schools used to be very strict but after the 1968 uprisings a much more free-and-easy spirit appeared. More sport was officially introduced, but little emphasis is placed on out-of-class activities. Teachers, highly unionized, see their role as confined to the classroom and few are prepared to stay on after hours to organize other pursuits.

In both primary and secondary schools, children are in mixed-ability classes, and there is little early specialization. Most children leave school at 16 to take up jobs or apprenticeships or to enter junior technical colleges.

Lycées At 15 or 16 the more academic children go to a *lycée* (high school). Many of these traditional schools have high social prestige, notably those in Paris such as Henri IV and Louis-le-Grand, and their intake is largely middle class. *Lycée* pupils prepare for the *baccalauréat* which they take at 18 or 19. This examination is less demanding than it used to be, but it still requires intensive study, especially for its mathematics and science options which carry much kudos. In itself the "*bac*" is not much of a job qualification in the eyes of employers and hence nearly all those who pass it choose to go on to university (and the *bac* remains the essential entrance qualification). The *lycées techniques*, newer and less academic than the classical *lycées*, prepare for a *bac technique* that leads to many skilled blue-collar jobs and is thus popular with the aspiring working class. It remains scorned by the bourgeoisie.

Universities

There are some 75 universities, nearly all state-run but with a measure of internal autonomy. Most are rather similar to each other, although a few have faculties distinguished in a particular field, such as medicine at Montpellier. Main cities now contain several universities, for under the post-1968 reforms the bigger institutions were split up into smaller, more manageable units.

The student population totals over 900,000: numbers have been swelling almost uncontrollably because it has proved politically impossible to introduce selection in the face of the traditional guarantee of university entry to successful *baccalauréat* candidates. Overcrowding and under-funding have led to a lowering of standards, with little personal contact between professors and students. The once proud Sorbonne is today simply a building that houses parts of the amorphous Paris universities.

A few gifted and ambitious students stay on to take a higher diploma, such as the prized *agrégation* which often leads the way to a well-paid academic career. But the vast majority take a two- or three-year degree course with little value on the job market. Graduate unemployment is high and the universities tend to have low prestige. Industrial and government research funds go mostly to separate research institutes, which are largely cut off from the business world and new technological development.

Grandes écoles

The sharp contrast between the universities and the *grandes écoles* is the most distinctive trait of higher education. These relatively small, autonomous colleges, which number about 250, draw off most of the best students and are devoted to training high-level specialists, mainly in engineering, applied science, administration and management studies. The entrance exam requires two or three years' rigorous study in special post-*bac* classes at the *lycées*. ("Those who come out top," one professor used to tell his class, "do not smoke, do not drink and are virgins.") Nine out of ten candidates fail this hurdle but successful students (of which only about 10% are women), lead a privileged existence. There is close contact with the teachers and graduates are virtually assured of a worthwhile career. Although they account for only 5% of those in higher education, the *grandes écoles* turn out a high proportion of the country's senior civil servants and its industrial and business leaders.

Top écoles One of the most prestigious *grandes écoles* is the Ecole Polytechnique. It was founded by Napoleon to train engineers for the armed forces and still comes under the aegis of the Ministry of Defence, with a serving general at its head. Graduates now mainly go into civil jobs, as engineers, scientists or executives. Other famous colleges include the Ecole Centrale and the Ecole des Hautes Etudes Commerciales, a superior business college. Equally elitist are the other postgraduate schools for engineers, the Ecole des Mines and Ecole des Ponts et Chaussées.

In a different category is the very influential Ecole Nationale d'Administration, a postgraduate college which was founded in 1946 to train senior civil servants. Its most talented alumni form the ranks of the *grands corps* which plays a dominant role in political life (see **The Political Scene**). They make up not only much of the diplomatic and prefectoral corps but also the Inspection des Finances, Conseil d'Etat and Cour des Comptes. Some of them join the personal staffs of ministers or become senior politicians themselves. In parallel, alumni of the engineering *écoles* fill the top posts in the state technical services, such as the railways and telecommunications.

City by City

The map below shows the cities featured in detail in the city by city guide. Each city follows a standard format: an introduction, information on arriving, getting around, city areas, hotels, restaurants, bars, entertainment, shopping, sightseeing, sports and fitness, and a directory of local business and other facilities such as secretarial agencies, couriers, hospitals, convention and exhibition centres and florists. In some cities entertainment, shopping, sightseeing and sports are combined under the heading relaxation. There is also a map locating recommended hotels and restaurants, and important buildings and sights.

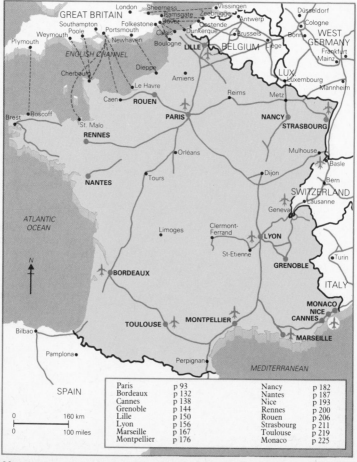

PARIS
Zip codes 75001–75020

Paris lies on the river Seine, encircling the Ile de la Cité where its life began, in a fertile basin of northeastern France. By tradition, Paris has always had greater political and cultural importance, as capital of a great empire and generator of ideas and artistic creativity, than as a centre of trade and finance. Since 1945, however, France's cultural influence has declined, and it is in industry and technology that the country has made most progress. The capital of this highly centralized nation has seized the opportunity to develop rapidly as a modern focus of business.

In world financial markets, Paris still does not play as strong a role as might be expected. Although the Bourse has been expanding and modernizing, it is still old-fashioned and only one-fifth the size of the London Stock Exchange. However, as a business centre Paris has been surging ahead. Several major convention centres have been built, notably the Palais des Congrès, and during the last decade Paris has been one of the world's most popular cities for international business conferences, staging well over 200 a year. Several multinationals such as IBM have their European headquarters in Paris, which is also the base for leading French groups such as Elf-Aquitaine, Saint-Gobain and Thomson. New high-rise business districts have been built, notably at La Défense, which lies to the west of the city, and at Quai de Bercy, which is east of the centre.

Industrially the city's importance is on the wane, but Paris still dominates most of French life. Nearly all the financial institutions and decision-making centres are based in Paris, including the state credit bodies and the main banks, and almost all the larger French firms have their head offices there. The recent decentralization policy has given a little more political and financial autonomy to the regions, but these moves are unlikely to reduce the importance of Paris as a business centre.

The business style of the capital is faster and tougher than is normal in the more easy-going provinces. If the French have a reputation in some quarters for arrogance, impatience and brusqueness, it is certainly the Parisians who have earned it. But they are industrious, competitive, quick to seize on new ideas and techniques, and more international in their outlook than provincials.

As its role changes, Paris continues to grow. The population of Greater Paris has almost doubled since 1945, and is now around 9m, although only 2.1m of these live within the city proper. The life of the city is vigorous, and its mood confident. People in business may worry about weakness in the French economy, but they are convinced that Paris is the most go-ahead of cities as well as the most beautiful. Certainly the government-led campaign to smarten up the capital has been highly successful. It is now very clean and more elegant than ever; and its new architectural showpieces, with their wide variety of styles, often highly controversial, are more striking than in any other European city.

Arriving

Paris has two large international airports, Roissy/Charles-de-Gaulle and Orly. It is also the hub of the country's excellent rail network, offering efficient services to all major national and international destinations. In addition, most of the country's autoroutes radiate from the capital.

Roissy/Charles-de-Gaulle airport

France's premier airport has two terminals, *Aérogare 1* and *Aérogare 2* (which has two separate sections, known as terminals 2A and 2B). As a general rule, Air France flies to Aérogare 2, using terminal 2A for intercontinental flights and some European destinations (particularly Italian cities) and terminal 2B for most European destinations; Aérogare 1 is mostly used by non-French airlines. Free shuttle buses link the terminals.

The futuristic design of the airport caused much comment when new and is enjoyed by some. Others find it confusing, even irritating. Be prepared for delays in collecting baggage and for long lines at passport control and the bureaux de change. Customs clearance, however, is usually fairly fast. Allow 45min to clear the airport.

Facilities include those you would expect of a major international airport: restaurants, bars, snackbars, bureaux de change, telephones, post offices, hairdressers, photocopying, information desks, rail inquiry office. A special *2A Service* ☎ 48 62 22 90 rents out meeting rooms and will provide secretarial assistance and other business services.

Flight information inquiries ☎ 48 62 22 80; recorded information on the day's Air France flights ☎ 43 20 12 55 (arrivals) and 43 20 13 55 (departures); general inquiries ☎ 48 62 12 12; freight inquiries ☎ 48 62 20 00.

Nearby hotels Arcade ☎ 48 62 49 49 🖳 212989 and *Sofitel*

☎ 48 62 23 23 🖳 230166 are both at the airport. Close by are *Ibis*, ave de la Raperie ☎ 39 88 00 40 🖳 699083; *Holiday Inn*, 1 allée du Verger ☎ 39 88 00 22 🖳 695143; *Patio*, 54 ave des Nations ☎ 48 63 26 10 🖳 232735. All these hotels accept major credit cards.

City link Charles-de-Gaulle is 25km/16 miles north of Paris, at Roissy-en-France. There are bus and rail links with Paris and with Orly airport, but a taxi is the most convenient way to travel.

Taxi Licensed cabs are available outside each terminal and usually plentiful, so you seldom have to wait long. Journeys are metered, and there is a special tariff as far as the Boulevard Périphérique, after which normal city rates apply. Check that the driver adjusts the meter rate when entering Paris, and beware of "cowboy" drivers in unlicensed cabs who charge exorbitant rates. The journey to central Paris takes 35–50min, depending on the traffic. Congestion is very severe during rush hours, especially on Friday evenings.

Bus Air France buses leave for Porte Maillot air terminal at 12min intervals between 6am and 11pm from gate 34 on the arrivals floor in Aérogare 1, gates A5 in terminal 2A and B6 in terminal 2B. The terminal has a bureau de change, tourist information and hotel reservations desk, restaurant and shops. Porte Maillot terminal is also close to the Palais des Congrès. Inquiries ☎ 42 99 20 70. The local 350 bus service leaves every 15–20 min for the Gare du Nord (journey time about 50min), 5.30–11pm. The 351 service leaves every 30min for Place de la Nation (journey time about 40min), 6am–8.30. Departures from boutiques floor in Aérogare 1 and gates A5 and B6 in terminals 2A and 2B.

Train A free shuttle bus leaves from gate 30 on arrivals level in Aérogare 1, and gates A5 and B6 in terminals 2A and 2B between 5.30am and 11.30pm, for Roissy-Rail station, from where trains run at 15min intervals to the Gare du Nord and other stations on the B line of the express Métro. Journey time to the Gare du Nord is 30min. Only worthwhile considering if you are travelling light.

Car rental Not recommended for those whose business is only in Paris, but convenient for the suburbs and provinces. All the leading companies have offices in each Aérogare.

Orly airport

Orly has two terminals: *Orly-Sud*, used by Air France and many foreign airlines; and *Orly-Ouest*, used for internal flights by Air Inter and small private French companies.

Facilities Both terminals have bars, restaurants, snackbars, banks, telephones, photocopying facilities, hairdressers, post offices, information offices and *2A Service* (see Charles-de-Gaulle airport) ☎ 46 86 74 82; Orly-Sud also has a bureau de change open 6.30am–11.30pm.

Flight information ☎ 48 84 32 10; general inquiries ☎ 48 84 52 52; freight inquiries ☎ 48 62 20 00.

Nearby hotels Altéa ☎ 46 87 23 37 Ⓣ 204345 and *Hilton International Orly* ☎ 46 87 33 88 Ⓣ 250621 are both at the airport and accept all or most major credit cards. Not far away are the *Holiday Inn* ☎ 46 87 36 36 Ⓣ 260738 and *Videotel Paris Orly* ☎ 45 60 52 52 Ⓣ 261004.

City link Orly is 16km/10 miles south of Paris. It is simplest to take a cab into the city.

Taxi Cabs wait outside both terminal exits; the journey rarely takes more than 45 min.

Bus Air France buses depart for Les Invalides air terminal (which has similar facilities to the Porte Maillot terminal) at 12min intervals from gate J at Orly-Sud and gate E on arrivals floor at Orly-Ouest between 5.50am and 11pm; additional buses meet flights landing after 11pm. Passengers may alight at the Porte d'Orléans and at Duroc Métro station on request and on the return journey may board at the Gare Montparnasse

rail station. Inquiries ☎ 43 23 87 75.
Train/Métro Trains run from Orly-Rail station (free shuttle bus) at 15min intervals (30min after 8pm) to the Gare d'Austerlitz and other stops on line C of the RER. Journey time to the Gare d'Austerlitz 35min.
Car rental Major firms have offices at Orly.

Railway stations

Paris has six main rail termini, all of them on the Métro (subway). All offer a wide range of services: bars and restaurants, refreshment stands selling tray meals and snacks, newsstands and information points (not always manned). Porters are rarely available but trolleys can usually be found at the automatic counters. (You need a Fr10 coin for the refundable deposit.) All stations have taxi ranks (there is usually a supplementary pick-up charge) and many operate a taxi reservations service. Baggage may be sent from all stations, on production of a ticket, to any destination in France or the rest of Europe.

Passenger inquiries ☎ 42 61 50 50; reservations ☎ 45 65 60 60; other inquiries ☎ 45 82 50 50.
Gare d'Austerlitz For arrivals from the southwest; from Bordeaux and Toulouse and from Spain via Orléans, Tours, Poitiers and Angoulême.
Gare de l'Est For arrivals from the east; from Nancy and Strasbourg and from Germany.
Gare de Lyon For arrivals from the southeast including the TGV (high-speed train) service, and from Switzerland and Italy.
Gare Montparnasse For arrivals from western France, especially Brittany.
Gare du Nord For arrivals from the north, including the Channel ports, where trains connect with ferries and hovercrafts from Britain; also services from Belgium, Holland and the Scandinavian countries.
Gare Saint-Lazare For arrivals from Normandy and boat trains from Dieppe.

Getting around

Paris is small by international capital standards and you may well be able to walk to many destinations. The public transport system (called RATP) is also excellent, with the various methods of transport fully integrated. The same RATP tickets are used on buses, the subway and the RER and are best bought in blocks of ten (*carnets*) at stations or tobacconists'. Driving is not recommended. The streets are like race tracks when not congested; Parisian drivers are not patient; and parking is very difficult.

A booklet called *Plan de Paris par arrondissement* is widely available and has good maps of each district or *arrondissement*, with subway stations clearly marked, and separate bus maps of each bus route. Fatter editions also include maps of inner suburbs. RATP information ☎ 43 46 14 14.

Taxis These are often hard to find in Paris, especially during rush hours and in wet weather, and drivers are not always willing to pick up passengers in the street. There are plenty of taxi ranks, recognized by a blue and white TAXI sign. Journeys starting from ranks at stations and airports are generally subject to a surcharge. Fares are metered and different rates apply in three separate zones (inner city, inner suburbs and outer suburbs). They are higher in the evenings and on Sundays and public holidays. Extra charges are made for baggage. Few drivers will take more than three passengers at a time. It is standard practice to add a 10–15% tip. Beware of unlicensed taxis: they are often uninsured and charge steep fares. Telephone numbers of taxi ranks can be found in the Yellow Pages but are not always answered.

Walking Central Paris is fairly safe for walking at most times, but beware of muggers and pickpockets in the main tourist areas (especially around the Champs-Elysées, the Opéra, Montmartre, Place Saint-Michel, Les Halles and the Beaubourg). The Bois de Boulogne should be avoided after dark.

Buses move faster in Paris than in many capital cities, thanks to a good network of bus lanes, though the evening rush hour (roughly 6.30–7.30) causes delays. They are a pleasant way of getting about central Paris and are relatively easy to use. Clear route maps are posted up at bus stops and inside buses. Most services operate at frequent intervals, but not at all after about 8.30pm or on Sundays and public holidays. You pay as you enter; short journeys require one RATP ticket, longer ones two or more. Route maps indicate the number of tickets needed.

Subway The Paris Métropolitain or Métro offers an efficient service between approximately 5.15am and 1.15am every day. Trains run at 90-second intervals during the daytime on most lines and only slightly less frequently at night (till about 1.15am). As the system is shallow, platforms are quickly reached, so it is often worth taking the Métro even for very short journeys. It is generally clean (no smoking is now the rule in all carriages) and safe, with police patrols deterring would-be muggers. Métro lines are known by the names of the stations at either end of the route; thus the central east–west line is called Vincennes–Neuilly.

There is only one fare in each class (each train has a first-class carriage), and a variety of bargain tickets is on offer, such as the one-day ticket valid on all forms of public transport.

Express Métro The three lines (called A, B and C) of the Réseau Express Régional (RER) are slotted into the ordinary Métro system and offer a very fast method of getting across Paris or out to the suburbs and nearby towns such as Versailles. Within the city limits use ordinary RATP tickets; for longer journeys use ticket machines inside RER stations.

Driving It is rarely sensible to drive in a capital city. Paris is no exception, but all the main car rental firms have offices.

Area by area

There is a sharp physical and political division in Paris, more than in most important capital cities, between the city and its suburbs. The former, the Ville de Paris, with its own local government and a population of 2.1m, is circumscribed by two concentric ring roads, the Boulevard Extérieur and a multilane highway, the Boulevard Périphérique, which can be very congested during rush hours. Outside lie the suburbs, each also with its own mayor and council, adding up to a conurbation of around 9m.

Most places of interest and centres of business are within the Ville de Paris, oval in shape and divided roughly in two by the curving Seine. Traditionally the southern part, known as the Left Bank (*Rive Gauche*) has been a byword for the city's intellectual life, while the Right Bank (*Rive Droite*) has been more opulent and commercial. But modern development has blurred these distinctions, and the major public buildings such as ministries, museums and palaces have always been dispersed fairly evenly on either side of the river. The business life of the city, too, is today somewhat scattered, without the clearly defined sectors to be found in London or New York. Some big banks and finance houses are close to the Bourse (stock exchange) in the old heart of the city; but many modern offices are in the smart Champs-Elysées area, or out at La Défense, the new high-rise complex in the western suburbs, or spread about elsewhere. There is no single powerful financial focus in the manner of Wall Street or the City of London.

The older parts of central Paris, on both banks, consist of a dense network of narrow streets dissected by the broad boulevards dating from the redevelopment of the city in the 1860s. And today there is still a sharp contrast between these stately tree-lined avenues and the congested older quarters. It is the broad area astride

the Seine, from the Eiffel Tower to Notre-Dame, that gives the most sweeping sense of space and grandiose urban planning; here mighty buildings stand back majestically from the river's banks – the Eiffel Tower, Trocadéro, Grand Palais, Invalides, Palais Bourbon, Louvre, Palais de Justice and others.

The Ville de Paris is divided into 20 *arrondissements*: these are postal districts numbering 75001 to 75020 (the last two digits indicate the *arrondissement*), but also administrative units each with its own *mairie*, and they spiral out from the centre to the edge. Each has its own personality, and Parisians will often say that they live in, say, the *seizième* (16e) or work in the *cinqième* (5e). Some older quarters of the city also have names, Montparnasse for example, and these mostly straddle the *arrondissements*.

The Champs-Elysées and the 16e

The smartest parts of the Right Bank are the 8e and 16e arr, along its western stretch. The 8e is partly residential but mainly an upmarket business area, home of the fashion and advertising industries and of many leading banks and hotels – even though its main thoroughfare, the Champs-Elysées, has itself moved downmarket and is today lined with fast-food eating places and split-screen cinemas as well as tourist cafés, travel agencies and car showrooms. Farther east, around the Madeleine church and the wide Place de la Concorde, is a highly fashionable area of boutiques, grand hotels and equally grand public buildings: here along the chic Rue du Faubourg Saint-Honoré lie the British and American Embassies and the presidential Palais de l'Elysée, while (just inside the 1er arr) the Ritz hotel faces the graceful 17thC Place Vendôme, and the elegantly arcaded Rue de Rivoli skirts the Tuileries gardens. Over to the west, the large 16e arr has long been the city's principal high-class residential quarter. Its late-19thC and early-

20thC apartment blocks are the homes of leading establishment figures; some, if they can afford it, join the oil sheikhs in the stately Avenue Foch, dubbed "millionaires' row." The 17e is also residential in a more modest way; at Porte Maillot is the city's main convention centre, the imposing new Palais des Congrès. The adjacent Bois de Boulogne, much the largest of Paris parks, is part of the 16e.

The Right Bank The 1er, 2e, 3e and 4e arr include the old heart of the city. Today this is a dense area of narrow commercial streets, much of it run-down and given over to small-scale commerce; but some parts are being redeveloped, and the area does contain several major buildings. Beside the river stands the vast Palais du Louvre which houses the Ministry of Finance as well as France's leading museum; close by are the Palais Royal and the Comédie Française theatre. Les Halles, to the east, was the site of the city's congested central food market until this was transferred to the suburbs in 1969; today Les Halles has been remodelled as a traffic-free shopping and leisure zone (it has a small park, a library, theatres and a sports centre) and it is full of lively activity. A short walk to the east, across Boulevard de Sébastopol, leads to the huge modernistic Pompidou arts centre, focus of a pedestrian zone (Beaubourg) that is usually full of street entertainers and is now becoming increasingly commercialized. Nearby, facing the river, is the Hôtel de Ville, and beyond it Le Marais, a famous historic quarter of elegant 16th–18thC mansions, now beautifully restored. Some are museums, such as the Carnavalet, but many are fashionable private houses: some well-known people live here, especially in and around the lovely Place des Vosges. The Rue des Rosiers area is a traditional Jewish quarter, with synagogues and kosher food shops. To the south lie the two famous islands in the Seine that were the kernel of Vieux Paris: the Ile de la Cité contains Notre-Dame, the Palais de Justice and the Préfecture de Police, while the quiet and charming little Ile Saint-Louis has long been a fashionable place to live.

Northwest of Les Halles, the Bourse and the Banque de France are a focus for banking and insurance activity. Farther west stands the majestic Opéra, close to the two large department stores, the Galeries Lafayette and Au Printemps. Eastward from here sweeps a rather tawdry main avenue, known in the plural as Les Grands Boulevards because it keeps changing its name before it finally reaches the big Place de la République, gateway to the eastern working-class Paris. One of the streets it crosses is Rue Saint-Denis, whose northern part, in the 2e, is the main red light district.

The Left Bank The central area towards the river comprises the 5e, 6e and 7e arr and it becomes steadily more bourgeois as it goes westward. The 5e, crowned by the Panthéon mausoleum, is the essence of the Latin Quarter, and the Sorbonne and other university buildings are here. This is a picturesque area of cheap student bistros, art movie houses and small apartments where many teachers and writers live. To the west, across Boulevard Saint-Michel ("Boul Mich"), the 6e is also a major centre of intellectual activity, but more prosperous: many bourgeois families live in the old streets around the Jardin du Luxembourg, while Saint-Germain-des-Prés with its bookshops, art galleries, trendy cafés and outdoor markets is well trodden by tourists seeking the "real" Paris. Many leading publishing houses are located here. Montparnasse, to the south, dominated by its much-criticized 200-metre/650-ft skyscraper, is today a lively entertainment area but has largely lost its artistic cachet of prewar years. The Faubourg Saint-Germain, forming the eastern part of the 7e, is the area where aristocrats lived in the pre-1914 period described by Marcel Proust. Today it is given over mainly to ministries and other public buildings including the Assemblée Nationale (Palais Bourbon). This is France's main governmental district. West of Les Invalides, the quiet streets around the Eiffel Tower and Ecole Militaire are where many of the well-off live. To the east, the refurbished Gare d'Orsay, now a museum, is by the river opposite the Tuileries.

The outer arrondissements

These are mostly of lesser interest. The 13e, 14e and 15e arr, sizable districts to the south, used to be largely working-class; but now, under pressure of rising land prices, they have become more middle-class as workers move out to suburban dormitories. Along the fringe of the 14e is the Cité Universitaire, a cluster of student hostels, and on the edge of the 15e, at the Porte de Versailles, is the main Paris exhibition centre. On the north side of central Paris, the mainly working-class 18e contains the picturesque hilltop "village" of Montmartre, as besieged by tourists as ever, and, lower down, the seedy *boîtes* and bars of the Place Pigalle area. The 9e is largely commercial and petit bourgeois, like the 10e, where the Gares du Nord and de L'Est are. The 11e, running down to the Place de la Bastille, is a zone of old workshops and workers' flats; the 12e is much the same, except for the imposing new business quarter which is springing up along the Quai de Bercy (the Ministry of Finance is due eventually to move there from the Louvre). The pleasant Bois de Vincennes is attached to the 12e. Lastly, the 19e and 20e have kept their old working-class character – except where there is a preponderance of immigrants.

The suburbs

The better residential suburbs lie out to the west where the prevailing winds bring a less polluted air. Much the smartest is Neuilly, home of many senior business people. Others, such as Saint-Cloud, Garches and Ville-d'Avray, lie farther out, stretching to Versailles and beyond, filling up the old fields and woodlands with smart new villas owned by young professionals.

Just west of Neuilly is La Défense with its 25 imposing skyscrapers, a new and highly impressive business complex that was built to provide an overspill for the crowded Champs-Elysées area: many big firms such as Esso, IBM and Saint-Gobain have their head offices at La Défense, where 40,000 people work. To the north, east and south of Paris, the inner suburbs are mainly working-class: these areas have often been dubbed the "Paris Red Belt," though not so many of them today remain Communist strongholds. Farther out, the suburbs have extended greatly since the war, as the conurbation has almost doubled in size. "New towns" were built somewhat at random in the 1960s, the best known being Sarcelles to the north, with a population of 40,000 which now includes a high proportion of immigrants. In more recent years five large "new towns" with pleasant architecture have been developed within 32km/20 miles of the city centre – Cergy-Pontoise to the northwest, Marne-la-Vallée to the east, Melun-Sénart and Evry to the southeast, Saint-Quentin-en-Yvelines to the southwest – and they have been attracting new light industry. Of older heavy industry, very little remains within the Ville de Paris, but there is plenty in the suburbs, led by the motor industries at Billancourt (Renault), Aulnay-les-Bois (Citroën) and Poissy (Talbot). Finally, the biggest new project in the Paris region today is the building of a Disneyland, the first in Europe, east of the city at Marne-la-Vallée: due to open in 1992, it will create some 30,000 permanent new jobs in the area.

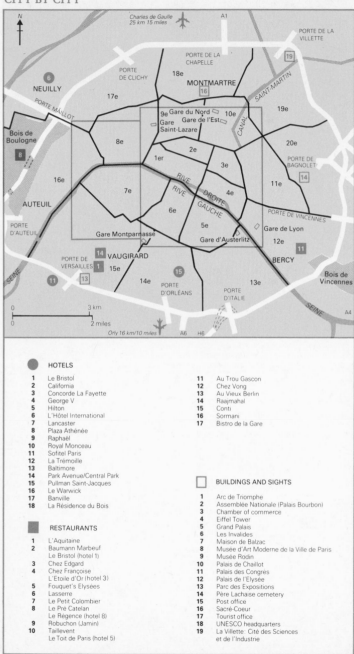

HOTELS

1   Le Bristol
2   California
3   Concorde La Fayette
4   George V
5   Hilton
6   L'Hôtel International
7   Lancaster
8   Plaza Athénée
9   Raphaël
10 Royal Monceau
11 Sofitel Paris
12 La Trémoille
13 Baltimore
14 Park Avenue/Central Park
15 Pullman Saint-Jacques
16 Le Warwick
17 Banville
18 La Résidence du Bois

11 Au Trou Gascon
12 Chez Vong
13 Au Vieux Berlin
14 Raajmahal
15 Conti
16 Sormani
17 Bistro de la Gare

RESTAURANTS

1   L'Aquitaine
2   Baumann Marbeuf
    Le Bristol (hotel 1)
3   Chez Edgard
4   Chez Françoise
    L'Etoile d'Or (hotel 3)
5   Fouquet's Elysées
6   Lasserre
7   Le Petit Colombier
8   Le Pré Catelan
    Le Régence (hotel 8)
9   Robuchon (Jamin)
10 Taillevent
    Le Toit de Paris (hotel 5)

BUILDINGS AND SIGHTS

1   Arc de Triomphe
2   Assemblée Nationale (Palais Bourbon)
3   Chamber of commerce
4   Eiffel Tower
5   Grand Palais
6   Les Invalides
7   Maison de Balzac
8   Musée d'Art Moderne de la Ville de Paris
9   Musée Rodin
10 Palais de Chaillot
11 Palais des Congrès
12 Palais de l'Elysée
13 Parc des Expositions
14 Père Lachaise cemetery
15 Post office
16 Sacré-Coeur
17 Tourist office
18 UNESCO headquarters
19 La Villette: Cité des Sciences
    et de l'Industrie

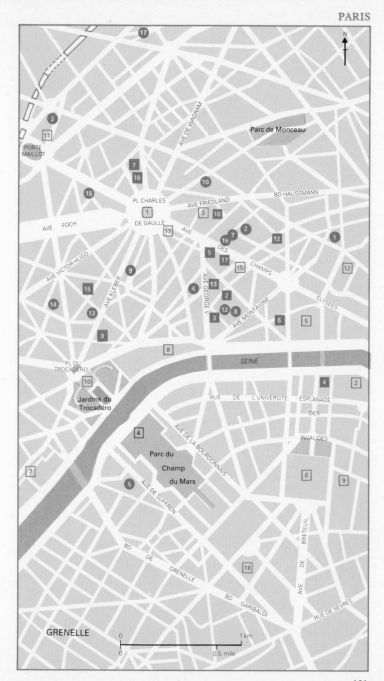

PARIS

N

Parc de Monceau

PORTE
MAILLOT

BD HAUSSMANN

PL CHARLES

AVE FOCH

DE GAULLE

AVE FRIEDLAND

AVE

DES

CHAMPS

ELYSEES

AVE VICTOR HUGO

AVE KLEBER

AVE GEORGE V

AVE MONTAIGNE

PL DU
TROCADERO

SEINE

Jardins du
Trocadéro

RUE DE L'UNIVERSITE

ESPLANADE

DES

INVALIDES

AVE DE LA BOURDONNAIS

Parc du

Champ

du Mars

AVE DE SUFFREN

AVE DE BRETEUIL

BD DE GRENELLE

BD GARIBALDI

RUE DE SEVRES

GRENELLE

0   1 km

0   0.5 mile

N

Gare du Nord

0 _____ 1 km
0 _____ 0.5 mile

Gare de l'Est

Gare Saint-Lazare ②

BD HAUSSMANN

①

⑩ ㉚
BD MONTMARTRE

⑰
⑬ PL DE
DES CAPUCINES
BD
L'OPERA
PL DE
L'OPERA

②①

BD POISSONNIERE BD BONNE NOUVELLE BD ST-DENIS BD ST-MART

BD DE STRASBOURG

PL DE LA
MADELEINE
⑦

⑪

⑧
⑫ ⑭
③
RUE DE RIVOLI
㉖ ④
⑤ ⑤

⑪

AVE DE L'OPERA

RUE REAUMUR

①

⑨
⑩

SEBASTOPOL

PL DE LA
CONCORDE

⑧ ⑱
㉔

③ ㉑
⑥

㉕

RUE DU LOUVRE

㉗ LES HALLES

②

Jardin des Tuileries

⑨

⑬

㉔
㉔

RUE DU TEMPLE

⑪

SEINE

FAUBOURG
SAINT-GERMAIN

⑫
㉕

RUE DE L'UNIVERSITE

RUE

DE

LE MARAIS

㉖ ⑩ ㉘
⑰
ST-GERMAIN

⑯ ㉒

㉓ ㉓ ㊲
㊱

㉒

④
⑱ ㉙

㉕ ④

㉓

RIVOLI

⑥
㊳ ⑮

ILE DE
LA CITE

⑦

QUARTIER LATIN

⑮

㉑

ILE
SAINT-
LOUIS

㉗

⑦

RUE DE SEVRES

⑲

⑨

㉘

㉘

㉜ ⑱

⑯
⑲

㉞

BD

RASPAIL

⑲

㉟

⑲
㉚ ㉝

⑥

⑳

Jardin du
Luxembourg

ST-MICHEL

㉒ ㉖

BD

Jardin de
Plantes

㉛
㉙

BD

DU

⑳ ㉗
MONTPARNASSE

MONTPARNASSE

Gare Montparnasse

⑦

BD DE PORT-ROYAL

⑤

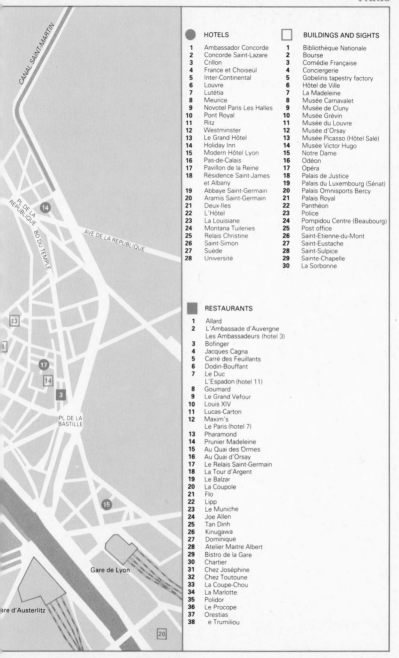

● HOTELS

1 Ambassador Concorde
2 Concorde Saint-Lazare
3 Crillon
4 France et Choiseul
5 Inter-Continental
6 Louvre
7 Lutétia
8 Meurice
9 Novotel Paris Les Halles
10 Pont Royal
11 Ritz
12 Westminster
13 Le Grand Hôtel
14 Holiday Inn
15 Modern Hôtel Lyon
16 Pas-de-Calais
17 Pavillon de la Reine
18 Résidence Saint-James et Albany
19 Abbaye Saint-Germain
20 Aramis Saint-Germain
21 Deux-Iles
22 L'Hôtel
23 La Louisiane
24 Montana Tuileries
25 Relais Christine
26 Saint-Simon
27 Suède
28 Université

□ BUILDINGS AND SIGHTS

1 Bibliothèque Nationale
2 Bourse
3 Comédie Française
4 Conciergerie
5 Gobelins tapestry factory
6 Hôtel de Ville
7 La Madeleine
8 Musée Carnavalet
9 Musée de Cluny
10 Musée Grévin
11 Musée du Louvre
12 Musée d'Orsay
13 Musée Picasso (Hôtel Salé)
14 Musée Victor Hugo
15 Notre Dame
16 Odéon
17 Opéra
18 Palais de Justice
19 Palais du Luxembourg (Sénat)
20 Palais Omnisports Bercy
21 Palais Royal
22 Panthéon
23 Police
24 Pompidou Centre (Beaubourg)
25 Post office
26 Saint-Etienne-du-Mont
27 Saint-Eustache
28 Saint-Sulpice
29 Sainte-Chapelle
30 La Sorbonne

■ RESTAURANTS

1 Allard
2 L'Ambassade d'Auvergne
Les Ambassadeurs (hotel 3)
3 Bofinger
4 Jacques Cagna
5 Carré des Feuillants
6 Dodin-Bouffant
7 Le Duc
L'Espadon (hotel 11)
8 Goumard
9 Le Grand Vefour
10 Louis XIV
11 Lucas-Carton
12 Maxim's
Le Paris (hotel 7)
13 Pharamond
14 Prunier Madeleine
15 Au Quai des Ormes
16 Au Quai d'Orsay
17 Le Relais Saint-Germain
18 La Tour d'Argent
19 Le Balzar
20 La Coupole
21 Flo
22 Lipp
23 Le Muniche
24 Joe Allen
25 Tan Dinh
26 Kinugawa
27 Dominique
28 Atelier Maitre Albert
29 Bistro de la Gare
30 Chartier
31 Chez Joséphine
32 Chez Toutoune
33 La Coupe-Chou
34 La Marlotte
35 Polidor
36 Le Procope
37 Orestias
38 e Trumiliou

Hotels

Paris has more classic luxury "palace" hotels than in other large city in the world. The top ones are the Bristol, Crillon, George V, Plaza Athénée, Ritz and Meurice, where period decor and Parisian elegance go hand in hand with courteous old-style service and modern comfort. Their relative formality may not suit all tastes, and their range of specific business services is usually limited. The few modern hotels in the same top class may lack charm, but they tend to be better equipped for business needs.

Even the new hotels will often lack many of the facilities that a global traveller may expect. Very few have swimming pools or private parking, while health and business centres are only just beginning to appear. Services that are standard in the modern hotels are television and minibars in all rooms, IDD telephones, room service, currency exchange and assistance with travel and theatre reservations.

Prices in the smart hotels are about average by world standards. Paris also has scores of medium-priced places suitable for business visitors on a limited budget. For those who dislike large hotels, and would prefer a much smaller place of character and charm, even at the expense of some amenities, Paris is well provided with very attractive smaller hotels, and a selection of these is given on pages 110 and 111. Many of these have no restaurant. These small hotels are very popular and reservations need to be made well ahead. The larger ones are less often full, except for the periods of the major trade shows and conventions in spring and autumn. If you have to make a last-minute reservation, you can find help at the tourist offices.

Most of the better hotels are very central, in the 1er or 8e arr, close to the main business areas. Some other good ones are on the Left Bank, such as the Lutétia and the Hilton, or near the Palais des Congrès. A few, such as the Holiday Inn, are in eastern central Paris or out on the periphery.

Best classic luxury palaces
Le Bristol • Crillon • George V • Lancaster • Lutétia • Meurice • Plaza Athénée • Ritz • Royal Monceau.
Best modern hotels Concorde La Fayette • Hilton • L'Hôtel International.
Best small hotels of charm
Abbaye Saint-Germain • Deux-Iles • L'Hôtel • Résidence du Bois • Saint-Simon.
Best for keeping fit Le Bristol • Royal Monceau • Sofitel.

Ambassador Concorde   *F*|||||
16 bd Haussmann, 9e ☏ *42 46 92 63*

TX *650912* • *AE DC MC V* • *305 rooms, 6 suites, 1 restaurant, 1 bar*
This "palace" built in 1927 is being sympathetically renovated by its new owners, the Concorde group. It has no great charm but is conveniently placed and efficient. Large, well modernized bedrooms, huge foyer and plenty of services. Limited parking. Hairdresser, gift shop • 8 meeting rooms (capacity up to 150).

Le Bristol   *F*|||||
112 rue du Faubourg St-Honoré, 8e
☏ *42 66 91 45* TX *280961* • *AE DC MC V* • *156 rooms, 44 suites, 2 restaurants, 1 bar*

Leading politicians and diplomats use this excellent hotel, conveniently near to the Elysée Palace. The Bristol is one of the three or four finest hotels in Paris, luxurious in a restrained and classic style, with service to match and with lovely marble bathrooms. It is also one of the few top Paris hotels to have a swimming-pool. The piano-bar carries echoes of prewar days, and the Bristol restaurant is superb (see *Restaurants*). 24hr room service, hairdresser, garage • rooftop pool, sauna • fax, 7 meeting rooms (capacity up to 180).

California *F*/////
16 rue de Berri, 8e ☎ *43 59 93 00*
Ⓣ *660634* • *Hôtels et Résidences du Roy* • *AE DC MC V* • *178 rooms, 3 suites; no restaurant*
This top-class hotel off the Champs-Elysées has a pleasant patio and spacious bedrooms with Louis XVI style furniture but modern comforts. Fax, 1 meeting room (capacity 30).

Concorde La Fayette *F*/////
3 pl du Général-Koenig, 17e
☎ *47 58 12 84* Ⓣ *650905* • *AE DC MC V* • *963 rooms, 27 suites, 2 restaurants, 1 coffee shop, 2 bars*
The city's second largest hotel at Porte Maillot makes an excellent venue for the business visitor. Not only is it in the same block as the air terminal and Palais des Congrès, sharing many facilities, but it has recently opened an executive "Top Club." Here, by paying a little more, the guest has a bedroom with various extra touches, including video programmes, as well as the use of a private lounge-clubroom with free drinks, newspapers, and polyglot hostesses providing advice and secretarial help. Service is personal and courteous; bedrooms are all well equipped, many with splendid views over western Paris. Amenities include a lively jazz bar, a panoramic top-floor bar, and good cuisine in the Etoile d'Or (see *Restaurants*). 24hr room service, parking • golf practice area, jogging track • fax, 7 meeting

rooms in hotel (capacity up to 150), others in Palais des Congrès (capacity up to 3,800).

Concorde Saint-Lazare *F*/////
108 rue St-Lazare, 8e ☎ *42 94 22 22*
Ⓣ *650442* • *AE DC MC V* • *324 rooms, 2 restaurants, 1 bar*
This huge old "palace" was built in 1889 to serve visitors arriving at the adjacent Saint-Lazare rail terminus. Today its clientèle consists mostly of Japanese and European tour groups coming by air, as well as French provincial businessmen. A recent facelift has modernized the spacious bedrooms but retained the period charm of the public rooms – notably the huge foyer with its high glass roof, marble galleries and many Art Nouveau flourishes. Its sophisticated bar opens late; the restaurant serves regional dishes. 24hr room service, hairdresser, duty-free boutique, gift shop • fax, 9 meeting rooms (capacity up to 180).

Crillon *F*/////
10 pl de la Concorde, 8e ☎ *42 65 24 24*
Ⓣ *290204* • *Concorde* • *AE DC MC V* • *149 rooms, 40 suites, 2 restaurants, 2 bars*
This is the only one of the city's classic luxury "palaces" to remain in French ownership. The 18thC decor is luxurious, with marble pillars and gilt-framed mirrors; the atmosphere discreet, as befits its very select clientele. Service is studiously attentive; the bedrooms facing Place de la Concorde are double-glazed, but those facing the formal inner courtyard are quieter. The banqueting rooms and the Ambassadeurs restaurant are excellent (see *Restaurants*), and the famous bar has been elegantly restyled. 24hr room service, shop, limited parking • fax, 6 meeting rooms (capacity up to 70).

France et Choiseul *F*////
239 rue St-Honoré, 1er ☎ *42 61 54 60*
Ⓣ *680959* • *Ladbroke* • *AE DC MC V* • *97 rooms, 23 suites, 1 brasserie/bar*

This classic hotel in a fashionable area, close to the Tuileries, has recently been renovated by its new British/plan owners. Its large open-plan bar/foyer has attractive decor in pale blue and gold, soft music plays, and there is a pretty courtyard for drinks. Snacks and light meals are served in the bar. Bedrooms are modern but not large; all have electric trouser-presses, rare in Paris. Fax, 5 meeting rooms (capacity up to 250).

George V   [F]//////
31 ave George V, 8e ☎ *47 23 54 00*
℡ *650082/290776 • THF • AE DC MC V • 288 rooms, 63 suites, 2 restaurants, 1 bar*
The George V has a quieter and more sedate atmosphere than its flamboyant stablemate around the corner, the Plaza Athénée. Its appeal is less to the showy star than to the serious tycoon, but its mainly 18thC decor is even more magnificent, and there are Flemish tapestries, sculptures and paintings, including a Renoir. Recent renovation has enhanced this splendour while adding to the modern comforts and amenities. Rooms have videos, and some have balconies facing the pleasant patio with its red parasols; the stylish restaurant, Les Princes, also looks onto this. The tearoom and bar are two of the smartest venues in town. 24hr room service, hairdresser, massage, florist, gift shop • fax, 7 meeting rooms (capacity up to 600).

Hilton   [F]//////
18 ave de Suffren, 15e ☎ *42 73 92 00*
℡ *200955 • AE DC MC V • 445 rooms, 29 suites, 3 restaurants, 2 bars*
The Hilton group has allowed its luxurious French showpiece to have a truly "Parisian" style that is all its own. The swift and polished service is up to the highest American standards, but there is little else about it that seems American; of the guests, about 25% are from the USA and over 50% European. The atmosphere is lively, informal and

cosmopolitan, and the bedrooms are both attractive and well planned, many facing the nearby Eiffel Tower. La Terrasse is an animated brasserie and coffee-shop; Le Western, the sole concession to American taste, serves Texan-style food; the elegant Toit de Paris (see *Restaurants*) offers panoramic views. The range of business and other amenities is excellent. 24hr room service, Air France reservation desk, hairdresser, shops, garage • fax, 3 meeting rooms (capacity up to 1,300).

Inter-Continental   [F]//////
3 rue Castiglione, 1er ☎ *42 60 37 80*
℡ *220114 • AE DC MC V • 380 rooms, 75 suites, 1 restaurant, 2 bars*
This palatial *belle époque* masterpiece celebrated its centenary in 1978 and has recently been renovated. Bedrooms now have every modern comfort (some top-floor ones have fine views over the Tuileries, some suites have jacuzzis), and the ornate salons have been refurbished. The patio, with its flowers and fountain, is a fashionable place for a business meal, although service is still rather variable for a hotel in this price range. Fax, 8 meeting rooms (capacity up to 1,000).

L'Hôtel International   [F]////
58 bd Victor-Hugo, 92200 Neuilly
☎ *47 58 11 00* ℡ *610971 • Tollman-Hundley • AE DC MC V • 323 rooms, 3 suites, 2 restaurants, 1 bar*
Built by the Club Méditerranée and now American-owned, this bright and breezy ultra-modern hotel is convenient for La Défense or the Palais des Congrès. It offers members a wide range of facilities at its new "Business Club," with newspapers, free drinks, photocopying, Minitel and hostesses. A garden and piano-bar are added attractions, while Le Club has bequeathed its famous formula of lavish buffet meals with unlimited wine. 24hr information desk, gift shop, garage • fax, 5 meeting rooms (capacity up to 125).

Lancaster [F]/////
7 rue de Berri, 8e ☎ *43 59 90 43*
☎ *640991* • *Savoy* • *AE DC MC V*
• *57 rooms, 10 suites, 1 restaurant,*
1 bar
The small but luxurious Lancaster
wears something of an upper-class
English air, owing to its discreet and
personal service. But the period decor
and furnishings are Parisian, and
many of the guests are publicity-shy
American stage and screen stars who
relish the quiet and privacy. Business
people too enjoy the private
atmosphere of the bar, and the
statue-filled patio where meals are
served in summer. 24hr room service
• 4 meeting rooms (capacity
up to 25).

Louvre [F]/////
Pl André Malraux, 1er ☎ *42 61 56 01*
☎ *220412* • *Concorde* • *AE DC MC V*
• *215 rooms, 4 suites, 1 restaurant,*
1 bar
Located just a few steps from the
Palais Royal and the Louvre, this is a
classic hotel with very well equipped
bedrooms (all have Minitels). It has a
highly cosmopolitan, mainly business
clientele, but it was not always so:
Camille Pissarro painted his famous
Avenue de l'Opéra from a second-
floor room when he stayed here in
1898. Today this can be rented as a
suite. 24hr room service, gift shop,
garage • fax, 2 meeting rooms
(capacity up to 200).

Lutétia [F]/////
45 bd Raspail, 6e ☎ *45 44 38 10*
☎ *270424* • *Concorde* • *AE DC MC V*
• *282 rooms, 18 suites, 1 restaurant,*
1 bar
The largest of the Left Bank's
traditional hotels was built in 1910
and has long been a fashionable place.
It is much admired for the Art Deco
elegance of its public rooms and
bedrooms, which have all been
recently refurbished in gentle pastel
colours; and today the large
conservatory-style bar, the brasserie
and the main restaurant, Le Paris
(see *Restaurants*) are all much

frequented by business people. The
salons are well equipped with video
and other amenities. 24hr room
service • 12 meeting rooms (capacity
up to 1,000).

Meurice [F]/////
228 rue de Rivoli, 1er ☎ *42 60 38 60*
☎ *230673* • *Inter-Continental* • *AE*
DC MC V • *151 rooms, 36 suites,*
1 restaurant, 1 bar
Queen Victoria and other monarchs
have stayed at the Meurice, oldest of
the city's luxury "palaces," built in
1816. The present British owners
have brought in renovation (such as
pink marble bathrooms) without
spoiling the majestic decor of
tapestries, great chandeliers and
gilded panelling. The atmosphere
might be a little too prim and sedate
for some tastes, but the old-style
service is impeccable and there is
high-quality decor and equipment in
all bedrooms, some of which overlook
the Tuileries. The main restaurant is
elegant but has no view. 24hr room
service • fax, 6 meeting rooms
(capacity up to 250).

Novotel Paris Les Halles [F]//
8 pl Marguerite-de-Navarre, 1er
☎ *42 21 31 31* ☎ *216389* • *AE DC MC*
V • *271 rooms, 14 suites, 1 restaurant,*
1 bar
Pleasantly situated beside the brand-
new park of Les Halles, this equally
new chain hotel has functional but
comfortable rooms and a spacious
open-plan layout with cheerful
decor. A good range of facilities
include satellite TV. Gift shop,
newsstand • 5 meeting rooms
(capacity up to 150).

Plaza Athénée [F]/////
25 ave Montaigne, 8e ☎ *47 23 78 33*
☎ *650092* • *THF* • *AE DC MC V* • *220*
rooms, 44 suites, 2 restaurants, 1 bar,
1 tearoom
At the ultra-glamorous Plaza movie
stars mingle with wealthy tourists of
the more flamboyant kind, many of
them South American. It's a place
where people go to be seen, in the

stylish gallery/tearoom beloved of Dietrich, the somewhat vulgar bar, the Régence restaurant (see *Restaurants*) and the Relais grillroom, a fashionable place for after-theatre suppers. Despite the razmatazz the business guest is not forgotten but the accent is more on luxury. 24hr room service, beauty parlour, massage, hairdresser • Fax, 4 meeting rooms (capacity up to 180).

Pont Royal   *F*////
7 rue de Montalembert, 7e
☎ *45 44 38 27* ☎ *270113* • *AE DC MC V* • *73 rooms, 5 suites, 1 restaurant, 1 bar*
Next to Gallimard the publishers, the Pont Royal has a literary pedigree, with William Faulkner and Ernest Hemingway among former guests, but it also offers solid comfort at less than top prices. The decor lacks charm, and rooms are small, but service is most efficient, and the meeting room by the small garden is especially attractive. The restaurant, Les Antiquaires, and the rather gloomy but well heated basement bar are still popular with literati • 5 meeting rooms (capacity up to 50).

Raphaël   *F*/////
17 ave Kléber, 16e ☎ *45 02 16 00*
☎ *610356* • *AE DC MC V* • *52 rooms, 36 suites, 1 restaurant, 1 bar*
Conveniently close to L'Etoile, the Raphaël is for those who want a marble-floored period-style, discreet luxury hotel; its clientele regularly includes senior business people as well as international film stars. In the bar and foyer, the dark panelling, Oriental tapestries and large oil paintings create an ambience that some may find snug, others a little heavy. The restaurant, too, is a bit dull. But there is a terrace overlooking all Paris, the bedrooms are elegant and well equipped, and service is efficient. 24hr room service • 2 meeting rooms (capacity up to 50).

Ritz   *F*/////
15 pl Vendôme, 1er ☎ *42 60 38 30*
☎ *220262/211189* • *AE DC MC V* • *164 rooms, 45 suites, 1 restaurant, 3 bars*
The most expensive hotel in Paris and arguably the most famous in the world, the Ritz numbers Proust, Churchill, Chaplin and Garbo among former guests. Today it is owned by the Al-Fayed family, who also own Harrods in London, and many of its visitors are Arab royalty. Indeed, the hotel has something of the hushed air of a royal palace, with long silent corridors and exquisite art treasures. But the facilities are modern and the service superb and unobtrusive. The famous bars, the lovely inner garden and the restaurant, L'Espadon (see *Restaurants*), are all ideal for discreet top-level talks. Hairdresser, florist, shops • health centre with sauna and massage • fax, 3 meeting rooms (capacity up to 120).

Royal Monceau   *F*/////
37 ave Hoche, 8e ☎ *45 61 98 00*
☎ *650361* • *CIGA* • *AE DC MC V* • *180 rooms, 40 suites, 3 restaurants, 2 bars*
This delightful Italian-owned luxury hotel caters well to the discerning senior business executive. In a quiet location near the Parc Monceau, it has well-equipped, elegant bedrooms and public rooms, a "business club" and good restaurants: Il Carpaccio, high-class Italian; Le Jardin, where sumptuous buffet-breakfasts are served in a pleasant garden setting; and a diet restaurant. Service could perhaps be more friendly. Limited parking. 24hr room service, hairdresser, beauty salon • health club with saunas, jacuzzi, massage, small pool • fax, 8 meeting rooms (capacity up to 300).

Sofitel Paris   *F*////
8–12 rue Louis-Armand, 15e
☎ *40 60 30 30* ☎ *200432* • *AE DC MC V* • *618 rooms, 17 suites, 2 restaurants, 2 bars*
This huge modern chain hotel is handy for the Héliport and the Porte

de Versailles exhibition centre, to which transport is provided. Rooms are smallish and the atmosphere not exactly personal, but the service is deft and facilities include a well-equipped business centre and 15 suites that are designed for daytime use as offices. Jazz club, piano-bar. 24hr room service, gift shops, garage • rooftop pool, jacuzzi, gym • fax, 42 meeting rooms (capacity up to 1,000).

La Trémoille _F/////_
14 rue de la Trémoille, 8e
☎ 47 23 34 20 ℡ 640344 • THF
• AE DC MC V • 97 rooms, 14 suites,
1 restaurant, 1 bar
Just off the Champs-Elysées, a British-owned hotel of dignified Parisian elegance, popular with businessmen seeking high standards of comfort and service in unpretentious surroundings. The new penthouse suites are superb, and many other rooms have pleasant balconies and luxurious bathrooms. The bar and restaurant are small but chic. Fax.

Westminster _F/////_
13 rue de la Paix, 2e ☎ 42 61 57 46
℡ 680035 • Warwick • AE DC MC V
• 84 rooms, 18 suites, 1 restaurant,
1 bar
Recent renovation has transformed this hitherto rather dull hotel near the Opéra into yet another stylish Parisian "palace." Some bedrooms are in period style, some more modern; many have marble bathrooms and videos. Friendly service; intimate piano-bar and restaurant. Limited parking. Jeweller's • 4 meeting rooms (capacity up to 50).

OTHER HOTELS
Baltimore _F/////_ _88 bis ave_
Kléber, 16e ☎ 45 53 83 33 ℡ 611591
• Cidotel • AE DC MC V. Comfortable, well renovated hotel of medium size, with an excellent restaurant, L'Estournel.
Le Grand Hôtel _F/////_ _2 rue_
Scribe, 9e ☎ 42 68 12 13 ℡ 220875

• _Inter-Continental_ • _AE DC MC V_. A large and fairly luxurious hotel by the Opéra, with lavish Second Empire decor. Gym, sauna.
Holiday Inn _F////_ _10 pl de la_
République, 11e ☎ 43 55 44 34
_℡ 210651 • AE DC MC V_. In eastern Paris, an old hotel, recently renovated, with pleasant patio and brasserie. Limited pay parking.
Modern Hôtel Lyon _F//_ _3 rue_
Parrot, 12e ☎ 43 43 41 52 ℡ 230369
• _AE MC V_. A useful small hotel near the Gare de Lyon, well modernized. No restaurant.
Park Avenue _F///_; **Central Park** _F///_ _55 ave Raymond-_
Poincaré, 16e ☎ 45 53 44 60
℡ 643862 • Cidotel • AE DC MC V. Two brand-new functional hotels with some shared amenities, built around the same inner courtyard. Garage.
Pas-de-Calais _F//_ _59 rue de_
Saints-Pères, 6e ☎ 45 48 78 74
_℡ 270476 • MC V_. A quiet, comfortable little Left Bank address. Some rooms overlook a pretty courtyard. No restaurant.
Pavillon de la Reine _F///_ _28 pl_
des Vosges, 3e ☎ 42 77 96 40
_℡ 216160 • AE DC MC V_. An old building on one of Paris' loveliest squares, recently converted into a smart little hotel. Garage. No restaurant or bar.
Pullman Saint-Jacques _F///_
17 bd St-Jacques, 14e ☎ 45 89 89 80
_℡ 270740 • AE DC MC V_. Gigantic and functional, with many facilities and small but comfortable bedrooms. Convenient for Orly airport. Garage.
Résidence Saint-James et Albany _F/////_ _202 rue de Rivoli,_
_1er ☎ 42 60 31 60 ℡ 213031 • AE DC MC V_. A classic hotel, now attractively modernized, with very quiet rooms, many of them studios with kitchenettes. Garage.
Le Warwick _F/////_ _5 rue de_
Berri, 8e ☎ 45 63 14 11 ℡ 642295
• _AE DC MC V_. Very modern, just off the Champs-Elysées but quiet. Bedrooms are large, and some suites have roof-terraces.

Small hotels of quality and character

Paris has a remarkable range of charming small hotels, some cheap, others less so. Quiet and intimate, comfortable and stylish, they offer personal service but often lack amenities such as 24hr room service, air conditioning or telex. Of those listed below, only L'Hôtel has a restaurant and several do not accept credit cards.

Abbaye Saint-Germain   [F]///
10 rue Cassette, 6e ☎ *45 44 38 11*
• 45 rooms, 1 bar
A former 17thC monastery in a small street near Saint-Germain-des-Prés is now an elegant little hotel. Bedrooms are fairly small but well furnished, with modern marble bathrooms. Business contacts could be entertained in the bar or the flagged courtyard. Service is friendly and efficient. Reservations should be made well in advance.

Aramis Saint-Germain   [F]//
124 rue de Rennes, 6e ☎ *45 48 03 75*
Ⓣ *205098 • Best Western • AE DC MC V • 42 rooms, 1 bar*
This very modern and efficient little place was recently opened by a graduate of the renowned Lausanne Hotel School. Its location, on a busy shopping street in Montparnasse, is noisy, but rooms have double glazing and air conditioning. Bedrooms are on the small side, but bathrooms are well equipped, some with jacuzzis. The neat breakfast room and cocktail bar is suitable for business talks • 2 meeting rooms (capacity up to 40).

Banville   [F]//
166 bd Berthier, 17e ☎ *42 67 70 16*
Ⓣ *643025 • AE MC V • 40 rooms; no bar*
Claiming to be the cheapest three-star hotel in Paris, the Banville has few special amenities but is run in a pleasant and personal way by very friendly people. Its large foyer is elegant, its bedrooms comfortable and prettily decorated, with modern marble bathrooms. The residential 17e lacks charm, but is convenient for the air terminal and Palais des Congrès. 24hr room service.

Deux-Iles   [F]//
59 rue St-Louis-en-l'Ile, 4e
☎ *43 26 13 35* Ⓣ *375974 • 17 rooms, 1 bar*
This elegantly converted 17thC house in the narrow main street of the city's smaller and quieter island retains much of the charm of Vieux Paris. The atmosphere is warm and friendly, and the intimate cellar bar with its log fire and deep sofas is just the place for a quiet chat, as is the little patio. Bedrooms are small, but are furnished with pretty Provençal fabrics and have elegant tiled bathrooms.

L'Hôtel   [F]/////
13 rue des Beaux-Arts, 6e
☎ *43 25 27 22* Ⓣ *270870*
• AE DC MC V • 25 rooms, 2 suites, 1 restaurant, 1 bar
When Oscar Wilde died here, broke, in 1900, this 18thC town house was a disreputable little place; now it is the most stylish and fashionable (and expensive) of the city's smaller hotels. Celebrity guests enjoy its intimacy and privacy and relish the plushy boudoir-like decor, with velvet and antiques in all rooms, pink Venetian marble in the bathrooms, and odd touches like the metal sculpture of a sheep in the very smart bar. Most rooms are quite small, except for the splendid penthouse suites with their balconies and rooftop views. You can apply for the room (and bed!) where Wilde died, or Mistinguett's room with her own Art Nouveau furniture. Reservations need to be made well in advance. The winter garden is now a chic little restaurant. 24hr room service.

La Louisiane [F]/
60 rue de Seine, 6e ☎ *43 29 59 30*
• *AE DC MC V* • *80 rooms; no bar*
Another Left Bank hotel with literary associations, this one, unlike L'Hôtel, has remained cheap and downmarket: it is recommended only for a businessman on a tight budget or nostalgically seeking communion with the great days when the likes of Sartre, Hemingway and Cyril Connolly used to stay here. Today it still has a cosmopolitan feel but absolutely no frills: rooms are plain but well modernized, with respectable plumbing, and are protected by double glazing from the noise of the colourful Buci street market below.

Montana Tuileries [F]//
12 rue St-Roch, 1er ☎ *42 60 35 10*
☎ *214404* • *AE DC MC V* • *25 rooms, 1 bar*
With its large, well modernized rooms and air of friendly efficiency, this is a useful address for those wanting to avoid the generally high prices of the smart and central Tuileries area. 24hr room service.

Relais Christine [F]////
3 rue Christine, 6e ☎ *43 26 71 80*
☎ *202606* • *AE DC MC V* • *39 rooms, 12 suites*
A 16thC abbey in a narrow street near Saint-Germain-des-Prés has been recently converted into a small luxury hotel where breakfast is served in the former chapel in the basement. Rooms vary in size but are all furnished with antiques; best are the penthouse suites, noisiest those by the lift, quietest those facing the pretty courtyard. 24hr room service, garage • 1 meeting room (capacity up to 25).

La Résidence du Bois [F]////
16 rue Chalgrin, 16e ☎ *45 00 50 59*
• *Relais et Châteaux* • *16 rooms, 3 suites, 1 bar*
A Third Empire mansion in a quiet residential street near L'Etoile has been transformed into one of the best small hotels in Paris, infinitely restful and run by friendly and helpful people. The compact bar, cheerfully decorated with murals, and the pretty walled garden with its creepers and canopies are ideal for a quiet business chat after a day in the city. Spacious bedrooms are furnished with silks and satins in gentle colours. Service is efficient. No restaurant, but simple meals are served to residents.

Saint-Simon [F]////
14 rue St-Simon 7e ☎ *45 48 35 66*
☎ *203277* • *29 rooms, 5 suites, no bar*
The tiny cobbled forecourt with its shrubs and trelliswork gives a rural air to this delightful 17thC house in a quiet Faubourg Saint-Germain street: a select hotel owned and run by a Swedish couple who have filled it with antiques. The elegant little bar and salons in the basement have tiled floors, old beams and rough stone walls with little alcoves. Some rooms have balconies.

Suède [F]//
31 rue Vaneau, 7e ☎ *47 05 00 08*
☎ *200596* • *AE MC V* • *40 rooms, 1 suite, 1 bar*
The upper back bedrooms of this discreet and rather formal Faubourg Saint-Germain hotel overlook the leafy gardens of the Prime Minister's office and residence, the Hôtel Matignon. Service is efficient and the place is quiet and comfortable, with a large lounge and a patio where business talks can be held. Light snacks are available till 10pm.

Université [F]//
22 rue de l'Université, 7e
☎ *42 61 09 39* ☎ *260717* • *27 rooms, 1 suite; no bar*
Another 17thC town house on the Left Bank converted into an intimate and attractive hotel, stylishly decorated with antiques and tapestries. Rooms have safes and plenty of modern comforts.

Restaurants

Paris certainly has more great restaurants than any other city on earth. Today as ever the quality of the cuisine is paramount, and most of the places considered suitable for high-level business entertaining will have really distinguished food: if your guests are French, the venue should be selected with this in mind.

Many of the best gourmet restaurants are in the smart hotels, such as the Bristol or Crillon. Others are run by famous *patron*/chefs, such as Alain Senderens, who at Lucas-Carton offers elegant surroundings and first-rate service as well as fine food: in Paris at least, if not in the provinces, it is rare to find top-level cuisine in a humble setting. The cooking, whether classical or *nouvelle* or a mix of the two, is almost always French: foreign restaurants seldom make the top grade and are not much used for business purposes. Most of the best restaurants are in the smarter central districts – the 1er, 6e, 7e, 8e and 16e *arrondissements* – though a few lie scattered elsewhere.

Lunch is the main business meal, while dinners are more likely to be social. Lunch appointments are for 1pm or a little later, dinners never before 8pm: Parisians often like to dine late. It is always advisable to make a reservation ahead in a serious restaurant, but this is less essential for the larger brasseries or for dinner in a hotel. Business eating is mostly à la carte, and expensive: but most of the top restaurants also offer interesting set menus at somewhat lower prices, and it would not be thought amiss to point these out to your guests, since the chef will be putting most effort into the day's "specials."

Some useful selections

For fine food in elegant surroundings Les Ambassadeurs
• Le Bristol • Carré des Feuillants • L'Espadon
• Le Grand Vefour • Lucas-Carton
• Lasserre • Le Pré Catelan
• Robuchon • Taillevent • La Tour d'Argent.
For eating outdoors L'Aquitaine
• L'Espadon • Le Pré Catelan
• Le Régence.
Open very late All brasseries
• Baumann Marbeuf • Chez Edgard
• Fouquet's.

Allard   *F*/|||
41 rue St-André-des-Arts, 6e
☎ *43 26 48 23* • *closed Sat, Sun, Aug, Dec 23–Jan 3* • *AE DC MC V*
The most famous bistro in Paris has confounded the pessimists by retaining its traditional character in spite of the death of André Allard in

1983 and the recent retirement of Madame. All is as before: the sawdust on the floor, the zinc-topped bar, the worn furniture, the waiters in long cotton smocks, the noisy cosmopolitan clientele. The food is still variable too, but much of it is excellent, notably the duck and the *turbot beurre blanc*, and portions are generous.

L'Ambassade d'Auvergne   *F*/
22 rue du Grenier-St-Lazare, 3e
☎ *42 72 31 22* • *MC V*
At this friendly "embassy" of Auvergnat tradition, the decor is carefully rustic, with great hams hanging from the ceiling, but the seating is comfortable. The hearty peasant cuisine includes *pot-au-feu, boudin* with chestnuts and other local dishes served in generous portions, and the aromatic cheeses come from the patron's family farm.

Les Ambassadeurs [F]|||||
Hôtel Crillon, 10 pl de la Concorde, 8e
☎ *42 65 24 24* • *AE DC MC V* • *jacket and tie*
The formal 18thC elegance of the Crillon's main dining room makes an ideal setting for a really special meal with important guests. Service is smooth and discreet in the grand manner, and the unfussy cooking is excellent. The lunchtime set menu offers good value. On fine days meals are served in the hotel's attractive courtyard.

L'Aquitaine [F]|||
54 rue Dantzig, 15e ☎ *48 28 67 38*
• *closed Sun, Mon* • *AE DC V*
The friendly yet sophisticated Aquitaine is owned and run by Christiane Massia. Service is gentle and courteous, decor beguiling, with pretty table-lamps, beamed ceiling and unusual murals. The upstairs room is best, leading onto an elegant paved terrace where meals are served under parasols in fine weather. Mme Massia provides light and original variations on the cuisine of her native Landes (in Aquitaine), with the accent on fish, duck and *foie gras*. An excellent place for lunchtime work or evening pleasure, out of the way but worth the trek.

Baumann Marbeuf [F]||
15 rue Marbeuf, 8e ☎ *47 20 11 11*
• *AE DC MC V* • *smart dress*
Until well past midnight Parisians crowd this lively Alsatian citadel of good *choucroute*, which is offered in various forms, with *pot-au-feu*, duck or even fish, as well as more classically with pork. Good meat dishes, too, and a fine selection of Alsatian wines and fruit spirits. Eye-catching glass and marble décor. Fine for a working lunch.

Bofinger [F]||
5 rue de la Bastille, 4e ☎ *42 72 87 82*
• *AE DC MC V* • *smart dress*
Allegedly the city's oldest brasserie, Bofinger is famous for its exuberant high-ceilinged Art Nouveau decor

and its draught beer. The food is brasserie-style but there are some more modern dishes from the *nouvelle cuisine* repertoire. A pleasant place for a relaxed meal with colleagues, if a little out of the way. It also has various private rooms seating up to a hundred.

Le Bristol [F]|||||
Hôtel Le Bristol, 112 rue du Faubourg-St-Honoré, 8e ☎ *42 66 91 45* • *AE DC MC V* • *jacket required*
Shirts without ties in summer, and more than a dash of *nouvelle cuisine*, are about the only concessions to modernity permitted by the Bristol's two superlative restaurants, much patronized by the upper echelons of international business, politics and the rich. Here all is grace and elegance in the grandest classical tradition. In winter you dine in a noble oval hall, with oak panelling and a superb Gobelin tapestry; in summer, in a lovely light room open to the garden. Meals are generous and very good, punctuated by all the right appetizers, sorbets and petits-fours; service, by battalions of waiters, is almost too perfect and deferential. The set menus are good value.

Jacques Cagna [F]||||
14 rue des Grands-Augustins, 6e
☎ *43 26 49 39* • *closed Sat (exc twice a month)*, *Sun, Aug, last week Dec* • *AE DC MC V* • *jacket and tie preferred*
Tucked away in a narrow street in Vieux Paris, Cagna's establishment is quiet at lunchtime and is a pleasant place for a business lunch, with its 16thC beams, salmon-coloured walls and Flemish still lifes. In the evenings it is very popular and reservations are essential. Cagna's cuisine is personal and imaginative, and the menu includes at least one recipe borrowed from his mother as well as unusual seafood dishes such as *coquilles Saint-Jacques au jus de truffe*. Good value set menus. Interesting wine list.

Carré des Feuillants [F]////
14 rue Castiglione, 1er ☎ *42 86 82 82*
• *closed Sat L, Sun* • *AE MC V* • *jacket
and tie preferred*
Opened in 1986, in a 17thC house
near the Tuileries, this newcomer to
the ranks of top Paris restaurants is
owned and run by a brilliant and
ambitious young chef from Gascony,
Alain Dutournier. His business and
diplomatic clientele is glossy; so is his
fancy modern decor, in an intimate
setting of small connecting rooms.
His cuisine is inventive and delicious,
drawing on the traditions and the
produce of his native southwest. The
fixed-price business lunch is fair
value.

Chez Edgard [F]///
4 rue Marbeuf, 8e ☎ *47 20 51 15*
• *closed Sun* • *AE DC MC V*
This is one of the best-known
middle-price restaurants in Paris, a
regular rendezvous for politicians of
all parties (even Communist leaders)
as well as film and media people. It is
typically Parisian, always crowded at
lunchtime (but quieter at night),
with brisk service and good
traditional food. Very fresh shellfish;
wines at reasonable prices.

Chez Françoise [F]/
*Aérogare des Invalides, esplanade des
Invalides, 7e* ☎ *47 05 49 03* • *closed
Sun D, Mon D and Aug* • *AE DC V*
Tucked discreetly away beneath the
Invalides air terminal, Chez
Françoise is frequented, especially at
lunchtime (when reservations are
essential), by diplomats and
politicians from the nearby Quai
d'Orsay and the Chambre des
Députés. The sober decor of wood
panelling and classical white linen in
the main dining room is offset by a
trellis effect in the smaller front area,
with cane chairs and plants. The
classical cuisine, with particularly
good fish, is served by discreet and
experienced waiters. Unusually, the
"business menu" is available in the
evenings as well as at lunchtime, and
the wine list reasonably priced.

Dodin-Bouffant [F]////
*Pl Maubert-Mutualité/25 rue Frédéric-
Sauton, 5e* ☎ *43 25 25 14* • *closed
Sun, Aug, Christmas and New Year
period* • *DC MC V*
A long-standing Left Bank restaurant
with a faithful local and international
clientele. Excellent fish and shellfish
(from the restaurant's own tanks)
feature prominently on the menu and
the game is to be recommended,
when in season. Like the long wine
list, the lunchtime fixed-price menu
offers good value. Reservations are
advisable at all times and essential on
summer evenings when the pretty
pavement terrace is very popular (last
orders at 1am). A lively after-theatre
crowd frequents both upstairs and
downstairs dining rooms in winter.
The first floor has a private room for
up to 50.

Le Duc [F]/////
243 bd Raspail, 14e ☎ *43 20 96 30*
• *closed Sat, Sun, Mon* • *no credit
cards*
Appropriately for a restaurant
specializing in fish and shellfish, the
decor is all mahogany and brass,
suggesting the dining room of a
luxury yacht. The Minchelli
brothers, who long ago rejected rich
sauces and are now seen as precursors
of *nouvelle cuisine*, rely entirely on
using the freshest food and the
simplest preparation. If, because of
storms, no fresh fish is available, the
restaurant does not open. The
approach is purist; the results, like
the wines, are well worth the price.

L'Espadon [F]/////
Hôtel Ritz, 15 pl Vendôme, 1er
☎ *42 60 38 30* • *AE DC MC V* • *jacket
and tie in winter*
The Ritz's restaurant is surprisingly
small and intimate, and its period
decor and furnishings have a
charmingly feminine flavour,
evoking Madame de Pompadour
herself. In fact, you are more likely to
find Arab oil sheikhs, American
tycoons or Parisian singing stars,
whether indoors or out in the formal

garden. Service is old-fashioned and masterly, and the equally superb cooking tends towards the traditional: venison in season is much recommended.

L'Etoile d'Or [F]////
Hôtel Concorde La Fayette, 3 pl du Général-Koenig, 17e ☎ *47 58 12 84* • *closed Aug* • *AE DC MC V* • *jacket and tie*

That this gigantic and somewhat functional modern hotel should sport so elegant and ambitious a restaurant is a sign that its business customers tend to appreciate true quality. Joël Renty's cooking is inventive without being fussy, the service is stylish and the seating spacious. There is live piano music in the evenings, and a dressy dinner-dance every Friday. The set menus are good value, especially at lunchtime.

Fouquet's Elysées [F]////
99 ave des Champs-Elysées, 8e ☎ *47 23 70 60* • *closed (1st floor) Sat, Sun, Aug* • *AE DC MC V* • *jacket and tie*

Fouquet's remains an oasis of chic and grandeur among all the fast-food places and the car showrooms. Pagnol and Simenon were habitués, and Fouquet's has retained its literary cachet; many well-known faces can still be spotted. The first-floor restaurant is rather grand; the luxurious ground-floor brasserie with its elegant glass-fronted terrace is cheaper and more entertaining. Here the food is defiantly traditional and the set menu is good value.

Goumard [F]////
17 rue Duphot, 1er ☎ *42 60 36 07* • *closed Sun, 1 week Aug, Dec 21–Jan 4* • *AE DC MC V* • *smart dress*

This elegant little restaurant near the Madeleine makes an ideal business venue. The two smallish dining-rooms are discreet and comfortable, the decor of blue and yellow tiles is pretty, and the service by waiters in naval-style uniform is impeccable. Excellent fish and shellfish dishes.

Le Grand Vefour [F]/////
17 rue de Beaujolais, 1er ☎ *42 96 56 27* • *closed Sat, Sun, Aug* • *AE DC MC V* • *jacket and tie*

This famous old showpiece of Vieux Paris stands tucked away down an arcade at the north end of the Palais Royal. It belonged for many years to the great *patron*/chef Raymond Oliver, but is now in the hands of Jean Taittinger, the champagne king, who has carefully restored its majestic early 19thC decor. Here the rich and famous come to enjoy some of the best cooking in Paris, mainly classical but with many *nouvelle* additions. Distinguished Bordeaux wines and a good value set menu.

Lasserre [F]/////
17 ave Franklin-Roosevelt, 8e ☎ *43 59 53 43 or 43 69 53 43* • *closed Mon L, Sun, Aug* • *no credit cards* • *jacket and tie*

The rituals of haute cuisine in fine surroundings are fully maintained at this classic establishment, still warmly in favour with a discerning international clientele. Impeccable waiters serve the food onto gold-rimmed plates, and at night the roof opens up to reveal the stars. The cuisine has lost its top ratings in the French guides, for this rich cooking is now out of fashion: but older gourmets remain delighted with it.

Louis XIV [F]/
1 bis place des Victoires, 1er ☎ *40 26 20 81* • *closed Sat, Sun, Aug, nat hols* • *MC V*

This lively traditional bistro near the Bourse is a good place for an unpretentious lunch with business colleagues in the area: it is used a lot by executives and journalists working nearby. Friendly service, a terrace out on the square for fine days, and very reliable Lyonnais cooking.

For general information about French restaurants, see the *Planning and Reference* section.

Lucas-Carton [F]/////
*9 pl de la Madeleine, 8e ☎ 42 65 22 90
• closed Sat, Sun, Aug, Dec 23–Jan
4 • DC MC V • jacket and tie D*
Alain Senderens, most celebrated of
Parisian practitioners of *nouvelle
cuisine*, has taken over the venerable
Lucas-Carton. He has kept the
magnificent *belle époque* decor with
red velvet banquettes and Art
Nouveau woodwork, and has added
his own individual style of cooking,
enticing fashionable diners back to a
place whose glory had begun to fade.
The duck is excellent; the food,
generally, which includes a
"dégustation menu," is as good as
anywhere in Paris.

Maxim's [F]//////
*3 rue Royale, 8e ☎ 42 65 27 94 • AE
DC V • jacket and tie; Fri D evening
dress*
With its gleaming mirrors and
chandeliers, its orchestra playing
waltzes in the evenings, its famous
private rooms and its glamorous
history, Maxim's remains the epitome
of "La Vie Parisienne." Nowadays
the crowds come as much for the
history as for the food, although that
is better than some like to make out.
The rosettes and the gourmets have
mostly gone, it is true, but perhaps
both were misplaced in a restaurant
catering to hundreds at a time. For all
its visual splendour, Maxim's was
regarded in earlier days simply as the
best brasserie in the world. It must
have been easier then, but Maxim's is
still a Parisian institution.

Le Paris [F]////
*Hôtel Lutétia, 23 rue de Sèvres, 6e
☎ 45 48 74 34 • closed Sun, Mon, Aug
• AE DC MC V • jacket and tie preferred*
Like the rest of the hotel, this
intimate and luxurious little
restaurant has recently been restored
to its original 1920s' splendour. Here
under the chandeliers, senior
politicians and publishers, for
instance, come to enjoy the inventive
and subtle cooking of Jacky Fréon.
Excellent set menu at lunch.

Le Petit Colombier [F]///
*42 rue des Acacias, 17e ☎ 43 80 28 54
• closed Sat, Sun L, first two weeks
Aug • MC V*
Useful either for a business lunch or
an intimate dinner, this snug little
place with its old-fashioned
woodwork has something of the
atmosphere of a provincial *auberge*.
Service is friendly, if sometimes slow,
and Bernard Fournier's excellent
cooking brings modern touches to
such classics as *navarin d'agneau*.
Good set menu.

Pharamond [F]//
*24 rue de la Grande-Truanderie, 1er
☎ 42 33 06 72 • closed Mon L, Sun,
Jul • AE DC V*
A noble survivor of the rebuilding of
the Les Halles quarter, this fine old
timbered building serves some of the
best Norman food in town, at
moderate prices and amid a splendid
Art Nouveau decor of mirrors and
ceramic tiles. Business and other
customers come to enjoy dishes such
as tripe or scallops in cider, served
classically or with modern variations.
Try the ciders and the calvados.

Le Pré Catelan [F]//////
*Route de Suresnes, Bois de Boulogne,
16e ☎ 45 24 55 58 • Sun D, Mon,
2 weeks Feb • V*
This palatial building in the leafy
setting of the Bois de Boulogne has
various salons which are much in
demand for smart receptions. It is
run by the celebrated patissier
Gaston Lenôtre and his nephew
Patrick whose food is exquisite. In
summer you can eat in the flowery
garden or in a bright and green *belle
époque* summerhouse; for winter
there is an elegantly snug dining-
room with open fire. An ideal place
for high-level entertaining.

Prunier Madeleine [F]/////
*9 rue Duphot, 1er ☎ 42 60 36 04
• MC V*
A rather tired old seafood restaurant
was recently revived by a change of
ownership and some redecoration.

The very young chef, Eric Cassegrain, serves an interesting mixture of exciting new dishes and Prunier standards like the *marmite dieppoise*. There are private rooms, the smallest intimate and charming, the largest holding up to 60.

Au Quai des Ormes [F]|||||
72 quai de l'Hôtel-de-Ville, 4e
☎ *42 74 72 22 • closed Sat, Sun, Dec 24–25, Jan 1 • V • smart dress*
This spacious and discreetly elegant restaurant offers a fine view of the Ile Saint-Louis from the small first-floor terrace. It is much used at lunchtime by a business clientele (a private room holding 30 people is available), who appreciate the reliable *nouvelle cuisine*, with its emphasis on fish, the rather grand but not pompous service and the relaxed atmosphere. The lunchtime fixed-price menu is popular, while the chic Parisian clientele in the evenings chooses between the low-calorie menu or the more expensive gourmet menu.

Au Quai d'Orsay [F]|||
49 quai d'Orsay, 7e ☎ *45 51 58 58 • closed Sun • AE DC MC V • smart dress*
Just along the Quai from the foreign ministry, this smart restaurant purrs at lunchtime with the confidential chatter of diplomats, and at night is graced by the *beau monde*, mainly couples. They come for the traditional *cuisine bourgeoise* and for the vast plateful of wild mushrooms served as a starter.

Le Régence [F]|||||
Hôtel Plaza Athénée, 25 ave Montaigne, 8e ☎ *47 23 78 33 • AE DC MC V • jacket and tie*
For those who want a glamorous setting for their business entertaining, with maybe a film star or two at the next table, then the tasteful opulence of "le Plaza" could be just right. The period furnishings are matched by extreme comfort and splendid service; at dinner there is candlelight and a pianist; and on fine days you can eat under red parasols in the flowery courtyard. The cuisine is mainly classical.

Le Relais Saint-Germain [F]
190 bd St-Germain, 7e ☎ *45 48 11 73 • V*
For a reasonably priced working lunch on the Left Bank, Le Relais is very good value and it is highly popular with middle-rank civil servants and publishers, for example. There is no carte, just a set menu of well-cooked classic dishes with plenty of choice. The air-conditioned basement is calmer than the crowded ground-floor room.

Robuchon (Jamin) [F]|||||
32 rue de Longchamp, 16e
☎ *47 27 12 27 • closed Sat, Sun • AE DC V • jacket and tie preferred*
Behind an unassuming façade, down a side-street near the Trocadéro, lies arguably the best restaurant in Paris today, thanks to the remarkable gifts of its *patron/chef* Joël Robuchon. It used to be called Jamin, but he has now changed its name to his own – but not out of vanity, for this rigorous perfectionist is a shy man who stays in his kitchen rather than parading among his guests after dinner. Reservations need to be made weeks in advance to secure a table in one of his two small and very comfortable dining rooms, where some might find the theatrically romantic decor a little fussy. But few would apply this word to a modern cuisine of great subtlety and invention.

Taillevent [F]|||||
15 rue Lamennais, 8e ☎ *45 61 12 94 • closed Sat, Sun, Aug, 1 week Feb, nat hols • no credit cards • jacket and tie*
Just east of L'Etoile, Robuchon's friend Jean-Claude Vrinat also runs a luxurious establishment in the top gourmet bracket, reckoned by the senior politicians and industrialists who use it to be one of the city's four or five best. Tables need to be reserved weeks ahead, but once there

you will not be patronized or intimidated. The decor is discreet and classical, the seating spacious and the atmosphere serious, as diners concentrate on business and their meal. The cuisine is constantly evolving and includes, for instance, hot oysters with leeks and truffles.

Le Toit de Paris $\boxed{F}$////
Hôtel Hilton, 18 ave de Suffren, 15e ☎ 42 73 92 00 • D only, closed Sun, Aug • AE DC MC V • jacket and tie
Hilton International has here created a glamorous restaurant that is Parisian in its cuisine and its clientele, only a third of whom are hotel guests. No lunches are served, except for business functions, and a champagne brunch on Sundays. For an elegant and leisurely evening "Le Toit" is a good choice, especially if anyone in the party feels like a fairly sedate old-fashioned dance to the music of the Ricotta trio (for serious talk, reserve a table at the far side of the room). The top-floor setting with its panoramic views is exhilarating, with the lights of Paris before you and the floodlit Meccano of the Eiffel Tower so close you could almost touch it. Appetizing *nouvelle cuisine* by Marc Thivet, whose forte is fish. The service is courteous, and the set menus good value.

La Tour d'Argent $\boxed{F}$/////
15–17 quai de la Tournelle, 5e ☎ 43 54 23 31 • closed Mon • AE DC MC V • jacket and tie
This is a penthouse where it is worth making a reservation well ahead to secure a table with a view across to the floodlit Notre-Dame and the Seine below. Security is tight and identities are carefully checked. Once inside, you are struck by the graceful dignity of this restaurant, where the waiters wear tails even at noon. The chandeliers, parquet floor and well-spaced yellow-clothed tables provide the setting for a cuisine of the highest quality that mixes modern and classical: duck is what the restaurant is famous for, but lamb and lobster

are also first-rate, and the set menu at lunch is good value. The wine list is the best in Paris, and afterwards you can enjoy an armagnac or cognac in the lovely, atmospheric cellars.

Au Trou Gascon $\boxed{F}$////
40 rue Taine, 12e ☎ 43 44 34 26 • closed Sat, Sun • AE V
This delightful old bistro is usefully located in an eastern area where a major new business quarter is fast growing up around Quai de Bercy but where there are few really good eating-places. Under a new chef the Gascon and Landais cooking is as excellent as ever, with some classic local dishes and some innovations. The set business lunch offers a good choice and the range of wines and armagnacs is spectacular.

Restaurant prices
The price symbol ($\boxed{F}$ to $\boxed{F}$//////) given after the restaurant name is based on the cost at the time of going to press of a typical *à la carte* meal including wine (see page 7). Most restaurants offer at least one, and often several, fixed-price menus at considerably lower prices.

Brasseries
Brasseries are today more in vogue than ever with Parisians. Though generally too hectic and congested for high-level entertaining, they could often be the right choice for a more down-to-earth business meal. Prices are usually moderate and the cooking straightforward.
   The fairly small *Le Balzar*, 49 rue des Ecoles, 5e ☎ 43 54 13 67, is a haunt of university professors and media people; *La Coupole*, 102 bd du Montparnasse, 14e ☎ 43 20 14 20, attracts into its famous high-ceilinged hall artists and ad-men, starlets and scribblers, tourists and grey-suited bourgeois, and the noise and fun go on into the small hours;

Flo, 7 cour des Petites-Ecuries, 10e ☎ 47 70 13 59, noted for its Alsatian food and draught beer, is trendy and lively but has rather cramped seating; *Lipp*, 151 bd St-Germain, 6e ☎ 45 48 53 91, remains the celebrated meeting-place of the city's political and intellectual elite; the bustling *Le Muniche*, 27 rue de Buci, 6e ☎ 46 33 62 09, is popular with the Left Bank media world (try for the quieter alcoves) and open till 3am.

Non-French cuisines

Paris does not have many good restaurants serving foreign cuisines, but they are on the increase and you may like to try one or two of the following places.

American *Joe Allen*, 30 rue Pierre-Lescot, 1er ☎ 42 36 70 13, is not a place for business, but fun for any homesick visitor seeking burgers and apple pie in an authentic (well, fairly) American atmosphere.

Chinese and Vietnamese These proliferate, two of the best being *Chez Vong*, 27 rue Colisée, 8e ☎ 43 59 77 12, which is fairly smart, and *Tan Dinh*, 60 rue de Verneuil, 7e ☎ 45 44 04 84, with its pretty decor and good French wines.

German The delightful *Au Vieux Berlin*, 32 ave George-V, 8e ☎ 47 20 88 96, has style and comfort, good German food, a pianist in the evenings, and clients include top French and German politicians.

Indian restaurants are still scarce, but there is excellent tandoori cooking at *Raajmahal*, 192 rue de la Convention, 15e ☎ 45 33 15 57.

Italian Best among the many good ones are probably *Conti*, 72 rue Lauriston, 16e ☎ 47 27 74 67, and *Sormani*, 4 rue du Général-Lanzerac, 17e ☎ 43 80 13 91.

Japanese *Kinugawa*, 9 rue du Mont-Thabor, 1er ☎ 42 60 65 07, is elegant and friendly.

Russian *Dominique*, 19 rue Bréa, 6e ☎ 43 27 08 80, run by a White Russian émigré family, serves bortsch, blinis and other specialities in an "old Russian" decor.

Good but casual

Paris has scores of atmospheric bistros and romantic restaurants, too down-to-earth or crowded for business but good for relaxing with friends. *Atelier Maître Albert*, 1 rue Maître Albert, 5e ☎ 46 33 13 78, offers low lighting, a log fire, a good set dinner and a young clientele. *Bistro de la Gare*, 59 bd du Montparnasse, 6e ☎ 45 48 38 01, and at 73 ave des Champs-Elysées, 8e ☎ 43 59 67 83, are both lively formula restaurants offering a good set meal at a fair price with a pretty decor. *Chartier*, 7 rue du Faubourg-Montmartre, 9e ☎ 47 70 86 29, is an authentic surviving late-19thC "soup kitchen" with Art Nouveau decor and very low prices. *Chez Joséphine*, 117 rue du Cherche-Midi, 6e ☎ 45 48 52 40, is a pleasantly atmospheric old bistro with a good-value menu and a formidable wine list. *Chez Toutoune*, 5 rue de Pontoise, 5e ☎ 43 26 56 81, is lively, friendly, very Parisian, with a copious Provence-inspired set menu. *Le Coupe-Chou*, 9 rue de Lanneau, 5e ☎ 46 33 68 69, is a romantic place in a very old beamed building, popular with couples. *La Marlotte*, 55 rue du Cherche-Midi, 6e ☎ 45 48 86 79, is animated, candle-lit, much in vogue with yuppies and has some well-known clients (Chirac and Giscard among them) and the food is good value. *Polidor*, 41 rue Monsieur-le-Prince, 6e ☎ 43 26 95 34 is a delightful warm bistro with good bourgeois cooking and upmarket clients. *Le Procope*, 13 rue de l'Ancienne-Comédie, 6e ☎ 43 26 99 20, is Paris's oldest café-restaurant (1686): once the haunt of Voltaire, Robespierre and Balzac, it now serves not too inspired food in enchanting surroundings. *Orestias*, 4 rue Grégoire-de-Tours, 6e ☎ 43 54 62 01, is Greek-run, down-to-earth, cheap and excellent. *Le Trumiliou*, 84 quai de l'Hôtel de Ville, 4e ☎ 42 77 63 98, provides Auvergne cooking in a warm friendly atmosphere.

Bars and cafés

The French tend to work late in their offices, and generally prefer to do business over a leisurely meal rather than in bars. Nearly all the best cocktail bars for business talks are in the big hotels, frequented by foreigners, or attached to leading restaurants. Café-going on the other hand is an old Paris tradition, but it has waned in recent decades as the French have become more comfortably housed. The city's 10,000 cafés offer much the same range of alcoholic drinks as bars (apart from elaborate cocktails). Unlike bars, they usually have open pavement terraces. But they tend to be more cramped, noisy and casual than hotel bars, and therefore less suitable for a quiet business drink. Several of the bars and cafés mentioned on this page also feature in *Restaurants*.

Smart bars The luxury hotels have the best: the Bristol, Crillon (much used by journalists), George V, Inter-Continental, Lancaster, Plaza Athénée, and the Ritz, whose very fashionable bar was "liberated" by Hemingway in 1944. The Concorde La Fayette has a stylish panoramic rooftop bar, as does the Hilton. The smooth and intimate bar of l'Hôtel is popular with film and theatre people, and that of the Pont Royal with publishers and writers.

Among the best-known café-bars in restaurants are *Fouquet's*, on the Champs-Elysées, which is old-fashioned but still smart, *La Coupole*, always the focus of a trendy crowd, the *Closerie des Lilas*, still a haunt of literati, and *Chez Francis* at the Pont de l'Alma. The Foyer Bar of the *Café de la Paix*, 12 bd des Capucines, 9e, and the *Alexandre*, 53 ave George V, 8e, are sophisticated and cosmopolitan. And the famous *Harry's New York Bar*, 5 rue Daunou, 2e, still dispenses its 160 types of whisky to wistful expatriates, as it did when Fitzgerald and Hemingway were regulars.

Wine bars These are bistros or taverns serving good wine by the glass, and also snacks and light dishes. *Le Henri-IV*, 13 pl du Pont-Neuf, 1er, is much used by actors, politicians and lawyers from the nearby courts; *Rubis*, 10 rue du Marché St-Honoré, 1er, is also popular. As the modern wine bar is less a Paris than a London phenomenon, it is not surprising that two of the best should be English-owned: Steve Spurrier's *Blue Fox*, Cité Berryer, 8e, and Mark Williamson's *Willi's*, 13 rue des Petits-Champs, 1er. Both are popular with the British and anglophile French.

Pubs Recent attempts to implant the British pub have been less successful. Several so-called pubs today serve English beers and pub food amid "typically English" decor. To English eyes these places may look phoney, yet some remain popular with Parisians – among them, *Le Pub St-Germain*, 17 rue de l'Ancienne Comédie, 6e, open all night, *Le Sir Winston Churchill*, 5 rue de Presbourg, 16e, and *Le Twickenham*, 70 rue des Saints-Pères, 6e, frequented by publishing people.

Cafés The most famous Paris cafés are side by side in St-Germain-des-Prés – the *Deux Magots* and *Le Flore*, 170 and 172 bd St-Germain, 6e, where Sartre and Camus used to meet. Today there are fewer writers and more tourists: but these are still lively places and could be suitable for a business chat in the mornings or mid-afternoons when they are least crowded. Much the same applies to the historic cafés on the bd de Montparnasse – *Le Select*, no. 99, *Le Dôme*, no. 108, and *La Coupole*, no. 102, which are still haunts of the art world. A similar role is played by the cafés of some brasseries, such as *Le Balzar* and notably *Lipp* (see *Brasseries*). The latest fashionable place for younger smart people is the slick and futuristic *Café Costes*, sq des Innocents, 1er, at Les Halles.

Entertainment

"Paris by night" (the term used even by the French) is mostly as glamorous as its reputation and certainly as varied. Full listings of events in the capital are published in two pocket-sized weeklies, *L'Officiel des Spectacles* and *Pariscope*. Your hotel should also have a copy of the free *Sélection Paris* booklet and you can dial ☎ 47 20 94 94 for a recorded message about current events in the city (☎ 47 20 88 98 in English, ☎ 47 20 57 58 in German).

Ticket agencies Obtaining tickets in advance is not an easy matter. Many theatres operate a system involving reservations and sales not more than one or two weeks in advance; they are reluctant to make telephone reservations and do not work with agencies. Your hotel may be able to obtain tickets for you and the following agencies are usually reliable: *Agence des Théâtres des Champs-Elysées* ☎ 43 59 24 60, *Allo Loisirs* ☎ 42 61 82 25, *Night and Day* (in Méridien-Etoile hotel) ☎ 47 59 92 82, *SOS Théâtre* ☎ 42 25 03 18.

Theatre Paris theatre is often a disappointment, with curiously old-fashioned and declamatory acting. The best-known subsidized theatre is the very beautiful *Comédie Française*, pl du Théâtre-Français, 1er ☎ 40 15 00 00, for which it is hard to obtain tickets; the *Odéon*, 1 pl Paul-Claudel, 6e ☎ 43 25 70 32, is subtitled "Théâtre de l'Europe" and often acts as a home for visiting foreign companies; the *Théâtre de la Ville*, 2 pl du Châtelet, 1er ☎ 42 74 22 77, is well known for its international theatre festival. The commercial theatres are mostly on the Right Bank, many near the Opéra, the experimental mostly on the Left Bank. The liveliest of the experimental theatres are Peter Brook's *Bouffes du Nord*, 209 rue du Faubourg St-Denis, 10e ☎ 46 07 73 73; the *Cartoucherie* in the Bois de Vincennes ☎ 48 08 39 74, a converted ammunition factory; and

the *Lucernaire Forum*, 53 rue Notre-Dame-des-Champs, 6e ☎ 45 44 57 34. Most of Paris's theatres close for at least a month during the summer.

The café-theatres – lively, uncomfortable and requiring a good knowledge of French and things French – are concentrated in the Beaubourg area: *Les Blancs Manteaux*, 15 rue des Blancs-Manteaux, 4e ☎ 48 87 15 84; *Café de la Gare*, 41 rue du Temple, 3e ☎ 42 78 52 51; *Petit Casino*, 17 rue Chapon, 3e ☎ 42 78 36 50; *Point Virgule*, 7 rue Ste-Croix-de-la-Bretonnerie, 4e ☎ 42 78 67 03. Others are on the Left Bank: *Café d'Edgar*, 58 bd Edgar-Quintet, 14e ☎ 43 20 85 11; *Le Cloître Saint-Séverin*, 19 rue St-Jacques, 5e ☎ 43 25 19 92; and *Edgar III*, 3 impasse de la Gaîté, 14e ☎ 43 20 85 11. *Au Bec Fin*, 6 rue Thérèse, 1er ☎ 42 96 29 35, usually offers a good dinner as well as a choice of several playlets.

Opera and dance The splendid *Opéra* ☎ 47 42 57 50 with its Chagall ceiling stages both opera and ballet but tickets are expensive and hard to obtain. The *Théâtre Musical de Paris*, pl du Châtelet, 1er ☎ 42 33 00 00, has lavishly staged opera and dance at prices affordable by wider audiences, an aim that is also behind the *Opéra Bastille*, a vast project in the developing Bastille district. Dance is also staged at the Opéra, where the country's ballet company is based, but dance companies can be found in many venues all over Paris during the excellent winter season (mainly Nov and Dec): primarily the *Théâtre des Champs-Elysées*, 15 ave Montaigne, 8e ☎ 47 20 36 37; and huge places such as the *Palais des Congrès*, Porte Maillot, 17e ☎ 42 66 20 75; the *Palais des Sports*, Porte de Versailles ☎ 48 28 40 90; even the sports complex *Palais Omnisports de Paris Bercy*, 6 bd Bercy, 12e ☎ 43 46 12 21. During the Marais Festival (June) and the Festival de l'Ile de France (in the summer months) dance can be enjoyed in the courtyards of the mansions in Le Marais and historic buildings outside Paris.

Cinema The latest films are a major topic of conversation in Paris and cinemas are frequently crowded throughout the week (reduced prices everywhere on Mon). The plush cinemas are on the Champs-Elysées, the art houses mostly on the Left Bank, in the Latin Quarter and Saint Germain-des-Prés. In both these categories foreign films are shown in the original language, generally with French subtitles (labelled *v.o.* for *version original* in the various listings); elsewhere in Paris films are dubbed (labelled *v.f.* for *version française*). On the Champs-Elysées you may find French films with English subtitles. The standard programme in the capital's 450-plus cinemas runs from 2pm to midnight (2am on Fri and Sat), with films showing at two-hour intervals. Paris has two *cinémathèques*, at the Palais de Chaillot, 16e ☎ 47 04 24 24 and in the Pompidou Centre, 4e ☎ 42 78 35 57, providing a non-stop feast of classics, both French and foreign. Usherettes generally expect to be tipped.

Music The main venue for classical music is the *Salle Pleyel*, 252 rue du Faubourg St-Honoré, 8e ☎ 45 61 06 30. Concerts are also held at the *Maison de la Radio*, 116 ave du Président-Kennedy, 16e ☎ 42 30 15 16 and at the *Théâtre des Champs-Elysées*, 15 ave Montaigne, 8e ☎ 47 20 36 37. Much the pleasantest way of listening to classical music is to attend one of the frequent concerts held in beautiful churches such as the Gothic *Sainte-Chapelle* (reserve well in advance), *Saint-Germain L'Auxerrois, Saint-Germain-des-Prés, Saint-Julien-le-Pauvre, Saint Merri* and *Saint-Roch*. The cathedral of *Notre-Dame*, the church of the *Madeleine* and various historic buildings also stage occasional concerts. For contemporary music the best place is *IRCAM*, the experimental music centre

inside the Pompidou Centre ☎ 42 77 12 33. The main pop and rock venues are the huge *Palais des Congrès* ☎ 42 66 20 75, the *Palais des Sports* ☎ 48 28 40 90 and the legendary *Olympia Music-Hall* ☎ 42 66 17 79.

Paris has dozens of jazz clubs, offering the whole range of styles. Well-known jazz clubs include *Caveau de la Huchette*, 5 rue de la Huchette, 5e ☎ 43 26 65 06; *Petit Journal*, 71 bd St-Michel, 5e ☎ 43 26 28 59; and *Slow Club*, 130 rue de Rivoli, 1er ☎ 42 33 84 30.

Nightclubs and casinos Paris has a number of very fashionable (and very expensive) private nightclubs whose doors tend to remain firmly closed to those not accompanied by habitués or famous faces. *Club Olivia Valère*, 40 rue du Colisée ☎ 42 25 11 68; *Elysée-Matignon*, 2 ave Matignon ☎ 42 25 73 13; and the famous *Régine's*, 49 rue de Ponthieu ☎ 43 59 21 60 are all in the 8e arr near the Champs-Elysées. *Castel*, 15 rue Princesse, 6e ☎ 43 26 90 22, is the most exclusive.

The best dinner-and-show places are mostly very stylish, very expensive and more popular with foreigners than the French. They include the long-famous *Folies-Bergère*, 32 rue Richer, 9e ☎ 42 46 77 11; *Lido* 116 bis ave des Champs-Elysées, 8e ☎ 45 63 11 61; and *Moulin Rouge*, pl Blanche, 18e ☎ 46 06 00 19. Other well-known places are *Alcazar de Paris*, 62 rue Mazarine, 6e ☎ 43 29 02 20; *Cabaret des Champs Elysées*, 78 ave des Champs-Elysées, 8e ☎ 43 59 09 99; *Don Camillo*, 10 rue des Saints-Pères, 6e ☎ 42 60 82 84; *Eléphant Bleu*, 49 rue de Ponthieu, 8e ☎ 45 25 20 84; and the *Paradis Latin*, 28 rue Cardinal-Lemoine, 5e ☎ 43 25 28 28. *Crazy Horse Saloon*, a very upmarket strip club at 12 ave George-V, 8e ☎ 47 23 32 32, is popular for business entertainment.

The only casino in the Paris area open to visitors is at Enghien to the northwest of the city.

Shopping

Despite the mushrooming of hypermarkets in the suburbs, Paris still has a huge variety of small specialist shops, and for many visitors shopping is one of its main attractions. Window displays are stylish, the range of goods is excellent and shopping hours are long: roughly 9–7, Mon–Sat, though smaller shops may close for two hours at lunchtime. Apart from the clusters of antique dealers and specialist bookshops on the Left Bank, Paris does not have as distinct shopping districts as some other cities.

Fashion is the main exception. The major old-established couturiers are in and around Avenue Montaigne, 8e (*Balmain, Dior, Courrèges, Givency, Laroche, Nina Ricci, Yves St Laurent, Ungaro*) or Rue du Faubourg St-Honoré, 8e (*Louis Férand, Lanvin, Torrente*, with *Chanel* nearby in Rue Cambon, 1er). The more avant-garde designers prefer the Left Bank: *Sonia Rykiel*, 71 rue des Saints-Pères, 6e; *Chantal Thomass*, 5 rue du Vieux-Colombier, 6e. Many of the trendiest fashion boutiques are in Saint-Germain-des-Prés or in and around Les Halles.

Department stores Standard opening hours are 9.30–6.30, Mon-Sat. *Au Bon Marché*, 38 rue de Sèvres, 7e ☎ 45 49 21 22, is the only department store on the Left Bank and has a well-known antiques department. The huge *Galeries Lafayette*, 40 bd Haussmann, 9e ☎ 42 82 34 56, and its neighbour *Au Printemps*, 64 bd Haussmann ☎ 42 82 50 00, are full of chic boutiques and have useful facilities for visitors: shopping cards enabling purchases to be grouped together; 24hr pick-up facility; tax-recovery documentation; bureau de change; travel and theatre agency; restaurants; hairdressers. *La Samaritaine*, 19 rue de la Monnaie, 1er ☎ 45 08 33 33, is less stylish but popular for its roof terrace with spectacular views over the city. Open till 8 Wed. *Aux Trois-Quartiers*, 17 bd de la Madeleine, 1er ☎ 42 60 39 30, is more select and expensive.

Drugstores These stylish mini-shopping centres are open daily 9–1.30am, selling newspapers and magazines, gifts, books and records; all have restaurants, some have takeaway food service. *Drugstore Saint-Germain*, 149 bd St-Germain, 6e ☎ 42 22 80 00; *Drugstore Champs-Elysées*, 133 ave des Champs-Elysées, 8e ☎ 47 23 54 34; *Drugstore Matignon*, 1 ave Matignon, 8e ☎ 43 59 38 70.

Shopping centres and arcades There is a whole series of upmarket shopping malls or arcades leading off the north side of the Champs-Elysées, with fashion boutiques, restaurants and snackbars. *Forum des Halles*, 1er, is a smart shopping centre built in the late 1970s to replace the colourful food market; chic fashion boutiques and beauty shops, restaurants, cafés, cinemas, sports facilities, and Fnac store. *Palais des Congrès*, Porte Maillot, 17e, has art and antique shops, temporary craft stalls, bookshop, fashion boutiques, post office, restaurants and cafés. *Tour Maine-Montparnasse*, ave du Maine, 14e ☎ 45 38 32 32 is a large shopping centre adjoining the vast skyscraper, with dozens of shops (including a branch of Habitat), restaurants and cafés plus various leisure facilities.

Street markets Paris has many colourful open-air food markets. The best known are in Saint-Germain-des-Prés (Rue de Seine and Rue de Buci), the Latin Quarter (Rue Mouffetard), the Invalides area (Rue Cler), and Neuilly (Place du Marché, close to the Palais des Congrès).

There is a picturesque flower market on the Ile de la Cité near Notre-Dame; a market for stamps and postcards is held on Avenue Marlguy and Avenue Gabriel, near the Champs-Elysées, on Thursdays, weekends and public holidays; and the famous flea market at Porte de Clignancourt is open from Saturday to Monday.

Sightseeing

Paris is full of monuments, old churches, elegant squares and picturesque streets, as well as scores of museums and galleries. Many of the major sights lie fairly close together near the stretch of the river between Notre-Dame and the Eiffel Tower. This central area is very compact and can be toured on foot. State museums are closed on Tuesday, many others on Monday: all are open on Sunday when many are free (on other days most charge modest admission fees). The tourist office ☎ 47 23 61 72 will give advice. For recorded details in English of the day's main events ☎ 47 20 88 98.

Arc de Triomphe Crowning the top of the Champs-Elysées, this impressive arch with its relief sculptures was built by Napoleon to commemorate French military victories. Below it, an eternal flame burns over the Tomb of the Unknown Soldier, honouring the dead of two world wars. Magnificent view from the platform at the top. *Pl Charles-de-Gaulle, 8e. Platform open 10–5.30.*

Assemblée Nationale (Palais Bourbon) The lower house of parliament meets in a semi-circular chamber in this 17thC mansion built by the Duchess of Bourbon. To attend a debate, and visit the fine library, apply in writing to 126 rue de l'Université, 75007.

Bibliothèque Nationale A fine 17thC mansion houses one of the world's greatest collections of maps, prints, manuscripts, and books (9m volumes). The medals collection and splendid Mazarin Gallery are open to the public. *58 rue de Richelieu, 2e. Open 12–6.*

Conciergerie The keeper (concierge) of the king's household used to inhabit this section of the great 14thC palace built by Philip le Bel on the Ile de la Cité. Later it became notorious as a prison, especially during the Revolution, and one can visit the cells where Marie-Antoinette, Robespierre, Danton and others awaited the guillotine. *1 quai de l'Horloge, 1er. Open Wed–Mon, 10–6.*

Eiffel Tower Built in 1889 for the World Exhibition, long reviled but now placidly accepted as the city's best-known symbol, engineer Gustave Eiffel's tower of iron girders rises 315 metres/1,052ft above the city. The two lower platforms can be reached by lift or stairs, the top one by lift only: splendid panoramas. *Pont d'Iéna 7e. Open 10am–11pm.*

Gobelins tapestry factory Founded by Louis XIV, this state-owned enterprise still weaves tapestries for public buildings and for use as official gifts. *42 ave des Gobelins, 13e. Guided tours 2 and 2.45 Tue, Wed, Thu.*

Grand Palais This huge porticoed structure, built for the Universal Exhibition of 1900, now houses large-scale temporary art exhibitions and a science museum, the Palais de la Découverte. *Ave Winston-Churchill, 8e. Open Wed–Mon, 10.30–6.30.*

Hôtel de Ville Seat of the city government and office of its mayor, this great pompous pile was built in the 1870s as a pastiche of its Renaissance predecessor, burned down in 1871 by the Communards. The debates of the city council are open to the public; on Mondays there are guided tours of the reception rooms. *Pl de l'Hôtel de Ville, 4e. Open Mon–Sat, 9–6; tours Mon 10.30.*

Les Invalides This massive complex of buildings was erected by Louis XIV in the 1670s to house his invalided soldiers. Today the main attraction is Napoleon's tomb. There are also museums of French military history and of the two world wars. *Open Apr–Sep, 10–6; Oct–Mar, 10–5.*

Jardin des Plantes Botanical garden dating from the 17th century and containing tropical plants, a natural history museum, including skeletons and fossils, and a small zoo. *Rue Geoffroy St-Hilaire, 5e. Open Wed–Mon, 10.30–5.*

La Madeleine A handsome 18th–19thC church with Corinthian columns, a lovely marble interior and a famous organ. It is often used for concerts and smart weddings. *Pl de la Madeleine, 8e. Open 8.30–7.*

Maison de Balzac Of the various Paris homes of the great novelist, this one is now a museum, full of his possessions and steeped in his personality. *47 rue Raynouard, 16e. Open Tue–Sun, 10–5.30.*

Musée d'Art Moderne de la Ville de Paris Housed in the grandiose Palais de Tokyo. Braque, Dufy, Modigliani and Picasso are well represented. *11 ave du Président Wilson, 16e. Open daily exc Mon, 10–5.40; Wed 10–8.30.*

Musée Carnavalet A graceful Renaissance building in the Marais, once the home of Madame de Sévigné, now a fascinating museum of Paris history, conveyed in models, paintings, maps and furniture. *23 rue de Sévigné, 3e. Open Tue–Sun, 10–5.30.*

Musée de Cluny One part of this museum is an archaeological site, the remains of the vast Gallo-Roman thermal baths of around AD200; the other part, the Hôtel de Cluny, built by rich abbots in the 15thC, houses a medieval collection including a set of marvellous 15thC tapestries. *8 pl Paul-Painlevé, 5e. Open Wed–Mon, 9.45–12.30, 2–5.15.*

Musée Grévin Waxworks of famous people ancient and modern; historical tableaux; distorting mirrors and other tricks. *10 bd Montmartre, 9e. Open Mon–Sat, 2–7; Sun, 1–7.*

Musée du Louvre France's leading museum, and one of the world's greatest, housed in a huge and majestic palace that was successively enlarged by various monarchs from François I to Napoleon III. The Greek, Roman and Egyptian antiquities include the Venus de Milo and Winged Victory of Samothrace; the Leonardo da Vinci collection, including Mona Lisa, is the world's finest; El Greco and Rembrandt are well represented. More galleries will open when the Finance Ministry moves out, and a controversial glass pyramid is going up in the main courtyard. *Quai du Louvre, 1er. Open Wed–Mon, 10–6.30.*

Musée d'Orsay A huge and ornate late-19thC railway station, left derelict, has recently been transformed into a very beautiful museum of the arts, covering the period 1848–1914. All the Impressionists formerly in the Jeu de Paume have been transferred here. *1 rue de Bellechasse, 7e. Open Tue–Sun, 10.30–6; Thu, 10.30–9.45; Sun, 9–6.*

Musée Picasso (Hôtel Salé) A 17thC mansion in the Marais houses the artist's private collection of his own work, and of some other artists, which passed to the state in lieu of tax on his death. All his periods are represented. *5 rue de Thorigny, 3e. Open Thu–Mon, 9.15–5; Wed 9.15–10pm.*

Musée Rodin Much of the best work of the great sculptor, including "The Kiss" and "The Burghers of Calais," is laid out in a fine 18thC mansion and its quiet garden. *77 rue de Varenne, 7e. Open Wed–Mon, 10–6.*

Musée Victor Hugo Memorabilia of the great novelist, with some of his own drawings and paintings. *6 pl des Vosges, 4e. Open Tue–Sun, 10–5.30.*

Notre-Dame Built in the 12th–14th centuries, sacked during the Revolution, then restored by Viollet-le-Duc, this architectural jewel lies at the heart of Vieux Paris. It has a richly sculptured facade and lovely rose windows; you can ascend either of its high twin towers. *Rue de l'Arcole, 4e. Open 8–9; towers open 10–5.30.*

Opéra Charles Garnier's ornate 1860s masterpiece has a marble stairway and an ornate auditorium, enhanced, or marred for some, by the addition of Chagall's painted ceiling. *Pl de l'Opéra, 9e. Open for visits 10–5; closed Sun and public holidays.*

Palais de Chaillot Built for the 1937 Exhibition, this huge colonnaded palace with its two curving wings today houses a state-run theatre and four interesting museums: the *Musée du Cinéma*, the

Musée de la Marine (maritime subjects, including model ships), the *Musée des Monuments Français* (replicas of French monumental sculptures), and the *Musée de l'Homme* (pre-history and anthropology). *Pl du Trocadéro, 16e. Varied opening times, all closed Tue.*

Palais de l'Elysée Built in 1718, and since 1873 the French President's official residence and workplace. Not open to the public, but the courtyard can be glimpsed from the street. *Rue du Faubourg-St-Honoré, 8e.*

Palais de Justice The main Paris law courts occupy a huge building on the Ile de la Cité that was once a royal palace, then the seat of parliament till 1789. *4 bd du Palais, 1er. All courts and halls, except juvenile court, open to public weekdays, 9–7.*

Palais du Luxembourg The seat of the Senate (upper house of parliament) is a palace built for Marie de Medici in the 17th century, then much altered in the 19th. Guided tours include the council chamber, library (with paintings by Delacroix) and other rooms. *15 rue de Vaugirard, 6e. Open for tours Sun 9.30–11, 2.30–4.30.*

Palais Royal Cardinal Richelieu's 17thC palace, with its elegant colonnaded courtyard, was later the scene of orgies, political rallies, and prostitution. The palace itself is now offices, and Président Mitterrand has had the courtyard adorned with 260 black-and-white striped columns, an avant-garde piece of art that horrifies many Parisians. *Rue de Rivoli, 1er. Open 7.30am–8.30pm.*

Panthéon The tombs of many illustrious Frenchmen, from Victor Hugo to Resistance leader Jean Moulin, are housed in this rather fusty museum with its huge dome. Interesting paintings by Puvis de Chavannes. *Pl du Panthéon, 5e. Open 10–6.*

Père Lachaise cemetery Hundreds of famous people, from Molière to Oscar Wilde and Edith Piaf, lie buried in the city's largest cemetery, laid out in 1804. *16 rue du Repos, 20e. Open daily.*

Pompidou Centre (Beaubourg) Sometimes described as "an arty oil refinery" because of its multi-coloured external piping, the giant cultural centre initiated by the late President Pompidou at first shocked Parisians. Now it pleases most of them, and attracts more visitors per day (25,000) than the Eiffel Tower and Louvre combined. As well as a library, industrial design centre and much else, it houses the splendid Musée National d'Art Moderne. *Rue St-Martin, 4e. Open Wed–Mon, 12–10; Sat, Sun, 10–10.*

Sacré-Coeur This famous Paris landmark, gleaming white on the hill of Montmartre, was built in the late 19th century in response to a national vow after defeat in the war of 1870–71. Its neo-Byzantine style is not to all tastes: but the interior is elegant, with a superb mosaic above the altar. *Rue du Cardinal Dubois, 18e. Open 6am–10.45. Access to crypt 9–5.30; summer 9–6.30.*

Saint-Etienne-du-Mont A 16thC Latin Quarter church in a strange variety of styles, with a notable roodscreen and fine stained-glass windows in the cloister. *Pl St-Geneviève, 5e.*

Saint-Eustache This large and lovely 17thC church at Les Halles is noted for its flying buttresses, lavish stained glass and superb organ. Often used for concerts. *2 rue du Jour, 1er. Open 8–7pm.*

Saint-Sulpice A great 17th–18thC church in classical style, with masses of space and fine murals by Delacroix. Recitals are often given on its massive organ. *Pl St-Sulpice, 6e.*

Sainte-Chapelle Fine 13thC church tucked away in a courtyard of the Palais de Justice; possibly the loveliest church in Paris as well as one of the oldest. It consists of two chapels one above the other – the lower one a little gloomy, the upper one lit by marvellous stained-glass windows. *4 bd du Palais, 4e. Open 10–6.*

La Sorbonne The University of Paris was founded here by Robert de Sorbon in 1253 and the present imposing buildings date from the 17th century. They are now used for lectures and administration by several of the 13 university faculties scattered around the city. The great courtyard thronged with students, the baroque library and ornate lecture rooms are worth visiting. *Rue Sorbonne, 5e*

UNESCO headquarters Imposing Y-shaped building dating from 1958 and containing works of art by Henry Moore, Picasso and others. Open to groups by prior arrangement. *9 pl de Fontenoy, 7e ☎ 45 68 10 00.*

La Villette: Cité des Sciences et de l'Industrie Just inside the Périphérique in the northeast of the city is an ambitious development which typifies the French love of grandeur. What is claimed to be the world's largest science museum of futuristic design, opened in 1986 in a huge building that was formerly the city's main abattoir. Displays are elaborate and ingenious, with the accent on French high-tech. The symbol of La Villette is the spherical Géode, next door, which houses a panoramic cinema using the Omnimax process. Nearby, on a 34ha/85-acre site, is a brand-new arts and leisure complex, with three concert halls and the new home of the Paris Conservatoire. *Ave Corentin-Cariou, 19e. Museum open Tue–Fri, 2–8; Sat, Sun, noon–8.*

Guided tours

A guided tour by bus can probably provide the best quick introduction to Paris. Several companies run circular tours of the main sights or of certain specialized sights. These usually last about 2hr and include commentary in various languages. Operators include *American Express* ☎ 42 66 09 99, *Cityrama* ☎ 42 60 30 14, *Paris-Vision* ☎ 42 60 31 25, SNCF ☎ 47 42 00 26.

River trips The banks of the Seine are best seen from one of the cruise-boats that ply mainly the central stretch between the Eiffel Tower and Quai de Bercy. They also go after dark when the main buildings are floodlit. Apply to *Vedettes de Paris* ☎ 43 26 92 55, *Vedettes Parisiens Tour Eiffel* ☎ 47 05 50 00, or *Vedettes du Pont Neuf* ☎ 46 33 98 38. *Bateaux Mouches* ☎ 42 25 22 55 also run cruises that serve lunch or dinner.

Walking lecture tours on cultural and historical themes, with expert guides, are organized by *Arcus* ☎ 45 67 68 01, and *Paris et son Histoire* ☎ 45 26 26 77.

Incentive tours Companies wanting to plan a group incentive visit for their staff could apply to *Incentive Congress Organization*, 22 rue Turbigo, 2e ☎ 42 96 81 11, or *Treasure Tours*, 15 rue de l'Arcade, 8e ☎ 42 65 05 69.

Parks and gardens

Central Paris has less greenery than many great cities, but there are quite big parks on its periphery. To the west, the Bois de Boulogne is rather heavily dissected by motor roads, but it contains several delightful and secluded smaller parks such as the Bagatelle and Pré Catelan as well as the Jardin d'Acclimatation, an amusement park. To the east, the Bois de Vincennes has a zoo, boating lakes, and on the north side a château with medieval keep and a chapel. Inside the city the best-known central parks are small and rather formal: the Jardin de Luxembourg with its baroque fountain and statues, and the Tuileries, elegant but a little dry and dusty. The charming little Parc Monceau in the 8e has been pleasantly landscaped and has some children's playgrounds. Those in search of more romantic green spaces should visit the Parc de Monsouris (14e) and the unusual Parc des Buttes Chaumont (19e) with its hilly woods and rocky island in a lake.

Spectator sports

Paris's major venue for spectator sports is the huge new complex called the *Palais Omnisports de Paris Bercy*, 8 bd de Bercy, 12e ☎ 43 46 12 21, which houses numerous sporting activities including boxing, cycling, motorcycle races and showjumping.

Cycling Paris–Roubaix race in the spring; Grand Prix Cycliste de la Ville de Paris, June; the Tour de France reaches its climax on the Champs-Elysées at the end of July.

Horse-racing The smart racecourses are *Auteuil* (steeplechasing) and *Longchamp* (flat racing), both in the Bois du Boulogne, 16e, and *Vincennes*, on the eastern edge of the city, is famous for its trotting races. The major race for aficionados is the *Prix de l'Arc de Triomphe*, which attracts the international set to Longchamp in early October.

Rugby and soccer The big Paris stadium is the *Parc des Princes*, Porte de Saint-Cloud, 16e ☎ 42 88 02 76. The top local soccer teams are *Paris Saint-Germain* and *Matra-Racing*.

Tennis The *Stade Roland-Garros*, ave Gordon-Bennett, 16e ☎ 47 43 48 00, hosts the French Open Championship in late May, early June.

Keeping fit

The French have recently taken to sport in a big way. Gyms, squash clubs and tennis clubs are now fashionable, especially with young business executives of both sexes, and are hard to get into. The places we list below will normally accept visitors, often for a high hourly or daily fee, but are usually crowded in the evenings and at weekends.

Gyms and health clubs The *Gymnase Club* requires payment for a minimum of ten visits to any one of their well-equipped clubs, which claim to offer 44 different activities ranging from aerobics to underwater gymnastics; most have pools, saunas, jacuzzi and UVA. Convenient addresses for business visitors are the

Gymnase Maillot, 17 rue du Débarcardère, 17e ☎ 45 74 14 04; and the *Salle des Champs-Elysées*, 55 bis rue de Ponthieu, 8e ☎ 45 62 99 76. The punningly named *Espace Vit'Halles*, 48 rue Rambuteau, 4e ☎ 42 77 21 71, which has plenty of space and facilities, offers anything from a day ticket to an annual subscription and is open seven days a week. The *Vitatop Fitness Club*, 118 rue de Vaugirard, 6e ☎ 45 44 38 01, has pool, sauna, steam bath, solarium with pleasantly garden-like decor. (See also *Hotels.*)

Golf Weekday playing for a green fee is usually possible at clubs in nearby towns. The most private, and oldest, is Mortfontaine, near CDG airport. The *Racing Club de France* is at La Boulie near Versailles ☎ 39 50 59 41. Others are at *Saint-Cloud*, 69 rue du 19 Janvier, Garches ☎ 47 01 01 85; at *Saint-Germain-en-Laye*, route de Poissy ☎ 34 51 75 90; and at *Saint-Nom-la-Bretéche*, Domaine de la Tuilerie ☎ 34 62 54 00.

Riding There are three riding stables in the Bois de Boulogne: *Centre Hippique du Touring-club de France* ☎ 47 22 88 48; *Société d'Equitation de Paris* at the Porte de Neuilly ☎ 47 22 87 06; and *Société Equestre de l'Etrier*, route de Madrid-aux-Lacs ☎ 46 24 28 02; and one in the Bois de Vincennes: *Bayard UCPA Centre Equestre* ☎ 43 65 46 87.

Squash and tennis Clubs willing to accept visitors are mainly on the outskirts. Two which offer both are *Tennis Club de la Défense*, 45 bd des Bouvets, Nanterre ☎ 47 73 04 40, which has 8 indoor tennis courts and 6 squash courts, plus gym and sauna; and *Tennis Country Club*, 58 bd du Président-Wilson, Saint-Denis ☎ 48 09 22 69, which has 20 indoor tennis courts and 5 squash courts.

Swimming Paris's public swimming pools are unpleasantly overcrowded. For pools in health clubs and hotels see above. *Piscine Keller*, 8 rue de l'Ingénieur-Keller, 15e ☎ 45 77 12 12, is a private pool with a sauna.

Local resources
Business services
Paris has excellent facilities for
conferences, seminars and meetings
and an increasingly good range of
services for individual business
visitors. Your hotel may have good
advice, since Paris hotel concierges
are rightly famous for their ability to
supply at speed (and for a
consideration) any services guests
require. *Assistance Démarches*
☎ 42 81 47 67 is a useful service
offering help with administrative
problems such as obtaining visas.

Companies offering short-term
office accommodation include: *Acte*,
17 rue de la Baume, 8e
☎ 45 62 23 23; *Ibos*, 15 ave Victor-
Hugo, 16e ☎ 45 02 18 00; *Locaburo*,
14 rue Anatole-France, La Défense
☎ 47 75 32 00; *Multiburo*, 34 bd
Haussmann, 9e ☎ 47 70 47 70
℡ MBI 290266; *Orion Locations*, 37
rue de Surène, 8e ☎ 42 66 33 26; and
Le Satellite, 8 rue Copernic, 16e
☎ 47 27 15 59. The *2A Service* at the
airports (see *Arriving*) can also
supply fully equipped and serviced
offices.
Photocopying and printing
Photocopiers are available in most
post offices, at stations and airports,
and in hundreds of copy shops,
photography studios and stationers
all over the city. *Rank Xerox* has copy
shops at 80 bd de Sébastopol, 3e
☎ 48 87 03 31; 128 rue de Rennes, 6e
☎ 45 49 04 10; and 40 bd
Malesherbes, 8e ☎ 42 66 10 53.
Organization Deb's, 139 ave Charles-
de-Gaulle, Neuilly ☎ 47 45 20 44
provides an efficient and
comprehensive service midway
between the Palais des Congrès and
La Défense and has another branch
at La Défense itself ☎ 47 78 40 65.
Secretarial For all temporary staff,
Manpower has offices all over Paris;
for the nearest to your hotel consult
the telephone directory or
☎ 47 66 03 03. *Intérim Nation*
☎ 43 45 50 00 is another company
with many branches. Most large
hotels can arrange for temporary

secretarial assistance. *Monique
Deberghes*, 92 rue Saint-Lazare, 9e
☎ 42 81 07 63 specializes in
supplying conference stenotypists
and typing from tapes.
Translation and interpreting
*Communications Internationales
Rozbroj* ☎ 47 64 10 00 ℡ 640252 fax
47 66 36 86; *Eclair Courrier
International* ☎ 42 25 86 10; *Express
Traductions* ☎ 48 74 65 73; *Opéra
Traductions* ☎ 47 42 06 43.

Communications
Local delivery Most Paris
businesses have their own messenger
or courier for collections and
deliveries in and around the city and
many also send their own staff to
provincial cities. So any company you
do business with will probably be
able to provide this service. Large
hotels can often supply a messenger
for errands within Paris. The city's
messenger services generally work on
a subscription basis, or require you to
buy a block of ten tickets. Also *Allo
Frêt* ☎ 46 55 88 80; *Allo Postexpress*
☎ 42 85 10 33; *Delta Courses*
☎ 42 71 15 07; *TTL* ☎ 47 93 36 06;
Vit' Courses ☎ 46 51 90 17.
Long-distance delivery *Calberson-
Calexpress* ☎ 42 00 11 66; *DHL*
☎ 45 01 91 00; *Securicor France*
(Europe only) ☎ 43 39 04 33.
Post offices Paris has one 24hr post
office, 52 rue du Louvre, 1er
☎ 40 28 20 00; the office at 71 ave
des Champs-Elysées is open Mon–Sat
8am–10pm. Outside Paris, the post
office at *Orly Sud* airport is open
24hr, that at *CDG* airport Mon–Sat
6.30am–11pm, Sun and public
holidays 8.30am–8.30pm. Normal
post office opening hours in Paris are
Mon–Fri 8–7, Sat 8–12.
Telex and fax 24hr public telex
office is at 103 rue de Grenelle, 7e
☎ 45 50 34 34; to dictate a telex by
telephone ☎ 42 47 12 12. The main
fax office is in the Palais des Congrès,
at Porte Maillot, 17e (on the lower
ground floor); telex and fax are also
available at the main post office in
each *arrondissement*.

Conference/exhibition venues

Paris is one of the world's leading conference centres, and can offer a huge range of venues, from major convention hotels to prestige rooms in historic mansions and châteaux.

Palais des Congrès, 2 pl de la Porte-Maillot, 17e ☎ 46 40 22 22, is the largest conference centre, holding up to 4,100 people, with 19 meeting rooms, 2 exhibition halls of 1,250 sq metres, simultaneous translation equipment (for up to 6 languages) and a wide range of other facilities. It is conveniently situated in the same building as the Roissy/CDG air terminal. The *Parc des Expositions* at the Porte de Versailles, 15e ☎ 48 42 87 00, is Paris's major exhibition centre, with 8 exhibition halls covering a total of 220,000 sq metres, 12 meeting rooms seating up to 800 people, restaurant facilities for over 4,000, and 5,000 parking spaces. Of the many other conference halls and rooms available (a full list is available from the *Comité Parisien des Congrès*, see *Information sources*), the best-known central ones include, in *arrondissement* order, the *Salle de l'Espace*, 1er ☎ 40 26 17 52; the *Maison de L'Europe de Paris*, 35 rue des Francs-Bourgeois, 4e ☎ 42 72 94 06; the *Centre de Conférence Panthéon*, 16 rue de l'Estrapade, 5e ☎ 43 25 11 85; *Maison de la Chimie*, 28 bis rue St-Dominique, 7e ☎ 47 05 10 73; *Centre Audiovisuel de l'Entreprise*, 21 rue Clément-Marot ☎ 47 20 65 32; *Centre Chaillot-Galliéra*, 28 ave George-V ☎ 47 20 71 50; *Maison des Centraux*, 8 rue Jean-Goujon ☎ 43 59 52 41; *Espace de Pierre Cardin*, 1 ave Gabriel ☎ 42 66 17 30 and *Pavillon Gabriel*, 5 ave Gabriel ☎ 42 68 18 18 – all in the 8e; and the new *Zénith* at La Villette, 19e ☎ 42 45 91 48. Outside Paris possibilities include historic châteaux such as *Vaux-le-Vicomte* ☎ 60 66 97 09 and *Breteuil* ☎ 30 52 05 11, the attractive *Moulin de Guérard* ☎ 64 04 77 55 and *Pavillon Henri IV* ☎ 34 51 62 62.

Emergencies

Bureaux de change Suprisingly few Paris banks have exchange counters and the few that do exist frequently close for lunch between 11.30 and 1.45, especially in July and Aug. The *Crédit Commercial de France* (CCF) has two special exchange offices at 115 ave des Champs-Elysées, 8e ☎ 40 70 27 22 (Mon–Sat, 8.30–8), and 2 carrefour de l'Odéon, 6e ☎ 43 25 38 17 (Mon–Sat, 9–7.30). The *Union de Banques à Paris* (UBP) bureau de change operates Sat, Sun and public holidays 10.30–6. Bureaux de change at airports and stations are open till at least 8.30pm, and often till 11.30pm in summer.

Credit card loss or theft American Express ☎ 47 08 31 21; *Access/Eurocard/MasterCard* ☎ 43 23 46 46; *Diners Club* ☎ 47 62 75 75; *Visa* ☎ 42 77 11 90.

Medical emergencies SOS *Médicins* ☎ 43 37 77 77 or 47 07 77 77; for cases of food or drug poisoning *Centre anti-poison* ☎ 42 05 63 29; for burns ☎ 47 72 91 91.

Hospitals British Hospital 48 rue de Villiers, 92300 Levallois-Perret ☎ 47 58 13 12; *Hôpital Américain de Paris* 63 bd Victor-Hugo, 92200 Neuilly-sur-Seine ☎ 47 47 53 00. *Hôpital Cochin* 27 rue du Faubourg St-Jacques, 14e ☎ 42 34 12 12. Automatic call boxes at main crossroads labelled *Police-secours* may also be used in emergencies.

Pharmacies Paris has one 24hr pharmacy: *La Pharmacie des Champs-Elysées* 84 ave des Champs-Elysées, 8e ☎ 45 62 02 41. The pharmacy counter in the *Drugstore Saint-Germain* (on the corner of Bd St-Germain and Rue de Rennes, 6e) is open daily to 2am. For details of pharmacists willing to make up prescriptions outside normal opening hours, contact the *Commissariat de police* of the *arrondissement*, where emergency prescriptions must also be stamped.

Police ☎ 17. Préfecture de Police, 7 bd du Palais, 4e ☎ 42 60 33 22.

Government offices

Centre Français du Commerce Extérieur (CFCE), 10 ave d'Iéna, 16e ☎ 45 05 30 00: information about France's foreign trade. *Institut National de la Statistique et des Etudes Economiques* (INSEE), 195 rue de Bercy, 12e ☎ 43 45 72 31 or 43 45 70 75: Paris's "economic observatory;" *Ministère de l'Economie, des Finances et de la Privatization*, 93 rue de Rivoli, 1er ☎ 42 60 33 00 (*Commerce extérieur*, 41 quai Branly, 7e ☎ 45 50 71 11; *Commerce, Artisanat et Services*, 80 rue de Lille, 7e ☎ 45 56 24 24): information on all forms of income and other planning assistance to small businesses. *Ministère de l'Industrie, des P et T et du Tourisme*, 101 rue de Grenelle, 7e ☎ 45 56 36 36: information on postal, telex and fax services and on industrial matters. *Ministère de l'Interieur*, pl Beauvau, 8e ☎ 45 22 90 90: inquiries on immigration and residence permits and security matters.

Information sources

Business information Chambre de Commerce et d'Industrie de Paris, *27 ave de Friedland, 8e ☎ 42 89 70 00*. Chambre de Commerce Internationale, *38 cours Albert 1er, 8e ☎ 45 62 34 56*. Assemblée Permanente des Chambres de Commerce et d'Industrie (APCCI), 45 ave d'Iéna, 16e ☎ 47 23 01 11, provides information on local chamber of commerce activities throughout France. *Comité Parisien des Congrès*, Office de Tourisme, 127 ave des Champs-Elysées, 8e ☎ 47 20 12 55, offers a very full information service, free of charge, on all the technical aspects of organizing conferences, seminars, meetings, incentives in Paris; meeting rooms available; conference services include interpreting, accommodation, special reduction on rail and air travel within France; meetings can be set up with companies providing a wide range of services and the Committee will also

put a whole conference project out to tender.

Local media The national press is based in Paris (see *The business media*). The city is the home of the *International Herald Tribune*, but has no local daily. *Ville de Paris*, a monthly published by the Hôtel de Ville, gives information on local development projects and occasionally on local businesses but is geared to ratepayers rather than visitors. *Pariscope* and L'Officiel des Spectacles are the best source of information on local events. *Europe 1* news flashes often give information on traffic trouble spots and *Radio Tour-Eiffel*, a local radio station, is light-hearted but informative.

Tourist information The main *Office de Tourisme de Paris* is at 127 ave des Champs-Elysées, 8e ☎ 47 23 61 72 or 47 20 60 20 ⊠ 611984; for a recorded message giving details of current events in and around the capital ☎ 47 20 94 94 (English version ☎ 47 20 88 98, German version ☎ 47 20 57 58). Subsidiary tourist offices at Orly and Roissy/CDG airports, Gare d'Austerlitz, Gare de l'Est, Gare de Lyon, Gare du Nord and at the Eiffel Tower (May–Sep only). RATP (public transport) information ☎ 43 46 14 14.

Thank-yous

Credit card orders are not usually accepted by telephone in France but the concierge in your hotel may be able to arrange for payment to be added to your hotel bill.
Florists *Jardin de Vaugirard* (*Interflora*), 239 rue de Vaugirard, 15e ☎ 43 06 11 91; *Pascal Martinet Fleurs Royal Vendome*, 231 rue St-Honoré, 1er ☎ 42 60 42 76.
Luxury foods *Fauchon*, 26 pl de la Madeleine, 8e ☎ 47 42 60 11.
Fruit It is chic these days to send baskets of exotic fruit instead of flowers: *Inter-fruits*, 89 ave de Wagram, 17e ☎ 47 63 10 55, does attractive arrangements.

BORDEAUX

Zip code 33000

Bordeaux, capital of the Aquitaine region, is France's second-largest port on the Atlantic seaboard, and, with a population of 600,000, its eighth-largest city. For many years major wine shippers, concentrated on the Quai des Chartrons, constituted Bordeaux's main economic strength. However, complacency and malpractice resulted in the reorganization of trade and the construction of a vast Cité Internationale du Vin: a complex of merchants' offices, shops and a promotional showcase for the wines of Bordeaux. Since 1981 the city has hosted the biennial Vinexpo-Vinitech, the world's biggest wine trade fair.

Apart from wine, Bordeaux is fast developing many high-tech industries, including missile production and aeronautics. Aérospatiale, Dassault, Matra, Sogema and others employ some 15,000 people. Research spin-offs have led to a broader specialization in composite materials. The electronics industry is growing and several major international firms have set up bases in Bordeaux (Pioneer, IBM, Sony, Siemens, TRW). The other main industrial sector is made up of pharmaceutical and chemical firms.

The former prime minister, Jacques Chaban-Delmas, has been mayor of Bordeaux since 1947. Twenty years ago he drained the marshes to the north of the city and created the Bordeaux-Lac district, now the home of the Parc des Expositions (exhibition centre) and the Palais des Congrès (conference hall). More recently, he revitalized the slums of Mériadeck and rehabilitated Vieux Bordeaux, the city's old quarter. However, he has postponed ambitious and expensive plans for a science and technology park for reasons of cost. The Bordeaux business community is reputed to be similarly hard-headed in its dealings.

Arriving
Mérignac airport
The terminal is expanding fast to meet the threat from the TGV (high-speed train) which in 1990 will cut the rail journey from Paris to three hours. There are scheduled direct flights to and from Brussels, Frankfurt, Geneva, London (daily) and Madrid, as well as Paris and most major French cities. The terminal has three cafés, a brasserie and a restaurant. The bureau de change is open Mon–Sat, 8.30–12 and 2–4.45; at other times up to 200Fr per passenger may be changed at the information counter. Airport information ☎ 56 34 84 84. Freight inquiries ☎ 56 34 00 26.
Nearby hotel *Novotel Bordeaux-Aéroport*, ave J.F. Kennedy, 33700

Mérignac ☎ 56 34 10 25 ☎ 540320
• AE DC MC V. Free 3min shuttle service (apply airport information counter). Le Grill is useful for casual business lunches.
City link The airport is 12km/7 miles west of the city centre. The most reliable way of getting into town is by taxi (15–20min). The bus timetable does not always coincide with flights.
Taxis are usually plentiful, but sometimes scarce at weekends. Reservations ☎ 56 97 11 27.
Car rental Avis, Europcar and Hertz have desks at the airport.

Railway station
Gare Saint-Jean There are 15 trains a day from Paris (journey time

about 4hr, longer at night). The station is not within walking distance of the city centre. There are usually taxis in front of the station. Buses 7 and 8 go to the centre. Passenger inquiries ☎ 56 92 50 50; reservations ☎ 56 92 76 56.

Getting around

The easiest and quickest way to get around Bordeaux's business district is on foot. Elsewhere, use a car, taxi or the efficient bus service.
Taxis Easily recognizable, but relatively expensive. Reservations ☎ 56 96 00 34 or 56 80 70 37.
Limousines *Ducourneau* ☎ 56 92 21 63.
Driving has become much easier as a result of the computerized traffic control system but great care is needed to choose the correct lane. Most of the centre has controlled parking and there are many underground garages. All the main car rental firms have city offices.
Walking is safe and the wide river Garonne makes orientation easy.

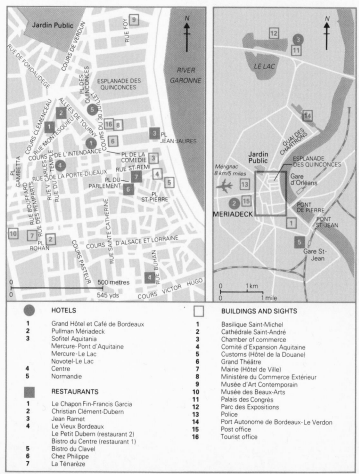

	HOTELS		BUILDINGS AND SIGHTS
1	Grand Hôtel et Café de Bordeaux	1	Basilique Saint-Michel
2	Pullman Mériadeck	2	Cathédrale Saint-André
3	Sofitel Aquitania	3	Chamber of commerce
	Mercure- Pont d'Aquitaine	4	Comité d'Expansion Aquitaine
	Mercure-Le Lac	5	Customs (Hôtel de la Douane)
	Novotel-Le Lac	6	Grand Théâtre
4	Centre	7	Mairie (Hôtel de Ville)
5	Normandie	8	Ministère du Commerce Extérieur
		9	Musée d'Art Contemporain
	RESTAURANTS	10	Musée des Beaux-Arts
		11	Palais des Congrès
1	Le Chapon Fin-Francis Garcia	12	Parc des Expositions
2	Christian Clément-Dubern	13	Police
3	Jean Ramet	14	Port Autonome de Bordeaux- Le Verdon
4	Le Vieux Bordeaux	15	Post office
	Le Petit Dubern (restaurant 2)	16	Tourist office
	Bistro du Centre (restaurant 1)		
5	Bistro du Clavel		
6	Chez Philippe		
7	La Ténarèze		

Area by area

The business district is contained within what is known as "the Triangle" (the area bordered by Cours Clemenceau, Cours de l'Intendance and Allées de Tourny). The major civic institutions are concentrated in Mériadeck, not far from the city hall (Mairie). Port activities are restricted to the Port Autonome de Bordeaux-Le Verdon, but the offices of the port authority and customs are centrally located. Vieux Bordeaux is in the southern-central part of town. Its mainly 18thC buildings are gradually being refurbished with civic help.

The suburbs The most desirable residential suburbs of Bordeaux are Caudéran and Le Bouscat to the west and northwest of the centre. Most high-tech industries are in the northern suburbs around Bordeaux-Lac or near Mérignac airport.

Hotels

Bordeaux's hotels are not really geared up to the needs of business travellers. None, for example, offers 24hr room service though the main ones have international direct dialling. But you can expect high culinary standards in hotel restaurants and, generally, friendly and efficient service. The best are the Pullman Mériadeck in the centre and the Sofitel Aquitania out at Bordeaux-Lac. During the biennial Vinexpo-Vinitech trade fair, next due in June 1989, rooms in Bordeaux are virtually impossible to find. Shuttles operate to hotels as far afield as Arcachon and Biarritz. As the French domestic airline, Air Inter, doubles its Paris flights during the fair, some executives simply fly down for the day. If you are attending an event at the Parc des Expositions or Palais des Congrès, you can ask Bordeaux-Congrès Services ☎ 56 50 84 49 to make your hotel reservation.

Grand Hôtel et Café de Bordeaux *F*//

2–5 pl de la Comédie ☎ *56 90 93 44* ⊤Ⓧ *541658 • AE DC MC V • 95 rooms, 3 suites, 1 restaurant, 1 bar*
The Grand Hôtel lies in the heart of Bordeaux's business district.
Bedrooms are well-appointed but on the small side. Those overlooking the busy Place de la Comédie are double-glazed; those at the back have air conditioning and offer extra comfort. The small brasserie is closed in the evening and at weekends. The bar is popular with local business people.
7 meeting rooms (capacity up to 80).

Pullman Mériadeck *F*//

5 rue Robert-Lateulade ☎ *56 90 92 37* ⊤Ⓧ *540565 • AE DC MC V • 194 rooms, 2 suites, 1 restaurant, 1 bar*
Within walking distance of the centre, the modern Pullman makes up for its rather bleak location in the Mériadeck district by offering the business visitor more than its rivals (special executive floor, secretarial services). The roomy Mériadeck restaurant is often used for business entertaining; the cocktail bar serves one or two dishes until 1am.
Bedrooms are well equipped; those at the back have the best outlook and some rooms have TV, minibar and hairdryer. 15 meeting rooms (capacity up to 130).

Sofitel Aquitania *F*//

33300 Bordeaux-Lac ☎ *56 50 83 80* ⊤Ⓧ *570557 • AE DC MC V • 212 rooms, 2 suites, 2 restaurants, 3 bars*
A modern hotel overlooking the lake, right between the exhibition centre and conference hall. There is a cocktail bar, Le Talbot, and late-night live jazz in Le Saint-Germain. Much business is done over lunch at the hotel's relatively inexpensive

restaurant, Le Flore. The Aquitania specializes in providing facilities for seminars, receptions and banquets (for up to 1,200 people). Newsstand • outdoor pool • 9 meeting rooms • (capacity up to 1,500).

OTHER HOTELS

Centre [F] *18 rue du Temple* ☎ *56 48 13 29 • AE DC MC V.* Very central, small, friendly and quiet hotel. Popular with business visitors on a small budget.

Normandie [F] *7 cours du 30-Juillet* ☎ *56 52 16 80* ⊤⊠ *570481 • AE DC MC V.* Reliable, large, old-fashioned hotel overlooking the Place des Quinconces.

Apart from the Sofitel Aquitania, Bordeaux-Lac has several hotels which cater specially for business visitors, including **Novotel-Le Lac** ☎ 56 50 99 70 **Mercure-Pont d'Aquitaine** ☎ 56 50 90 14 **Mercure-Le Lac** ☎ 56 50 90 30.

Out of town

La Réserve [F]/
74 ave du Bourgailh, 33600 Pessac ☎ *56 07 13 28* ⊤⊠ *560585 • AE DC MC V • closed mid-Nov–mid-Mar* There is great competition for the 19 rooms at this hotel among those who prefer rural surroundings (it is only a 12min drive from the centre). Excellent cuisine. Tennis court.

Restaurants

Fifteen years ago Bordeaux was one of the very few major French cities with a poor gastronomic reputation. Nowadays, however, there are many restaurants including those of top hotels where formal or casual business entertaining can be combined with gastronomy. All the establishments mentioned here offer fixed-price menus as well as *à la carte*. All but Le Vieux Bordeaux are in or near the business district.

Le Chapon Fin-Francis Garcia [F]///
5 rue Montesquiou ☎ *56 79 10 10 • closed Sun, Mon, 1 week each Jan and Easter, 3 weeks Jul • AE DC MC V* Already famous for its decor – a turn-of-the-century riot of papier-mâché – this restaurant was taken over in 1987 by the ebullient, talented Garcia: a move welcomed by business executives who no longer have to make a pilgrimage to the station to sample his superb cuisine, as he is now on their doorstep.

Christian Clément-Dubern [F]///
42 allées de Tourny ☎ *56 48 03 44 • closed Sat L, Sun • AE DC V* Ideal for important business occasions (though the service can be a little slow). The cuisine is *nouvelle*, with the emphasis on imaginative fish dishes, and the wine list naturally strong on Bordeaux. Tables are well spaced, and private dining rooms are available.

Jean Ramet [F]///
7 pl Jean-Jaurès ☎ *56 44 12 51 • closed Sat L, Sun, 1 week each Christmas and Easter, 2 weeks mid-Aug • V* This small, elegant restaurant offers some of the city's finest food, with imaginative interpretations of classical dishes. The wine list is unashamedly chauvinistic (*nothing* but the best Bordeaux).

Le Vieux Bordeaux [F]
27 rue Buhan ☎ *56 52 94 36 • closed Sat L, Sun, Aug, 1 week mid-Feb • AE DC MC V.* Michel Bordage's restaurant has built up a faithful clientele appreciative of his original, frequently changing menu and impeccable service. Ideal for secluded business lunches and less formal evening occasions.

Good but casual

You can be sure of above-average simple food at two offshoots of restaurants described above: *Le Petit Dubern*, 42 allées de Tourny ☎ 56 48 03 44, and Francis Garcia's *Bistro du Centre*, 5 rue Montesquiou ☎ 56 51 28 81. Garcia's sister has turned his former restaurant near the station into the attractive *Bistro du Clavel*, 44 rue Charles-Domercq ☎ 56 92 91 52.

In the central Place du Parlement are *Chez Philippe* ☎ 56 81 83 15, regarded by many as the city's best fish restaurant, and the much less pricey *La Ténarèze* ☎ 56 44 43 29, which serves Gascon fare.

Entertainment

Lists of main events can be found in the local daily, *Sud-Ouest*, in the weekly *Le Courrier Français*, or from the Office de Tourisme (which also provides a 24hr telephone listing in English of certain events ☎ 56 48 04 61).

Theatre, opera, music Plays and operas are regularly staged at the imposing *Grand Théâtre*, pl de la Comédie ☎ 56 90 91 60, as are many of the events of Bordeaux's music festival, the Mai Musical. In November a festival of avant-garde theatre, music and film, SIGMA, is held in the multipurpose cultural centre, *Entrepôt Lainé* ☎ 56 44 60 27.

Shopping

Most of the best shops are in the roads leading off Place Gambetta, and in Allées de Tourny. The Mériadeck shopping centre also contains a wide variety of stores. There are several interesting markets in Place St-Pierre on different weekdays. Antiques can be found in Rue Bouffard and Rue des Remparts near Place Gambetta, or at the flea market by the Basilique Saint-Michel. *Au Printemps*, pl Gambetta, and *Galeries Lafayette*, 11–19 rue Ste-Catherine, are the main department stores.

Food and wine Several good food shops cluster around the covered market in Place des Grands-Hommes. Excellent chocolates are made by *Saunion*, 56 cours Clemenceau. Wines (free tasting) and wine accessories are available from *Maison du Vin*, 1 cours du 30-Juillet, or from *Hôtel des Vins*, 106 rue de l'Abbé-de-l'Epée.

Sightseeing

Bordeaux is rightly proud of its Cathédrale Saint-André, Grand Théâtre, Basilique Saint-Michel, Place de la Bourse and its handsome old buildings in the Vieux Bordeaux district.

Musée d'Art Contemporain Special exhibitions of modern painting and sculpture. *Entrepôt Lainé, rue Foy. Open Tue 11–10, Wed–Sun 11–7.*

Musée des Beaux-Arts A fine permanent collection of classical and modern art. *20 cours d'Albret. Open Wed–Mon, 10–12, 2–6.*

Out of town

Arcachon, Bordeaux's own seaside resort, is a 40min drive away, and there are many good beaches elsewhere along the Côte d'Argent. Guided tours of prestigious wine châteaux (May–Oct) are organized by *Loisir Accueil Gironde*, 21 cours de l'Intendance ☎ 56 52 61 40.

Spectator sports

Soccer The local team, Les Girondins, have an immense following. Home games are played at the *Stade Municipal* ☎ 56 93 25 83.

Keeping fit

Fitness centres There are no fitness centres in hotels, but visitors can use the *Gymnase des Quinconces*, 5 rue Blanc-Dutrouilh ☎ 56 81 90 61.

Golf There is an 18-hole course at *Bordeaux-Lac* ☎ 56 50 92 72.

Tennis Courts are available by the hour at *Mériadeck* (covered) ☎ 56 93 05 85 and *Le Lac* ☎ 56 50 92 40.

Local resources

Business services

The major hotels can supply or arrange for most services you are likely to need. *Burocarte* ☎ 56 93 05 06 provides photocopying, fax, secretarial services and temporary office accommodation.
Translation *Cabinet Gallagher* ☎ 56 97 93 25.

Communications

Local delivery *DEB Courses* ☎ 56 39 70 69.
Post office Main office: rue Georges-Bonnac, open 8–7.
Telex and fax *Télex Publique* ☎ 56 81 18 12 ⊠ 540127, open 8.30–6.

Conference/exhibition centres

The Bordeaux-Lac exhibition and conference facilities are next to the A10 autoroute, a 10min drive from the city centre or, by expressway, from Mérignac airport. Bus 31 runs regularly from Place des Quinconces in the city centre. During major trade fairs and conventions, special shuttle services connect with the centre and the airport.

The huge *Parc des Expositions* has 15 or so trade fairs and 2 public exhibitions a year which draw some 800,000 visitors. There is also a 17-ha/42-acre outdoor exhibition area, plus a restaurant, meeting rooms, banks and a post office.

The *Palais des Congrès* accommodates some 70 events each year, attracting 25,000 visitors. Its three auditoria can seat a total of 1,600. Extension work to double the capacity is expected to begin in 1988.

For information contact the *Comité des Expositions de Bordeaux* ☎ 56 39 55 55 (trade fairs), or *Bordeaux-Congrès* ☎ 56 50 84 49 (conventions).

Emergencies

Bureaux de change Most hotels will change currency, but give poor rates. *Thomas Cook*, Gare St-Jean, opens daily, 8–7.
Hospitals 24hr emergency medical and dental treatment: *Hôpital Pellegrin*, pl Raba-Léon ☎ 56 96 83 83.
Pharmacies Pharmacies stay open late in turn. For information ☎ 56 90 92 75 ext. 1501.
Police Main station: *Commissariat Central*, 87 rue de l'Abbé-de-l'Epée ☎ 56 90 92 75.

Government offices

Mairie (city hall), Palais Rohan ☎ 56 90 91 60. *Douanes* (customs), quai de la Douane ☎ 56 44 47 10. *Port Autonome de Bordeaux* (head office), pl Gabriel ☎ 56 90 58 00. The regional office of the *Ministère du Commerce Extérieur* (foreign trade ministry) is at 9 rue Condé ☎ 56 48 27 25.

Information sources

Business information The helpful Bordeaux *Chambre de Commerce*, 12 pl de la Bourse ☎ 56 90 91 28 is very knowledgeable about local business. Further information can be obtained from the *Comité d'Expansion Aquitaine*, 2 pl de la Bourse ☎ 56 52 65 47.
Local media The daily newspaper *Sud-Ouest* gives good local business coverage.
Tourist information *Office de Tourisme de Bordeaux*, 12 cours du 30-Juillet ☎ 56 44 28 41 is open daily, 9–6.30 (7.30 in summer). It also provides an accommodation reservation service.

Thank-yous

Chocolates *Saunion* ☎ 56 48 05 75 (see *Shopping*).
Florist *Marc Postulka* ☎ 56 44 00 31 takes telephone orders by credit card.

CANNES
Zip code 06400

Cannes is a town of only 72,000 people, but the size and splendour of its tourist industry make it seem much bigger. Set around a lovely bay, it has leisure and business tourism as the basis of its economy. However, since World War II it has dynamically developed its convention and festival trade. The focal point is the Palais des Festivals, opened in 1982, France's largest convention centre outside Paris. This hosts many big annual events, notably the Film Festival in May which today is less a cultural event than a brash commercial fair. The only industry is an Aérospatiale high-tech satellite plant and a few small boatbuilding firms.

Sophia Antipolis, the largest and fastest-growing "technology park" in France, is on a rural site about 11km/7 miles inland. After a slow and difficult start, this "silicon valley" has now attracted a large number of French and foreign investors, notably Digital Equipment with a big research and production centre; Dow Corning with a management centre; research laboratories of Rohm & Haas, Searle and Toyota; a production unit of Wellcome; and the central reservation centre of Air France. There are new hotels and banks, and a much wider range of modern business services than in Cannes itself which, it could almost be said, is now a dormitory for the business visitor to Sophia-Antipolis.

Arriving
The autoroute A8 goes within 4km/2 miles of Cannes, linking it with Nice, Marseille and other cities. Cannes is on the TGV express train route and shares a big international airport with Nice.

Airports
The Nice-Côte-d'Azur Airport (for details see *Nice*) is 25km/16 miles away. There is a minibus shuttle every 15min from Place Mérimée ☎ 93 21 30 83; travel time about 30min. Taxis do the journey a little quicker. At Mandelieu, 8km/5 miles west of Cannes, there is a small airport for private business flights: its *Service 2A* offers such facilities as photocopying, telex and furnished offices for rent. All airport inquiries ☎ 93 47 11 00.

Railway station
The very central main station is linked to Paris by the same three daily TGV express trains as Nice, doing the journey in 6–7hr. There are frequent fast trains along the coast in summer, east to Nice and Monaco, west to Marseille. The station has a taxi rank and a tourist office. Passenger inquiries and reservations ☎ 93 99 50 50.

Getting around
Visitors staying at the major hotels on Boulevard de la Croisette often find little need for transport as the new Palais des Festivals and the main shopping area are within easy walking distance.

Taxis These can be hailed in the street or found at one of the 12 ranks ☎ 93 38 09 76.

Driving Traffic in central areas is very heavy in summer and at festival times: coming to or from the autoroute, it is best to avoid the main Boulevard Carnot and take side roads. Large new undergound parking areas include one below the Palais des Festivals. All major car rental firms have offices in the city: *Avis* ☎ 93 94 14 86, *Budget* ☎ 93 43 48 87, *Europcar* ☎ 93 39 75 20, *Hertz* ☎ 93 99 04 20.

Walking A delight along the sea

front, and in the old part of the town; no security risks.

Bus There is a network, centring on Place de l'Hôtel de Ville and going out into the suburbs. Bus information ☎ 93 39 54 40.

Area by area

As in any resort, life gravitates towards the seafront, now dominated by the Palais des Festivals. East from the Palais runs Europe's most glamorous promenade, the palm-shaded Boulevard de la Croisette, backed by a succession of majestic hotels, luxury boutiques and crowded terrace-cafés. Inland are other hotels and, farther back, parallel to the front, Rue d'Antibes, the town's main shopping artery. West of the Palais is the old part of Cannes: the former fishing port, now a smart yachting marina, and the hill of Le Suquet crowned by an 11thC tower.

In the narrow alleys, here and around the colourful Forville market, many elderly people still live in poverty.

At the other end of the promenade stands the stately Palm Beach Casino on its promontory, Pointe de la Croisette: an area full of luxury flats and villas. This elite sector extends up the wooded slopes to the north, past the well-named Californie to Super-Cannes and Le Pézou. Le Cannet, a separate commune north of the town centre, is mainly petit-bourgeois, while such working class as Cannes possesses is over to the west, at Rocheville and around La Bocca, a centre of light industry.

The surrounding area

Cannes lies at the heart of the most intensely varied part of the Côte d'Azur, now savagely overbuilt but still fascinating. To the east is the noisy and rather downmarket resort

HOTELS

1. Carlton
2. Majestic
3. Martinez
4. Novotel Montfleury
5. Madone
6. Sofitel Méditerranée
7. Splendid
8. Univers

RESTAURANTS

1. Gaston Gastounette
2. Mère Besson
   Palme d'Or (hotel 3)
3. Royal Gray
   La Côte (hotel 1)
4. La Mirabelle
5. La Brouette de Grand-Mère
6. Blue Bar
7. Le Festival
8. Le Ragtime
9. Le Refuge
10. Au Bec Fin

BUILDINGS AND SIGHTS

1. Chamber of commerce
2. Forest Hill Montfleury
3. Hôtel de Ville
4. Musée de la Castre
5. Palais des Festivals
6. Palm Beach Casino
7. Police
8. Post office
9. Tourist office

of Juan-les-Pins, a sharp contrast to the serenity of beautiful pine-forested Cap d'Antibes with its luxurious villas, or to the ancient seaport of Antibes with its castle and Picasso museum. Many well-known hill villages are just inland: Biot and Valbonne; Vallauris, where Picasso lived and worked; and delightful Mougins, where many Cannes executives have their homes. To the west is the smart boating resort of La Napoule and the rugged red-rock coast of the Esterel. Offshore are the two Lérins islands.

Hotels

Of the enormous range of good hotels, the bigger ones are geared largely to the business-plus-holiday convention trade: most are on or near the front, and most have pools. Prices soar by up to 50% between April and September. The main hotels below will exchange currency.

Carlton $[F]////$
58 bd de la Croisette ☎ *93 68 91 68*
Ⓣ*470720* • *Inter-Continental* • *AE DC MC V* • *325 rooms, 30 suites, 3 restaurants, 2 bars*
Built in 1912 in *belle époque* style, the Carlton is the grandest, most famous and still undeniably the best of La Croisette's great white wedding-cake palaces. Despite all the marble and luxury, the hotel has a relaxed atmosphere, helped along by a clientele that is very sophisticated but informal: the Film Festival's top stars stay here often. Comfortable bedrooms are in light, pretty colours, and many have balconies with superb sea views. 24hr room service, travel agency, hairdresser, jewellery shop • private beach • fax, 9 meeting rooms (capacity up to 140).

Majestic $[F]////$
14 bd de la Croisette ☎ *93 68 91 00*
Ⓣ*470787* • *AE DC MC V* •
248 rooms, 12 suites, 3 restaurants, 2 bars
Of the big luxury hotels this is the closest to the Palais des Festivals; it

also has much the best swimming-pool, in an idyllic palm grove where buffet lunches are served in summer. The hotel's decor is a bit old-fashioned and the service not always perfect, but the spacious rooms are superbly equipped, the best having balconies facing the sea. 24hr room service, travel desk, hairdresser, jewellery and fashion shops • private beach • fax, 4 meeting rooms (capacity up to 350).

Martinez $[F]////$
73 bd de la Croisette ☎ *93 68 91 91*
Ⓣ *470708* • *Concorde* • *AE DC MC V* • *411 rooms, 15 suites, 2 restaurants, 1 bar*
Built in 1929, the luxurious Martinez was bought by Concorde in 1982, since when the group has done a lot of renovation. The public rooms and the spacious, well-equipped bedrooms, some of which have sea-facing balconies, have been restored to their original Art Deco style. Service is attentive and courteous. Its Palm d'Or restaurant is first-class (see *Restaurants*), and meals are also served under the palms by the pool in the front garden. 24hr room service, hairdresser, jewellery and clothes shops • 7 tennis courts, private beach • fax, 8 meeting rooms (capacity up to 800).

Novotel Montfleury $[F]////$
25 ave Beauséjour ☎ *93 68 91 50*
Ⓣ *470039* • *AE DC MC V* • *181 rooms, 2 restaurants, 2 bars*
Less central but also less pricey than La Croisette's palaces, this recent Novotel acquisition is up on a hill in its own big gardens. It is breezily modern, with a relaxed atmosphere, and is popular with convention groups who enjoy the leisure amenities. Rooms, most with balconies, are spacious and well-appointed. Hairdresser • heated outdoor pool, physiotherapy centre, billiards, reduced rates at adjacent Forest Hill Montfleury sports club • 6 meeting rooms (capacity up to 400).

OTHER HOTELS

Madone *F* *5 ave Justinia*
☎ *93 43 57 87* • *AE DC MC V*. Only a
5min walk from La Croisette but in a
different world: a small but very
comfortable family hotel in a quiet
street, with a pretty garden full of
palms and mimosa. Some rooms have
kitchenettes. Outdoor pool.

Sofitel Méditerranée *F//* *2 bd
Jean-Hibert* ☎ *93 99 22 75* ⊤ₓ *470728*
• *AE DC MC V*. A large, lively and
comfortable modern hotel by the
port, with a heated rooftop pool and
good facilities; many rooms have
balconies with sea views.

Splendid *F//* *4 rue Félix-Faure*
☎ *93 99 53 11* ⊤ₓ *470990* • *AE DC MC
V*. Centrally located near the Palais
des Festivals, but rooms are
soundproofed; attentive service.

Univers *F//* *2 rue Maréchal-Foch*
☎ *93 39 59 19* ⊤ₓ *470972* • *AE DC MC
V*. A modernized, central hotel with a
pleasant roof-terrace.

Restaurants

Cannes has a predictably wide range
of good restaurants, two of them
serving top-flight cuisine. In high
season, reservations are advisable.

Gaston Gastounette *F//*
7 quai St-Pierre ☎ *93 39 47 92*
• *closed 3 weeks Jan* • *AE DC MC V*
Fresh fish, efficient service, and an
airy open terrace are the attractions
of this comfortable and lively place
by the port. Suitable for a working
lunch, or for a convivial evening,
when musicians play. Good value
fixed-price menu.

La Mère Besson *F//*
13 rue des Frères-Pradignac
☎ *93 39 59 24* • *closed Sun L in Jul,
Aug* • *AE MC V*
With a high reputation locally, this
staunch citadel of true Provençal
cuisine sticks to classic dishes – *aïoli,
cuisses de grenouilles* and so on – and
does them well. It is a serious, rather
formal place with demure waitresses;
being in a side street, its outdoor
terrace is quiet.

Palme d'Or *F////*
73 bd de la Croisette ☎ *92 98 30 18*
• *closed Feb, mid-Nov–late Dec* • *AE
DC MC V* • *jacket and tie*
The inventive modern cooking of
chef Christian Willer at this
luxurious first-floor restaurant of the
Martinez is considered a close
runner-up to the Royal Gray in the
view of most gastronomes. A
glamorous venue for high-level
entertaining, its wide front dining-
terrace, facing the sea, is open to the
stars. Good value fixed-price menus
available. The somewhat cheaper
Orangerie, downstairs by the pool, is
ideal for a working lunch.

Royal Gray *F/////*
rue des Serbes ☎ *93 68 54 54* • *closed
Mon, Sun (exc D Jul, Aug), Feb 1–
Mar 5* • *AE DC MC V* • *jacket preferred*
The somewhat flashy Hôtel Gray
d'Albion has recruited a chef,
Jacques Chibois, who by common
acclaim is the most brilliant in town.
His light and varied dishes can be
enjoyed in spacious comfort, either in
the ornate dining room or out on the
palm-shaded terrace which lacks a sea
view but is otherwise pretty. The
middle-priced set menu at lunch is
very good value.

OTHER RESTAURANTS

Also very suitable for a business meal
are the elegant *La Côte* in the Carlton
hotel and *La Mirabelle*, 24 rue St-
Antoine ☎ 93 38 72 75, both
expensive. Somewhat cheaper, *La
Brouette de Grand-Mère*, 9 rue
d'Oran ☎ 93 39 12 10, is a lively and
charming place for dinner. Three
middle-price terrace restaurants
along the Boulevard de la Croisette
are fashionably crowded with people
who come to see and be seen: *Blue
Bar* ☎ 93 39 03 04, *Le Festival*
☎ 93 38 04 81, and *Le Ragtime*
☎ 93 68 47 10, which has loud live
music. *Le Refuge*, 13 quai St-Pierre
☎ 93 39 34 54, is one of the best of
the touristy but inexpensive fish
restaurants around the port, while for
really good local dishes at low prices

you should not miss the ever-animated *Au Bec Fin*, 12 rue du 24-Août ☎ 93 38 35 86.

Out of town
There are many fine hotels and eating places around Cannes. Their doyen is the exclusive *Hotel du Cap* and *Restaurant Eden Roc* ☎ 93 61 39 01 at Cap d'Antibes where Scott Fitzgerald used to stay. In a medium price range, the *Mas Candille* ☎ 93 90 00 85 at Mougins is a converted 17thC farmhouse on a hillside. Mougins also contains one of France's finest restaurants, Roger Vergé's *Le Moulin* ☎ 93 75 78 24; another is Louis Outhier's *L'Oasis* at La Napoule ☎ 93 49 95 52. (See also *Nice*.)

Bars
The elegant bar of the *Carlton* remains the town's smartest social rendezvous. Other big hotels also have terraces suitable for a business drink, notably the *Martinez* and *Majestic*. Jet-setters make for *Blue Bar* and *Le Festival*.

Entertainment
Theatre, music Cultural listings appear in the weekly *7 jours 7 nuits*. The *Palais des Festivals* ☎ 93 39 01 01 is used for some visiting drama productions (no resident company) and for winter concerts by the local Orchestre Provence-Côte-d'Azur. Summer concerts are given at *Le Suquet* and on the Iles des Lérins.
Cinema Despite its Film Festival, Cannes has no "art" cinema! But there are festivals of all kinds during the year.
Nightclubs and casinos There is plenty of nightlife. Best of the town's many discos are *Le Galaxy*, in the Palais des Festivals ☎ 93 68 00 07, and the youthful and trendy *Whisky à Gogo*, 115 ave des Lérins ☎ 93 43 20 63. You can dine and

dance more calmly at *Jane's* in the Hôtel Gray d'Albion ☎ 93 99 04 94. In summer, by far the most attractive nightspot in the area is the huge and very stylish *La Siesta* ☎ 93 33 31 31, on the coast north of Antibes, where you can dine and dance outdoors among waterfalls and flaming torches; it also has a casino. The smart and imposing *Palm Beach*, bd de la Croisette ☎ 94 43 91 12, is the summer casino, replaced in Nov–May by the *Palais des Festivals*. The *Casino des Fleurs* ☎ 93 68 00 33 is open all year.

Shopping
There are very smart boutiques along Boulevard de la Croisette and in the Hôtel Gray d'Albion; bigger stores are in Rue d'Antibes. Rue Meynadier has traditional shops for local products: *Ceneri* is one of France's finest cheese stores. Nearby is the colourful *Forville* market (open Tue–Sun, am only).

Sightseeing
The only worthwhile museum is *La Castre* (closed Tue and Nov), on Le Suquet hill, devoted to antiquities and ethnography. The *Observatoire* at Super-Cannes offers stunning views of the coast.

Spectator sports
Soccer The city's first-division football team plays at the *Stade Pierre de Courbertin* ☎ 93 47 03 55.
Pelota This Basque ball game is played at the *Fronton Municipal*, 175 rte d'Antibes, Mougins ☎ 93 43 66 99.

Keeping fit
Fitness centres are not a feature of the big hotels; among the many private ones, try *Top-fit Fitness*, Les Terriers ☎ 93 74 44 44.
Golf There are several renowned golf clubs in the area, notably the smart and exclusive *Country Club de Cannes-Mougins*, rte de Golfe, Mandelieu ☎ 93 75 79 13, and *Cannes-Mandelieu*, Domaine de la

Paoute ☎ 93 49 55 39.
Riding The best centre is *Club d'Eperon*, Plan de Grasse ☎ 93 70 55 41.
Sailing and board sailing *Centre Nautique Municipal*, 2 quai St-Pierre ☎ 93 38 21 16; *Club Nautique de la Croisette*, Plage Jardin Pierre-Longue, bd de la Croisette ☎ 93 43 09 40.
Swimming The beach at Cannes is long and sandy. Most of the beach at *La Croisette* is divided into over 20 paying beaches with neat rows of parasols and mattresses; best and most fashionable are those run by the big hotels but open to all. There are public beaches west of *Le Suquet*. The *Palm Beach* ☎ 93 43 91 12 has a fine large swimming pool.
Tennis Courts can be rented at *Cannes Tennis Club*, Martinez hotel, 11 rue Lacour ☎ 93 43 58 85, and at the big *Forest Hill Montfleury*, 19 ave Beauséjour ☎ 93 38 75 78, which also has a swimming pool.

Local resources
Business services
Some of the big hotels have offices to rent and will supply secretarial help, while the *Palais des Festivals* can offer advice on where to find these facilities. The *Accès Network* in Antibes ☎ 93 34 33 72 is an Anglo-American venture that helps foreign companies and business visitors.
Photocopying *Bureaux Copies* ☎ 93 39 19 49; *Palais des Festivals*.
Secretarial *Bis* ☎ 93 39 00 36, *Manpower* ☎ 93 39 70 82.
Translation *R-M Matordes* ☎ 93 43 57 26, *Jenny Abitbol* ☎ 93 38 94 57.

Communications
Local delivery *Exocet* ☎ 93 69 41 00.
Long-distance delivery *DHL* ☎ 05 20 25 25, *PTT* ☎ 93 39 13 16.
Post office Main office: rue Bivouac Napoléon ☎ 93 39 14 11.
Telex and fax At the main post office, and Palais des Festivals.

Conference/exhibition centres
Much of the town's business life revolves around the huge new *Palais des Festivals*, 1 bd de la Croisette ☎ 93 39 01 01, ☎ 470749 fax 93 99 37 34. This is the largest French convention centre outside Paris and is superbly equipped: a main auditorium seating 2,400, with Dolby stereo sound and simultaneous translation in seven languages; 14 other halls seating from 40 to 1,000; a salon that can take up to 3,000 for cocktails, 1,200 for a banquet; a telecommunications room; and 14,000 sq metres of exhibition space. The *Palais Croisette*, esplanade Georges-Pompidou ☎ 93 39 01 01, also has conference facilities.

Emergencies
Bureaux de change *Change Office*, 12 quai St-Pierre, open daily 9.30–7.30; *American Express*, 8 rue des Belges, 9–7, closed Sat pm, Sun.
Hospitals Main hospital: *Pierre Nouveau*, ave des Broussailles ☎ 93 69 91 33. *Anglo-American Hospital*, Sunny Bank, 133 ave Petit Juas ☎ 93 68 26 96. Emergencies: ☎ 93 99 55 55 or 93 38 39 38 or 93 99 12 12. Dental emergencies ☎ 93 39 10 78.
Pharmacies These open at night on a rota basis; see press or ask police.
Police Main station: 15 ave de Grasse ☎ 93 39 10 78.

Government offices
Hôtel de Ville, pl de l'Hôtel de Ville ☎ 93 68 91 92. *Préfecture*: see *Nice*.

Information sources
Business information The *Chambre de Commerce*, always helpful, is at Allée de la Liberté ☎ 93 99 08 28.
Local media See *Nice*.
Tourist information *Office du Tourisme*, Palais des Festivals ☎ 93 39 24 53; branch office at main station ☎ 93 99 19 77.

Thank-yous
Florist *Primavera Fleurs*, 54 rue d'Antibes ☎ 93 39 01 15.

GRENOBLE
Zip code 38000

Grenoble, encircled by snowy peaks and the craggy summits of the Vercors and Chartreuse, is Europe's only big industrial town *within* the Alpine massif. Long known for its dynamism, Grenoble was the fastest-growing French city in the postwar boom years. Although the growth has now levelled off, it is still the main French pace-setter in high-tech research and production along with Toulouse.

In the 1860s hydro-electricity was invented nearby and industry moved in. It is now highly diversified. The older firms are based on mechanics and electro-engineering, notably Neyrpic (turbines and hydraulics), Merlin-Gerin (electro-metallurgy), and more recently Caterpillar (tractors). But since the 1960s the emphasis has switched to nuclear physics, electronics and computers. The government chose Grenoble for its principal nuclear research centre; other major state research bodies followed, in telecommunications and data processing; and now Synchroton, the big new Anglo-German particle accelerator complex, is being built.

Private manufacturing firms have also moved to Grenoble, including Hewlett-Packard (computers) and Becton, Dickinson (paramedical). There are no fewer than 46 foreign-owned companies in Grenoble, and the ancient university, with 35,000 students, has a high proportion of foreigners. In fact, newcomers from Paris and elsewhere account for 80% of the city's population and provide virtually all of its industrial elite. The local business style is thus far from provincial. Although other towns are catching up with its progress, Grenoble remains one of the most impressive French cities outside Paris.

Arriving
Grenoble has good links with Lyon and Geneva by autoroute, but the roads to the south are much slower. Rail links too are better to the north.

Grenoble Saint-Geoirs airport
The airport is 40km/25 miles away to the northwest. It has regular daily flights to and from Paris and Nice. From other cities flights arrive at the big airport at Satolas (see *Lyon*) which is only 30km/19 miles farther by autoroute. Geneva airport is 2hr away by car.

Grenoble's airport has limited facilities: a snack bar, information desk and meeting room (capacity 20) with telex and fax. All inquiries ☎ 76 65 48 48.

City link A bus shuttle from the station connects with all flights, taking 40min. Taxis take a little less.

There is a rank at the airport ☎ 76 54 42 54, and major car rental firms have desks.

Railway station
The centrally located station has five TGV express trains a day to Lyon and Paris. The journey to Paris takes about 3hr, marginally faster than by air. There are also good services to Geneva and Marseille. The station has a bureau de change and taxi rank. Passenger inquiries ☎ 76 47 50 50; reservations ☎ 76 47 54 27.

Getting around
The compact nucleus of the old town can be tackled on foot, but transport is needed to reach other parts.

Taxis These are easy to spot and plentiful ☎ 76 54 42 54, or go to one of several ranks. In the suburbs ☎ 76 54 17 18.

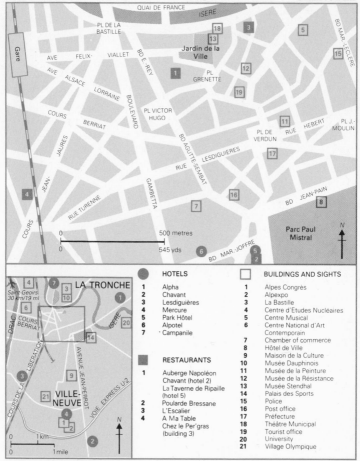

	HOTELS		BUILDINGS AND SIGHTS
1	Alpha	1	Alpes Congrès
2	Chavant	2	Alpexpo
3	Lesdiguières	3	La Bastille
4	Mercure	4	Centre d'Etudes Nucléaires
5	Park Hôtel	5	Centre Musical
6	Alpotel	6	Centre National d'Art
7	Campanile		Contemporain
		7	Chamber of commerce
		8	Hôtel de Ville
	RESTAURANTS	9	Maison de la Culture
		10	Musée Dauphinois
1	Auberge Napoléon	11	Musée de la Peinture
	Chavant (hotel 2)	12	Musée de la Résistance
	La Taverne de Ripaille	13	Musée Stendhal
	(hotel 5)	14	Palais des Sports
2	Poularde Bressane	15	Police
3	L'Escalier	16	Post office
4	A Ma Table	17	Préfecture
	Chez le Per'gras	18	Théâtre Municipal
	(building 3)	19	Tourist office
		20	University
		21	Village Olympique

Driving Driving in the city centre is not easy, but elsewhere there are few problems. There is plenty of garage parking in the centre. All major car rental firms have offices in town.

Walking Pleasurable and safe in the pedestrian centre, but tedious elsewhere because of the distances.

Bus and tram There is an efficient bus service, but it runs less frequently after 9pm. Pale blue trams, frequent, fast and silent, link 21 stations, from Langevin and Fontaine in the west, via the centre, to Alpes Congrès in the south.

Area by area

The compact historic centre beside the river Isère has been neatly restored and mostly closed to traffic. The focal point is Place Grenette with its boutiques and open-air cafés.

Just across the river, the narrow Rue St-Laurent is a lively Italian quarter, at the foot of the ruined fortress of La Bastille. To the south of the old centre, a grid of dull 19thC streets is now the main commercial and administrative area.

Farther south, the monumental Maison de la Culture stands close to

the controversial high-rise blocks of
La Villeneuve. Beyond, encircled by
hypermarkets and big new factories
such as Hewlett-Packard, stands the
major convention and conference
centre of Alpes Congrès and Alpexpo.

The smartest housing is up the
valley to the northeast, at La
Tronche, Meylan and Saint-Ismier.

Nearby, east of the city, is the vast
new university campus of Saint-
Martin-d'Hères.

Much of the city's modern
industry is south of town, at
Echirolles and Eybens, or to the
northwest, up the Isère valley
towards Saint-Egrève.

Hotels

The supply of first-rate modern hotels in Grenoble has not yet caught
up with the city's industrial and economic expansion. Of the few really
good ones, only one is close to the centre: others are farther out, but
within easy reach of the main business areas. IDD telephones and
currency exchange are generally available.

Alpha *F*|
34 ave de Verdun, 38240 Meylan
☎ *76 90 63 09* TX *980444* • *Mapotel*
• *AE DC MC V* • *60 rooms, 1 restaurant,*
1 bar
A light and modern hotel just outside
the town, but easily accessible. The
spacious rooms have balconies with
splendid views, and some have
kitchenettes. There is a pleasant
restaurant and a piano-bar. Pool • 6
meeting rooms (capacity up to 200).

Chavant *F*|||
Bresson, 38320 Eybens ☎ *76 25 15 14*
• *AE MC V* • *7 rooms, 1 restaurant,*
1 bar
Secluded, yet only 10min by car from
Alpes Congrès. It is chiefly a famous
luxury restaurant (see *Restaurants*),
but the bedrooms are all comfortable
and elegantly furnished. Warm
family atmosphere and personal
service. 1 meeting room (capacity up
to 20).

Lesdiguières *F*|
122 cours de la Libération
☎ *76 96 55 36* TX *320306* • *AE DC MC*
V • *36 rooms, 1 restaurant, 1 bar*
This big handsome villa is one of
Grenoble's most agreeable hotels. It
is used as a training centre for
catering students, hence its low
prices. The big stylish bar and the
bright attractive restaurant are both
suitable as business venues.

Mercure *F*|
1 ave d'Innsbruck ☎ *76 09 54 27*
TX *980470* • *AE DC MC V* • *98 rooms,*
1 restaurant, 1 bar
This modern chain hotel may be
somewhat impersonal but service
is efficient and many bedroom
balconies have mountain views. The
restaurant is suitable for modest
business entertaining. Outdoor pool
• 5 meeting rooms (capacity up to
250).

Park Hôtel *F*||||
10 pl Paul-Mistral ☎ *76 87 29 11*
TX *320767* • *AE DC MC V* • *56 rooms,*
3 suites, 1 restaurant, 1 bar
The best hotel for business purposes:
some bedrooms convert into daytime
offices and many are supplied with
Minitels; typewriters available.
Service is deft and the restaurant is
useful for business entertaining (see
Restaurants). 3 meeting rooms
(capacity up to 60).

OTHER HOTELS
Alpotel *F*| *12 bd Maréchal-
Joffre* ☎ *76 87 88 41* TX *320884* • *AE
DC MC V*. Central and efficient with
good conference facilities (rooms for
up to 300).
Campanile *F* *ave de l'Ile Brune,
38120 St-Egrève* ☎ *76 75 57 88*
TX *980424* • *Concorde* • *V*. Just
outside town, a comfortable and
friendly modern hotel.

Restaurants

The choice is thinner than one might expect. Some of the finest restaurants, very popular for business meals, are rural *auberges* just outside town but close to the new industrial and scientific areas. Reservations are advisable.

Auberge Napoléon [F]//

7 rue Montorge ☎ *76 87 53 64 • closed Sat, Sun • AE DC MC V*
This auberge in the old town has recently been converted into an elegant restaurant. The cooking is careful and ambitious and the wines are very well chosen.

Chavant [F]///

Bresson ☎ *76 25 15 14 • closed Sat L, Wed, Dec 25–31 • AE MC V*
This enchanting auberge is in a village just outside town but quickly reached (see *Hotels*), and is the best place for top-level business entertaining. Emile Chavant, a former pupil of Escoffier, provides classic dishes while his sister Danielle is the charming maîtresse d'hôtel. In winter meals are served in a panelled room before a log fire, and in summer out under the chestnut trees. The set menu is excellent value and there is a splendid range of old armagnacs.

La Taverne de Ripaille [F]/

10 pl Paul-Mistral ☎ *76 87 29 11 • closed Sun L, 3 weeks Aug, Dec 24– Jan 3 • AE DC MC V*
The small restaurant of the Park Hôtel is pleasantly intimate and a sound choice for business entertaining, though the food is not remarkable.

Other good restaurants

The *Poularde Bressane*, 12 pl Paul-Mistral ☎ 76 87 08 90, is comfortable if rather formal, with good classical cooking. *L'Escalier*, 6 pl de Lavalette ☎ 76 54 66 16, offers Guérard-inspired *nouvelle cuisine*. More traditional is *A Ma Table*, 92 cours Jean-Jaurès ☎ 76 96 77 04, a little bistro whose friendly warmth and high-quality cooking make it ideal

for a more casual dinner. And up on the summit of La Bastille, *Chez le Per'gras* ☎ 76 42 09 47 (closed Nov–Mar) is a fine place to eat while enjoying the dramatic view.

Out of town

At Montbonnot, a village 8km/5 miles out on the N90 to Chambéry, *Les Mésanges* ☎ 76 90 21 57 is a handsome auberge where business people enjoy Georges Achini's excellent food. A little farther north, at Le Sappey up in the Chartreuse hills, the even more popular *Le Pudding* ☎ 76 88 80 26 is named after its splendid array of homemade desserts. The set menus offer superb value and at weekends reservations are essential.

Bars and cafés

The best hotel bars for a business drink are those of the Park and the Mercure. Of the cafés that line Place Grenette, the smartest is the *Cintra*, popular with the young professionals. The bars and cafés around Place St-André tend to be student haunts, the *Tribunal* being very trendy. A pleasant place for a quiet drink at any hour is *Le Pub Cambridge*, pl Victor-Hugo.

Entertainment

The main focus of Grenoble's cultural life is the huge *Maison de la Culture* ("*Le Cargo*"), rue Paul-Claudel ☎ 76 25 05 45, which stages homegrown as well as imported productions. The daily *Dauphiné Libéré* lists other offerings.
Theatre, dance Jean-Claude Gallotta's Groupe Emile Dubois, one of France's leading modern ballet companies, has its base at the *Maison de la Culture*, which also stages plays by the resident Centre Dramatique

National des Alpes. Lighter comedies come on tour to the *Théâtre Municipal*, rue Hector-Berlioz ☎ 76 54 03 08. Small local troupes include *Théâtre-Action* and the *Serge Papagalli* café-theatre.

Cinema Several "art" houses show foreign films with subtitles, notably *Le Méliès*, rue de Strasbourg ☎ 76 47 99 31, *Le Club*, 9 bis rue de Phalanstère ☎ 76 87 46 21 and *La Nef*, 18 bd Edouard-Rey ☎ 76 46 53 25.

Music The *Centre Musical*, rue du Vieux-Temple ☎ 76 42 43 09, holds concerts by the Ensemble Instrumental de Grenoble and visiting orchestras. Grenoble's new Orchestre National de Jazz has a high reputation. Each June there is an outdoor music festival.

Nightclubs The smartest of the discos suitable for business people is *La Mare au Diable* ☎ 76 89 15 38, out at Uriage. Of the cabarets, *Le Canotier*, 18 Grande Rue ☎ 76 54 51 11, is chic and has a lively show; while *Espace Drac-Ouest*, 135 bd Paul-Langevin ☎ 76 26 19 63, is a large popular nightclub with dancing, dining and even swimming.

Shopping

The main shopping area runs from Avenue Alsace-Lorraine via Place Grenette to Rue de la République: here there are big department stores, two shopping centres and a variety of smart boutiques. Try *Genty-Hediart*, 1 rue de Bonne, for local products such as Grenoble nuts and Chartreuse liqueurs. The largest new stores and hypermarkets are at La Villeneuve, in the southern suburbs.

Sightseeing

The best panoramic view of the city is obtained from *La Bastille*. A cable-car goes up daily from 9am till midnight (till 7.30pm Sun, Mon and winter).

Musée Dauphinois A record of local rural life. *30 rue Maurice-Gignoux. Open Wed–Sun, 9–noon, 2–6.*

Musée de la Peinture Including Canaletto, Monet, Renoir, Matisse and Picasso, but hardly their best work. *Pl de Verdun. Open Wed–Mon, 10–noon, 2–6 (till 9 Thu).*

Musée de la Résistance Remarkable photos and souvenirs of Resistance battles. *14 rue J.-J.-Rousseau. Open Wed–Sat, 3–6.*

Musée Stendhal A rather disappointing collection of the writer's memorabilia. *1 rue Hector-Berlioz. Open Tue–Sun, 2–6.*

Spectator sports

Rugby and soccer The city's rugby team, which plays at the *Stade Lesdiguières*, cours de la Libération ☎ 76 96 43 97, is more successful than its soccer team, which plays at *Stade Bachelard*, rue Reynier ☎ 76 96 19 78.

Palais des Sports This big stadium, built for the 1968 Winter Olympics, is used for professional ice hockey, skating, cycling and tennis championships. Bd Clemenceau ☎ 76 54 72 09.

Keeping fit

Skiing on the nearby Alpine slopes is the major local sport, but the city has good facilities for other sports too. Among the best fitness clubs are *Santa Monica*, 3 ave Jeanne-d'Arc ☎ 76 51 03 68 and *Club Antinéa*, 10 rue des Eaux Clairs ☎ 76 96 92 43.

Golf The 18-hole *Golf de Grenoble* ☎ 76 90 24 70 opened in 1987 at Saint-Quentin-sur-Isère, 24km/15 miles to the northwest.

Skiing The best nearby slopes are at Chamrousse, 29km/18 miles southeast. The big resorts of Alpe d'Huez and Deux-Alpes, about 65km/40 miles away, offer better skiing at higher altitudes.

Swimming Try the *Stade Nautique* ☎ 76 22 26 36 at Echirolles.

Tennis and squash There are 28 clubs and centres, the best being *Sporting Tennis*, 128 cours de la Libération ☎ 76 96 42 99, and *Tennisquash Meylan*, 47 bd des Alpes, Meylan ☎ 76 90 16 45.

Local resources
Business services
Grenoble is reasonably well geared to business people. *Acte* ☎ 76 87 44 00 and *Aire à Bureau* ☎ 76 09 70 00 can rent out furnished offices and provide a range of services.
Photocopying and printing *Aire à Bureau, Acte.*
Secretarial *Bis* ☎ 76 87 75 41, *Dactyl-office 2000* ☎ 76 43 37 16.
Translation *ITBS* ☎ 76 21 73 04, *Inlingua* ☎ 76 44 39 45.

Communications
Local delivery *Top Service* ☎ 76 48 25 25.
Long-distance delivery
DHL ☎ 05 20 25 25 (toll free); *Swiss Air Cargo* ☎ 76 87 33 07.
Post office Main office: 17 rue Beyle-Stendhal ☎ 76 43 53 08.
Telex and fax At main post office; *Aire à Bureau* ☎ 76 09 70 00.

Conference/exhibition centres
The city has more than 300 conference rooms, and the chamber of commerce ☎ 76 47 20 36 will give advice and help. The main centre is *Alpes Congrès*, ave d'Innsbruck ☎ 76 22 18 18 ⓕ 980682, which has eight rooms, seating up to 1,200, with audiovisual equipment. The *Maison de la Culture* and the *Palais des Sports* also have conference rooms. The chamber of commerce has some well-equipped rooms in its own premises and can provide secretarial assistance. For exhibitions, the new *Alpexpo*, ave d'Innsbruck ☎ 76 39 66 00, has some 40,000 sq metres of space. (See also *Hotels.*)

Emergencies
Bureau de change At main station, 7–7 daily.
Hospitals *Michallon* ☎ 76 42 81 21, and *Echirolles* ☎ 76 09 80 50, both have emergency services.
Pharmacies Open Sundays on a rota basis; for details see newspapers or ask police.
Police Main station: bd Maréchal Leclerc ☎ 76 60 40 40.

Government offices
Hôtel de Ville, bd Jean-Pain ☎ 76 42 81 42; *Préfecture de l'Isère*, pl de Verdun ☎ 76 54 81 31.

Information sources
Business information The *Bureau d'Implantation d'Entreprises Nouvelles (BIEN)*, 4 pl de Verdun ☎ 76 44 23 26, is a great source of advice on local economic activity and so is the *Chambre de Commerce et d'Industrie*, 1 pl André-Malraux ☎ 76 47 20 36.
Local media The only local daily is the very right wing *Dauphiné Libéré*, part of the Hersant group, whose local business coverage is poor: it might be better to read the Grenoble pages of the Lyon papers (see *Lyon*). The state TV network *FR* has a nightly news magazine, while *Radio France Isère* is good for local news.
Tourist information *Office du Tourisme*, 14 rue de la République ☎ 76 54 34 36. Open 9–6; 9–7 in summer.

Thank-yous
Chocolates *Zugmeyer*, 4 bd Agutte-Sembat ☎ 76 46 32 40.
Florist *Thévoux-Chabuel*, 3 rue de la République ☎ 76 44 13 52.

LILLE
Zip code 59000

Lille, the capital of the heavily populated Nord Pas-de-Calais region of northern France, comes as a surprise to many visitors, expecting to find only a grim industrial town. It is the centre of a conurbation of over a million inhabitants usually referred to as "La Métropole du Nord," or simply "La Métropole," which includes the towns of Roubaix and Tourcoing and a host of suburbs and satellite towns. In recent years the region has successfully diversified from heavy industry to electronics, and 75% of France's mail-order sector is based in the Lille area.

The prospects for the 1990s are generally good: plans include an international business district, an exhibition centre and a technopark which, combined with the Channel Tunnel and the TGV Nord, should enable Lille to attain the European role for which it has been striving.

Arriving

Lille has fast road and rail links in all directions. The journey from Paris takes about 3hr. The city also has expanding air services.

Lille-Lesquin airport

Open 24hr, Lille's airport is 12km/7 miles southeast of the city, only 10–20min away. It handles international flights from Basle, Frankfurt, London, Milan and North Africa, 5–6 flights a day from Paris-Orly (flight time 1hr), and regular domestic flights.

Terminal facilities include a restaurant ☎ 20 87 52 05, duty-free shop, chamber of commerce office and seven car rental desks. Information ☎ 20 87 92 00 ℡ 130053.

Nearby hotels *Holiday Inn* ☎ 20 97 92 02 ℡ 132051 has free shuttle bus service to airport. *Novotel* ☎ 20 97 92 25 ℡ 820519.

City link Taxis normally coincide with flight arrivals but can be ordered in advance ☎ 20 06 06 06.

Railway station

Lille has direct trains to Basle, Brussels, Milan and Rome, and 12 a day to Paris (journey time about 2hr). A TGV service to Lyon takes about 4hr. Taxi rank outside. Passenger inquiries ☎ 20 74 50 50; reservations ☎ 20 06 26 99.

Getting around

All parts of town are covered by public transport. A car is useful for visiting outlying areas.

Taxis The main taxi rank is at the station ☎ 20 06 06 06.

Driving *Avis* ☎ 20 31 03 78, *Citer* ☎ 20 57 84 16, *Europcar* ☎ 20 30 64 44, *Hertz* ☎ 20 06 85 50.

Walking A good way of getting about the lively city centre.

Bus Lille has buses, and a tram service linking it with Roubaix and Tourcoing. Information ☎ 20 98 50 50.

Subway Lille's Métro is the world's first fully automatic system. Line 1 has 18 stations and runs through the centre of town; a second line is due to open in 1989. Information ☎ 20 98 50 50.

Area by area

The heart of Lille is Place Général-de-Gaulle, known locally as the "Grand-Place." The pedestrian area around Place Rihour and Rue de Béthune is now the city's liveliest shopping and entertainment district. To the east the Place du Théâtre houses the chamber of commerce, the Bourse, the opera house and the main post office, while to the north lies the old town, known as Vieux Lille. Rue Nationale and Rue Esquermoise are lined with shops, offices and banks; between them is the modern

HOTELS

1 Carlton
2 Grand Hôtel Bellevue
3 Novotel
4 Royal
5 Ibis
6 Paix
7 Urbis Opéra

RESTAURANTS

1 La Belle Epoque
2 Le Compostelle
3 La Devinière
4 Le Flambard
5 L'Huîtrière
6 Le Restaurant
7 Le Restaurant de Paris
8 Le Gastronome
9 Le Club Clément-Marot
10 Brasserie Jean
11 Brasserie André
12 Brasserie de la Paix
13 Le Lutterbach
14 L'Houblonnière
   Queen Victoria
   (restaurant 1)

BUILDINGS AND SIGHTS

1 Ancienne Bourse
2 Citadelle
3 Chamber of commerce
4 Foire Internationale de Lille
   (exhibition grounds)
5 Hospice Comtesse
6 Mairie
7 Musée des Beaux-Arts
8 Musée Charles de Gaulle
9 Musée Industriel et
   Commercial
10 Palais des Congrès et de
   la Musique
11 Palais Rihour
12 Police
13 Post office
14 Préfecture
15 Regional chamber of
   commerce
   Tourist office (building 11)

Nouveau Siècle complex, containing the conference centre.

To the south, near the town hall, a new business area has been created in the once grim Saint-Sauveur district. The Préfecture and the city's main museum are to the west in Place de la République. To the south, around Boulevard Vauban, is a smart residential area.

Marcq-en-Baroeul to the east is an upmarket suburb. Many executives commute from here, and from Lambersart and Bondues. Villeneuve d'Ascq was built in the 1960s and has various university faculties. Roubaix and Tourcoing, both heavily industrialized, lie close to the Belgian border; they include the Mercure, a high-tech industrial zone.

Hotels

Until recently Lille had only three central hotels suitable for top-level business travellers, but since the opening of the conference centre in 1983 four new hotels have opened, and for those with a car there are a number of large modern hotels on the outskirts. Provision for parking is adequate. Currency exchange is standard.

Grand Hôtel Bellevue *F/*
5 rue Jean-Roisin, 59800
☎ *20 57 45 64* ⊤ᴇ *120790* • *AE V* • *80 rooms, 1 bar; no restaurant*
A traditional French provincial hotel. Rooms are spacious and furnished with reproduction antiques. The bar is popular with local business people. 24hr room service • 4 meeting rooms (capacity up to 80).

Carlton *F/*
3 rue de Paris, 59800 ☎ *20 55 24 11* ⊤ᴇ *110400* • *AE DC MC V* • *64 rooms; no restaurant, no bar*
Another traditional city-centre hotel, known for its good service. Rooms are comfortable and double-glazed. The famous Brasserie Jean (see *Restaurants*) is on the same corner. 3 meeting rooms (capacity up to 150).

Novotel *F///*
116 rue de l'Hôpital Militaire, 59800 ☎ *20 30 65 26* ⊤ᴇ *160859* • *AE DC MC V* • *120 rooms, 8 suites, 1 restaurant (open 24hr), 1 bar*
This new hotel is very central and has the usual Novotel facilities, but no pool. Individual safes • 1 meeting room (capacity up to 30).

Royal *F/*
2 bd Carnot, 59800 ☎ *20 51 05 11* • *Accor* • *AE DC MC V* • *102 rooms, 1 restaurant (closed weekends), 1 bar*
The best of the traditional, central hotels is right by the opera house. Business people like the comfortable rooms (some equipped as offices) and welcoming bar. Rooms overlooking the busy boulevard are double-glazed. The *Royal Grill* restaurant is convenient for simple meals. 7 meeting rooms (capacity up to 60).

OTHER HOTELS
Ibis *F/ ave Charles-St-Venant, 59800* ☎ *20 55 44 44* ⊤ᴇ *136950* • *MC V*. Close to the station, this hotel has a 24hr bar and underground parking. Rooms are functional and small, but there is a large restaurant. 5 meeting rooms (capacity up to 150).
Paix *F 46 bis rue de Paris, 59800* ☎ *20 54 63 93* • *MC V*. A modest but convenient hotel, with some spacious rooms. Those overlooking the street are double-glazed.
Urbis Opéra *F 21 rue Lepelletier, 59800* ☎ *20 06 21 95* ⊤ᴇ *136846* • *V*. A new hotel in the old town behind the "Grand-Place."

Restaurants
Lille has several top-class restaurants, which are widely used for business entertaining, though the Lillois tend to see meals as a way of concluding rather than negotiating business. Reservations are essential. All the restaurants listed have private dining rooms available.

La Belle Epoque *F///*
10 rue de Pas ☎ *20 54 51 28* • *closed Sun D* • *AE DC MC V*
This tiny Art Nouveau restaurant above an English-style pub offers good quasi-*nouvelle* cuisine, with an excellent fixed-priced lunch menu.

Le Compostelle *F///*
4–6 rue St-Etienne ☎ *20 54 02 49* • *closed Sun D (also Sun L May–Oct)* • *AE DC MC V*
This intimate restaurant with several different dining rooms is always crowded. The cuisine is based on

traditional French dishes with some *nouvelle* touches; good wine list.

La Devinière *F///*
61 bd Louis-XIV ☎ *20 52 74 64* • *closed Sat L, Sun, 2 weeks Aug* • *AE DC MC V*
Inventive *nouvelle cuisine* has made the reputation of this restaurant close to the new business district.

Le Flambard *F////*
79 rue d'Angleterre ☎ *20 51 00 06* • *closed Sun D, Mon, Aug* • *AE DC V*
The city's finest restaurant is in

Vieux Lille and serves beautiful *nouvelle cuisine*. The lowest fixed-price menu offers outstanding value.

L'Huîtrière [F]////
3 rue des Chats-Bossus ☎ *20 55 43 41*
• *closed Sun D* • *AE DC V*
Fronted by a superb fishmonger's, L'Huîtrière has no less superb fish and shellfish and the wine list is excellent. Too noisy for business, but excellent for a relaxed meal.

Le Restaurant [F]////
1 pl Sébastopol ☎ *20 54 23 13* •
closed Sat L, Sun, first half Jan •
AE DC MC V
One of the area's top restaurants, very popular for high-level business entertaining. It mainly serves *nouvelle cuisine*.

Le Restaurant de Paris [F]////
52 bis rue Esquermoise ☎ *20 55 29 41*
• *closed Sun D, Aug* • *AE DC*
Lille's grandest restaurant is popular for its mixture of classical and modern cuisine. Elegant service.

Good but casual
Le Gastronome, 67 rue de l'Hôpital Militaire ☎ 20 54 47 43, and *Le Club Clément-Marot*, 16 rue de Pas ☎ 20 57 01 10, are good small restaurants near the conference centre. Of Lille's many lively brasseries the best-known is the *Brasserie Jean*, 2 rue Faidherbe ☎ 20 55 75 72, which specializes in Flemish food. *Brasserie André*, 71 rue de Béthune ☎ 20 54 75 51, is the archetypal French brasserie. *Brasserie de la Paix*, 25 pl Rihour ☎ 20 54 70 41, is stylish and lively. *Le Lutterbach*, 10 rue Faidherbe ☎ 20 55 13 74, is another classic brasserie. *L'Houblonnière*, 42 pl Général-de-Gaulle ☎ 20 74 54 34, specializes in beer and regional dishes; modest but friendly. The *Queen Victoria*, 10 rue de Pas ☎ 20 54 51 28, looks like an English pub but also serves real meals from kitchens shared with the *Belle Epoque* restaurant upstairs.

Bars
The bars in the Royal and Bellevue hotels are popular with business people. The *Brasserie Jean* is a local institution and the English pub-style *Queen Victoria* is rather smart. The bar of the Ibis hotel is open 24hr.

Entertainment
Lille has an unusually lively cultural scene.
Theatre, dance, opera The *Théâtre National de la Salamandre*, 4 pl Général-de-Gaulle ☎ 20 54 52 30 (also at 21 rue Boileau, Tourcoing ☎ 20 25 25 82), offers a good mix of classical and modern plays. The dance company *Ballet du Nord* is based at Rue de l'Epaule, Roubaix ☎ 20 24 66 66. *Opéra de Lille*, 2 rue des Bons-Enfants ☎ 20 55 48 61, is the city's opera house, but the *Atelier Lyrique de Tourcoing*, 82 bd Gambetta ☎ 20 26 66 03 may well have a livelier programme.
Cinema The city has no fewer than 60 cinemas, 24 of them in Rue Béthune.
Music The *Orchestre National de Lille*, 3 pl Mendès-France ☎ 20 54 67 00, is one of France's top orchestras. Concerts and recitals are held at the *Conservatoire National de la Région*, 48 rue Royale ☎ 20 74 57 50, and the *Palais des Congrès et de la Musique*, 20 rue du Nouveau-Siècle ☎ 20 30 89 40.
Tickets can be bought from the tourist office and the *Fnac* store, 9 pl Général-de-Gaulle.

Shopping
Lille's busy commercial centre is based around Place Général-de-Gaulle. Here you will find *Galerie des Tanneurs* and *Galeries de l'Opéra*, two smart new shopping arcades, the *Fnac* and France's largest single bookshop, the famous *Furet du Nord*. Rue des Chats-Bossus and the area around the church of Notre-Dame-de-la-Treille is the antique dealers' district. The local spirit, *genièvre*, is sold at delicatessens.

Sightseeing
Guided tours are arranged by the tourist office.
Ancienne Bourse (also known as the Vieille Bourse). A 17thC building whose courtyard is now filled with stalls selling flowers and books.
Citadelle Designed by France's greatest military architect, Sébastian Vauban.
Hospice Comtesse A complex of medieval and 17th–18thC buildings, now a museum of local history. *32 rue de la Monnaie* ☎ *20 51 02 62. Open Wed–Mon, 10–12.30, 2–5.*
Musée des Beaux-Arts A varied collection of paintings and decorative arts. *Pl de la République* ☎ *20 57 01 84. Open Wed–Mon, 9.30–12.30, 2–6.*
Musée Charles de Gaulle The General's birthplace is now a museum devoted to his life and times. *9 rue Princesse* ☎ *20 31 96 03. Open Wed–Sun, 10–12, 2–5.*
Musée Industriel et Commercial An exhibition of 19thC trade and industry. *2 rue du Lombard* ☎ *20 06 31 27. Open daily 10–12.30, 2–6.*
Palais Rihour A 15thC Gothic palace which now houses the tourist office.

Spectator sports
Horse-racing Le Croisé-Laroche racecourse ☎ 20 72 03 68 is at Marcq-en-Baroeul.
Soccer The Lille Olympic Sporting Club (LOSC) plays at the *Stade Grimonprez-Jooris* ☎ 20 57 56 45.

Keeping fit
Several outlying hotels have pools, and the Mercure offers free access to tennis courts. The Bois de Boulogne is ideal for jogging.
Fitness centres *Nauticlub Forest Hill*, ave de la Marne, Marcq-en-Baroeul ☎ 20 98 97 97, takes visitors; it has squash courts, sauna, jacuzzi, gym and aerobics. In town try the *Salle des Champs-Elysées*, 5 rue du Court-Debout ☎ 20 30 00 20.
Golf *Golf du Sart*, 5 rue Jean-Jaurès,

Flers ☎ 20 72 02 51; *Golf de Brigoude*, 36 ave du Golf, Villeneuve d'Ascq ☎ 20 91 17 86.
Riding *Centre Equestre de Bousbecque*, 59 rue de Linselles ☎ 20 23 52 99; *L'Etrier du Croisé Laroche*, 137 bd Clemenceau, Marcq-en-Baroeul ☎ 20 72 33 08.
Squash and tennis *L'Arbonnoise*, rue du Lieutenant-Colpin, Villeneuve d'Ascq ☎ 20 05 15 15, has squash and tennis courts. *Citizen Squash*, in town at 177 bis rue des Stations ☎ 20 57 58 18; *Tennis Club des Flandres*, 103 rue Jean-Baptiste Lebas, Croix ☎ 20 72 36 52.
Swimming Apart from the hotel pools, there is an Olympic-sized pool at 36 ave Marx-Dormoy ☎ 20 92 80 22.

Local resources
Business services
The Holiday Inn at the airport has the fullest hotel business facilities in the area. *Acte*, 40 bd de la Liberté ☎ 20 54 35 48, and *France Domiciliation Service*, 141 rue de Douai ☎ 20 52 60 36, both provide a wide range of services, including telex, fax, secretarial help and word processing.
Photocopying and printing *Copy 2000* ☎ 20 57 61 44 (also does mailings); *Copy Eclair* ☎ 20 57 92 88, open 8–8; *Document Service* ☎ 20 06 32 72; *Prontaprint* ☎ 20 06 56 36.
Translation *Nord Traductions*, 260 rue des Postes ☎ 20 57 40 80; *Nortelex*, 28 pl de la Gare ☎ 20 06 82 38 also offers secretarial service and office rental.

Communications
Local delivery *Abeille Rush* ☎ 20 06 48 10; *Taxi-Colis* ☎ 20 53 18 72.
Long-distance delivery *DHL* ☎ 20 47 60 50; *Securicor* ☎ 20 52 27 08.
Post office Main office: 7 pl de la République ☎ 20 54 70 13.
Telex and fax At main post office; *OREM*, 3–5 sq Dutilleul ☎ 20 57 95 66.

Conference/exhibition centres

Lille's conference centre, which doubles as a concert hall, is *Palais des Congrès et de la Musique*, 30 pl Mendès-France ☎ 20 30 89 40. The main auditorium takes up to 2,000 delegates and has five booths for simultaneous translation; the *Salle Québec* can be used for small conferences (capacity up to 400) or for trade exhibitions; another 14 rooms are available (capacity up to 120); the centre has 1,100 sq metres of exhibition space.

The chamber of commerce (see *Information sources*) can supply meeting rooms. *Château de Villers* at Lompret ☎ 20 44 45 46 is an attractive place for seminars. The tourist office runs a conference advisory service, *Tourlille Services* ☎ 20 30 81 00 ⊠ 110213.

The city's exhibition grounds, *Foire Internationale de Lille*, BP 523, 59022 Lille ☎ 20 52 79 60 ⊠ 132606, are quite central, and house several major trade fairs and the international fair in September.

Emergencies

Bureaux de change *Crédit Agricole*, 10 ave Foch, is open Sat (8.15–11.30am); the main post office has an exchange counter open Mon–Fri to 7pm, and Sat 8–12.

Medical emergencies *SAMU* ☎ 20 54 22 22; for doctors outside normal hours ☎ 20 30 11 11; *Centre Hospitalier Régional*, 1 ave Oscar-Lambret ☎ 20 96 92 80 or 20 51 92 80.

Pharmacies The police list those open outside normal shopping hours.

Police Main station: 6 bis bd de Maréchal-Vaillant ☎ 20 86 17 17. Emergencies ☎ 17.

Government offices

Conseil Général du Nord, 2 rue Jacquemars Giélée ☎ 20 30 59 59; *Conseil Régional Nord/Pas-de-Calais*, 7 sq Morrison ☎ 20 60 60 60; *Mairie*, pl Roger-Salengro ☎ 20 49 50 00; *Préfecture*, 171 bd de la Liberté ☎ 20 30 59 59.

Information sources

Business information The *Chambre de Commerce*, pl du Théâtre ☎ 20 74 14 14, has a full information service. *Chambre Régionale de Commerce et d'Industrie du Nord/Pas-de-Calais* is at 2 Palais de la Bourse ☎ 20 74 14 14. Other organizations are *Agence Régionale de Développement*, 185 bd de la Liberté ☎ 20 30 82 81; *Association pour la Promotion Industrielle de la Métropole Nord* (APIM), 37 rue Thiers ☎ 20 57 03 79; and *Association pour le Renouveau Industriel* (ARI), 16 Résidence Breteuil ☎ 20 55 98 82. All will help with setting up offices or plants in the area. The regional office of *INSEE* is at 10–12 bd Vauban ☎ 20 30 89 87. There is an *Internat-Commercial Club* (ICC) at 40 rue Eugène-Jacquet, Marcq-en-Baroeul ☎ 20 98 92 01.

Local media The main local daily is *La Voix du Nord. La Gazette* is an economic weekly, *Face* a business and economic monthly published by the chamber of commerce. *Plein Nord*, another monthly, is designed for executives new to the area. *Fréquence Nord* and *France Inter Lille* are Lille-based radio stations. The regional television channel is *FR3 Nord-Picardie*.

Tourist information *Office de Tourisme*, Palais Rihour, pl Rihour ☎ 20 30 81 00; there is an information desk at the station. Regional tourist office, 13 rue du Palais-Rihour ☎ 20 60 60 60.

Thank-yous

Confectionery *Allaeys*, 95 rue Colbert ☎ 20 57 10 32 runs a nationwide *Intergâteaux* service; *Jean Trogeneux*, 57 rue Nationale ☎ 20 54 74 42 sells fine chocolates.

Florist *Véronique*, 125 rue Nationale ☎ 20 57 15 93.

LYON
Zip code 69000

Secretive, cautious, prosperous, self-confident – Lyon has always been, and remains, all of those things. But it has also recently become one of Europe's fastest growing and most innovative cities. About 12 years ago its ageing industrial base was steered through a radical overhaul by its long-serving mayor, Francisque Collomb. Today Lyon boasts no fewer than three dynamic *technopoles* (industrially-oriented research centres), at La Doua, Ecully and Gerland. Similarly, three major new industrial sites, at L'Isle d'Abeau, Plaine de l'Ain and Limonest, have been created close by. The new industrial climate has attracted a number of international firms to Lyon (among them Hewlett Packard, Schering-Plough and Lever). Another feather in the city's cap was the decision to move the headquarters of Interpol from Paris to Lyon. In addition, Lyon's celebrated silk industry, which started in the 15th century, continues to flourish alongside the growing man-made fibre industry.

Lyon is the capital of the thriving Rhône-Alpes region, and France's second most important city economically with a population of only 1.2m. Its banks, which first rose to prominence in the 16th century, remain thriving concerns. It has long been the base of big French corporations such as Rhône-Poulenc (chemicals) and Berliet (now Renault Véhicules Industriels). It also teems with smaller, high-growth French companies which have benefited from Lyon's booming unlisted securities market, which opened in 1983. However, the Bourse, founded in 1464, still has a long way to go before becoming an international financial market on the scale of Frankfurt, Milan, or Zürich.

Another tradition of Lyon is gastronomy. It is no myth that senior Lyonnais executives prefer to spend their money on lavish dining at top restaurants than on flashy status symbols. Lyon is a city, then, where the ice-breaking function of business entertainment can prove crucially important. While popular belief says it is hard to make an initial deal with Lyonnais business people, they are unswervingly loyal once you strike up a relationship and gain their trust.

Arriving

Lyon likes to call itself "the crossroads of France." The city is connected by the A6 autoroute to Paris (the Dijon–Lyon section can be congested in summer), Marseille, Grenoble, Saint-Etienne and Clermont-Ferrand. The autoroute linking Lyon with Geneva will be virtually completed by 1988. There is a good range of direct scheduled air services to major European cities and all important French cities. But the quickest means of travel from Paris to Lyon (centre to centre) is the TGV (high-speed train).

Lyon-Satolas International airport

This is very much a business traveller's airport, as it offers connections to business cities and schedules departures and arrivals early and late in the day. Being 27km/17 miles from the centre of Lyon, and under competition from the TGV, means that it is not much used to and from Paris. But there is considerable traffic with all other major French cities, as well as daily weekday direct flights from Amsterdam, Brussels, Copenhagen, Düsseldorf, Frankfurt, London,

Milan, Munich, Turin, Vienna and Zürich. The airport has two light, airy terminals containing cafés and bars, two brasseries and one high-class restaurant, La Grande Corbeille. Banking and currency exchange facilities are available in the central building Mon–Sat, 8.35–5; at other times up to 500Fr per passenger will be changed by the hostesses near Bloc 2 in the international terminal. There is a post office open weekdays, 8–8 and Sat, 8–noon. The airport's *2a Service* (☎ 72 22 72 21 or 72 22 75 26) offers good business facilities including individual offices, meeting rooms with a capacity of up to 30, telephones, telex, secretarial services, slide projection and catering. Airport information and freight inquiries ☎ 72 72 72 21.

Nearby hotels *Sofitel Lyon Satolas* ☎ 78 71 91 61 ⊤Ⅹ 380480 • AE DC MC v. Modern hotel in the airport's central building overlooking the runways and mountains beyond; all rooms soundproofed and air-conditioned. *Climat de France* ☎ 78 40 96 44 ⊤Ⅹ 306725 • AE MC V. Modest modern hotel in the airport's freight section; free shuttle.

City link The long trip into town by taxi is expensive. Buses are frequent and nearly as quick as taxis.

Taxi The ride takes about 30min. There is a taxi rank in front of each terminal. For reservations ☎ 78 71 90 90.

Car rental All the main car rental firms have desks at the airport. A car is necessary if you are making trips to the outskirts of Lyon.

Bus The bus fare is about one-fifth of the cost of a taxi. Buses leave every 20min (every 30min Sat pm and Sun) from Bloc 2 of the international terminal and Bloc 3 of the domestic terminal. You should get off either at Gare de la Part-Dieu (35min), or at Gare Perrache (45min), depending on your final destination. The bus driver can reserve a taxi (by radio), which will meet you at one of the stops in town and take you on.

Lyon-Bron airport
This private airport is 10km/6 miles east of Lyon, next to the European exhibition centre. *2a Service* offers on-the-spot business facilities (fewer than at Satolas airport). All inquiries ☎ 78 26 81 09.

Railway stations
The TGV has revolutionized rail travel. The 425km/266-mile trip from Paris now takes a mere 2hr. Over 20 TGVs a day run in each direction from about 6am to midnight. Lyon has two main stations: Gare de Perrache and Gare de la Part-Dieu. You must decide when buying your ticket which station is the more convenient for you (all seats on TGVs have to be reserved). For both stations: passenger inquiries ☎ 78 92 50 50; reservations ☎ 78 92 50 70.

La Part-Dieu This is the first stop for passengers from Paris. It has among other things an Avis desk and a currency exchange bureau. The station is in the middle of one of Lyon's two business quarters. To reach the other one, Cordeliers, take either the Métro (subway), changing at Charpennes, or a taxi. Leave by the station's Vivier-Merle exit for the taxi rank (turn left outside) and airport bus stop (straight ahead).

Perrache TGVs from Paris reach this station 10min after leaving Gare de la Part-Dieu. There is a 3-stop subway connection with Cordeliers. Use the Terre-plein Central exit for taxis and for the airport bus (which is poorly signposted – look out for the vehicle itself rather than for a bus stop).

Getting around
The centre of Lyon is quite large and often congested with traffic. Getting around usually requires a car, the subway, a taxi or a bus. Just crossing the river Rhône by one of the several bridges entails a walk of some 180 metres. But once you are in either of the two business quarters, La Part-Dieu or Cordeliers, the easiest way to get around is on foot.

HOTELS

1 Carlton
2 Cour des Loges
3 Grand Hôtel Concorde
4 Holiday Inn
5 Pullman Part-Dieu
6 Royal
7 Sofitel Lyon
8 Artistes
9 Grand-Hôtel des Beaux-Arts
10 Mercure Part-Dieu

RESTAURANTS

1 L'Assiette Lyonnaise
2 Le Bistrot de Lyon
3 Henry
4 Jean Vettard
5 Léon de Lyon
6 Pierre Orsi
7 La Tour Rose
8 La Tassée
9 Café des Fédérations
10 Bar du Musée
11 La Meunière

BUILDINGS AND SIGHTS

1 Bourse
2 Cathédrale Saint-Jean
3 Chamber of commerce
4 Espace Tête d'Or
5 Hôpital Saint-Joseph
6 Hôtel de Ville
7 Musée des Beaux-Arts
8 Musée de la Civilisation Gallo-Romaine
9 Musée Historique des Tissus
10 Notre-Dame-de-Fourvière
11 Tourist office (also in stations)
12 Palais des Congrès Internationaux
13 Post office
14 Préfecture

Taxis Although easily recognizable and plentiful, it is not immediately clear whether cabs are vacant. If one of the very small coloured lights under the word "taxi" is on, it means the taxi is occupied; if none of the lights is on, it is vacant. Taxis may be hailed or found at ranks (there are not many of these). They are relatively expensive. Radio cabs: *Taxi-Allô* ☎ 78 28 23 23, *Télé-Taxi* ☎ 78 28 13 14, *Taxi-Radio* ☎ 78 30 86 86.

Limousines *Compagnie Lyonnaise des Limousines* ☎ 78 85 64 10; *Avis* ☎ 72 33 99 14.

Driving Once you have got the hang of the traffic system (almost all streets are one-way), driving is easy except at rush hours and in the centre. Parking may prove difficult, but many hotels have their own parking facilities. All major car rental firms have offices in the city centre.

Walking This is safe in central Lyon and easy, as the Rhône and Saône rivers make orientation straightforward.

Subway Lyon's newish Métro network is clean, quiet and efficient. Tickets are best bought in sheets of six from vending machines, and should be stamped in the stamping machines on platforms before boarding the train. There are useful 2- and 3-day rover tickets valid for both the subway and buses.

Bus Certain bus lines are useful, particularly if you need to get to the suburbs. Subway and bus tickets are interchangeable and can be bought from the driver. They should be stamped in one of the machines on the bus. There are maps of bus lines at stops and in vehicles.

Area by area

The real centre of Lyon is located on what is known as Presqu'île (literally "peninsula"), a narrow tongue of land that runs between the Rhône and Saône rivers just before they join each other. Its districts, from north to south, are Terreaux, Cordeliers, Bellecour and Perrache. The older of Lyon's two business quarters lies on the east side of Presqu'île, in Cordeliers and adjoining parts of Terreaux and Bellecour. This is where the Lyon Bourse and the big finance and insurance companies are located.

The other main business quarter is in the new district of La Part-Dieu, on the east side of the Rhône. Here the emphasis is on engineering, computers and high-tech industries.

The largely 18thC quarter of Croix-Rousse, once the centre of Lyon's silk industry, lies to the north of Presqu'île. The oldest part of the city, Vieux-Lyon, huddles under the hill of Fourvière on the west bank of the Saône. The most desirable residential quarter in central Lyon is the northern part of Brotteaux, on the edge of the Parc de la Tête d'Or.

Districts Lyon is divided into nine *arrondissements*, and their numbers form the last digit of their zip codes. But the Lyonnais themselves prefer to use the old names of districts rather than the *arrondissement* number. To help you to find your bearings, here are the zip code equivalents of the districts mentioned above: Terreaux = 69001; Cordeliers = 69001 and 69002; Bellecour and Perrache = 69002; La Part-Dieu = 69003; Croix-Rousse = 69004; Vieux-Lyon = 69005; Brotteaux = 69006. Villeurbanne, although a different commune from Lyon itself (zip code 69100), is so close to the northeast of central Lyon that it is effectively an inner suburb.

The suburbs

The most sought-after residential areas on the outskirts of Lyon are to the northwest (Ecully, Dardilly). But many commute farther afield from the attractive hills (Monts du Lyonnais) southwest of the city.

Much heavy industry is based to the south of Lyon, particularly along the Rhône. There are three major new industrial sites within a 37km/23-mile radius of the city:

manufacturing firms (in particular Lever) are at Plaine de l'Ain, while major computer and service companies are at L'Isle d'Abeau (Hewlett Packard) and Limonest.

Hotels

Lyon hotels are generally of a high standard, but there are relatively few of them. As though waking up to this fact, the city gained two new luxury hotels in 1987, the Cour des Loges and the Holiday Inn. All hotels given full entries have IDD telephones in every room. Most major hotels offer currency exchange. Parking is not a problem unless stated otherwise. Normally hotel accommodation is easy to find. If you experience problems, the tourist office ☎ 78 42 25 75 may be able to help you reserve a room (but not more than five days before your arrival).

Because of keen competition from the city's many restaurants, hotel catering is kept on its toes. All the main hotel restaurants referred to by name serve high-class cuisine in spacious and elegant surroundings.

Carlton [F]|
4 rue Jussieu, 69002 ☎ *78 42 56 51*
TX *310787 • Mapotel • AE DC MC V • 87 rooms, 1 bar, no restaurant*
The Carlton is one of Lyon's most pleasant older hotels, and is much appreciated by business travellers and visiting actors and musicians for its quiet, central location and discreet, friendly service. Its large rooms (including rotundas, a feature of turn-of-the-century French architecture) have traditional or modern furniture. Limited parking • 1 meeting room (capacity 10).

Cour des Loges [F]||||
6 rue du Boeuf, 69005 ☎ *78 42 75 75*
TX *330831 • AE DC MC V • 53 rooms, 10 suites, 1 restaurant, 1 bar*
This new hotel in Vieux-Lyon within easy walking distance of Cordeliers, is an imaginatively converted series of Renaissance buildings. The less expensive rooms are on the small side, but this is made up for by the quality of their fittings and facilities (eg electronic safes, hairdryers, videos). Some larger rooms and suites have a private garden or fireplace. The bar-cum-restaurant, Tapas des Loges, managed by Philippe Chavent of La Tour Rose down the road (see

Restaurants), serves till 2am. 24hr room service, gift shop, newsstand, video library • pool, sauna, jacuzzi, gym • 4 meeting rooms (capacity up to 40).

Grand Hôtel Concorde [F]||
11 rue Grôlée, 69002 ☎ *78 42 56 21*
TX *330244 • AE DC MC V • 140 rooms, 3 suites, 1 restaurant, 1 bar*
A big, conveniently central hotel housed in a late-19thC building which is much used for seminars and conferences. The most congenial of its large, traditionally-furnished rooms (all of which have cable TV) overlook the Rhône. There is a particularly spacious and pleasant public area ideal for small informal meetings. 9 meeting rooms (capacity up to 200).

Holiday Inn [F]||
29 rue de Bonnel, 69003 ☎ *72 61 90 90*
TX *330703 • AE DC MC V • 157 rooms, 1 suite, 1 restaurant, 1 bar*
Opened in mid-1987, this is without doubt the Lyon hotel that best caters for business travellers. There are computer facilities, as well as the usual range of business services. Rooms are well equipped and there is a special executive floor.

The building and decor are cautiously modern. Its Nouvelles Orléans restaurant bravely proposes genuine Louisiana cuisine. 24hr room service • sauna, jacuzzi, gym • 16 meeting rooms (capacity up to 400).

Pullman Part-Dieu F////
129 rue Servient, 69003 ☎ *78 62 94 12* ℡ *380088 • AE DC MC V • 245 rooms, 7 suites, 2 restaurants, 1 bar*
Perched at the top of the huge Crédit Lyonnais skyscraper (locally nicknamed "the pencil") in the middle of the Part-Dieu quarter, this is Europe's tallest hotel. Its snug rooms are reached by galleries running around an atrium which is draped with tropical plants. They afford stunning views (ask for the Fourvière side when making your reservation), as does the restaurant, which is ideal for business entertaining at senior level. The bar, Le Panache, is also popular with business people. There are good business facilities and a special executive floor. Modular meeting room (capacity up to 250).

Royal F/
20 pl Bellecour, 69002 ☎ *78 37 57 31* ℡ *310785 • Mapotel • AE DC MC V • 90 rooms, 1 restaurant, 1 bar*
The Royal, like its sister hotel, the Carlton, is one of the city's older hotels, with spacious rooms including some rotundas. On the whole its decor is pleasantly sober and the Royal enjoys a superb location overlooking one of Europe's largest squares, Place Bellecour. 1 meeting room (capacity 10).

Sofitel Lyon F////
20 quai Gailleton, 69002
☎ *78 42 72 50* ℡ *330225 • AE DC MC V • 195 rooms, 3 suites, 2 restaurants, 2 bars*
This large modern hotel is on the banks of the Rhône, not far from the Place Bellecour. Although rather unprepossessing from the outside, it is most congenial within, with

pleasant bedrooms, a delightful interior palm garden, luxury boutiques, an excellent rooftop restaurant, Les Trois Dômes, and a fashionable cocktail bar, Le Melhor. Simple food is served till 2am in the smart Sofi Shop restaurant on the ground floor, whose tables are separated by smoked-glass partitions. Hairdresser • 17 meeting rooms (capacity up to 400).

OTHER HOTELS
Artistes F/ *8 rue Gaspard-André, 69002* ☎ *78 42 04 88* ℡ *375664 • AE DC MC V.* Quiet hotel near Place Bellecour.
Grand-Hôtel des Beaux-Arts F/ *75 rue du Président-Herriot, 69002* ☎ *78 38 09 50* ℡ *330442 • AE DC MC V.* Recently modernized traditional hotel in the middle of Presqu'île.
Mercure Part-Dieu F/ *47 bd Vivier-Merle, 69003* ☎ *72 34 18 12* ℡ *306469 • AE DC MC V.* Large modern hotel in the middle of the Part-Dieu business quarter and a 3min walk from the Gare de la Part-Dieu.

Out of town
Those who prefer rural surroundings should consider the possibility of commuting to *Ostellerie du Vieux Pérouges* ☎ *74 61 00 88* in Pérouges (see *Sightseeing*), 39km/24 miles northeast – a beautiful country hotel whose main St Georges et Manoir section is a perfectly preserved 15thC building.

Hotel prices
In many hotels, particularly older ones, room rates vary considerably. The price symbol (F to F/////) given after the hotel name is based on the cost at the time of going to press of a typical room for one person (see page 7). Although the actual prices will go up, the relative price category is likely to remain the same.

Restaurants

The Lyonnais regard their city as the gastronomic capital of the world. A slight exaggeration, perhaps, even if top-notch restaurants do lie extraordinarily thick on the ground. While members of the local business community, like all Lyonnais, love to linger over sophisticated *haute cuisine*, they also congregate in humbler establishments known as *bouchons*. Reservations are always advisable, even in these. All the major restaurants listed here have excellent wine lists and offer attractive set menus. (See also Cour des Loges, Pullman and Sofitel hotels.)

L'Assiette Lyonnaise *F*
19 pl Tolozan ☎ *78 28 35 77 • closed Sat L, Sun, Aug 1–14 • AE DC MC V*
This recently redecorated, unpretentious restaurant full of potted plants and ventilated by a huge ceiling fan is ideal for the not-too-formal business lunch or late supper (last orders 11.30). There is a small terrace in summer, a rarity in Lyon. The food is traditional Lyonnais and very good value.

Le Bistrot de Lyon *F/*
64 rue Mercière ☎ *78 37 00 62 • V*
This establishment in the lively Rue Mercière attracts a smarter clientele and serves more sophisticated cuisine than its bistro atmosphere and friendly prices would seem to indicate. Most unusually in a city that tends to pull down the shutters early, it serves until 1.30am.

Henry *F/*
27 rue de la Martinière ☎ *78 28 26 08 • closed Sat L, Mon • AE DC V*
One of the very few Lyonnais restaurants suitable for important entertaining occasions which also takes orders until 11.30pm and is open on Sunday. In addition, its two private dining rooms with independent telephones make it possible to have lingering business lunches. Chef Pierre Balladone, a highly skilled but unflashy cook who is particularly at home with fish, offers good value top-flight cooking. The decor is sober and tasteful, the tables well spaced, and the service very friendly.

Jean Vettard *F/*
7 pl Bellecour ☎ *78 42 07 59 • closed Sun, Jul 24–Aug 31 • AE DC V • smart dress preferred*
A long established family-run restaurant on Place Bellecour whose superb *belle époque* decor and celebrated Lyonnais dishes – *quenelles de brochet financière, poularde en vessie* – have remained unchanged down the generations. But Jean Vettard also offers several excellent and intelligently "modern" dishes of his own devising (eg *turbot au fumet de menthe*). The place for really important business entertaining.

Léon de Lyon *F/*
1 rue Pleney ☎ *78 28 11 33 • closed Mon L, Sun, Dec 20–Jan 6 • V*
Jean-Paul Lacombe is a brilliant practitioner of generously served *nouvelle cuisine* that is inventive without being far-fetched. His wide-ranging menu, which explains each dish in detail, changes completely twice a year. The decor is typically Lyonnais, with stained-glass windows, wood panelling and low ceilings, and the service impeccable. For business discussions, ask for a table in the quieter ground-floor section.

Pierre Orsi *F/*
3 pl Kléber ☎ *78 89 57 68 • closed Sun (also Sat, May–Sep) • AE MC V • no smoking till end of meal preferred*
Located between the two most chic shopping streets in Lyon, Cours Franklin-Roosevelt and Cours Vitton, this is the only really top-class restaurant close to the Part-

Dieu business quarter, and is much frequented by senior managers at lunch time. Pierre Orsi's classical cuisine is as refined and elegant as his salmon-pink decor.

La Tour Rose [F]////
16 rue du Boeuf ☎ *78 37 25 90*
• *closed Sun* • *AE DC MC V*
Owner-chef Philippe Chavent is an exponent of the highly imaginative – and occasionally over-the-top – *nouvelle cuisine* and a fan of rare Côtes-du-Rhône vintages. But dining at La Tour is more than a gastronomic event: Chavent is a discriminating collector of modern art, which graces his walls; the tablecloths are made of silk, no less; and the restaurant building itself is a fine example of Lyonnais Renaissance.

Bouchons
These café-restaurants generally serve expertly cooked local dishes and Beaujolais of a quality rarely found outside the Lyon area, all for very reasonable prices. Business people traditionally organize informal meetings in their local *bouchon* over a bottle of wine and *mâchons* (a substantial snack taken at any time of day), or else sit down for an often lengthy set lunch, sometimes conducting business into the afternoon over the *bouchon*'s own telephone. Although such restaurants are casual, reservations are advisable; they are always closed on Sundays. The most celebrated *bouchon*, which has almost graduated to the status of a restaurant proper, is *La Tassée*, 20 rue de la Charité ☎ 78 37 02 35. The one where there is the greatest competition for a table is *Café des Fédérations*, 8 rue du Major-Martin ☎ 78 28 26 00. Two lesser known *bouchons* much frequented by bankers and insurance brokers are the convivial *Bar du Musée*, 2 rue des Forces ☎ 78 37 71 54 and, for those who like a Gargantuan atmosphere, *La Meunière*, 11 rue Neuve, ☎ 78 28 62 91.

Out of town
Some 12km/7 miles out of Lyon, in Collonges-au-Mont-d'Or, there is a restaurant whose fame has travelled the world – as indeed has its eponymous owner, Paul Bocuse. The cuisine at *Restaurant Paul Bocuse* ☎ 78 22 01 40 is undoubtedly sublime, if you can bear the vulgarity of the decor. But the demure Lyonnais are not too keen on those who, like Bocuse, excel at self-publicity. So if you want to entertain an important local client out of town, head rather for Mionnay, 20km/12 miles north of Lyon, which boasts one of the very finest restaurants in the whole of France, *Alain Chapel* ☎ 78 91 82 02. But take the precaution of reserving well ahead.

Bars
The two hotel bars most favoured by business people for a quiet drink are *Le Panache*, in the Pullman, and more particularly *Le Melhor*, in the Sofitel, which specializes in cocktails (see *Hotels*). Those in search of a really discreet atmosphere make for *Le Cintra*, 43 rue de la Bourse (opposite the Stock Exchange), a veritable cavern of leather seats, polished brass and varnished wood panelling. But many Lyonnais business people like to do their talking in *bouchons*.

Lyon also has two excellent wine bars which offer a wide range of vintages, from the humble to the most prestigious, by the glass: *Le Comptoir du Boeuf*, 3 pl Neuve-St-Jean and *Le Bouchon aux Vins*, 62 rue Mercière. The Rue Mercière has many other bars, which are more suitable for an evening off.

Entertainment
Lyon has quite a lively cultural scene. For essential listings buy the weekly *Lyon Poche*.
Theatre One of France's most celebrated theatres is Roger Planchon and Georges Lavaudant's *Théâtre National Populaire* (TNP), 8 pl Lazare-Goujon, Villeurbanne

☎ 78 84 70 74. Lyon is also regularly visited by touring companies.

Cinema The inventors of the cinema, Louis and Auguste Lumière, were from Lyon. Their house has been turned into *L'Institut Lumière*, 25 rue du Premier-Film ☎ 78 00 86 68. It holds photographic exhibitions and houses the Lyon Cinémathèque, which organizes regular showings of rare films. In commercial cinemas, many English-speaking films are shown with subtitles (*version originale*, or *v.o.*).

Music Lyon is a very musical city and attracts many big names in every department, from classical to jazz and rock. There are regular concerts by its own orchestra, the Orchestre National de Lyon (conductor: Serge Baudo), usually at the *Auditorium Maurice-Ravel*, 149 rue Garibaldi ☎ 78 71 05 73. The important Festival International Berlioz alternates with the Biennale de la Danse (Sep). There are frequent organ recitals in churches.

Nightclubs Lyon was once famed as a city of early-to-beds. Things have changed, and there are now many nightspots. Among the more chic are *Le Piano*, 53 rue Mercière ☎ 78 92 89 16 and *Le Saint-Antoine*, 37 quai St-Antoine ☎ 78 37 01 35. The trendiest discos, which attract a younger, more dynamic crowd, are *L'Aquarius*, 47 quai Pierre-Scize ☎ 78 28 84 86, and especially *L'Actuel*, 30 bd Eugène-Deruelle ☎ 78 95 12 93 (Wed–Sat).

Casino There is a charming *belle époque* casino in the tiny spa of Charbonnières-les-Bains, ☎ 78 87 02 70, 8km/5 miles west of Lyon on the N7.

Shopping

Fashion Not surprisingly in view of its tradition as a textile city, Lyon has a natural feel for clothes (especially silk). The best fashion shops are to be found in Cours Franklin-Roosevelt and its continuation Cours Vitton, not far from La Part-Dieu, and in Rue du Président-Herriot, in Presqu'île. For good-value silk articles try *Maison des Canuts*, 10 rue d'Ivry, which is also a small museum.

Food Wander around the mouthwatering central food market, *Halles de Lyon*, 192 cours La Fayette, to see if anything takes your fancy. *Maurice Bernachon*, 42 cours Franklin-Roosevelt, is certainly the best known, and doubtless the best, maker of chocolates in Europe.

Department stores *Au Printemps*, 42 rue du Président-Herriot, and two *Galeries Lafayette* stores, at 6 pl des Cordeliers and in the Centre Commercial de la Part-Dieu, a shopping centre which also houses a wide variety of other stores.

Antique markets Good ones include *Stalingrad*, 115 bd de Stalingrad, Villeurbanne, and *Le Carré Saint-Jean*, quai Romain-Rolland. Top antique dealers operate in Rue Auguste Comte.

Sightseeing

The recently-renovated *Vieux-Lyon*, with its many 16th–17thC buildings, galleried courtyards, Florentine towers and interesting shops, is well worth exploring. Parts of it have been pedestrianized. Above Vieux-Lyon is perched the immense church of *Notre-Dame-de-Fourvière*, an important centre of pilgrimage and an unparalleled example of late-19thC extravagance (rare stones used in its construction, and a mixture of Byzantine, Assyrian, Gothic and Romanesque styles). At the south end of Vieux-Lyon is the stately Gothic *Cathédrale Saint-Jean*, which is remarkable for its three highly ornate doors and 13thC stained-glass windows.

To the north of Presqu'île the *Croix-Rousse* quarter, once the home of *canuts* (silk workers), should on no account be missed: it is honeycombed with *traboules*, covered passages, galleries or flights of steps connecting streets or houses to one another. These *traboules*, a word derived from the Latin *transambulare* (to walk through), enabled silk to be carried to and from workshops without being rained on – and *résistants* to escape their pursuers during the last war (a map of the *traboules* is available from the Office de Tourisme).

Lyon has only one central park, the pleasant *Parc de la Tête d'Or*, just north of Brotteaux. It has a small zoo, a lake and a superb rose garden.
Musée des Beaux-Arts A large collection of sculpture and paintings, particularly strong in French 19thC and 20thC art. *20 pl des Terreaux. Open Wed–Mon, 10.45–6.*
Musée de la Civilisation Gallo-Romaine An intelligent display of relics from the time when Lyon was called Lugdunum. *17 rue Cléberg. Open Wed–Sun, 9.30–12, 2–6.*
Musée Historique des Tissus A fine collection of tapestries, fabrics and, above all, silks. *34 rue de la Charité. Open Tue–Sun, 10–12, 2–5.30.*

Guided tours
Office de Tourisme ☎ 78 42 25 75 offers a number of interesting walks and, in summer, river cruises. The 2hr tour of floodlit Vieux-Lyon includes access to private courtyards. *Taxi-Radio* ☎ 78 30 86 86 runs tours of Lyon by taxi with commentary, lasting up to 3hr, depending on the number of sights taken in.

Out of town
Vienne, 30km/19 miles south and easily reached by train or motorway, has superb Roman remains (temples, theatre, mosaics). Pérouges (see also *Hotels*), 39km/24 miles northeast, with a good motorway connection, is a perfectly preserved tiny medieval village, often used as a ready-made film set.

Spectator sports
Racing There are regular horse races at Hippodrome de Bron-Parilly ☎ 78 38 09 69.
Soccer *Olympique Lyonnais* (OL), a 2nd-division club, plays at the Stade Gerland, ave Jean-Jaurès. For information ☎ 78 58 64 22.

Keeping fit
Fitness centre The best and most comprehensively equipped centre open to visitors is *Le Mandala*, 9 rue Boissac ☎ 78 42 74 28.
Golf Two 18-hole golf courses are open to nonmembers (weekdays only): *Golf du Clou* ☎ 74 98 19 65, in Villars-les-Dombes, 30km/19 miles northeast; and *Golf de Lyon-Verger* ☎ 78 02 84 20, 14km/9 miles south.
Squash The *Squash Club de Lyon*, 20 rue Essling ☎ 78 95 13 25 has 4 courts and is open to nonmembers.
Tennis The only club that regularly accepts nonmembers (if you reserve 24hr ahead) is LET ☎ 78 55 63 66. It is 8km/5 miles northeast on exit slip-road 5 (for Beynost) off the A42 motorway. There are outdoor and covered courts.

Local resources
Business services
The major hotels listed can either provide or organize most of the services you are likely to need.
Photocopying and printing *Copy 200* ☎ 78 30 62 69, *J'Imprime* ☎ 78 95 10 92 and 78 24 45 04.
Secretarial *Marcelle Genevier* ☎ 78 86 04 09.
Translation *Peter Brook* ☎ 78 52 74 30.

Communications
Local delivery RAC ☎ 78 58 36 52, *Taxi-Colis* ☎ 72 04 68 00.
Long-distance delivery *Taxi-Colis* ☎ 72 04 68 00.
Post office Main office: Hôtel des Postes, pl Antonin-Poncet.
Telex and fax *International Télex Assistance* ☎ 78 83 46 87.

Conference/exhibition centres
Eurexpo ☎ 72 22 33 44 is Lyon's main exhibition centre. It is just off the A43 autoroute 13km/8 miles east, next to Bron private airport and halfway to Satolas airport. Opened in 1984, it has 9 ha/23 acres of exhibition halls and, as befits Lyon, no fewer than six restaurants.

Eurexpo can also accommodate conferences. During all exhibitions there is a bus shuttle service between Eurexpo and Gare de la Part-Dieu. For major events there is also a shuttle between Eurexpo and Satolas airport.

Central Lyon has two major conference centres: *Palais des Congrès Internationaux*, quai Achille-Lignon, 69006 ☎ 78 93 14 14 whose biggest auditorium has a capacity of 1,000; and the brand-new *Espace Tête d'Or* 103 bd Stalingrad, 69100 Villeurbanne ☎ 78 94 69 00 which has a modular hall that can hold up to 3,000 people. For other conference inquiries, contact the *Bureau des Congrès* in the Office de Tourisme ☎ 78 42 25 75.

Emergencies

Bureaux de change Most major hotels will change currency, but give a rather poor rate. *Thomas Cook*, Gare de la Part-Dieu, daily, 8.30–6.30. *AOC*, 13 rue du Griffon, Mon–Sat, 9–6.

Hospitals 24hr emergency department: *Hôpital Saint-Joseph*, 9 rue du Professeur Grignard ☎ 78 69 81 82; *Hôpital Edouard-Herriot*, 5 pl d'Arsonval ☎ 78 53 81 11. These hospitals will give details of how to get emergency dental treatment during the day.

Pharmacies *Pharmacie Blanchet*, 5 pl des Cordeliers; open all the time. *Pharmacie Perret*, 30 rue Duquesne; open Mon–Sat, 8.30am–7pm.

Police Main station: *Hôtel de Police* 40 rue Marius-Berliet ☎ 78 00 40 40.

Government offices

Worth contacting are the city hall, *Hôtel de Ville*, pl des Terreaux ☎ 78 27 71 31, and the *Préfecture*, cours de la Liberté ☎ 78 62 20 26.

Information sources

Business information By far the most useful organization is Aderly (Association pour le Développement Economique de la Région Lyonnaise), which is a department of the *Chambre de Commerce et de l'Industrie de Lyon*, 20 rue de la Bourse, 69002 ☎ 78 38 10 10. *Aderly* will not only advise the visiting business traveller but give incoming firms practical help on the siting of their business, rental of premises, building permits, housing, schooling, and so on.

Local media The main daily newspaper is the *Progrès de Lyon*, which regularly carries local and national business news. There is also a monthly business magazine, *Entreprises Rhône-Alpes*.

Tourist information The *Office de Tourisme* has a single telephone number ☎ 78 42 25 75 and three bureaux, two of which open longer hours in summer (Jun 15–Sep 15): pl Bellecour (in the middle of the square), Mon–Fri, 9–6 (9–7 in summer), Sat, 9–5 (9–6 in summer); Gare de Perrache, Mon–Sat, 9–12.30, 2–6 (Mon–Sat, 9–7, Sun, 11–6 in summer); and Gare de la Part-Dieu (Mon–Sat, 10–1, 2–6.30). Information about local events and cultural listings will be found in the weekly *Lyon Poche*.

Thank-yous

Chocolates *Maurice Bernachon*, 42 cours Franklin-Roosevelt ☎ 78 24 37 98 (open Sun, closed Mon). Your Lyonnais client will appreciate a gift purchased from this world-famous maker of chocolates who has stubbornly turned down all offers to entice him away from his native city of Lyon.

Florists *Interflora*, 22 pl des Terreaux ☎ 78 28 85 39 will take telephone orders with credit card payment.

MARSEILLE   Zip code 13000

Handsomely set around a wide bay and circled by limestone hills, Marseille with over 900,000 people is France's second largest municipality, as well as the country's foremost port and capital of the Provence and Côte-d'Azur region. It is a potent place, intensely Mediterranean and cosmopolitan. Despite the decline of its port and of much local industry, it remains a major trading centre.

New modern industries, such as electronics, aeronautics and petrochemicals, have developed extensively to the north around Aix and the wide Etang (lagoon) de Berre. Major oil refineries, steel and chemical works have grown up at the big new port of Fos, some way west of the city. Much of the city's own manufacturing industry is in older traditional sectors such as textiles, soaps and heavy engineering, and many firms have closed. But food-processing still does well; Nestlé and Générale Sucrière both employ over 1,000 staff.

Marseille is now setting its cap at a high-tech future. It is building a big new science park ("technopole"), to house various advanced research bodies, including the institute of robotics. And the success of Comex, the famous diving firm, has kept the city at the fore in oceanography.

The city impressively modernized its infrastructure during the 33-year administration of its famous former mayor, Gaston Defferre. He built a Métro system, new autoroutes, beaches, hospitals and much else. But with his death in 1986 an era ended, and the future seems uncertain. Although gangsterism and drug-trafficking, long endemic in the city, are beginning to wane, there are still problems with racial tension and an above-average crime rate. Jean Anouilh called Marseille a "human ant-heap." In some ways it still is.

Arriving

Marseille is well served by a network of autoroutes: one goes east to Toulon and Nice, another north to Aix and Lyon. There are numerous scheduled air services and a rapid TGV rail link to Paris.

Marseille Provence airport

This sizable international airport is out at Marignane, 28km/17 miles northwest of the city. With some 4.5m passengers a year, it claims to be the busiest in the French provinces with flights from about 70 international destinations, as well as the main French towns (an average of 20 daily flights from Paris). There are three terminals linked by a central building with excellent services: bureau de change (open daily till 10.30pm), bank, post office, shops, bars and restaurants (the *Romarin* ☎ 42 89 04 76 is rather good). The *2a Service* ☎ 42 78 21 00 ☎ 420760 provides business facilities useful for those stopping over or not wanting to be in the centre, including private offices, telex, secretarial help, and meeting rooms for up to 300 people. Airport information and freight inquiries ☎ 42 89 90 10.

Nearby hotels Sofitel, 13700 Marignane ☎ 42 89 91 02 ☎ 401980 ● *AE DC MC V*. Large modern hotel next to the airport (free bus shuttle), with attractive, soundproofed bedrooms; big pool, sauna, tennis, boutiques, rooms for seminars, and a gourmet restaurant, *Le Clipper*.

Novotel, 13127 Vitrolles ☎ 42 89 90 44 ᵀˣ 420670 • *AE DC MC V.* Useful cheaper alternative, 3km/2 miles east of airport on D9. Modern and comfortable, it has a grill room and heated pool.
City link The journey into town takes 20–30min, 35–40min in rush hours.

Taxi Cabs are plentiful; reservations ☎ 42 89 03 65.
Car rental All main car rental firms have desks at the airport.
Bus There is a shuttle service between the airport and Gare Saint-Charles in the city centre. Buses leave every 15min, 5.30–10.

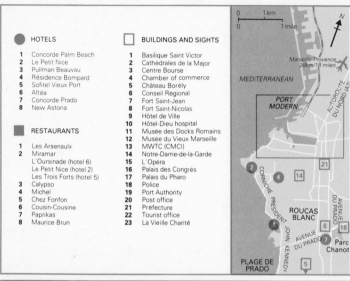

● HOTELS

1   Concorde Palm Beach
2   Le Petit Nice
3   Pullman Beauvau
4   Résidence Bompard
5   Sofitel Vieux Port
6   Altéa
7   Concorde Prado
8   New Astoria

■ RESTAURANTS

1   Les Arsenaulx
2   Miramar
    L'Oursinade (hotel 6)
    Le Petit Nice (hotel 2)
    Les Trois Forts (hotel 5)
3   Calypso
4   Michel
5   Chez Fonfon
6   Cousin-Cousine
7   Paprikas
8   Maurice Brun

□ BUILDINGS AND SIGHTS

1   Basilique Saint Victor
2   Cathédrales de la Major
3   Centre Bourse
4   Chamber of commerce
5   Château Borély
6   Conseil Régional
7   Fort Saint-Jean
8   Fort Saint-Nicolas
9   Hôtel de Ville
10 Hôtel-Dieu hospital
11 Musée des Docks Romains
12 Musée du Vieux Marseille
13 MWTC (CMCI)
14 Notre-Dame-de-la-Garde
15 L'Opéra
16 Palais des Congrès
17 Palais du Pharo
18 Police
19 Port Authority
20 Post office
21 Préfecture
22 Tourist office
23 La Vieille Charité

168

Railway station

The only mainline station is the big, fairly central Gare Saint-Charles. The new Paris–Lyon super-express TGV continues at a slower speed to Marseille, which is linked to Paris by 11 TGVs each way daily. At present the journey takes over four hours.

Facilities at Saint-Charles include a bank, photocopying and plentiful taxis; there is also a Métro station. Inquiries ☎ 91 08 50 50; reservations ☎ 91 08 84 12.

Getting around

The central business zone round La Canebière is fairly compact and can be tackled on foot, but the city extends over a wide area, and to visit the commercial port, the Palais des Congrès in the Prado area or the hotels along the coast road you will need to go by taxi, bus or Métro.

Taxis It is rarely difficult to find a cab in Marseille, but local drivers are not renowned for their courtesy or helpfulness. There are some 40 ranks in the city; or you can call *Marseille Taxi* ☎ 91 02 20 20 or *Taxi-Radio France* ☎ 91 49 91 00.

Driving Narrow streets and reckless double-parking frequently lead to traffic jams, which can be heavy at rush hours, despite the building of ring roads and a tunnel under the Vieux Port. There are plenty of parking facilities but street parking is not easy. Thieving is rife: *never* leave anything visible in your car. All major rental firms have offices in the city. *Avis* ☎ 91 80 12 00, *Budget* ☎ 91 64 40 03, *Europcar* ☎ 91 79 05 29, *Hertz* ☎ 91 56 24 55.

Walking The traffic and the narrow, dusty streets seldom make this a pleasure, but the Vieux Port, La Canebière and hilltop Notre-Dame at least make orientation easy, in this symmetrical city. Women especially should not walk alone after dark in the red-light district north of La Canebière.

Bus and subway The new Métro system is clean, efficient and frequent, and usually the fastest way to get about. There are only two lines, one running from north to south across the city, the other from the northeast suburbs to the centre. The Métro links in with the bus network, which is dense and effective, except that buses become few and infrequent after 9pm, while the Métro is open till 12.30am. Bus and Métro tickets are best bought in sheets of six, from machines. For information ☎ 91 91 92 10.

Area by area

The ancient heart of the city and still its central focus is the narrow inlet of the Vieux Port. To its south rises a high hill topped by the church of Notre-Dame-de-la-Garde, the city's main landmark. The hill was once a smart area but is now very mixed, with much run-down housing. Just north of the Vieux Port, the former medieval heart of Marseille has been rebuilt after wartime bombing; there are some finely restored old palaces and museums and the curious twin cathedrals called Cathédrales de la Major – one 12thC, Romanesque and very small, the other 19thC, Byzantine and huge. Farther north is the vast modern commercial port with its 19km/12 miles of quays, and inland from here stretches a wide industrial area of warehouses and old factories.

Inland from the Vieux Port runs the famous La Canebière, once one of the world's most fashionable boulevards, today tawdry and downmarket. But the compact area around its lower end is still the forum of the city's business and cultural life: here is the World Trade Center, Bourse, opera house and much else. To the south of La Canebière are the major shopping streets; to the north, the main station and a run-down Arab quarter.

The city is divided into 16 numbered *arrondissements*, but the districts informally keep their old names too. The principal well-to-do residential area is the 8e arr, between

Boulevard Michelet and the sea and in the Roucas-Blanc and Périer districts, some 3km/2 miles south of the centre. Here business executives and others live in handsome old villas or smart modern flats. Farther south, other middle-class housing stretches through Sainte-Marguerite and Le Cabot to the vast new university campus at Luminy. The city's main working-class districts are inland, towards Saint-Antoine and La Rose, where ugly postwar blocks of flats crowd the plain and hillsides. There is middle-class housing to the east, in Saint-Barnabé and Saint-Julien.

The suburbs

Nearly all the newer postwar industry is outside the city proper, some in the valley east towards Aubagne, much more to the northwest towards Marignane and the vast expanse of the Etang de Berre. The enclosing chain of rocky hills has prevented Marseille from spreading, so there is little of the semi-rural commuterland found outside many big cities. However, some people do commute daily from the charming resort of Cassis or from the lovely country around Aubagne.

Hotels

The city's business hotels are a varied and scattered assortment, some modern and functional, some much smaller but classically elegant. There are few good ones in the downtown area, but some out along the Corniche (coast road), overlooking the Mediterranean.

Concorde Palm Beach [F]///
2 prom de la Plage, 13008
☎ *91 76 20 00* ⊠ *401894 •* AE DC MC
V *• 161 rooms, 2 restaurants, 1 bar*
This unusual modern hotel is right by the sea, some 5km/3 miles south of the centre – and it pleasantly combines business and leisure features. It is built on the site of a mineral spring, formerly a smart spa centre. A spring still bubbles out of the rocky cliff *inside* the foyer! The place has a breezy club-like atmosphere; the bedrooms are cheerful, and all have sea-facing balconies. A large attractive bar opens onto the sun-terrace and pool, which has warm water supplied by the spring. Good lunchtime buffet in restaurants overlooking the sea. 24hr room service, currency exchange, hairdresser, clothes shop • pool, solarium, private beach, board sailing • 12 meeting rooms (capacity up to 500).

Le Petit Nice [F]////
Anse de Maldormé–Corniche J.F. Kennedy, 13007 ☎ *91 52 14 39*
⊠ *401565 •* AE V *• 15 rooms, 2 suites, 1 restaurant, 1 bar*

This tiny and very superior family-run hotel (a *Relais et Châteaux* member) contrasts sharply with the rest of this teeming city: it is a 19thC villa in Hellenic style about 3km/2 miles from the centre, and is ideal for the executive wanting luxury plus privacy. Classical-style bedrooms and suites are spacious and all have minibars; a pretty palm-shaded garden overlooks the sea, and there is a superb restaurant (see *Restaurants*). Currency exchange, newsstand, hairdryers available on request • sea-water pool, solarium • 1 meeting room (capacity up to 20).

Pullman Beauvau [F]///
4 rue Beauvau, 13001 ☎ *91 54 91 00*
⊠ *401778 •* AE DC MC V *• 71 rooms, 1 suite, 1 bar, no restaurant*
Chopin, Georges Sand, Cocteau and Hemingway were among past visitors to this celebrated 18thC *relais de poste*, surrounded by the bustle of the Vieux Port. Exquisitely restored, with inviting bedrooms in period style, it has real warmth and character and is patronized by opera singers and other celebrities. A pianist performs in the snug,

English-style bar where good buffet breakfasts are served. Light meals available in the bar or bedrooms. All rooms have minibars and hairdryers. Currency exchange • 3 meeting rooms (capacity up to 40).

Résidence Bompard   *F*
2 rue des Flots-Bleus, 13007
☎ *91 52 10 93* ⊤ˣ *400430* • *AE DC V* •
47 rooms, 1 bar; no restaurant
The idyllic Bompard offers a tranquil escape from frenetic downtown Marseille, yet is within a 10min drive of it. High on the hill above the Vieux Port, it is a quiet villa in a big garden, where you can breakfast on a lovely patio. Bedrooms are bright and modern; some are in small bungalows in the garden and have sun-terraces and kitchenettes. 1 meeting room (capacity up to 40).

Sofitel Vieux Port   *F*||||
36 bd Charles-Livon, 13007
☎ *91 52 90 19* ⊤ˣ *401270* • *AE DC MC V* • *130 rooms, 1 restaurant, 1 bar*
This is the city's most prestigious modern hotel. It is a large airy building of attractive design, finely situated on the headland at the entrance to the Vieux Port; on its top floor, the pleasant conference rooms, pretty breakfast room and excellent Les Trois Forts restaurant (see *Restaurants*) all have panoramic views of the port. The bright and spacious Verandah bar is popular for business chats. The bedrooms, some with balconies, are also spacious. Currency exchange • heated pool • fax, 5 meeting rooms (capacity up to 190).

OTHER HOTELS
Altéa   *F*|| *rue Neuve-St-Martin, 13001* ☎ *91 91 91 29* ⊤ˣ *401886* • *AE DC MC V*. A large, well-equipped, modern chain hotel. Very central, with an excellent restaurant (see *Restaurants*), but otherwise impersonal, unbeautiful and with erratic service.
Concorde Prado   *F*|| *11 ave Mazargues, 13008* ☎ *91 76 51 11* ⊤ˣ *420209* • *AE DC MC V*. Efficient modern four-star business hotel, close to Palais des Congrès.
New Astoria   *F*| *10 bd Garibaldi, 13001* ☎ *91 33 33 50* ⊤ˣ *400430* • *AE DC MC V*. Attractively renovated city centre hotel offering outstanding value for money. Large, well-equipped bedrooms and a pleasant conservatory-style foyer.

Restaurants

Really good eating places are legion. Many are smart and comfortable, suitable for business meals; but the seafood can be even better at the simpler, more traditional places down by the coast, and some local clients might prefer to be taken there. Fish, Marseille's forte, comes cooked simply or in one of a hundred complex ways: *bouillabaisse*, queen of the Provençal kitchen, is always very expensive, and not always correctly prepared.

Les Arsenaulx   *F*
25 cours d'Estienne-d'Orves
☎ *91 54 77 06* • *closed Sun and Mon D* • *AE V*
Jeanne and Simone Laffitte, local trendsetters, have recently converted an old arsenal on a peaceful square into a stylish little cultural forum, with bookshop, art gallery, tearoom and restaurant. The latter, open till 1am, has become a fashionable meeting place for the city's intelligentsiae, and is popular for business meals too. The decor is invitingly unusual, with books lining the walls, and the regional cooking has many an inventive flourish.

Miramar   *F*|
12 quai du Port ☎ *91 91 10 40* •
closed Sun, 3 weeks Aug, Dec 24–Jan 6 • *AE DC MC V*

A seedy bistro on the Vieux Port has been newly reborn as a comfortable and smart little restaurant, much admired locally for its fish dishes (including *bouillabaisse*) and its *cassoulet* and desserts. Cordial and attentive service. Good for business meals, including the fixed-price menu, but the outdoor terrace has traffic noise.

L'Oursinade   *F*///
Rue Neuve-St-Martin ☎ *91 91 91 29* • *closed Sun, nat hols, Aug* • *AE DC MC V*
Tucked away in the dull Hotel Altéa is this exciting gastronomic haunt, where a famous chef, René Alloin, offers *nouvelle* variations on Provençal dishes. The modern decor, spacious seating and stylish service all help to make this an ideal spot for a discreet business meal. You can also eat outdoors on the shady patio. Good value fixed-price menu.

Le Petit Nice   *F*////
Anse de Maldormé–Corniche J.F. Kennedy ☎ *91 52 14 39* • *closed Mon (exc D, Jun 1–Sep 30), Jan* • *AE V* • *smart dress*
A distinguished clientele is drawn to this hotel's renowned little restaurant, not only for its extreme comfort and lovely setting, but for the sublime cooking of owner/chefs Jean-Paul and Gérald Passedat. Fish dishes are specially remarkable, and fixed-price menus are good value. You can enjoy wide sea views, whether eating outdoors in the pretty garden or in the intimate dining room. It is very expensive, but worth it.

Les Trois Forts   *F*///
36 bd Charles-Livon ☎ *91 52 90 19* • *AE DC MC V*
On the top floor of the Sofitel hotel, Les Trois Forts enjoys panoramic views of the city, port and sea. Comfort and spaciousness, deft service, cheerful modern decor and interesting cooking by a very talented chef, Marc Bayon, make this an excellent business venue. Very good value fixed-price menus.

Good but casual
Of the many classic fish restaurants along the coast road beyond the Vieux Port, three are specially prized by the Marseillais: *Calypso*, 3 rue des Catalans ☎ 91 52 64 00 (best *bouillabaisse* in town); *Michel*, 6 rue des Catalans ☎ 91 52 64 22, directly opposite Calypso and under same ownership; and *Chez Fonfon*, 140 vallon des Auffes ☎ 91 52 14 38, down in a cottage-lined creek, which looks like a fishing-village yet is right inside the city. None of the three are cheap (good fish seldom is); all are down-to-earth but just right for a leisurely dinner. In the town centre, *Cousin-Cousine*, 102 cours Julien ☎ 91 48 14 50, serves good *nouvelle cuisine*, meat and game as well as fish, in pretty surroundings. For a change you might try *Paprikas*, 24 rue Sainte ☎ 91 33 64 37, which serves authentic Hungarian dishes, with candlelight and soft music in the evenings. Finally, for real Provençal cooking at its best, do not miss the idiosyncratic *Maurice Brun*, 18 quai Rive-Neuve ☎ 91 33 35 38: up a gloomy stairway by the Vieux Port, a gargantuan but unchanging set menu (not cheap) is served with panache.

Out of town
Hemmed in by arid rocky hills on one side, sea and industry on the other, Marseille has fewer good out-of-town venues than most big French cities. However, 22km/14 miles southeast along the coast near Cassis, the elegant and expensive *Presqu'île* ☎ 42 01 03 77 serves high-quality modern cooking in the lovely setting of a *calanque* (cove). At Gémenos, 22km/14 miles due east of the city, *Le Relais de la Magdeleine* ☎ 42 82 20 05 is a beautiful and friendly country-house hotel with garden and pool, perfect for a quiet weekend.

Bars
The bars of the Beauvau, Sofitel and Concorde Palm Beach hotels are all much used for business drinks, although some might find their

evening piano-playing a little intrusive. For a late drink in a friendly youthful atmosphere, try the jazz bar *Le Pelle-Mêle*, 45 cours d'Estienne-d'Orves, or *Le Petit Pernod*, on the quay of the Vieux Port, frequented by *jeunesse dorée*.

Entertainment

The cultural scene is lively, notably for theatre and music; the weekly *Marseille Poche* lists events.

Theatre, dance, opera The well respected regular company of the venerable *Opéra*, pl Reyer ☎ 91 55 14 99, performs all year except in summer; the famous Roland Petit national ballet also has its base here. The leading dramatic repertory company, directed by Marcel Maréchal, is the state-backed *Théâtre La Criée*, 30 quai Rive-Neuve ☎ 91 54 70 54; the city has about ten other theatres and troupes, including a satirical café-théâtre *La Maison Hautée*, 10 rue Vian ☎ 91 92 09 40. A handsome new cultural centre near the cathedral, *La Vieille-Charité*, rue de la Charité ☎ 91 54 77 75, is used for both plays and concerts.

Music and festivals The Orchestre Philharmonique de Marseille, created in 1987, has made a promising debut. Various music groups often give concerts in *Saint-Victor* and other churches; in summer there are outdoor concerts and ballet at the *Palais du Pharo*, bd Charles-Livon ☎ 91 52 90 90. Other annual events include an international folklore festival in July at Château-Gombert, and in December a picturesque fair of *santons* (Provençal clay figurines) on La Canebière.

Cinemas "Art" and subtitled foreign movies are shown at the *Paris* ☎ 91 33 41 54 or 91 33 15 59.

Nightlife Of the dozen leading discos, *Le Duke*, 6 rue Lulli ☎ 91 33 14 88, is the most trendy and sophisticated and *Satellite*, corniche J.F. Kennedy ☎ 91 52 00 11, the most decorous. *L'Abbaye de la Commanderie*, 20 rue Corneille

☎ 91 33 45 56, is a snug cabaret/bar with Marseillais songs and jokes for those familiar with the patois. The nearest casino is *Casino Municipal*, La Rostague, ave du Docteur Leriche, at Cassis ☎ 42 01 78 32, besieged by Marseillais gamblers at weekends.

Shopping

The smartest boutiques are in the streets running south from La Canebière – Rue St-Ferréol, Rue de Rome, Rue Paradis. Nearby, the *Centre Bourse* is a lavish new shopping-centre with a good department store, *Nouvelles Galeries*, and 70 other shops. Other big centres are at Bonneveine, on the coast, and off the autoroute to Aubagne.

Small shops selling local products include *Bataille*, 18 rue Fontange, and *Marrou*, 15 pl Castellane (wines, cheeses and other foods), *La Taste*, 73 cours Julien (Provençal herbs and spices), and *Les Olivades*, 3 rue Moustier (fabrics and *santons*). Good open-air markets (mornings only) are in Avenue du Prado (food and clothes) and the Vieux Port fish market.

Sightseeing

Though not generally thought of as a major tourist city, Marseille contains almost as much of interest as nearby Aix or Arles. Right next to the Centre Bourse, the remains of the ancient Greek port and town have been turned into a small public garden where you can walk amid the ruins.

Basilique Saint-Victor 5thC fortified church, rich in early Christian history; the crypt holds the tomb of two 3rdC martyrs. *Rue Sainte. Open daily.*

Château Borély Lovely 18thC mansion in a park, housing remarkable collections of Egyptian, Greek and Roman antiquities, and French 18thC drawings. *Ave Borély. Open Wed, 1–5.30; Thu–Mon, 9.30–12.15, 1–5.30.*

Musée des Beaux-Arts Splendid collection including Daumier caricatures and Puget sculptures (both artists were Marseillais), as well as works by Rubens and Brueghel; Serre's horrific canvasses of the city during the 1721 plague. *Palais Longchamp. Open Wed, 2–6; Thu–Mon, 10–12, 2–6.*

Musée des Docks Romains The original Roman docks in their actual setting on the Vieux Port, near the Greek remains, along with numerous Roman amphorae and grain storage jars. *4 pl Vivaux. Open Wed, 2–6; Thu–Mon, 10–12, 2–6.*

Musée du Vieux Marseille Absorbing local folk-art museum in a 16thC house. Vivid arrays of figurines. *2 rue de la Prison. Open Wed, 2–6; Thu–Mon, 10–12, 2–6.*

Château d'If Notorious 16thC fortress, on islet 3km/2 miles offshore, long used as a State prison, for the "Man in the Iron Mask" and others. Walls have the carvings left by Huguenot prisoners. *Boats leave from Vieux Port every 30min, 9–12, 2–7 in summer; every hour, 9–12 in winter.*

Guided tours
Valadou-Mottet, 73–75 La Canabière ☎ 91 91 90 02, runs morning tours of the city in summer, lasting 2–3hr.

Spectator sports
Horse-racing Regular meetings at the Borély course ☎ 91 77 88 91.
Motor-racing One of the best circuits in France, with events nearly every weekend, is the *Circuit Paul Ricard* ☎ 94 90 74 90, at Le Beausset, 40km/25 miles east of the city.
Soccer *Olympique Marseillais* (OM), a successful 1st-division team, plays at the Stade Vélodrome, 3 bd Michelet ☎ 91 77 07 28.

Keeping fit
There is no suitable fitness or health centre open to visitors, but many other sports are available.
Golf The nearest 18-hole course is 22km/14 miles north at *Les Milles*, Domaine Riquetti, Aix ☎ 42 24 20 41.
Sailing *Centre Municipal de Voile*,

prom de la Plage ☎ 91 76 31 60.
Squash This sport is now much in fashion. *Set Squash de Marseille*, 265 ave du Mazargues ☎ 91 71 94 71 and *Le Fitness*, ave de St-Roch, Le Rove ☎ 91 09 92 92 are clubs with sauna and pool as well as squash courts.
Swimming Best sea-bathing is at the municipal beach, often crowded, at Promenade de la Plage. Best pool is *Luminy*, rte Léon-Lachamp ☎ 91 41 26 59, in southern suburbs. Or try the Concorde Palm Beach hotel.
Tennis The clubs in town are mostly exclusive, rarely admitting nonmembers, but try *Raquette Club*, 139 chemin Pont de Vivaux ☎ 91 75 19 33. Best club open to the public is 15km/9 miles north: *Arbois*, quartier la Mere, Plan de Campagne ☎ 42 22 20 84, with 30 courts.

Local resources
Business services
While the main hotels can advise or help, it is also well worth contacting the big new *Mediterranean World Trade Center* (MWTC), 2 rue Henri Barbusse, 13241 ☎ 91 08 61 23 ✉ 441247: this will give advice on all matters, has an information bureau, and can rent out furnished offices and supply secretaries and translators. Users must belong to one of the 119 World Trade Center clubs.
Photocopying and printing *Sécretariat Service* ☎ 91 33 81 77 and *Gestetner* ☎ 91 79 91 30 offer prompt service.
Secretarial *Sécretariat Service*, *Manpower* ☎ 91 91 09 22.
Translation *Pierre Franchi* ☎ 91 53 36 47, *SEFIP* ☎ 91 64 42 56.

Communications
Local delivery *Marseille Courses* ☎ 91 37 57 82.
Long-distance delivery DHL ☎ 42 75 25 90.
Post office Main office: 1 pl Hôtel des Postes ☎ 91 90 00 16.
Telex and fax At main post office; also MWTC.

Conference/exhibition centres

The *Palais des Congrès*, Parc Chanot, 13226 ☎ 91 76 19 00 ℻ 410021, has two exhibition halls totalling 2,900 sq metres, seven meeting halls seating up to 1,250. Métro and bus lines run to the city centre, 3km/2 miles away. International trade fairs are held here in April and September. *Mediterranean World Trade Center* (see above) is smaller but more central and modern: two exhibition halls, totalling 990 sq metres, six meeting rooms seating up to 430. Like the Palais des Congrès, it has film-projecting and simultaneous translation amenities; it also has video and satellite liaison facilities. Some other conference venues: *Château des Fleurs*, 16 bd Michelet, 13008 ☎ 91 77 75 14; *Salle Saint-Georges*, 97 ave de la Corse, 13007 ☎ 91 52 51 01.

Emergencies

Bureaux de change *Thomas Cook*, Gare Saint-Charles, weekdays 6–8, weekends 6–6; *Change de la Bourse*, Centre Bourse, Mon–Sat, 8.30–6.30. **Hospitals** The most central of the city's many hospitals is *Hôtel-Dieu*, 6 pl Daviel ☎ 91 91 91 61. *SAMU* urgent 24hr medical service ☎ 91 49 91 91; *SOS Médecins* (doctors on call) ☎ 91 52 84 85; *SOS Dentistes* ☎ 91 25 77 77. **Pharmacies** *Garbit et Michel*, 166 La Canebière, *Brémond*, 183 rue de Rome, both open till 9.30pm, closed Sun. For rota of places open Sun and at night, see press or notice on any pharmacy door. **Police** Main station: 1 quai Joliette ☎ 91 91 90 40.

Government offices

Hôtel de Ville, quai du Port ☎ 91 91 90 00; *Préfecture*, 1 rue E. Rostaud ☎ 91 57 20 00; *Conseil Régional de Provence/Côte-d'Azur*, 322 ave Prado ☎ 91 76 55 35.

Information sources

Business information The city's *Chambre de Commerce et d'Industrie*, Palais de la Bourse, La Canebière, 13001 ☎ 91 91 91 51 ℻ 410091 fax 91914225, has excellent information and international relations services for the visitor, as does the *MWTC* ☎ 91 08 61 23.

Local media *Le Méridional*, right-of-centre, and *Le Provençal*, pro-Socialist, are the city's main dailies, with fairly good economic coverage; *Le Soir* is an evening paper, *La Marseillaise* a Communist daily. The local state TV station, *FR3*, has a nightly news magazine; *Radio Monte-Carlo* and the local *Radio France* station are also good for local news.

Tourist information The city's *Office du Tourisme*, 4 La Canebière ☎ 91 54 91 11, is open daily 8–9. Its branch at the Gare Saint-Charles is open Mon–Sat, 8–8. *Le Mois à Marseille* is a monthly events listing.

Thank-yous

Chocolates *Lucien Boyer*, 196 rue de Rome ☎ 91 37 78 61; *Puyricard*, 315 corniche J.F. Kennedy ☎ 91 31 31 32. **Florists** *Digitale*, 14 rue Breteuil ☎ 91 54 37 00; *Florelia*, 425 rue Paradis ☎ 91 22 81 12 and 187 rue de Rome ☎ 91 48 72 52.

MONTPELLIER
Zip code 34000

Montpellier's recent transformation from sleepy old wine-town to trendy modern technopolis has been astonishing. It has now seized from Grenoble and Toulouse the title of fastest-growing French boom city; and though its industrial base is still modest compared with theirs, it is pulsating with new research and high-tech ventures, helped by its university tradition and its attractive location in the sunny south. It lies on the historic plain of Languedoc, between the Mediterranean coast and the stony foothills of the Cévennes.

Until the 1960s, the economy of this lovely medieval city depended largely on the vineyards of the Languedoc plain which produce 40% of France's cheaper table wine. Then several events began to stir it out of its lethargy. The arrival of some 25,000 repatriated French settlers from Algeria produced a wave of dynamism. The government marked out the area for special development, building huge new coastal resorts which have brought new jobs and more modern and outward-looking attitudes. And in 1965 IBM built a plant which has since expanded into its largest in France, with a staff of 2,900 at work on the giant 308x and 3090 computers. Indeed, IBM has blazed the trail for other high-tech companies; these are active not only in the field of electronics, but also in pharmaceuticals, medical equipment and food processing. The population of the urban area has trebled since the mid-1960s, to reach 300,000. But unemployment is high, for the boom reputation is drawing too many job-seekers from outside.

The university's renowned medical school, founded in the 12th century, has provided another base for expansion. Today the city has 45,000 students in a diverse range of faculties, and 4,000 researchers in laboratories and institutes that collaborate with local firms. The research effort is fourfold: medical, notably molecular biology and anti-cancer studies; agronomic, especially tropical produce; electronics and computers, based on IBM; new media – an optical fibre 15-channel TV cable network is being installed, due to reach every home by 1989.

Economic growth is being matched by some striking new town planning projects, ever since the Socialists won power locally in 1977 under Georges Frèche, the most ambitious and grandiloquent mayor in France. He hired the famous Barcelona architect Ricardo Bofill to build "Antigone," a downtown housing complex of monumentalist design, now nearing completion. Some local people enjoy Antigone with its massive porticos and colonnades, others find it "Mussolinian": but at least it has put the city on the world architectural map. A huge new business and cultural complex is also being built and the airport is about to be doubled in size. It's all very exciting. But is it all too much? The other cities of the Languedoc/Roussillon region, notably Nîmes and Perpignan, have become vocally jealous and critical of their capital. They feel that it is now "colonizing" them, just as Paris used to do in the days before regional reform.

Arriving

Montpellier lies right beside the main south coast autoroute which goes west to Toulouse and on into Spain, east to Lyon and Marseille. It also has good rail and air links with many cities.

Fréjorgues airport

There are five daily flights to Paris (flight time about 1hr), and scheduled services to most major European destinations. But the terminal is too small for the needs of this fast-expanding city and is to be doubled in size by 1989. Until then, facilities are few: a good restaurant, a chamber of commerce information office ☎ 67 65 60 65, but no bureau de change and just one small shop. Airport information ☎ 67 65 60 65.
Nearby hotels Novotel, 125 bis ave de Palavas ☎ 67 64 04 04 ⊠ 490433 • *AE DC MC V*. A useful modern chain hotel at the A9 autoroute exit, 3km/2 miles south of the city and 6km/4 miles northwest of the airport (bus shuttle). Swimming pool, restaurant, conference rooms.
City link The airport is 8km/5 miles southeast. Bus links with the city are unreliable so a taxi is best. These are plentiful; or you can reserve one ☎ 67 29 52 21. All major car rental firms have airport desks.

Railway station

The TGV express Paris–Lyon goes on at a slower rate to Montpellier, which is linked to Paris by six TGVs a day – a journey of about 5hr. There are good rail links with many other cities, French and foreign. The station is very near the city centre. Passenger inquiries ☎ 67 58 50 50.

Getting around

The central area is very compact, partly pedestrianized and best negotiated on foot. Most public buildings are here. But a car or taxi would be needed to go farther out to the university or IBM, for example.
Taxis There are several ranks, the best being at the station. To reserve a

taxi: TRAM ☎ 67 92 04 55 or 67 58 10 10; *Radio Taxis* ☎ 67 58 74 82.
Driving The city's layout makes this very confusing at first, for the inner ring road round the Vieille Ville is one-way clockwise; and as the central area has been largely closed to traffic, you can get to it only to park. If you need to go there, use one of the big new underground garages, which have ample space, and colour codes to help you keep your bearings. Driving in the suburbs presents fewer problems and traffic jams are fairly rare. All the major car rental firms have offices in the city: *Avis* ☎ 67 64 61 84, *Budget* ☎ 67 64 37 29, *Europcar* ☎ 67 58 16 17, *Hertz* ☎ 67 58 65 18.
Walking In the Vieille Ville and other central areas of a city where the pedestrian is paramount, walking is enjoyable and presents no safety problems.
Bus A good network covers all the suburbs. One new service circles the inner ring road at 10min intervals – but it may be quicker to walk. Bus information ☎ 67 92 01 43.

Area by area

Modern Montpellier radiates out from its medieval kernel, the enchanting Vieille Ville. This has been restored, its narrow streets closed to through traffic, and today in true Midi style it remains a lively social forum, full of outdoor cafés and markets. Here the local nobility and older bourgeoisie still live in their handsome 17thC and 18thC mansions; here too are the Préfecture, the main museums and many university buildings. To the west is the stately belvedere of Promenade du Peyrou.

On the south side the broad Place de la Comédie, now paved over and filled with cafés, is the city's main social focus; it is known locally as "Place de l'Oeuf" because of its oval shape. Since the 1970s a modern piazza, called Le Polygone, has been grafted onto it. This is skirted by the new town hall and a big shopping centre. Beyond it, Bofill's vast "Antigone" descends majestically to the river Lez. And an ambitious new business and cultural complex is being completed at the end of the Esplanade leading from Place de la Comédie. Just inside the eastern edge of the Vieille Ville lies the Jardin du Champ de Mars.

While this whole central area is striking and unusual, the rest of the city is more humdrum. A drab commercial zone round the station leads to the middle-class Cours Gambetta district. Beyond, the modern town has expanded on every side – new working-class suburbs to the south (Saint-Martin) and northwest (La Paillarde); new

hospitals and huge university campuses to the north; and new industry, notably IBM, to the east.

The surrounding area

The hilly country just north of the town has been filling up with the homes of university and IBM staff and other commuters; some live in modern villa estates, others in old villages or converted farmhouses. To the south, other often ugly new suburbs sprawl across the plain towards the lagoons by the sea. And on all sides roll the endless vineyards.

The city is only 12km/7 miles from the cluttered, old-established beach resorts of Palavas and Carnon, and

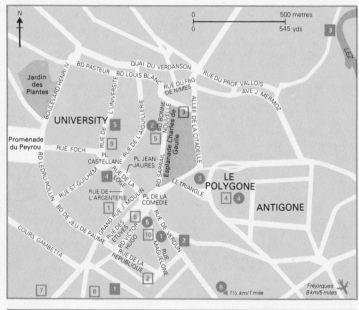

	HOTELS		RESTAURANTS		BUILDINGS AND SIGHTS
1	Métropole	1	Le Chandelier	1	Chamber of commerce
2	Noailles	2	Janus	2	Conseil Régional
3	Sofitel	3	La Réserve Rimbaud	3	Le Corum
4	Altéa	4	Le Louvre	4	Hôtel de Ville
5	Grand Hôtel du Midi	5	Le Bouchou	5	Musée Fabre
6	Novotel			6	Théâtre Municipal
				7	Police
				8	Post office
				9	Préfecture
				10	Tourist office

18km/11 miles from La Grande Motte, a huge and famous new resort built in modernistic style with a busy marina. Many city workers commute from all these places. Farther off, to the southwest, is the delightful old port of Sète, its little canals lined with excellent fish restaurants.

Hotels

For a boom city Montpellier is still somewhat under-equipped with good hotels, but there are some perfectly acceptable places in the town centre.

Métropole *F*///

3 rue du Clos-René ☎ *67 58 11 22* Ⓣ *480410* • *Mapotel* • *AE DC MC V* • *84 rooms, 4 suites, 1 restaurant, 1 bar*
Centrally located near the station, the city's premier hotel is sedately classical, with period furnishings and tapestries and a discreet, old-fashioned atmosphere: but most bedrooms have been comfortably modernized (the price-range is huge, for some are still quite simple). Best feature is the quiet shady garden where drinks and meals are served in summer. Currency exchange • jacuzzi • 7 meeting rooms (capacity up to 200).

Noailles *F*/

2 rue des Ecoles-Centrales ☎ *67 60 49 80* • *closed mid-Dec–mid-Jan* • *AE DC MC V* • *30 rooms; no restaurant*
A 17thC mansion in the heart of the Vieille Ville, now a graceful little hotel with friendly and helpful service. Quiet rooms at the back.

Sofitel *F*///

Le Triangle ☎ *67 58 45 45* Ⓣ *480140* • *AE DC MC V* • *98 rooms, 1 bar; no restaurant*
This functional but comfortable modern hotel is very central, next to Le Polygone: some of its bedrooms give onto the Esplanade gardens. The keep-fit club below the hotel has sauna, gym • 1 meeting room (capacity up to 20).

OTHER HOTELS

Altéa *F*/ *Le Polygone*
☎ *67 64 65 66* Ⓣ *480362* • *AE DC MC V.* A modern chain hotel, with central location, good restaurant and good facilities, making up for the ugly design and decor.
Grand Hôtel du Midi *F*/ *22 bd Victor-Hugo* ☎ *67 92 69 61* Ⓣ *490752* • *AE DC MC V.* An old building of character, recently renovated, with period furnishings but modern comforts.
Novotel *F*/ *125 bis ave de Palavas* ☎ *67 64 04 04* Ⓣ *490433* • *AE DC MC V.* A standardized but cheerful and efficient chain hotel, convenient for the autoroute, airport and beaches. Grill room, pool.

Out of town

The best choice is *La Demeure des Brousses* ☎ 67 65 77 66, only 4km/2 miles east of the city, within earshot of motorway hum but otherwise entirely bucolic – a lovely 18thC mansion in a big park with tall, ancient trees. Elegant bedrooms in "period" style and a good restaurant. *Les Reganeous* ☎ 67 92 52 18, just south of the city on the road to Palavas, is a small, single-storey hotel adjacent to a ranch-like roadhouse with grill room, disco and pool – a good place for relaxing.

Restaurants

Three places at least provide good regional cuisine in a suitable setting for a working meal; for informal eating, the choice is much wider.

Le Chandelier *F*//

3 rue Leenhardt ☎ *67 92 61 62* • *closed Mon L, Sun, 1 week in Feb, 3 weeks in Aug* • *AE DC V*
A drab street near the station is the unpromising setting for this really elegant restaurant, decked out with Hellenic decor of columns, statues and ornamental pool. Service is gracious and table seating spacious: but a business clientele is drawn, above all, by the excellent, creative cooking of *patron*-chef Gilbert

Furlan, who adapts classic regional dishes.

Janus [F]/
11 rue Aristide-Ollivier ☎ *67 58 15 61 • closed Sun • AE DC MC V*
Affable *patron*-chef François Lucéna serves the dishes of his native Gascony, and those of the Languedoc region, at his stylish and very animated new restaurant, which is much in vogue for business lunches and convivial dinners alike. The decor is bright and modern, with lots of mirrors; the first-rate cuisine mixes modern and traditional, with a good value fixed-priced menu changing daily.

La Réserve Rimbaud [F]/
820 ave de St-Maur ☎ *67 72 52 53 • closed Sun D, Mon, Jan • AE DC MC V*
A delightful outdoor terrace by the river is the best feature of this restaurant where the decor is pleasant, the service friendly, and the traditional cooking is usually – but not always – good. The fixed-price menu is very good value.

Good but casual
The narrow streets of the Vieille Ville contain many lively and informal eating places. One of the best is the intimate and friendly *Le Louvre*, 2 rue de la Vieille ☎ 67 60 59 37, with good regional cooking and a modestly-priced set menu. *Le Bouchou*, 7 rue de l'Université ☎ 67 66 26 20, is a warm and relaxed place, good value, and popular with students. On a fine day, it is fun to eat outdoors at one of the many inexpensive places in Place Jean-Jaurès or Place de la Chapelle Neuve.

Food and wine
Information and guidance on French food, including regional cooking, and on wine types and vintages are given in the *Planning and Reference* section.

Bars
Best of the hotel bars is *La Louisiane*, the piano-bar of the *Midi*, which is light and spacious. *César*, in "Antigone," is on the quiet Place du Nombre d'Or. *La Comédia*, rue de Verdun, is modern and trendy, and serves snacks as well as drinks. *Le London Tavern*, in the Vieille Ville, has comfortable upholstered banquettes in "English" style. All these bars have outdoor terraces.

Entertainment
Theatre, dance, music Cultural listings appear in the weekly *Sortir*. *Théâtre Municipal*, pl de la Comédie ☎ 67 66 00 92, is used for an opera season, Oct–Jun, for ballet (Dominique Bagouet's local company is good), and for concerts by the local philharmonic orchestra and others. A state-backed theatre company, Treize Vents, performs at the *Domaine de Grammont* ☎ 67 64 14 42, just out of town on the road to Mauguio. In July there is an international dance festival and an ambitious Radio France music festival. The *Salle Zénith*, Domaine de Grammont, is used for jazz and pop concerts.
Cinema Best cinemas for subtitled foreign films are *Le Club*, 5 ave Docteur-Pezet ☎ 67 63 49 93, and *Diagonal* 2 rue Marcellin-Albert, Celleneuve ☎ 67 75 41 90.
Nightclubs and casinos A good bar with music is *Les Chandelles*, 18 rue de l'Aiguillerie ☎ 67 66 32 05. Best nearby casino is at La Grande Motte ☎ 67 56 54 03.

Shopping
The central *Polygone* shopping centre has *Galeries Lafayette* and 80 boutiques; other centres are on the outskirts. Small shops selling local crafts such as porcelain and sculpted olive wood can be found in Rue de la Loge and Rue St-Guilhem.

Sightseeing
There are few striking museums, apart from the excellent *Musée Fabre*, bd Sarrail ☎ 67 66 06 34 (closed

Mon), which includes paintings by Greuze, Delacroix and Courbet. The *Jardin des Plantes* has many fine tropical trees and plants. Open daily.

Spectator sports
Bullfights Go to nearby Palavas or, better, to Nîmes or Arles.
Soccer The city's first-division team plays at *La Paillarde* ☎ 67 75 24 01.

Keeping fit
Fitness centres There are several good centres with sauna and gym: *Espace Carmette*, Le Polygone ☎ 67 58 45 72; *Occikiai*, 27 rte de Nîmes ☎ 67 79 65 22.
Golf There are two new 18-hole courses at Baillargues and La Grande Motte.
Sailing Best places are Mèze and Sète, to the southwest; for board sailing, La Grande Motte.
Swimming Try the Palavas or Grande Motte beaches, or the pool at the Reganeous hotel.
Tennis *Club de Grammont*, rte de Mauguio ☎ 67 64 29 55.

Local resources
Business services
The Hôtel Altéa has offices for rent. *Acte* ☎ 67 64 00 07 and *Sesame* ☎ 67 58 41 51 can provide offices, bilingual secretaries, telex, fax and other services.
Photocopying and printing *Sesame* ☎ 67 58 41 51; *Quick Print* ☎ 67 63 32 05.
Secretarial *Acte* ☎ 67 64 00 07; *Sesame* ☎ 67 58 41 51; also *Bis France* ☎ 67 58 36 24.
Translation *Sesame; Photex Bureau du Polygone* ☎ 67 65 05 90.

Communications
Local delivery *Ducros* ☎ 67 42 40 50.
Long distance delivery DHL offices in Marseille and Toulouse will pick up from Montpellier.
Post office Main office: pl Rondelet ☎ 67 34 50 00.
Telex and fax At main post office.

Conference/exhibition centres
A big new conference and cultural centre, *Le Corum*, is being built at the Esplanade in the heart of town and is due to open in stages during 1988–89: for details, ask at the town hall. In the meantime, the best centre is the *Parc des Expositions*, rte de Carnon ☎ 67 64 12 12.

Emergencies
Bureaux de change *Crédit Agricole*, passage Lonjon, open Mon–Sat, 10.30–12.30, 2–6.
Hospitals Main hospital is *Lapeyronie*, 555 rte de Ganges ☎ 67 33 80 08. Emergencies: ☎ 67 33 81 68. For dental emergencies ☎ 67 33 82 35.
Pharmacies For pharmacies open late and on Sun ☎ 67 58 74 22.
Police Main station: 22 ave Clemenceau ☎ 67 58 74 22.

Government offices
Mairie, Le Polygone ☎ 67 34 70 00; *Préfecture*, pl du Marché aux Fleurs ☎ 67 61 61 61.

Information sources
Business information The PR department of the *District de Montpellier*, 14 rue Marcel-de-Serres ☎ 67 52 18 19 ⊤ˣ 490531, can be just as helpful as the *Chambre de Commerce et de l'Industrie*, 32 Grand'rue Jean-Moulin ☎ 67 66 01 34.
Local media The local daily is *Midi Libre*, centre-right; *Le Méridien* is a useful economic weekly and *La Lettre M* is an economic intelligence report, sold on subscription only. *Radio France Hérault* is good for local news, while the TV channel FR*3* has an evening local news magazine.
Tourist information Office du Tourisme, 6 rue Maguelonne ☎ 67 58 26 04.

Thank-yous
Florist *Roger Pingeon*, 44 cours Gambetta ☎ 67 92 13 64.

NANCY
Zip code 54000

Unlike much of the Lorraine region, Nancy has never been dependent on the heavy industry whose recent sharp decline has had such a serious effect on the local economy. The city has respected universities, with important science and medical faculties, and various *grandes écoles* (including the recently established Institut National Polytechnique de Lorraine, with five associated engineering schools. The city's strength lies in the links it has forged between these academic centres and the developing high-technology sector. Nancy-Brabois-Innovation, one of France's first technoparks, has managed to attract some big names – Alsthom-Atlantique, Bouygues, Olivetti, Philips – and an extension is planned close to the city centre.

Nancy is a frequent choice of location for companies' eastern regional headquarters, and its dynamic conference centre is bringing an increasing amount of business. The age-old rivalry with Metz, only 60km/38 miles away, has been largely superseded by an awareness of the need jointly to combat the economic problems facing Lorraine as a whole.

Arriving
At present Nancy has only a small domestic airport, 4km/2 miles east of the city, though a new international airport is being built at Louvigny, 42km/26 miles to the north (due to open 1991). Journey time from Paris by fast train is about 3hr; by motorway, about 4hr.

Nancy-Essey airport There are regular flights to and from Paris and Lyon; summer flights from Nice. Taxis are generally available when scheduled flights arrive. Reservations ☎ 83 21 56 90.

Railway station There are 12 services a day to and from Paris and direct services to Strasbourg and Metz. Passenger inquiries ☎ 83 56 50 50; reservations ☎ 83 35 08 58.

Getting around
Traffic jams are rare, but a network of one-way streets makes driving in the centre impractical for those unfamiliar with the city. If your business takes you outside the city, renting a car may be worthwhile. All leading companies have offices. The central area is small and the business area, the conference centre, main hotels and station are all within walking distance of one another.

Taxis ☎ 83 37 65 37. The main rank is outside the station.

Buses Nancy has a good bus network and electric trolley buses. Services run to outlying districts, including the technopark. The central information kiosk at Place Maginot ☎ 83 37 12 12 sells maps and tickets, which can also be bought at various café-tobacconists or newsagents.

Area by area
The heart of Nancy is the lovely 18thC Place Stanislas, which links the medieval Ville Vieille and the Ville Neuve. To the north Rue Héré and Place de la Carrière lead to the old town and Parc de la Pépinière. The busy shopping and business area lies to the west around Rue Saint-Dizier, Rue Saint-Jean and Place Thiers. The mainly residential districts lie farther out beyond the railway line.

The arts faculty and the developing Manufacture des Tabacs complex lie to the west of the old town, while the science faculties are up above the city to the south, on the edge of Vandoeuvre, a new satellite town. Nearby are the big teaching hospital and the technopark.

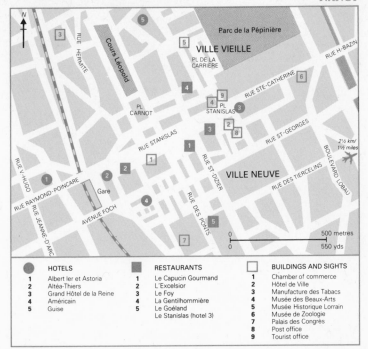

	HOTELS		RESTAURANTS		BUILDINGS AND SIGHTS
1	Albert 1er et Astoria	1	Le Capucin Gourmand	1	Chamber of commerce
2	Altéa-Thiers	2	L'Excelsior	2	Hôtel de Ville
3	Grand Hôtel de la Reine	3	Le Foy	3	Manufacture des Tabacs
4	Américain	4	La Gentilhommière	4	Musée des Beaux-Arts
5	Guise	5	Le Goéland	5	Musée Historique Lorrain
			Le Stanislas (hotel 3)	6	Musée de Zoologie
				7	Palais des Congrès
				8	Post office
				9	Tourist office

Hotels

Nancy's top hotel, the Grand Hôtel de la Reine, is right in the town centre. The other hotels catering to the business traveller are all near the station, though the two Novotels attract some people travelling by car.

Albert 1er et Astoria *F*|
3 rue de l'Armée-Patton ☎ *83 40 31 24* ⊤Ⅹ *850895 • Albastor-Nancy • AE DC MC V • 132 rooms, 4 suites, 1 bar; no restaurant*
This twin hotel near the station is built round a quiet central courtyard. The rooms are well planned and the service good. 3 meeting rooms (capacity up to 40).

Altéa-Thiers *F*|
11 rue Raymond-Poincaré ☎ *83 35 61 01* ⊤Ⅹ *960034 • AE DC MC V • 108 rooms, 4 suites, 1 restaurant, 1 bar*
Originally called the Frantel, this

hotel in a tower block opposite the station is very popular with business travellers and conference delegates, so advance reservations are advisable. The rooms are modern and functional, with good working space, air conditioning and double glazing. The hotel's restaurant, *La Toison d'Or*, is much used for business entertaining (see *Keeping fit*) • 3 meeting rooms (capacity up to 250).

Grand Hôtel de la Reine *F*||
2 pl Stanislas ☎ *83 35 03 01* ⊤Ⅹ *960367 • Concorde • AE DC MC V • 49 rooms, 3 suites, 1 restaurant, 1 bar*
This very grand hotel gets its name from Marie Antoinette, who stayed there in 1770. Its very comfortable rooms are decorated and furnished in Louis XV style. The salons are ideal for top-level business meetings. The pleasant restaurant (see *Restaurants*)

overlooks the square; the bar, furnished in "London club" style, is popular with business people. 5 meeting rooms (capacity up to 120).

OTHER HOTELS

Américain [F] 3 pl André-Maginot ☎ 83 32 28 53 ⊤ˣ 961052 • AE DC MC V. A modernized, central hotel, with two well-equipped meeting rooms.

Guise [F] 18 rue de Guise ☎ 83 32 24 68. A modestly equipped but charming little hotel in the Ville Vieille with a quiet atmosphere.

Out of town

Novotel Nancy Ouest ☎ 83 96 67 46 ⊤ˣ 850988 at Laxou and the smaller *Novotel Nancy Sud* ☎ 83 56 10 25 ⊤ˣ 961124 at Houdemont are both 5km/3 miles from the city. Both have meeting rooms, seating up to 300 and 200 respectively, and the usual Novotel amenities, including a pool.

Restaurants

Nancy's two top hotels have good restaurants frequently used for business entertaining, but the city also has several other suitable restaurants, including the top-class Le Capucin Gourmand. Rue des Maréchaux, locally known as "rue gourmande," is lined with lively restaurants for social evenings.

Le Capucin Gourmand [F]///
31 rue Gambetta ☎ 83 35 26 98 • *closed Sun D, Mon, Aug* • AE V
Nancy's top restaurant, with Art Nouveau decor and mostly *nouvelle cuisine*, is in the town centre. Private dining room available. The cheaper set menus are exceptional value.

L'Excelsior [F]
50 rue Henri-Poincaré ☎ 83 35 24 57 • AE DC MC V • *reservations essential L*
A fashionable brasserie with original Art Nouveau decor, known locally as the Flo, after the group who own it. The service is cheerfully speedy and the food is reliable with a

strong line in seafood. Popular for business lunches, it is also pleasant for relaxed evenings. Private dining rooms available.

Le Foy [F]
1 pl Stanislas ☎ 83 32 21 44 • *closed Wed, Jan* • V
Overlooking Place Stanislas, this quiet restaurant is a good place for business lunches. The set menus offer good value.

La Gentilhommière [F]//
29 rue des Maréchaux ☎ 83 32 26 44 • *closed Sat, Sun, 1 week in Feb, 2 weeks in Aug, Christmas and New Year period* • MC V
This well-run restaurant has a pleasant lounge bar and serves a mixture of classical and *nouvelle* cuisine. It has a loyal business clientele at lunch time and an equally loyal local following in the evening.

Le Goéland [F]//
27 rue des Ponts ☎ 83 35 17 25 • *closed Mon L, Sun* • AE DC V • *reservations essential*
An excellent fish and seafood restaurant, convenient for the nearby conference centre.

Le Stanislas [F]///
2 pl Stanislas ☎ 83 35 03 01 • AE DC MC V
The elegant restaurant of the Grand Hôtel de la Reine has a discreet atmosphere. There is an interesting regional flavour to the *nouvelle*-influenced cuisine and an excellent, though very expensive, wine list.

Out of town

Les Vannes et sa Résidence ☎ 83 24 46 01, at Liverdun, 16km/10 miles northwest of Nancy, is well known for its *nouvelle cuisine*. Also in Liverdun, the *Golf et Val Fleuri* ☎ 83 24 54 17 serves good classical dishes. The *Château d'Adomenil* ☎ 83 74 04 81, 35km/22 miles away in the countryside close to Lunéville, is used for important entertaining, mainly in the evening.

Bars

The top hotels' bars may be used for business discussions and more casual social drinking: the *Stan*, in the Grand Hôtel de la Reine, is narrow but stylish; *Le Club*, in the Altéa, is large and busy; the Albert 1er's bar is frequented by local business people.

Relaxation

Entertainment The beautiful *Opéra-Théâtre de Nancy*, 1 rue Ste-Catherine ☎ 83 32 08 54, has an interesting programme of opera and operetta. It also has a dance season (Oct–May) by the Ballet Théâtre Français de Nancy ☎ 83 36 78 07. The town offers a reasonable drama repertory, mostly performed by the Comédie Lorraine in the restored *Manufacture des Tabacs*, 6 rue Baron-Louis ☎ 83 30 25 34. The Orchestre Symphonique et Lyrique de Nancy stages concerts in the *Salle Poirel* ☎ 83 32 31 25. Nancy has a well-known jazz festival in October and a popular jazz club, *Le Caveau des Dominicains*, 21 bis rue St-Dizier (no reservations).

Shopping Luxury shops are mostly in the streets surrounding Place Stanislas. *Daum* in Rue Héré sells lovely glass, and *Lalonde* sells chocolates and traditional confectionery, such as *craquelines*, *bergamotes de Nancy* and *macarons des religieuses*.

Sightseeing The Ville Vieille and the beautiful 18thC Place Stanislas with its fine wrought-ironwork are not to be missed. Nancy also has fine Art Nouveau buildings. The *Musée de l'Ecole de Nancy*, 36-38 rue du Sergent-Blandan ☎ 83 40 14 86, is a genuine Art Nouveau house with superb furniture and glass by Emile Gallé and Louis Majorelle (closed Tue). *Villa Majorelle*, rue Majorelle ☎ 83 28 93 21, was built by the cabinet-maker for himself (open Mon–Fri). The *Musée des Beaux-Arts*, pl Stanislas ☎ 83 32 86 16, includes engravings by Jacques Callot, among others, a display of Daum glass (closed Tue). The *Musée*

de Zoologie, 34 rue Ste-Catherine ☎ 83 32 99 97, houses France's biggest zoology collection and a tropical aquarium. The *Musée Historique Lorrain* in the *Palais Ducal*, 64 Grand'Rue ☎ 83 32 18 74, is devoted to the history of Lorraine (closed Tue).

Guided tours of the Ville Vieille set out from the tourist office, which has brochures on Art Nouveau buildings.

Spectator sports The local soccer club, AS Nancy-Lorraine, plays at the *Stade Marcel-Picot*, 90 bd Jean-Jaurès, Tomblaine ☎ 83 29 42 38. Nancy's racecourse, *Hippodrome de Nancy-Brabois* ☎ 83 27 17 39, is at Vandoeuvre, to the south.

Keeping fit The *Vitatonic* fitness club, 10 pl Thiers ☎ 83 32 32 18, is in the tower block housing the Altéa hotel, opposite the station. Nancy has an Olympic swimming pool in Avenue Raymond-Pinchard, Gentilly and both indoor and outdoor pools at *Piscine Thermale*, rue du Sergent-Blandan. Three tennis clubs that will usually accept visitors are *Tennis du Clair-Chêne* ☎ 83 56 00 80, on the RN74 road at Chavigny; *Tennis Club Montplaisir*, 205 ave Général-Leclerc ☎ 83 51 47 47; and *Tennis Club de Nancy* in Forêt de Haye, where there is also a jogging track. The *Squash Club de Nancy* in the suburb of Maxéville ☎ 83 37 49 62 accepts visitors.

Local resources

Business services

SM Services ☎ 83 35 00 00 offers telex, fax, word processing; *Tap'vite* ☎ 83 37 44 16 offers full secretarial service plus photocopying, telex, binding of reports and documents; *JP Formation* specializes in word processing. The *Palais des Congrès* has an office that can be rented on a short-term basis.

Photocopying and printing Copy 2000 ☎ 83 37 45 29, *Copie Shop* ☎ 83 37 13 74, *Hélio-Service* ☎ 83 32 00 97, *Imprimerie Jeanne-d'Arc* ☎ 83 36 40 35 and at Laxou ☎ 83 28 35 33.

Translation *Centre d'Etudes de Langues* 3 rue Monzou, Laxou ☎ 83 96 19 36 also offers interpreting.

Communications
Local delivery *Motexpress* ☎ 83 35 88 88, *Taxi-Colis SMTS* ☎ 87 51 60 60.
Long-distance delivery *Chronopost* service from main post office; *Sernam* ☎ 83 35 35 93 ℡ 850644F.
Post office Main office: 8 rue Fournier ☎ 83 36 51 47.
Telex and fax At main post office.

Conference/exhibition centres
Nancy has a central and well-equipped conference centre, *Palais des Congrès de Nancy*, rue du Grand-Rabbin-Haguenauer ☎ 83 36 65 10. It covers 4,800 sq metres on four floors and will extend a further 1,200 sq metres by the end of 1988. Two auditoria seat up to 800, and ten smaller meeting rooms seat up to 150. Two restaurants are available. The Palais can organize conferences, exhibitions and meetings and supply all necessary equipment and services.

The *Chambre de Commerce* ☎ 83 36 46 43 has a conference room (capacity 100).

Just outside Nancy, on the N57 road to Epinal, is the *Parc des Expositions* ☎ 83 51 09 01, which houses Nancy's International Fair in late May and early June. It has eight exhibition halls covering a total of 29,000 sq metres.

Emergencies
Bureaux de change 24hr service at the station; main post office, Mon–Fri 8–7, Sat 8–noon.
Hospitals *SAMU* ☎ 83 32 85 79; night-time emergencies ☎ 83 37 24 24; emergency room at *Hôpital Central*, 29 ave Maréchal-de-Lattre-de-Tassigny ☎ 83 57 61 61; *CHU de Brabois*, Vandoeuvre ☎ 83 55 81 20.
Pharmacies The main police station has a list of those open at night.

Police Main station: 38 bd Lobau ☎ 83 32 72 35. Emergencies: ☎ 17.

Government offices
The *Hôtel de Ville*, pl Stanislas ☎ 83 37 65 01; *Préfecture*, rue Maurice-Barrès ☎ 83 34 26 26. The *Association pour le Développement de Nancy et de son Agglomération*, 8 rue Baron-Louis ☎ 83 30 14 26, offers local relocation advice, but a *Maison de l'Entreprise et du Développement Local* is due to open in late 1988 in the former Manufacture des Tabacs complex. *Nancy-Brabois Innovation* (technopark) ☎ 83 37 22 29.

Information sources
Business information The departmental *Chambre de Commerce et d'Industrie*, 40 rue Henri-Poincaré ☎ 83 36 46 43 ℡ 960070, has a *Service Industrie* offering on-line consultation of data on local companies. Its *Service de Documentation* will provide a wide range of information and prepare dossiers on specific subjects. For the regional *INSEE* office ☎ 83 27 03 27. For customs information ☎ 83 36 64 25.
Local media *L'Est Républicain* is the main local daily, with 17 different editions and a circulation of over 250,000. The *CCI*'s weekly, *Les Tablettes Lorraines* is a good source of information on small businesses. *Les Décideurs en Lorraine* is a useful annual publication giving details of companies and public bodies. The regional television station is *FR3 Lorraine-Champagne-Ardennes* and *Radio France Nancy* is the local state-run radio.
Tourist information Office du Tourisme, 14 pl Stanislas ☎ 83 35 22 41 ℡ Essincy 960414.

Thank-yous
Chocolates *Léonidas*, 24 rue St-Dizier ☎ 83 30 32 71.
Florists *Le Jardin d'Alice*, 19 rue de la Visitation ☎ 83 30 45 20; *La Licorne*, pl Malval ☎ 83 35 28 26.

NANTES   Zip code 44000

No longer officially part of Brittany, Nantes is now the capital of the
Pays de le Loire economic region and bidding energetically to fight its
way out of the recession. It is a city which has seen hard times recently.
Its once flourishing shipyards are no more, since the closure of
Dubigeon, and the food industry has also declined. All that remains of
the city's sugar industry is the Beghin factory, and the sole upholder of
its long tradition of biscuit manufacture is the Biscuiterie Nantaise. A
recent blow was the decision to withdraw production of the famous Petit
Lu biscuits, once synonymous with Nantes, from the old factory in the
city centre to the outskirts.

To attract new international business, the decision was taken in 1986
to set up a techno park, the Technopole Atlantique, on the attractive La
Chanterie site on the banks of the river Erdre. The following year saw
the opening of the Institut de Recherche et de l'Enseignement à
l'Electronique (IRESTE), financed by the city and regional authorities.
Also in 1987 the Centre Atlantique du Commerce International (CACI),
a World Trade Center member, opened in the Centre des Salorges,
housing the city and regional chambers of commerce and the customs
and port authorities. Now the Association Communautaire de l'Estuaire
de la Loire (ACEL) is negotiating a range of tax and other incentives for
new investors in an area to be known as the Atlantic International Zone
(AIZ). Altogether Nantes gives the impression of a city that is starting to
go places.

Arriving

Nantes has a small international
airport, a good train service (soon to
be better still thanks to the TGV) and
improving access roads.

Nantes Château-Bougon airport
There are frequent flights to many
French destinations and international
flights to a few European cities. For
air taxis service ☎ 40 73 76 94, 40 84
82 60 or 40 04 04 62. 24hr
information/welcome point
☎ 40 84 80 00 also provides currency
exchange, a hotel reservation service,
tourist information and rental of
airport meeting rooms and offices.
There is a bar, a restaurant (open
11.30–3, 6.30–10), a newsstand,
tobacconist, and shops, including
duty-free.
City link Most business travellers
take a cab into town; the 10km/6 mile
journey takes 15–25min.
Taxis The rank is on the esplanade

and there is a telephone from which
to call taxis. Advance reservations
☎ 40 69 22 22 or 40 56 00 44.
Bus Services leave for the station and
Place du Commerce at fairly frequent
intervals between 7.50am and
9.50pm; takes about 25min.

Railway station
Gare de Nantes There are services
to all France's major cities. Journey
time to Paris is about 3hr, but this
will be reduced to 2hr when the TGV
Atlantique service starts operating in
1989 or 1990. The station has a taxi
rank ☎ 40 74 18 02, parking area, a
hotel reservation service, a car rental
office ☎ 40 48 09 09 ext 1208, a
baggage office ☎ 40 74 95 95, and a
currency exchange desk. Passenger
inquiries ☎ 40 50 50 50.

Getting around
Taxis There are several ranks in
town. The three main taxi firms are

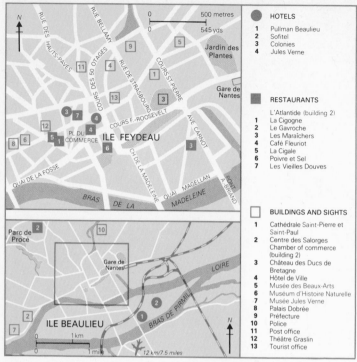

HOTELS
1 Pullman Beaulieu
2 Sofitel
3 Colonies
4 Jules Verne

RESTAURANTS
L'Atlantide (building 2)
1 La Cigogne
2 Le Gavroche
3 Les Maraîchers
4 Café Fleuriot
5 La Cigale
6 Poivre et Sel
7 Les Vieilles Douves

BUILDINGS AND SIGHTS
1 Cathédrale Saint-Pierre et Saint-Paul
2 Centre des Salorges Chamber of commerce (building 2)
3 Château des Ducs de Bretagne
4 Hôtel de Ville
5 Musée des Beaux-Arts
6 Muséum d'Histoire Naturelle
7 Musée Jules Verne
8 Palais Dobrée
9 Préfecture
10 Police
11 Post office
12 Théâtre Graslin
13 Tourist office

Allô Radio Taxis ☎ 40 69 22 22, *Allô Service Taxis* ☎ 40 56 00 44, *Atlantique Taxi* ☎ 40 63 66 66.

Driving The centre of Nantes is frequently clogged with traffic. City-centre streets all have meters, but there are six 24hr multilevel garages (map available from tourist office). For car rental: *Avis* ☎ 40 74 07 65, *Budget* ☎ 40 35 75 75, *Europcar* ☎ 40 20 32 00, *Hertz* ☎ 40 74 18 29, *interRent* ☎ 40 76 90 76.

Walking It is usually safe to walk, but Quai de la Fosse, with its somewhat seedy bars, is best avoided at night.

Bus and tram Nantes has an excellent service. Tickets can be bought anywhere displaying the TAN logo. Information ☎ 40 29 99 00.

Area by area

The busy centre of the modern city is Place du Commerce. The area to the north, including Place Royale and Place Graslin, is full of smart shops and restaurants. Opposite is the curious Ile Feydeau, an attractive district of 18thC buildings. To the east are the medieval streets leading to the château, the cathedral and the station. To the west is the docks area, now sadly deserted but due for refurbishment. On the other side of the river the Ile Beaulieu is now an important business district, housing many companies operating in the tertiary sector, various local government offices and the top business hotels. The area northwest of the centre, around the Parc de Procé, is a chic residential district.

Suburbs The smart residential areas are places along the banks of the river Erdre, like La Chapelle-sur-Erdre. Orvault, officially a separate town, is also popular with young executives.

Hotels

The city's two best-equipped business hotels are the Pullman Beaulieu and the Sofitel, both slightly away from the city centre on the characterless Ile Beaulieu. Both have restaurants, IDD telephones, currency exchange, laundry service, conference and meeting rooms, photocopying and secretarial services; all rooms have TV and minibar. The old-established city-centre "grand hotel," the Central, is being modernized and will not reopen until 1989. However, the city has several new small hotels that combine personal service with modern amenities.

Pullman Beaulieu _F_|
3 rue du Dr-Zamenhof, 44200
☎ _40 47 10 58 • AE DC MC V • 150 rooms, 1 suite, 1 restaurant, 1 bar_
A well-run modern hotel in the city's new business district. It has a particularly pleasant reception area-cum-lounge, some beautifully decorated "privilège" rooms and a noticeably friendly welcome • fax, 13 meeting rooms (capacity up to 400).

Sofitel _F_||
bd Alexandre-Millerand, 44200
☎ _40 47 61 03_ ⊤ˣ _710990 • AE DC MC V • 98 rooms, 2 suites, 1 restaurant, 1 bar_
Also in the business district, the Sofitel has good facilities, and its

rooms are comfortable; some overlook the Loire. The poolside terrace, where drinks and light meals are served in fine weather, is a popular meeting place. The service can be impersonal. Outdoor pool, tennis court • fax, 3 meeting rooms (capacity up to 40).

OTHER HOTELS

Colonies _F_ _5 rue du Chapeau-Rouge_ ☎ _40 48 79 76_ ⊤ˣ _711874 • AE MC V_. Well-renovated, friendly and central hotel; rooms are small. No restaurant.
Jules Verne _F_| _3 rue du Couëdic_ ☎ _40 35 74 50_ ⊤ˣ _701166 • Mapotel • AE DC MC V_. Very attractive new hotel in the much improved Place du Commerce area.

Restaurants

Nantes has one excellent restaurant, Les Maraîchers, several good ones and the chic business-oriented L'Atlantide, at the top of the much-vaunted new Centre des Salorges complex. Several prestige places for business entertaining are within 10km/6 miles of the city.

L'Atlantide _F_
Centre des Salorges, 15 quai E.-Renaud
☎ _40 73 23 23 • closed Sun D • V_
This light and airy restaurant opened in 1987 and soon became popular for its stylish decor and its fixed-price meals, which are good value. The cuisine is _nouvelle_-influenced and biased towards fish.

La Cigogne _F_|
16 rue Jean-Jacques Rousseau
☎ _40 89 12 64 • closed Sat L, Sun, Aug • MC V_

This tiny bistro in the town centre has long been known for its reliable classical cuisine with a Lyonnais flavour. Good wine list.

Le Gavroche _F_||
139 rue des Hauts-Pavés
☎ _40 76 22 49 • closed Sun D, Mon, Aug • V_
Although outside the city centre, the Nantais like entertaining in this discreetly elegant place, where the _nouvelle cuisine_ is beautifully served and the atmosphere restful.

Les Maraîchers [F]‖
21 rue Fouré ☎ *40 47 06 51 • closed
Sat L, Sun • AE DC V • reservations
essential*
The city's best-known restaurant is
in an unprepossessing street but it's
well worth the journey, across a
traffic-laden viaduct, for the
excellent *nouvelle cuisine*. The set
menus are very good value.

Good but casual
Café Fleuriot, pl Fleuriot
☎ 40 20 35 20, is a stylish new bistro
in the heart of Nantes; popular at
lunchtime with lively youngish
business clientele; tables outside in
summer. *La Cigale*, 4 pl Graslin
☎ 40 69 76 41, is too bustling for
entertaining but should not be missed
for its splendid Art Nouveau decor
and its good value, mainly fish
cuisine. On the Ile Feydeau, *Poivre et
Sel*, 13 rue Kervégan ☎ 40 47 02 35,
is good for a relaxed evening in fun
surroundings. *Les Vieilles Douves*,
3 rue des Vieilles-Douves
☎ 40 89 04 74 (evening only), serves
only cheese dishes.

Out of town
Two very pleasant small hotels
with excellent restaurants are
used by the business community:
Abbaye de Villeneuve, rte de Sables
d'Olonne ☎ 40 04 40 25, is in a
beautiful 18thC building 10km/6
miles south at Les Sorinières,
with pool, grounds and meeting
rooms; *Le Domaine d'Orvault*, ch
de Marais du Cens ☎ 40 76 84 02,
another peaceful hotel with
garden and tennis courts, is
only 7km/4 miles northwest at
Orvault.
   The *Delphin* restaurant,
9km/5 miles east at Bellevue
☎ 40 25 60 39, is delightfully set
beside the Loire. The expensive
cuisine is a judicious mixture of
classical and *nouvelle*, and popular
for business entertaining.

Bars
The bars of the *Pullman Beaulieu* and
Sofitel hotels are the only ones used
for business discussions, but the *Café
Fleuriot* is attracting an early-evening
business clientele.

Relaxation
Entertainment A monthly events
listing is published by the tourist
office. The *Théâtre Graslin*, pl
Graslin ☎ 40 89 36 78, has a good
winter season of opera, operetta and
dance, while the *Maison de la Culture
de Loire Atlantique*, 10 passage
Pommeraye ☎ 40 48 70 06, attracts
many theatre-goers. *L'Espace 44*, 84
rue du Général-Buat ☎ 40 29 25 86,
has a good middle-of-the-road
theatre programme. The *Orchestre
Philharmonique des Pays de Loire*
☎ 40 69 33 17 holds concert seasons
in Nantes.
Shopping The busiest shopping
district is around Rue Crébillon and
Passage Pommeraye, a splendid
19thC glass-roofed arcade. The
traffic-free Quartier Decré around
the department store *Les Nouvelles
Galeries*, 2 rue de Marne, is full of
attractive little shops and fashion
boutiques.
Sightseeing Nantes has many fine
old buildings, including the 15thC
Cathédrale Saint-Pierre et Saint-Paul,
and some excellent museums. Do not
miss the medieval streets of the
Change and *Juiverie* districts and the
baroque buildings of *Ile Feydeau*. The
moated *Château des Ducs de Bretagne*,
1 pl Marc-Elder, open Wed–Mon,
10–12, 2–6, dates from the late 15th
and early 16th centuries. It now
houses three interesting museums:
Musée des Arts Décoratifs, with the
emphasis on modern textile design;
Musée Régional des Arts Populaires, a
regional folklore collection; and the
Musée des Salorges, which is devoted
to the maritime, trading and
industrial history of post-18thC
Nantes.
   Other museums worth a visit are
the *Musée des Beaux-Arts*, best
known for its Courbets, Ingres and

De la Tours; the *Musée Jules Verne* (he is the city's most famous son); and the *Muséum d'Histoire Naturelle*. The *Palais Dobrée*, pl Jean-V, open Wed–Mon, 10–12, 2–6, houses an eclectic collection of art and antiquities.

Guided tours of the city take place throughout the year; programme available at the tourist office. There are sightseeing trips down the river Erdre in a stylish glass-enclosed boat, with meals served on board. *Bateaux de l'Erdre*, 24 quai de Versailles ☎ 40 20 24 50.

Spectator sports The main venue is *Stade de la Beaujoire*, bd de la Beaujoire ☎ 40 30 11 22. The local soccer club is frequently high in the French league. Weekly race meetings take place at *Hippodrome Le Petit-Port* ☎ 40 74 19 71, Easter–Oct (generally at weekends).

Keeping fit *Central Form*, 7 rue Clemence-Royer ☎ 40 73 16 16, has pool, jacuzzi, saunas, solariums, squash courts, golf practice area, table tennis and a wide range of exercise classes, plus a health-food restaurant. *Profil 2000*, 8 bd Georges-Mandel, Ile Beaulieu ☎ 40 47 76 66 puts the accent on beauty as well as health and is popular with women. Just outside Nantes at Orvault *Edipsos*, rue du Commandant-Charcot ☎ 40 94 82 52, has a well-equipped gym, sauna, dance and aerobic classes. Visitors can play golf at *Golf de Nantes* ☎ 40 63 25 82, an 18-hole course on the road to La Baule; closed Tue. There are also golf courses at La Baule itself and at Le Pornic. *Golf Center* ☎ 40 94 76 58 at Les Cochardières on the road to St-Etienne-de-Montluc has an indoor driving range. Courts are available at *Le Squash Nantais*, 20 rue Fouré ☎ 40 35 66 55, which also has sauna, gym, jacuzzi, aerobic and dance classes, and *Vita Squash*, 12 rue de la Havane ☎ 40 74 08 79. You can play tennis at *Country Club* ☎ 40 86 40 90 and *Les Forestries* ☎ 40 86 54 23, both on the road to St-Etienne-de-Montluc.

Local resources
Business services
The *Pullman Beaulieu* and *Sofitel* hotels can provide many services. The following companies all rent out office space and supply telephone, telex, photocopying and secretarial services: *Centre d'Affaires Nantais*, 5 bd Vincent-Gâche ☎ 40 35 71 10 (also offers fax, messenger service, telephone and letter-answering, financial and legal advice, accounting, debt-collecting); *Centrale Bureau Service* ☎ 40 89 76 75; *Iso Bureaux* ☎ 40 48 09 44; *L2A* ☎ 40 73 81 50 also handles formalities involved in setting up a business.

Photocopying and printing *Copy Service System*, 2 rue de l'Heronnière; *Imprimerie Chiffoleau* ☎ 40 95 04 36.

Translation *International Phoning* ☎ 40 58 04 92. *Atlantique Traduction* ☎ 40 37 03 93 ᵀˣ 700181F also provides technical secretarial service and printing of texts in foreign languages. The chamber of commerce's information service can supply a list of freelance translators and secretarial services. Both companies named here offer rapid service.

Communications
Local delivery *Taxi-colis* ☎ 40 46 65 65.
Long-distance delivery SERNAM (the SNCF's express service within France) ☎ 40 89 00 89. Also *Taxi-colis* ☎ 40 46 65 65 for service within France and abroad.
Post office Main office: pl de Bretagne ☎ 40 20 65 00
Telex and fax At main post office and *Office Général du Telex*, 1 rue Jean-Jacques-Roussseau ☎ 40 48 60 65 or 40 48 77 24.

Conference/exhibition centres
A new conference centre is badly needed. The best at present is the *Centre des Congrès Neptune*, 3 bis pl Neptune ☎ 40 35 72 44, whose main auditorium can hold 500 people;

three other rooms hold 100 each; the Tour Neptune block containing the centre also has a post office, banks, restaurant, snack bar and bar, boutiques, newsstand, Air France office and garage. The *Centre de Communication de l'Ouest*, pl Bretagne ☎ 40 20 23 23, has a 250-seat auditorium and four other meeting rooms. The stylish and well-equipped new *Centre Atlantique de Commerce International* (see *Information sources*) has an 80-seat meeting room and six others that can be joined to accommodate up to 250. The *Palais de la Beaujoire* ☎ 40 52 08 11 has 50,000 sq metres of exhibition space plus three conference rooms with seating for up to 500. *Nantes-Congrès*, Tour Bretagne, 44047 ☎ 40 35 30 20, can arrange all types of conference in these various centres.

Emergencies
Bureaux de change The exchange counter at the main post office is open Mon–Fri, 8am–7pm; Sat, 8–noon.
Hospitals Emergencies: *SAMU* ☎ 40 48 33 33 or 40 48 35 35.
Pharmacies For those open late and on Sun ☎ 40 74 11 11 or 40 74 21 21.
Police Main police station: pl Waldeck-Rousseau ☎ 40 74 11 11 or 40 74 21 21. Emergencies: ☎ 17.

Government offices
Mairie, rue de l'Hôtel-de-Ville ☎ 40 20 90 00, has an Economic Development Service. The *Préfecture de Loire-Atlantique* is on Quai Ceineray ☎ 40 47 39 80.

Information sources
Business information *Chambre de Commerce et d'Industrie de Nantes*, in the smart new Centre des Salorges, 16 quai Ernest-Renaud, 44100 ☎ 40 44 60 60 ⓉⓍ 700693 fax 40 44 60 90, has an information service about local businesses ☎ 40 44 60 43; a well-stocked reference library including on-line access to economic data and a wide range of periodicals ☎ 40 44 60 42

(1–5.30pm); an export advisory service ☎ 40 44 60 94. *Centre Atlantique de Commerce International* (*CACI*) is in the same complex ☎ 40 44 60 80 ⓉⓍ 710586 fax 40 44 60 90; affiliated to the international chain of World Trade Centers, it offers member companies a wide range of facilities and information services. It has also set up the CACI Business Club and a language-learning centre where local business people meet. *Chambre Régionale de Commerce et d'Industrie* ☎ 40 73 32 14 is also in the same complex. The *Service des Relations Extérieures* (public relations office) ☎ 40 44 60 91 can help you to decide which service you need in this huge centre. Local or regional statistics can be provided by *INSEE* at *Observatoire Economique de l'Ouest*, 5 bd Louis-Barthon ☎ 40 89 36 02. The *Atlantic International Zone* (*AIZ*) office, again in the Centre des Salorges ☎ 40 69 27 20, offers full information for potential investors in the region.
Local media The regional daily *Ouest France* covers national, international and local news and is France's biggest morning daily. *Presse Océan* is another, smaller-circulation, regional daily. *Plein Ouest* is a local economic news quarterly published by the chamber of commerce. *News West* is a bi-monthly business magazine aimed at the local business community. *FR3* has a regional television station. The local Radio France station is called *Radio France Loire Océan*.
Tourist information *Office du Tourisme*, pl du Commerce ☎ 40 47 04 51.

Thank-yous
Chocolates *Georges Gautier*, 9 rue de la Fosse ☎ 40 48 23 19.
Florists *Quelque Fleurs*, 10 rue Franklin ☎ 40 48 68 63; *Brin Fleurs*, 12 pl de la Bourse ☎ 40 35 42 16.

NICE

The doyen of Europe's beach resorts, and capital of the Côte d'Azur, is a large and busy commercial city that today is almost as important for the convention trade as it is for tourism.

Nice was under Italian rule till 1860, and today the lifestyle and character of the Niçois are still close to the Italian. English influences remain evident too, for it was they who created Nice as a winter resort in the late 18th century. Today the tourist industry has expanded to cater for other needs. There is a huge new convention centre, Acropolis, and most larger hotels depend on this trade.

The mayor, Jacques Médecin, has done much to modernize his city. Its business style is somewhat "Mediterranean" with its potent, Mafialike networks and frequent corruption scandals. But the arrival of so many outside interests has begun to modify this tradition.

Like other towns along the Côte d'Azur, Nice is today trying to develop as a centre of high technology and research. New institutes deal with health care (INSERM), oceanography (CERBOM) and astronomy (the Observatory). The town has very little industry, but modern light factories dealing with robotics, for example, are now growing up to its west in the Var valley. Farther west, IBM and Texas Instruments are among established foreign investors.

Arriving

The autoroute bypassing Nice leads west to Marseille and Paris, east into Italy. Nice is connected with Lyon and Paris by TGV and has an international airport.

Nice-Côte d'Azur airport

This is one of the busiest airports in France, with direct scheduled flights to some 80 cities worldwide. There are over 20 daily flights to and from Paris. Services include banks, bureau de change (open daily 8.30–7, 8.30–9 in summer), post office, shops, bars, restaurants (best is Le Ciel d'Azur ☎ 93 21 36 36) and a *2a Service* ☎ 93 21 30 73 that can provide business facilities. Airport information and inquiries ☎ 93 21 30 12.

Nearby hotel Holiday Inn ☎ 93 83 91 92 ⊠ 970202 • AE DC MC V. Large and well equipped, with big soundproofed bedrooms, pool, restaurant and meeting rooms. Offers a free bus shuttle.

City link The airport is on the coast 7km/4 miles southwest of the centre:

a bus runs every 15min to the main rail station, taking 15–20min. Airport taxis ☎ 93 52 32 32 are plentiful and take 10–15min.

Car rental All major firms have desks at the airport.

Railway station

Gare Nice-Ville is quite central and has three TGVs a day to Paris: the journey takes over 7hr, so flying (3hr 30min) is much faster. There are also good connections with Milan and Marseille. Services at the station include bank, information office, taxi rank. Passenger inquiries ☎ 93 87 50 50; reservations ☎ 93 88 89 93.

Getting around

Apart from a small central area by the seafront, Nice is quite spread out and a taxi or bus will be needed to visit most districts.

Taxis Numerous and easy to spot, with several ranks. Central taxi pool ☎ 93 52 32 32.

Driving Not enjoyable, as traffic is very heavy along the seafront and in the whole central area, especially in summer. The local driving style is competitive, so you need quick reflexes. Street parking is difficult in the centre, and even the big garages are often full. Thieving is rife: never leave anything visible in your car. All major rental firms have offices.

Buses A good network covers city and suburbs, but buses are few after 9pm. Information ☎ 93 85 61 81.

Walking Very pleasant in the Vieille Ville, along the promenade, and in the pedestrian area of Rue Masséna. There is some mugging, and women should avoid walking alone after dark in quieter areas.

Area by area

The central area is in two contrasting parts, divided by the dried-out bed of the river Paillon. On the east side is the fascinating Vieille Ville, a little network of medieval alleys full of old shops and bistros. Between here and the sea, a small area of 17thC streets contains the open-air markets and many of the major public buildings. Above it looms the rocky promontory where the feudal castle once stood, and beyond is the port. To the west of the Paillon, the broad Promenade des Anglais sweeps for two miles along the bay, backed by a succession of grand hotels and smart apartment blocks. The stately 19thC Place

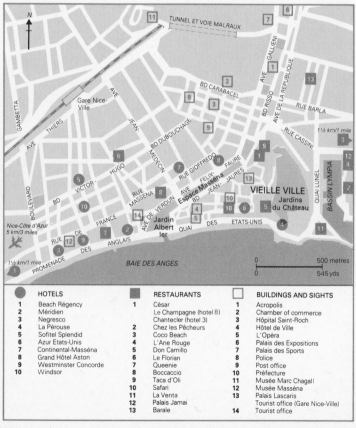

	HOTELS		RESTAURANTS		BUILDINGS AND SIGHTS
1	Beach Régency	1	César	1	Acropolis
2	Méridien		Le Champagne (hotel 8)	2	Chamber of commerce
3	Negresco		Chantecler (hotel 3)	3	Hôpital Saint-Roch
4	La Pérouse	2	Chez les Pêcheurs	4	Hôtel de Ville
5	Sofitel Splendid	3	Coco Beach	5	L'Opéra
6	Azur Etats-Unis	4	L'Ane Rouge	6	Palais des Expositions
7	Continental-Masséna	5	Don Camillo	7	Palais des Sports
8	Grand Hôtel Aston	6	Le Florian	8	Police
9	Westminster Concorde	7	Queenie	9	Post office
10	Windsor	8	Boccaccio	10	Préfecture
		9	Taca d'Oli	11	Musée Marc Chagall
		10	Safari	12	Musée Masséna
		11	La Venta	13	Palais Lascaris
		12	Palais Jamai		Tourist office (Gare Nice-Ville)
		13	Barale	14	Tourist office

Masséna, next to the Paillon, is the focal point of modern Nice: from here busy commercial streets stretch inland on either side of Avenue Jean-Médecin, and much of the city's business life is here.

The dried-out Paillon has recently been filling up with important new public buildings, such as the huge Acropolis convention complex and, farther north, the main exhibition centre.

The suburbs The hilly Mont Boron peninsula to the east is a middle-class residential area. Many business executives live to the north, at Mont Alban and Mont Vinaigrier, or on the hill of Cimiez to the west. Recent industrial growth is all to the west, on the Var plain, where several modern high-tech factories and big commercial centres have developed. A major business centre, l'Arénas, is being built close to the airport.

Hotels

This sprawling resort has some 350 hotels, of which at least 100 are suitable for business people. Some date from the *belle époque* period, others are breezily modern. Most of the best are either along the seafront or fairly close to it. All the larger hotels listed here can supply or organize a variety of business facilities. Currency exchange is standard, but hotel parking is generally limited.

Beach Régency *F*||||
223 prom des Anglais ☎ *93 83 91 51*
℡ *461635* • *AE DC MC V* • *318 rooms, 17 suites, 3 bars*
This huge modern hotel is some way from the centre, but is popular with business visitors. Bedrooms are dull but comfortable and many have sea-facing balconies. There is a piano-bar, and the main restaurant offers Lebanese as well as French dishes. 24hr room service, hairdresser, shops • pool, gym, jacuzzi, massage • fax, 7 meeting rooms (capacity up to 380).

Méridien *F*||||
1 prom des Anglais ☎ *93 82 25 25*
℡ *470361* • *AE DC MC V* • *305 rooms, 9 suites, 1 restaurant, 2 bars*
Central and sophisticated, this big new chain hotel is an excellent choice for the business visitor who also wants to relax. There are panoramic views of the sea and city from front bedrooms, the bar and La Brasserie, which is a popular eating place. The staff are unusually friendly and efficient. 24hr room service, airline desk, hairdresser, gift shop • rooftop pool, gym, yoga classes, hydrotherapy • fax, 4 meeting rooms (capacity up to 530).

Negresco *F*||||
37 prom des Anglais ☎ *93 88 39 51*
℡ *460040* • *AE DC MC V* • *135 rooms, 15 suites, 2 restaurants, 1 bar*
One of the world's greatest hotels, the privately-owned Negresco still maintains the grand traditions of *belle époque* luxury, offering immaculate service and genuine warmth. Picassos and Légers line the walls and the bedrooms are incredibly sumptuous in various period styles. The Chantecler restaurant is first-class (see *Restaurants*), and the piano-bar is the smartest venue in town for a business drink. A hotel with all modern comforts but few special facilities. Shopping arcade • fax, 8 meeting rooms (capacity up to 500).

La Pérouse *F*|||
11 quai Rauba-Capeu ☎ *93 62 34 63*
℡ *461411* • *Hôtels du Roy* • *AE DC MC V* • *63 rooms, 2 suites, 1 grill room (summer only), 1 bar*
This is the most delightful of Nice's medium-priced hotels, with a prime position high up on the side of the castle hill. Bedrooms are not large, but most have glorious views across the bay and some have private terraces. The atmosphere is friendly

with very good service. The little garden is used for breakfast and light lunches in summer; the bar has a log fire in winter. Outdoor pool, solarium, jacuzzi • 3 meeting rooms (capacity up to 25).

Sofitel Splendid   [F]///
50 bd Victor-Hugo ☎ *93 88 69 54* ⊠ *460938* • *AE DC MC V* • *115 rooms, 14 suites, 1 restaurant, 2 bars*
Although affiliated to the Sofitel chain, this hotel has been owned and run by the Tschann family since 1905. It has been modernized, with no loss of character, and service is excellent. Most rooms have balconies. On the roof is a sun-terrace and below it a panoramic bar. Hairdresser • pool, sauna • 4 meeting rooms (capacity up to 140).

OTHER HOTELS
Azur Etats-Unis   [F]/   *91 quai des Etats-Unis* ☎ *93 85 74 19* ⊠ *462619* • *AE DC MC V*. A modest, well-run hotel on the front. Rooms are small, but some have balconies with sea views.

Continental Masséna   [F]/
58 rue Gioffredo ☎ *93 85 49 25* ⊠ *470192* • *DC MC V*. Medium-sized, very central hotel near the sea; highly efficient, including 24hr room service.
Grand Hôtel Aston   [F]/   *12 ave Félix-Faure* ☎ *93 80 62 52* ⊠ *470290* • *AE DC MC V*. Fairly large, central hotel; smart and well modernized, with fine views from its roof-garden. Le Champagne restaurant is good for business meals (see *Restaurants*).
Westminster Concorde   [F]///
27 prom des Anglais ☎ *93 88 29 44* ⊠ *460 872* • *AE DC MC V*. A classic seafront "palace," less fully modernized than some, but with spacious, comfortable rooms and excellent service.
Windsor   [F]/   *11 rue Dalpozzo* ☎ *93 88 59 35* ⊠ *970072* • *AE DC MC V*. A friendly and unusual little hotel with odd Oriental furnishings. The rooms are small but comfortable and the hotel has a pool, sauna and gym. There are even office facilities. Remarkable value for money.

Restaurants
Oddly enough, Nice has fewer top-class gourmet restaurants than many big French towns (only two have *Michelin* rosettes); but for business or leisure purposes there are scores of pleasant places. The accent is on fish, including the famous Provençal dishes such as *bouillabaisse*; Nice's own cuisine features widely too, with such starters as *salade niçoise, anchoïade* and ravioli.

César (l'Univers)   [F]/
54 bd Jean-Jaurès ☎ *93 62 32 22* • *AE DC MC V*
The ebullient César runs a large, lively establishment that is truly Niçois. Good local fish. A fun place for a relaxed lunch or dinner.

Le Champagne   [F]///
12 ave Félix-Faure ☎ *93 80 62 52* • *closed Sun* • *AE DC MC V*
The Grand Hôtel Aston's elegant restaurant has well-spaced tables and a garden on one side. Chef Jean-Jacques Bissière won the Grand Prix

Escoffier in 1987 for a cuisine inspired by his native southwest.

Chantecler   [F]/////
37 prom des Anglais ☎ *93 88 39 51* • *closed Nov* • *AE DC MC V*
The restaurant of the Negresco is the smartest place in town. Chef Jacques Maximin serves inventive variations of Niçois dishes that some might find a little too fanciful. On a hot night, the outdoor terrace is preferable to the fussily ornate dining room. Half-price set menus available.

Chez les Pêcheurs *F*/
18 quai des Docks ☎ *93 89 59 61*
• *closed Wed, Tue D (winter), Thu L
(summer), Nov 1–mid-Dec* • *AE MC V*
A cheerful and friendly place down
by the port, notable for its local
dishes of fresh fish, such as
bouillabaisse and *bourride*.

Coco Beach *F*///
2 ave Jean-Lorrain ☎ *93 89 39 26*
• *closed Sun, Mon, mid-Nov to mid-
Dec* • *AE DC MC V*
Carmen Coco's quaint fish
restaurant, a local institution and for
many years a favourite haunt of the
rich and famous, is built like a boat
on the rocks above the shore, and has
lovely views. The fish is fresh (good
bouillabaisse) but the prices are
somewhat inflated.

Good but casual
Comfortable places suitable for a
business meal include *L'Ane Rouge*,
7 quai des Deux-Emmanuel
☎ 93 89 49 63 (good fish and
shellfish); the Italian *Don Camillo*,
5 rue des Ponchettes ☎ 93 85 67 95;
and *Le Florian*, 22 rue Alphonse-
Karr ☎ 93 88 86 60. For a quicker
meal, *Queenie*, 19 prom des Anglais
☎ 93 88 52 50, is a popular seafront
brasserie, while *Boccaccio*, 7 rue
Masséna ☎ 93 87 71 76, serves Italian
and fish dishes at outdoor tables. For
a relaxed dinner in a lively
atmosphere, try the unusual *Taca
d'Oli*, 35 rue Pairolière
☎ 93 62 07 40; the trendy *Safari*,
1 cours Saleya ☎ 93 80 18 44; or,
down by the port, the cheap and
romantic *La Venta*, 4 bd Guynemer
☎ 93 55 05 74. *Palais Jamai*, 3 quai
des Deux-Emmanuel ☎ 93 89 53 92,
serves excellent Moroccan food.
Lastly, no one should miss the
famous and eccentric *Barale*, 39 rue
Beaumont ☎ 93 89 17 94; here the
elderly Hélène Barale serves a set
menu (no choice) of genuine local
dishes, amid a bizarre collection of
antiques, then tells risqué stories and
gets her guests to sing (dinners only;
reservations essential).

Out of town
The best places are to the east on
or near the coast. There are two
famous luxury hotels at Beaulieu:
the *Métropole* ☎ 93 01 00 08 and
La Réserve ☎ 93 01 00 01, both
with good restaurants. Also in the
luxury class, the *Voile d'Or* hotel
at St-Jean-Cap-Ferrat
☎ 93 01 13 13 has a charming
setting by the harbour and
excellent food; at Villefranche,
the *Welcome* ☎ 93 76 76 93 is
another good place to stay or to
eat beside a picturesque quayside,
and is somewhat cheaper. In the
hill village of St-Paul-de-Vence is
the expensive but lovely *Colombe
d'Or* ☎ 93 32 80 02. Here you can
eat excellent local dishes
surrounded by an impressive
collection of modern art.

Bars
Among the best are those in the
Negresco, Méridien, La Pérouse and
Westminster (see *Hotels*). *Queenie* on
the seafront (see *Restaurants*) is a
fashionable meeting place but can be
crowded.

Entertainment
Opera, dance, music *L'Opera*, rue
St-François-de-Paule ☎ 93 92 81 81,
and the *Acropolis* convention centre,
espl Kennedy, are both used for
productions by the town's opera and
ballet companies and for concerts
every autumn by the Nice
Philharmonic Orchestra (reservations
☎ 93 80 59 83). The *Théâtre de
Verdure*, Jardin Albert 1er
☎ 93 82 38 68, has many outdoor
concerts.
Theatre Rather poor. A state-backed
company performs Oct–Apr in the
ugly *Nouveau Théâtre de Nice*, espl
des Victoires ☎ 93 56 86 86. *Au
Pizzaiolo*, rue de Pont Vieux
☎ 93 62 34 70, is a lively cabaret-
theatre performing in local dialect.
Cinema Best "art" houses with
subtitled foreign films are *Meliès*,

56 bd Risso ☎ 93 55 37 27, and the *Acropolis Cinemathèque*, espl Kennedy ☎ 93 92 81 81.

Festivals The famous carnival is just before Lent, with the Bataille des Fleurs on the day after Ash Wednesday. There is a major dog show and a festival of church music in April, a folkloric Fête des Maïs in May, and Europe's leading jazz festival is held at Cimiez in July.

Nightclubs and casinos Best discos are *Le Jock Club*, at Casino Ruhl ☎ 93 87 95 87; *Les Ecossais*, rue Halévy ☎ 93 87 92 00; and *La Camargue*, pl Charles-Félix ☎ 93 85 74 10, trendy and noisy. The famous *Casino Ruhl* ☎ 93 87 95 87 has recently reopened and offers nightly gambling and dinner-dance with floor show.

Shopping

The major department stores are around Place Masséna, and the best luxury boutiques in the nearby pedestrian streets. There are huge hypermarkets west of town near the airport. The Vieille Ville's colourful street markets are in Cours Saleya and Rue St-François, both mornings only. There are good antique markets at 7 prom des Anglais and 28 rue Ségurane.

Sightseeing

Nice has several fine collections of modern art, and some other good museums too.

Musée des Beaux-Arts A wide range of paintings, including works by Fragonard, Renoir, Braque and Dufy; Picasso ceramics. *33 ave des Baumettes. Open Tue–Sun, 10–12, 3–6 (winter 10–12, 2–5).*

Musée Marc Chagall The world's fullest collection of Chagall's work. *Ave Dr-Ménard. Open Wed–Mon, 10–7 (winter 10–12.30, 2–5.30).*

Musée Masséna A 19thC palace which has fascinating depictions of local history and folklore. *65 rue de France. Open Tue–Sun, 10–12, 3–6 (2–5 in winter).*

Palais Lascaris A sumptuous

17thC mansion, finely restored and furnished. *15 rue Droite. Open Wed–Sun, 9.30–12, 2.30–6.*

Also worth a visit is the ornate Russian Orthodox Cathedral, bd du Tsarevitch.

Spectator sports

Ice hockey Nice has a good team, playing in the *Palais des Sports*, espl de Lattre de Tassigny ☎ 93 13 13 13.
Soccer The rather mediocre local team plays in *Stade du Ray*, 25 ave du Ray ☎ 93 84 46 56.

Keeping fit

There is plenty to suit all tastes, especially watersports.

Health and fitness centres The best are in the *Beach Régency* and *Méridien* hotels, open to the public. Or try the private *Bio Club*, 15 bd Delfinot ☎ 93 56 54 00.

Golf The best local courses are outside Cannes and Monaco.

Ice skating An Olympic rink is at the *Palais des Sports* (see above).

Skiing The smart resorts of Auron, Isola 2000 and Valberg are within a 90min drive.

Squash *Club Vauban*, rue Maréchal Vauban ☎ 93 89 29 83.

Swimming and watersports Several hotels have good pools; the public ones, such as that at the *Palais des Sports*, are larger but more crowded. The shingle beach in front of the promenade is public. The best private sections are Galion Plage, Opéra Plage, Régence Plage and, notably, Ruhl Plage, which offers waterskiing and water-parachuting with trained instructors.

Tennis The private *Nice Lawn Tennis Club*, 5 ave Suzanne Lenglen ☎ 93 96 77 00, and municipal *Club Vauban* (see above) are best.

Local resources

Business services

The larger hotels will provide many services, while advice and help can be obtained from the *Nice Convention Bureau* in the Acropolis building ☎ 93 92 80 71 and *Côte d'Azur*

Développement ☎ 93 92 42 42. Private companies renting out furnished offices with full services are *Acte* ☎ 93 80 04 44, *Nice Etoile* ☎ 93 80 68 22, *Nice Europe* ☎ 93 80 04 10, and the *2a Service* at the airport. *L'Arénas*, a huge business centre now under construction near the airport, is due to open in 1988–89.
Photocopying and printing *Copy 2000* ☎ 93 62 38 84.
Secretarial *Acte* ☎ 93 80 04 44, *Manpower* ☎ 93 87 16 23.
Interpreting *Mme de Cruz-Santos* ☎ 93 79 08 54.
Translation *Mme Blanchet* ☎ 94 70 74 41.

Communications
Local delivery OK *Service* ☎ 93 87 87 87.
Long-distance delivery DHL ☎ 05 20 25 25 (international), *Of'Courses* ☎ 93 80 50 60 (national).
Post office Main office: rue Hôtel des Postes ☎ 93 85 98 63.
Telex and fax At main post office, or *Acropolis*, 1 espl Kennedy ☎ 93 92 83 00.

Conference/exhibition centres
The new and ultra-modern convention centre, *Acropolis*, 1 espl Kennedy ☎ 93 92 83 00, has 4 auditoria (capacity up to 2,500). The efficient *Nice Convention Bureau*, in the same building ☎ 93 92 80 71 ☒ 461861, offers help in organizing conferences there. They will also help with mounting an exhibition at the adjacent *Palais des Expositions* ☎ 93 92 83 83, which has a big hall of 14,000 sq metres. Convention facilities are also available at the larger hotels.

Emergencies
Bureaux de change *Change Or Charrière*, 10 rue de France, open daily 9–7; *Maison de la Presse*, 1 pl Masséna, open daily 8.45–8.30.
Hospitals Main hospital is *St-Roch*, rue Pierre-Dévoluy ☎ 93 13 33 00. Emergency medical service ☎ 93 85 01 01; emergency dental

service ☎ 93 53 03 03. See *Cannes* for the British and American hospitals.
Pharmacies All-night pharmacy: 7 rue Masséna ☎ 93 87 78 94.
Police Main station: 1 ave Maréchal Foch ☎ 93 55 91 22.

Government offices
Hôtel de Ville, 5 rue de l'Hôtel de Ville ☎ 93 13 20 20; *Préfecture des Alpes-Maritimes*, rte de Grenoble ☎ 93 72 20 00.

Information sources
Business information Three public organizations will provide free advice: the *Chambre de Commerce et d'Industrie*, 20 bd Carabacel ☎ 93 55 91 55; *Côte d'Azur Développement*, 10 rue de la Préfecture ☎ 93 92 42 42; and the *Nice Convention Bureau* ☎ 93 92 80 71.
Local media *Nice Matin*, the right-wing local daily, has some business coverage. *L'Action* is a monthly produced by the town hall. The state TV network *FR3* has a nightly news magazine. *Riviera 104*, a local English-language private radio station, has regular news bulletins including City reports from London.
Tourist information *Office du Tourisme* at main rail station, ave Thiers ☎ 93 87 07 07; also a branch at 5 ave Gustave V.

Thank-yous
Florists *L'Art et Les Fleurs*, 9 rue de la Buffa ☎ 93 87 11 84; *Carlin*, 11 pl Garibaldi ☎ 93 55 36 29.

RENNES
Zip code 35000

Rennes, the historic capital of Brittany and now the official capital of the Bretagne economic region, exemplifies the dynamism and adaptability that have recently enabled the region to head France's league table for economic growth after a long period of decline. The decision to detach Nantes from Brittany undoubtedly helped to foster Rennes's growth as a regional economic centre and the improving economic climate has created an aura of optimism, making the once staid city an increasingly lively and attractive place.

Formerly an administrative town, acting as an important legal, military and religious centre with a thriving commercial sector, Rennes never benefited from 19thC industrialization. Its only true industrial activity was printing, still represented by Oberthur, now mainly manufacturing banknotes and traveller's cheques, and by France's highest-circulation daily, *Ouest-France*, and it therefore suffered less than many French cities from the 1970s recession. In recent years it has managed to carve out a niche for itself as a centre of high-tech research, mainly in the communications field, and much local pride centres on its technopark, grandly christened Rennes-Atalante, on which the city is pinning many of its hopes for future prosperity.

A major factor in economic development over the last 20 years has been the presence of Citroën, whose workforce of 13,000, employed in two plants, has helped to absorb the pool of local labour formerly employed in agriculture ("The only immigrant worker at Citroën is the general manager" is a popular local quip). The other major factors are the city's large university (in fact two separate universities), housing 36,000 students and 2,500 research workers, and the decision by the French telecommunications authority to set up the Centre Commun d'Etudes de Télédiffusion et Télécommunications (CCETT). The CCETT has acted as a catalyst, attracting many high-tech research units from both the public and the private sector. The major areas of high-tech specialization are communications (the Ille-et-Vilaine was the pilot *département* for the Minitel system, Rennes has the world's first numeric television studio and was the first French city to have cable television via optical fibres); data processing; medicine (the Ecole Nationale de la Santé Publique is in Rennes, and diagnostic imaging is a key research field); and agricultural economics and agri-business.

Arriving
Rennes has fairly good communications. Journey times to Paris are 1hr by plane, 3hr by train (2hr from 1989 with the TGV), 3–4hr by car.

Rennes Saint-Jacques airport
There are several weekday flights to Orly-Ouest, but service is infrequent at weekends and in July and August. There are also direct flights to Le Havre and Lyon and (seasonal) to Caen and Cork; flights via Le Havre, Quimper or Brest to London–Gatwick; and via Cork, Le Havre, Lyon or Paris to other major destinations. This small airport has a good restaurant *Le Mermoz* ☎ 99 31 92 19, but few other

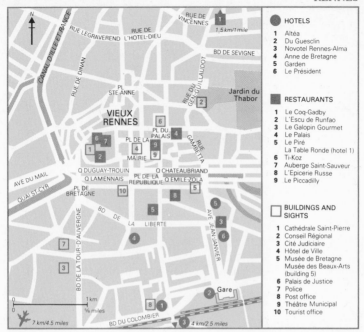

HOTELS

1 Altéa
2 Du Guesclin
3 Novotel Rennes-Alma
4 Anne de Bretagne
5 Garden
6 Le Président

RESTAURANTS

1 Le Coq-Gadby
2 L'Escu de Runfao
3 Le Galopin Gourmet
4 Le Palais
5 Le Piré
La Table Ronde (hotel 1)
6 Ti-Koz
7 Auberge Saint-Sauveur
8 L'Epicerie Russe
9 Le Piccadilly

BUILDINGS AND SIGHTS

1 Cathédrale Saint-Pierre
2 Conseil Régional
3 Cité Judiciaire
4 Hôtel de Ville
5 Musée de Bretagne
Musée des Beaux-Arts (building 5)
6 Palais de Justice
7 Police
8 Post office
9 Théâtre Municipal
10 Tourist office

facilities. The leading car rental firms have counters, which are staffed only when flights arrive. The airport is 7km/4 miles southwest of the city centre; for taxis to the city ☎ 99 30 79 79. Airport information ☎ 99 31 91 77.

Railway station
There are good services to Brest, Caen, Quimper and Saint-Malo, as well as Paris, but the service to Nantes usually involves a change at Redon. Inquiries ☎ 99 65 50 50.

Getting around
The centre of Rennes is small and has a number of pedestrianized streets, so a combination of walking plus the occasional taxi is recommended. The local bus service, *Sitcar* ☎ 99 28 55 55, has 14 city-centre lines, 16 suburban services, 6 lines to outlying districts and 3 evening services (normal service runs 6.30am–8.30pm). For taxis ☎ 99 30 79 79 or 99 53 60 60 (both 24hr); the main taxi

ranks are at the station and in Place du Parlement. A car is of little use in the centre but may be convenient for visits to outlying districts. All the leading car rental firms have offices: *Avis* ☎ 99 30 01 19, *Budget* ☎ 99 65 13 21, *Europcar* ☎ 99 59 50 50, *Hertz* ☎ 99 54 26 52.

Area by area
The main part of the city centre lies north of the river Vilaine, which was canalized in the 19th century and no longer flows right through the centre. The medieval heart, Vieux Rennes, lies north of Quai Duguay-Trouin, around the cathedral; this area, together with the streets leading east towards the busy Place de la Mairie, is the main shopping and restaurant area. East of the Place du Palais and the Palais de Justice (now law courts, once the home of the parliament of Brittany), lies Square de la Motte, surrounded by administrative buildings. Slightly farther east is Jardin du Thabor, attractive public

gardens surrounded by quiet residential streets.

The inner area south of the Vilaine, bordered by Boulevard du Colombier, contains the station, the new Maison de la Culture and the startlingly modernistic Cité Judiciaire. Since 1987 the Beauregard area northwest of the centre has been another administrative centre, housing the new Préfecture and the chamber of commerce.

There are various industrial zones on the outskirts. To the west is the ZI de la route de Lorient, including the Citroën factory. To the east in Rennes-Beaulieu lies the main university campus and the science faculties.

Between the campus and the residential suburb of Cesson-Sévigné, an area known as Coësmes-Beaulieu is the site of the new Rennes-Atalante technopark.

Hotels

Rennes badly needs a top-class city-centre hotel. The business-oriented Altéa is south of the centre, and the Novotel is too far out to be convenient for those without a car. There are several fairly well-equipped hotels near the station. The three hotels below all can provide currency exchange as well as limited business services such as photocopying and typing.

Altéa _F_/
pl du Colombier ☎ _99 31 54 54_
TX _730905_ • _AE DC MC V_ • _140 rooms, 1 restaurant, 1 bar_
This modern hotel, in the new Colombier district south of the centre but not far from the station, was formerly called the Frantel. The Table Ronde restaurant is popular for business entertaining (see _Restaurants_), and the bar is frequently used as a meeting place. The rooms are functional and comfortable, well suited to the mainly business clientele. All rooms have a minibar. 6 meeting rooms (capacity up to 300).

Du Guesclin _F_/
5 pl de la Gare ☎ _99 31 47 47_
TX _740748_ • _Accor_ • _AE DC MC V_ • _68 rooms, 1 bar; no restaurant_
An old-established, well-modernized hotel opposite the station, popular with business visitors. It is well served by restaurants nearby, and may reopen one of its own in 1989. Service is pleasant and rooms are well-planned, though some are small; the quietest overlook an inner courtyard. Parking difficult • 3 meeting rooms (capacity up to 40).

Novotel Rennes-Alma _F_/
ave du Canada ☎ _99 50 61 32_
TX _740144_ • _AE DC MC V_ • _98 rooms, 1 restaurant, 1 bar_
All the usual Novotel facilities are here, but the hotel is well away from the city centre, close to the Alma shopping centre and convenient for the autoroute. The grill room is open daily, until midnight. Rooms are air-conditioned. Outdoor pool • 6 meeting rooms (capacity up to 70).

OTHER HOTELS
Anne de Bretagne _F_/ _12 rue Tronjolly_ ☎ _99 31 49 49_ TX _741255_ • _MC V_. A well-run modern hotel near the Colombier district with its own (paying) garage. Mainly used by business people.
Garden _F_/ _3 rue Duhamel_ ☎ _99 65 45 06_ • _AE DC MC V_. A modest little hotel (single rooms are spartan) in a fairly central location; friendly service.
Le Président _F_/ _27 ave Jean-Janvier_ ☎ _99 65 42 22_ TX _730004_ • _AE DC MC V_. A modern hotel near the station attracting mainly business people. The avenue is noisy, but all rooms overlooking it are double-glazed. Deft service. No restaurant.

Restaurants

The city's two gourmet restaurants, both used extensively for business entertaining, are Le Piré and Le Palais. But there are a number of other good restaurants, several being in the medieval town centre.

Le Coq-Gadby [F]|
156 rue d'Antrain ☎ *99 38 05 55*
• closed 3 weeks in Aug • AE DC MC V
A Rennes institution, run by the same family for almost a century and popular for local celebrations as well as business entertaining, with private dining rooms available. Classical cuisine at reasonable prices.

L'Escu de Runfao [F]|
5 rue du Chapitre ☎ *99 79 13 10 • AE DC V*
A tiny wood-panelled restaurant in the heart of Vieux Rennes. Good *nouvelle cuisine* and an excellent wine list, with even one or two of the better wines available, unusually, by the glass.

Le Galopin Gourmet [F]|
21 ave Jean-Janvier ☎ *99 30 09 51 or 99 31 55 96 • closed Sun and mid-Jul–mid-Aug • AE DC V*
This spacious and comfortable restaurant is conveniently near the station and offers a well-balanced mixture of classical and *nouvelle* cuisine and particularly attentive service. The set menus are generally good value.

Le Palais [F]||
7 pl du Parlement ☎ *99 79 45 01*
• closed Sun D, Mon, 1 week in Feb and last 3 weeks in Aug • AE DC MC V
One of the city's two finest restaurants, Le Palais is conveniently central. Its decor matches the elegance of the 18thC Place du Parlement, and it offers exciting cuisine with the emphasis on seasonal produce cooked in mainly *nouvelle* style.

Le Piré [F]||
18 rue du Maréchal-Joffre
☎ *99 79 31 41 • closed Sat L, Sun*
• AE DC V
A delightful farmhouse-style building in a flower-filled courtyard just south of the river makes an unexpected setting for the city's other top-class restaurant. Run by a dynamic young couple, it has a diverse and loyal clientele. The inventive cuisine, at reasonable prices, is complemented by a good wine list.

La Table Ronde [F]||
pl du Colombier ☎ *99 31 54 54 • closed Aug • AE DC MC V*
The air-conditioned restaurant of the Altéa is mainly used for business entertaining and is particularly pleasant in summer when meals are served on a terrace beneath an awning. It has an interesting modern cuisine, with a leaning towards seafood dishes.

Ti-Koz [F]||
3 rue St-Guillaume ☎ *99 79 33 89*
• closed Sun, first half Aug • AE DC MC V
Dining rooms on two floors of this historic building in a picturesque part of Vieux Rennes are full of attractive furniture and ornaments. Fish and shellfish are the staples of the usually reliable cuisine.

Good but casual
Auberge Saint-Sauveur, 6 rue St-Sauveur ☎ 99 79 32 56, is a 15thC building near the cathedral and marks the spot where the great fire of 1720 was halted; the atmosphere is charming, and the cuisine often interesting. For an unusual evening, *L'Epicerie Russe*, 42 rue Vasselot ☎ 99 79 56 86, is a popular choice: it serves the usual Russian dishes, plus a huge range of vodkas. Late meals are often hard to find in provincial cities, but *Le Piccadilly*, 15 Galerie du Théâtre ☎ 99 78 17 17, never closes; a conveniently central place for a brasserie-type meal.

Out of town
Hostellerie du Lion d'Or
☎ 99 68 31 09, 17km/11 miles
northeast at Liffré, has excellent
food. *Auberge de la Hublais*
☎ 99 83 11 06 is only 5km/3 miles
east at Cesson-Sévigné and is popular
at lunch time. *Ar Milin'*
☎ 99 00 30 91, 22km/14 miles away
at Châteaubourg, is a stylish
restaurant in a converted mill, often
used for seminars.

Relaxation
Entertainment With its large
student population Rennes has a fair
amount of lively theatre and "art"
cinemas, and is one of France's major
centres for rock music. Known as *Le
Grand Huit* (because of its figure-of-
eight shape), the new *Maison de la
Culture*, 1 rue St-Hélier
☎ 99 31 55 33, has a busy
programme of plays, dance, music
and occasionally cinema. The very
pretty *Théâtre Municipal*, pl de la
Mairie ☎ 99 28 55 87, has middle-of-
the-road plays, opera and operetta.
The most interesting cinema is at
L'Arvor, 29 rue d'Antrain
☎ 99 38 72 40. The main concert
venues are *Le Grand Huit*, the
Théâtre Municipal and, for jazz and
rock, the *Salle Omnisports*, bd de la
Liberté ☎ 99 30 86 35; classical
concerts are sometimes held in the
city's churches. Details available
from the tourist office.
Shopping Fashion boutiques and art
galleries cluster together in the old
streets of Vieux Rennes while the
main area for antiques is Rue
Vasselot. The city's only department
store, *Nouvelles Galeries*, is on the
corner of Rue de Rohan and Quai
Duguay-Trouin; it stays open all
day, whereas many other shops shut
for the traditional two-hour lunch
break. The smart new city-centre
shopping complex called *Le Colombia*
has dozens of small shops. There is a
picturesque food market in Place des
Lices (Sat am) and an indoor
market, *Halles Centrales*, which also
has bric-à-brac stalls on Thursdays;

open-air flower market daily in Place
de la Mairie.
Sightseeing Strenuous efforts have
been made to restore the heart of the
city and make it an attractive place
for strolling. There is much medieval
architecture to be seen in *Vieux
Rennes*; while the 17th–18thC period
is best exemplified in Place de la
Mairie and Place du Parlement. The
Musée des Beaux-Arts, 20 quai Emile-
Zola ☎ 99 28 55 85, has an
interesting fine art collection; the
Musée de Bretagne, at the same
address and number, is devoted to
regional history. The *Cathédrale
Saint-Pierre* is mostly 18th–19thC; it
has many lovely paintings, including
a 16thC altarpiece.
  Guided tours of Vieux Rennes set
out from the tourist office. There are
also day trips along the river Vilaine
in small motorboats.
Spectator sports The city's
basketball, rugby and soccer teams
are all successful. The *Stade Rennais*,
111 rte de Lorient ☎ 99 54 25 25,
holds 25,000 people, the *Salle
Omnisports* 6,000.
Keeping fit The jokingly named
Jules et Gym, 12 rue Duhamel
☎ 99 31 75 00, a modern fitness club
covering 1,000 sq metres, has an
arrangement with most of the city's
hotels for temporary membership.
Club Jean de Beauvais, 12/14 rue du
Pré-Botté ☎ 99 78 17 66, also accepts
visitors. The city's 9-hole *golf course*
is 5km/3 miles away at Saint-
Jacques-de-la-Lande ☎ 99 64 24 18;
advance reservations essential. There
are two large public indoor pools:
Piscine Brequigny, 12 bd Albert-
Premier ☎ 99 31 80 33, and the
splendid Art Deco *Piscine Saint-
Georges*, rue Gambetta
☎ 99 28 55 55. Both also have saunas.
Tennis Club du Bois de Soeuvres, rte
de Chantepie in nearby Vern-sur-
Seiche ☎ 99 00 41 59, is open seven
days a week, 7am–midnight: 4 indoor
and 4 outdoor tennis courts,
2 squash courts, pool, sauna and
gym; visitors accepted when courts
available.

Local resources

Business services

Companies which offer the widest range of services are *Accès Créative* ☎ 99 53 65 55, which can even handle debt-collecting and assist in setting up companies; *Buroscope* ☎ 99 38 43 43; and *Servitel* ☎ 99 31 77 12.

Photocopying and printing *Bis Répétita* ☎ 99 78 14 95 or 99 38 61 38 will collect and deliver; *Copy 2000* ☎ 99 30 28 78.

Translation and interpreting *Atir*, 15 rue Marie-Rouault ☎ 99 32 31 18, also offers secretarial service.

Communications

Local delivery *TAT* ☎ 99 31 90 92 ⊠ 740305.

Long-distance delivery *TAT* ☎ 99 31 90 92 ⊠ 740305; *TNT-IPEC* ☎ 99 32 37 38.

Post office Main office: 27 bd Colombier ☎ 99 31 67 67.

Telex and fax At main post office where *Office Général du Telex* also operates ☎ 99 54 15 65.

Conference and meeting rooms

It is hoped that a new conference centre will be opened in the 1990s. Meanwhile, the new *Chamber of Commerce* ☎ 99 33 66 66 has some conference rooms for rent; and the *Maison des Compagnons du Devoir*, 9 rue du Bois-Rondel ☎ 99 38 42 15, has four small meeting rooms (capacity up to 50). (See also *Hotels*.)

Emergencies

Bureaux de change The main post office has an exchange counter open Mon–Fri, 8–7; Sat, 8–noon.

Hospitals *Domus Médica* (24hr) ☎ 99 79 48 33. Emergencies: *Centre Hospitalier*, 2 rue de l'Hôtel-Dieu ☎ 99 28 43 21.

Pharmacies Outside shop hours contact the police station, where emergency prescriptions can be stamped.

Police Main station: bd de la Tour-d'Auvergne ☎ 99 65 00 22. Emergencies ☎ 17.

Government offices

Hôtel de Ville, pl de la Mairie ☎ 99 28 55 55; *Préfecture*, 3 ave de la Préfecture ☎ 99 02 82 22.

Information sources

Business information The smart new *Chambre de Commerce et d'Industrie de Rennes*, 2 ave de la Préfecture, 35042 cedex ☎ 99 33 66 66 ⊠ 730091 fax 99 33 24 28, is away from the centre but has a well-stocked *Centre de documentation*, its *Bureau d'information sur les entreprises*, which has on-line access to details of all local businesses, and its *Centre de formalités des entreprises*, which helps with all administrative formalities involved in doing business in the area. The *Commerce extérieur* department ☎ 99 33 66 50 is particularly concerned with attracting and assisting foreign companies. Other useful sources include the *Conseil Régional de Bretagne*, 3 ave de la Préfecture ☎ 99 02 82 22; *Conseil Général d'Ille et Vilaine*, Hôtel du Département, 1 ave de la Préfecture ☎ 99 02 81 35; *Association Rennes-Atalante*, 11 rue Clos Courtel ☎ 99 63 28 28; and the local branch of INSEE, 36 pl du Colombier ☎ 99 30 91 90.

Local media *Ouest-France*, based in Rennes, is France's largest-circulation daily. The Breton chamber of commerce publishes *La Bretagne Economique*, a monthly with features on local companies.

Tourist information *Office du Tourisme*, 3 rue des Portes-Mordelaises ☎ 99 30 38 01.

Thank-yous

Chocolates *La Bonbonnière*, 15 quai Lamennais ☎ 99 79 42 83; *Corne Toison d'Or*, 7 rue Vasselot ☎ 99 79 35 54; *Léonidas*, rue de l'Hermine ☎ 99 79 49 01.

Florists *Bellier*, 7 rue Châteaurenault ☎ 99 79 44 12; *Aux Lys de Bretagne*, 5 rue de Toulouse ☎ 99 79 40 49.

ROUEN
Zip code (centre) 76000

Rouen is the capital of Haute-Normandie and has a population of about 500,000. Close to the Seine estuary and only 140km/88 miles from Paris, the historic and attractive city is also Europe's largest cereal-exporting port and France's third-largest river port. Local industries include textiles, metalworking, electronics, chemicals and pharmaceuticals, food, rubber and plastics. Shell and Esso have research centres here and the Centre National pour la Recherche Scientifique (CNRS) employs about 300 people. The city's long-serving mayor is the charismatic Jean Lecanuet. His policy of putting the city's cultural life and the reconstruction of its war-damaged centre before investment in industry has allowed Rouen to fall behind rival French towns in economic prosperity, but the emphasis is now changing. Formerly dependent on heavy industry – textiles, metalworking and oil-refining – Rouen is making a determined effort to attract investment in research and high technology. The local authorities also believe that recent improvements to accessibility and, in due course, the Channel Tunnel, which is expected to put Rouen on a main artery from the Channel ports to the Atlantic coast, will help the city to recover lost ground.

Arriving
Rouen is about an hour by car or train from Paris. There are also direct rail services to Caen, Dieppe and Le Havre, and a TGV link with Lyon (4hr). The station is a 10min walk from the centre. Inquiries ☎ 35 98 50 50.

Rouen-Boos airport
This small airport is 11km/7 miles southeast of the city. There are direct scheduled flights to and from Nantes and Lyon (with connecting flights to several other French cities) and London–Gatwick. It is best to call ahead for a taxi ☎ 35 88 50 50 or 35 80 34 34 (the journey to town takes 15–30min). For a radio-taxi charter service to Paris airports reserve well in advance ☎ 35 88 50 50. Airport inquiries ☎ 35 80 24 28.

Getting around
Walking is the most sensible and pleasant way to get around the mainly pedestrianized centre of Rouen on the right bank of the Seine. In left bank areas and the suburbs it is better to travel by car or taxi.

Taxis are plentiful. For 24hr reservations ☎ 35 88 50 50 or 35 80 34 34.
Car rental Avis ☎ 35 72 77 50, *Budget* ☎ 35 03 01 11, *Europcar* ☎ 35 70 18 30 and *Hertz* ☎ 35 98 16 57. Driving is not recommended in the centre.

Area by area
The Seine divides Rouen into the Rive Droite and the Rive Gauche. The Old Town, on the right bank, is one of the most attractive city centres in France. The right bank is the main shopping area and houses the big banks, the town hall and the law courts. On the left bank are the city's main administrative buildings.

Rouen's industrial districts are spread along the Seine valley, near the port; the main areas are Grand and Petit Couronne, Grand and Petit Quevilly, Sotteville and Saint-Etienne-du-Rouvray, all on the left bank. There is an important *parc d'activités technologiques* at Mont-Saint-Aignan on the right bank. The smart residential areas are the right bank hills of Bihorel, Bonsecours and Bois-Guillaume.

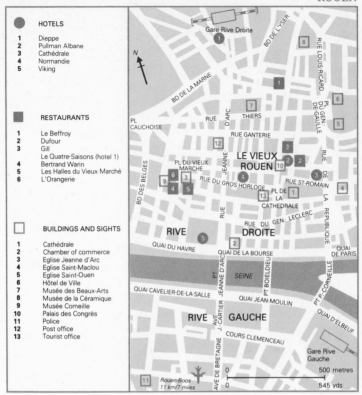

HOTELS

1 Dieppe
2 Pullman Albane
3 Cathédrale
4 Normandie
5 Viking

RESTAURANTS

1 Le Beffroy
2 Dufour
3 Gill
  Le Quatre-Saisons (hotel 1)
4 Bertrand Warin
5 Les Halles du Vieux Marché
6 L'Orangerie

BUILDINGS AND SIGHTS

1 Cathédrale
2 Chamber of commerce
3 Eglise Jeanne d'Arc
4 Eglise Saint-Maclou
5 Eglise Saint-Ouen
6 Hôtel de Ville
7 Musée des Beaux-Arts
8 Musée de la Céramique
9 Musée Corneille
10 Palais des Congrès
11 Police
12 Post office
13 Tourist office

Hotels

Most of Rouen's hotels are small and modest. In central Rouen the choice at the top of the range is between the modern and well-equipped Pullman Albane and the old established Dieppe.

Dieppe [F]|
pl Bernard-Tissot ☎ *35 71 96 00*
TX *180413* • *AE DC MC V* • *38 rooms, 2 restaurants, 1 bar*
This family-run 19thC hotel opposite the station has a loyal clientele. On weekdays its bar and restaurant Le Quatre-Saisons (see *Restaurants*) are much used by local businessmen. All the rooms are double-glazed and have modern bathrooms; some have minibars. Service is willing and efficient. Currency exchange • 1 meeting room (capacity up to 50).

Pullman Albane [F]||
rue Croix-de-Fer ☎ *35 98 06 98*
TX *180949* • *AE DC MC V* • *125 rooms, 4 suites, 1 bar; no restaurant*
This modern hotel, formerly called Frantel, is beside the cathedral and has an underground garage. The Wagons-Lit group has completely renovated it. About 10% of the rooms are now delightful (and relatively expensive) *chambres privilèges*, decorated in 1930s style. The hotel also runs the conference centre (Palais des Congrès) next door. The

rather dark bar is a popular meeting place. Service is more personal than in many chain hotels. All rooms have TV, radio, minibar, working space and air conditioning; "privilege" rooms have hairdryers. Direct dialling, currency exchange, gift shop, newsstand • 15 meeting rooms (capacity up to 600).

OTHER HOTELS
Cathédrale *F* *12 rue St-Romain*
☎ *35 71 57 95* • *MC V*. A small hotel in a 16thC building. Few modern amenities, but friendly service, pretty courtyard garden and a quiet, central location.

Normandie *F* *19 rue du Bec*
☎ *35 71 55 77* TX *771350* • *AE DC MC V*. Modest but well-run modern hotel in a pedestrianized street in the heart of the Old Town.
Viking *F* *21 quai du Havre*
☎ *35 70 34 95* TX *180503* • *AE MC V*. Functional modern hotel overlooking the Seine on the right bank.

Out of town
Convenient for the Parc des Expositions, 6km/4 miles south of the city, is the *Novotel Rouen-Sud* ☎ 35 66 58 50, a modern chain hotel with a pool. *Le Saint-Pierre* (see *Restaurants*) has excellent food as well as pretty rooms.

Restaurants
The old heart of Rouen has several top-flight restaurants and a good choice of bistros. The top restaurants normally serve only one sitting, so reservations are essential for lunch and dinner.

Le Beffroy *F*//
15 rue Beffroy ☎ *35 71 55 27* • *closed Sun, Mon, week at Christmas, week in Feb, 3 weeks in Aug* • *AE MC V*
A delightful atmosphere in which to enjoy *nouvelle* versions of Norman dishes. The accent is on fish and poultry, and the reasonably priced set meals attract a loyal clientele.

Dufour *F*/
67 rue St-Nicolas ☎ *35 71 90 62* • *closed Sun D, Mon and Aug* • *AE MC V*
This comfortable restaurant serving classical cuisine is used for business lunches (the Pullman Albane hotel and Palais des Congrès are opposite) or leisurely evening meals. No fixed-price menus but the *à la carte* and the wine list (with particularly good Bordeaux) are competitively priced. Private dining rooms available.

Gill *F*//
60 rue St-Nicolas ☎ *35 71 16 14* • *closed Mon, Sun, nat hols, Feb 1–15, first 3 weeks in Sep* • *AE DC V*
Behind a plain façade near the

cathedral lies a stylish, high-tech interior. The Gill offers *nouvelle cuisine*, with many fish dishes. Good for an important business lunch or smart evening entertainment.

Le Quatre-Saisons *F*/
pl Bernard-Tissot ☎ *35 71 96 00* • *AE DC MC V*
The restaurant of the Dieppe hotel, famous for its Norman cooking, is frequently used for business entertaining.

Bertrand Warin *F*//
7–9 rue de la Pie ☎ *35 89 26 69* • *closed Sun D, Mon, first half Jan, Aug* • *AE MC V*
Rouen's "in" restaurant, just off the Place du Vieux-Marché, is elegant and offers superb *nouvelle cuisine*. Suitable for top-flight business entertaining.

Good but casual
Around the Place du Vieux-Marché are lots of small restaurants. At 41, *Les Halles du Vieux Marché* ☎ 35 71 57 73 has fixed-price menus.

At 2 rue Thomas-Corneille is *L'Orangerie* ☎ 35 98 16 03, which serves mainly fish.

Out of town
Le Saint-Pierre ☎ 35 23 80 10 in the village of La Bouille, 20km/12 miles away, is one of the best restaurants in the Rouen area, offering *nouvelle* Norman cuisine.

Bars
The bar most used by both local and visiting business people is the small one in the *Hôtel de Dieppe*. The *Pullman Albane* hotel bar is popular with conference participants. In the Place du Vieux-Marché, *Le Bouchon de Rouen* is a wine bar which is also good for light meals.

Relaxation
Theatre, dance, opera, cinema
The *Théâtre des Arts*, 111 rue Général-Leclerc ☎ 35 98 50 98, specializes in opera (and occasionally ballet) and is well known for its annual Wagner production. Widely varied plays are performed at the *Théâtre des Deux Rives*, 48 rue Louis-Ricard ☎ 35 70 22 82, though it is hard to get tickets at short notice. The modern *Espace Duchamp-Villon*, in the Saint-Sever arts centre ☎ 35 62 31 31, offers a broad range of concerts, plays, ballet and films.
Shopping Central Rouen is a good shopping area. The department store *Au Printemps* is near the cathedral, and there are many fashion boutiques nearby. The city is famous for its *faïence* and the best shop is *Carpentier* in Rue St-Romain. Also renowned is its *sucre de pomme* (apple candy) – best from *Rolland*, rue des Carmes, or *Perier*, rue du Gros-Horloge. Calvados can be bought at the *Caves Jeanne d'Arc*, 31 rue Jeanne-d'Arc, and cheeses at *Leroux*, 40 rue de l'Hôpital. The Place du Vieux-Marché has an open-air market.
Sightseeing The *Cathédrale* is one of the most beautiful Gothic buildings in France (the crypt, the Lady Chapel and the tombs of the dukes of Normandy can be seen only during the regular guided visits ☎ 35 71 00 48). The *Eglise Saint-Maclou* with its *flamboyant* tracery and the abbey church of *Saint-Ouen* are both used for concerts, and there is the modern *Eglise Jeanne d'Arc*, on the spot where she was burnt at the stake. The *Musée des Beaux-Arts*, sq Verdrel ☎ 35 71 28 40, houses a good collection of paintings and its famous ceramics are now in the new *Musée de la Céramique*, 1 rue Faucon ☎ 35 71 28 40. The birthplace of the great classical dramatist Pierre Corneille, *Le Musée Corneille*, is in Rue de la Pie ☎ 35 71 63 92. Outside the city, at Croisset, is *Flaubert's house* ☎ 35 36 43 91.
Rouen is within a 45min drive of many of the Norman abbeys in the Seine valley. *Caudebec-en-Caux* has a fine Gothic church and the *Abbaye de Bec-Hellouin* is only 42km/26 miles away.
Spectactor sports The local soccer club is well down the French league. Local sporting pride centres on Stephen Caron, a half-Scots European swimming champion. Popular water sports include jousts on the Seine.
Keeping fit There are no sports or fitness clubs open to visitors in the city centre. Nearby, however, the *Sporting Club de la Fôret Verte* ☎ 35 59 15 47 offers tennis, squash, swimming and sauna. Squash can also be played at *Rouen Squash* ☎ 35 89 47 80. The most convenient golf courses are at *Mont Saint-Aignan* ☎ 35 74 05 41 and *Le Vaudreuil* ☎ 32 59 02 60, but telephone first.

Local resources
Business services
Of the hotels, only the Pullman Albane provides good business services. Services offered by *ITS*, 1 rue Champmeslé ☎ 35 88 41 21, include photocopying, mailing, word processing, some printing, laminating, and market research or marketing by telephone; their office

in Mont-Saint-Aignan ☎ 35 59 89 89 offers a full data-processing service. Also away from the centre, business services are offered by *Auxitec*, 8 rue de Buffon ☎ 35 70 04 40 and *Société Rouennaise de Service*, 144 rue Beauvoisine ☎ 35 07 50 03.
Photocopying *Xerox Copies Service* ☎ 35 70 62 54.
Translation and interpreting *Centre d'études des langues* (CEPPIC) ☎ 35 71 75 25.

Communications
Local and long-distance delivery *Radio Colis Express* ☎ 35 34 96 72.
Post office The main office is at 45 rue Jeanne-d'Arc ☎ 35 71 33 86.
Telex and fax Available at the main post office.

Conference/exhibition centres
The *Palais des Congrès* has eight conference rooms, the largest of which holds up to 600 people. Meeting rooms can also be rented in the *Halle aux Toiles*, pl de la Vieille-Tour ☎ 35 70 11 95, the *Salle Sainte-Croix-des-Pelletiers*, 20 rue Ste-Croix-des-Pelletiers ☎ 35 71 59 90, and the *Palais des Consuls*, quai de la Bourse ☎ 35 71 71 35.

Just outside the city at the Madrillet, the *Parc des Expositions* ☎ 35 66 52 52 has nearly 100,000 sq metres of exhibition space and a number of conference rooms.

Emergencies
Bureaux de change The main banks are in Rue Jeanne-d'Arc and the post office in the same street has an exchange counter open until 7. The *Banque Franco-Portugaise* in Place de la Calade stays open on weekdays to 6.30 and on Sat to 4.
Hospitals For medical emergencies ☎ 35 88 44 22 or go to the Pavillon Félix-Dévé, part of the *Hôpital Charles-Nicolle* (24hr).
Pharmacies The police have a list of those open late and will stamp emergency prescriptions.
Police Main station: 9 rue Brisout-de-Barneville ☎ 35 63 81 17.

Government offices
The *Hôtel de Ville*, pl du Général-de-Gaulle ☎ 35 89 81 40, is the city's main official centre. The *Chambre de Commerce et d'Industrie de Rouen* (CCIR), Palais des Consuls, quai de la Bourse, BP 641, 76007 Rouen ☎ 35 71 71 35 is very active in promoting the local economy.

Information sources
Business information The *Association pour la promotion économique du Grand Rouen* ☎ 35 71 71 35 acts as an economic development office and issues 3-month "welcome cards" to potential investors in the area, offering free accommodation and detailed information on the city's economy. The chamber of commerce (see above) supplies information on local industries and publishes a *Bulletin économique* every two months. The local *INSEE* office, 8 quai de la Bourse ☎ 35 98 43 50, publishes *Données Statistiques pour la Haute-Normandie*.
Local media *Paris-Normandie* is the main regional daily. *Liberté Dimanche* is the popular local Sunday paper. The town hall's monthly *Mieux Vivre à Rouen* often includes features on local industries and companies.
Tourist information *Office de Tourisme*, 25 pl de la Cathédrale ☎ 35 71 41 77.

Thank-yous
Chocolates *Beyer*, rue Grand-Pont ☎ 35 71 09 36.
Florists *Monville* ☎ 35 70 09 23 and *Paucod* ☎ 35 71 10 09 take telephone orders made through your hotel.

STRASBOURG   Zip code 67000

The pleasant and prosperous capital of Alsace is so attractive that many people think of it as a picture-postcard tourist spot; some even think of it as being in Germany. The local authorities are working hard to dispel Strasbourg's folksy image and to emphasize its importance as a major economic centre, an important port on the Rhine and the seat of such institutions as the Council of Europe, the European Court of Human Rights and the European Parliament.

Although not as industrialized as Mulhouse to the south, Strasbourg has a number of thriving industries, especially brewing (Kronenbourg, Heineken, Adelshoffen and Pêcheur), food (Suchard Tobler), cars (General Motors) and textiles. Some 500 new factories have been set up in Alsace since the early 1960s, many of them with foreign capital attracted by the Alsatian reputation for hard work.

The city is a major service centre, with particular importance in banking, finance and insurance; three large regional banks, the Sogénal, Crédit Industriel d'Alsace-Lorraine and the Banque Fédérative du Crédit Mutuel (BFCM) have their headquarters in Strasbourg. The presence of the European institutions has fostered the growth of a large diplomatic community: over thirty countries have consulates in the city. The city is also an academic centre; it has three universities and famous schools of medicine and theology.

Increasing emphasis is being put on high-tech research: a technopark is being set up in the southern suburbs at Illkirch. France's first World Trade Center was opened in Strasbourg in 1979, and the conference centre attracts more conferences than any other French city except Paris. Despite all this economic activity, despite the regular influx of Eucocrats, life seems to proceed at a pleasantly leisurely pace and this is not the least of Strasbourg's successes.

Arriving

Strasbourg's central position in Europe gives it good road links with Austria, the Benelux countries, Germany, Italy and Switzerland, as well as Paris. The journey from Paris takes 4–5hr by car or train. The airport has some international flights but occasionally it may be more convenient to use Basle airport (145km/90 miles away).

Strasbourg-Entzheim airport

There are domestic flights to Paris, Lille, Lyon, Marseille and Nice, and international flights to major European and some North African destinations (not all direct). Information *Strasbourg-Aviation*

☎ 88 68 91 99; helicopter services ☎ 88 68 97 97.

Although small, this airport has a restaurant, bar, meeting room for up to 25 people, bureau de change, travel agency and duty-free shop. Airport information and reservations ☎ 88 78 40 99.

City link The airport is 12km/7 miles southwest of the city on the D392; road journey takes about 20min by car, 30min by bus.

Taxis are normally available when scheduled flights arrive or may be ordered in advance ☎ 88 36 13 13.

Car rental All major rental companies have desks at the airport.

Bus There is an efficient service coinciding with scheduled flights.

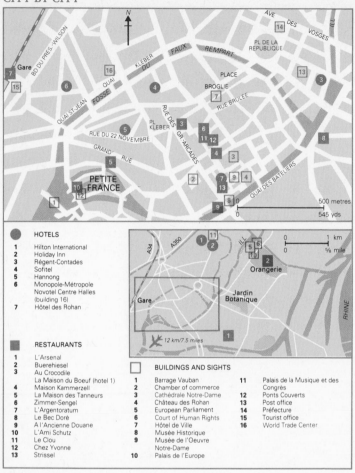

HOTELS

1 Hilton International
2 Holiday Inn
3 Régent-Contades
4 Sofitel
5 Hannong
6 Monopole-Métropole
  Novotel Centre Halles
  (building 16)
7 Hôtel des Rohan

RESTAURANTS

1 L'Arsenal
2 Buerehiesel
3 Au Crocodile
  La Maison du Boeuf (hotel 1)
4 Maison Kammerzell
5 La Maison des Tanneurs
6 Zimmer-Sengel
7 L'Argentoratum
8 Le Bec Doré
9 A l'Ancienne Douane
10 L'Ami Schutz
11 Le Clou
12 Chez Yvonne
13 Strissel

BUILDINGS AND SIGHTS

1 Barrage Vauban
2 Chamber of commerce
3 Cathédrale Notre-Dame
4 Château des Rohan
5 European Parliament
6 Court of Human Rights
7 Hôtel de Ville
8 Musée Historique
9 Musée de l'Oeuvre
  Notre-Dame
10 Palais de l'Europe
11 Palais de la Musique et des
   Congrès
12 Ponts Couverts
13 Post office
14 Préfecture
15 Tourist office
16 World Trade Center

Railway station

Strasbourg's large and busy station
handles numerous international as
well as domestic trains. It has an
exchange counter, lockers and
photocopying facilities. Taxi rank
outside. Passenger inquiries
☎ 88 22 50 50; reservations
☎ 88 32 07 51.

Getting around

Walking is quick and pleasant in the
city centre. There are several taxi
ranks and an efficient bus service.

Taxis The main rank is in Place de
la République. Other useful ones are
in Place Kléber and outside the
Novotel. For radio taxis
☎ 88 36 13 11 or 86 36 13 13.
Driving Traffic is not a major
problem and parking is relatively
easy. All the main car rental
companies have offices.
Buses *The Compagnie des Transports
Strasbourgeois* (CTS) has information
kiosks outside the station and beside
the town hall, or call *Allobus*
☎ 88 28 20 30.

Area by area

Strasbourg lies to the west of the Rhine, and the centre is encircled by the river Ill and its canals. At its heart is the lovely cathedral, and between here and the river are the city's major museums. The bustling commercial area runs from the cathedral west and north to Place Kléber and Place Broglie. The picturesque Petite France area is to the west.

Beyond the river to the west lies the station surrounded by hotels and small businesses, and to the north the leafy Place de la République, with monumental 19thC public buildings and the Palais du Rhin.

Avenue de la Paix leads north from the centre towards the modern conference centre and exhibition grounds. To the east of here are the European institutions and the lovely Orangerie park, whose surrounding streets form an exclusive residential area.

Another upmarket area is La Robertsau beyond the Orangerie, though some executives prefer the large western suburb of Oberhausbergen or the wine villages in the surrounding countryside. The northern suburb of Schiltigheim is industrial and several big breweries are based here.

Hotels

The business traveller is spoilt for choice in Strasbourg. During the European Parliament sessions, however (roughly one week per month), hotel accommodation becomes markedly scarce. Advance reservations are advisable at all times, as Strasbourg is a major tourist city as well as a business and Eurocrat centre. All hotels listed here have IDD telephones, 24hr room service, currency exchange and parking facilities. The first two are conveniently close to the conference centre.

Hilton International [F]//
ave Herrenschmidt ☎ *88 37 10 10*
Ⓣ *890363* • *AE DC MC V* • *247 rooms, 5 suites, 2 restaurants, 1 bar*
The rooms are comfortable and air-conditioned; eight are reserved for nonsmokers. The hotel has a first-class restaurant, La Maison du Boeuf (see *Restaurants*); Le Jardin is more casual and serves lighter meals. The piano-bar, Le Bugatti, is convenient for meeting business colleagues travelling by car. Shops, courtesy coach to European Parliament • sauna, jacuzzi, relaxation room • fax, 5 meeting rooms (capacity up to 450).

Holiday Inn [F]//
20 pl de Bordeaux ☎ *88 35 70 00*
Ⓣ *890515* • *AE DC MC V* • *170 rooms, 2 suites, 2 restaurants, 2 bars*
The atmosphere here is comfortable and relaxed. All rooms are air-conditioned and fairly spacious, with good working areas. Some, mainly on a special executive floor, have extra business facilities. The Louisiane restaurant is relaxed and cheerful; the two bars and the coffee shop are always busy. Shops • pool, sauna, jacuzzi, steambath, tennis, table-tennis • modular meeting room (capacity up to 800).

Régent-Contades [F]///
8 ave de la Liberté ☎ *88 36 26 26*
Ⓣ *890641* • *AE DC MC V* • *31 rooms, 1 suite, 1 bar; no restaurant*
This lovingly restored and very grand late 19thC mansion overlooking the Ill offers luxurious accommodation. The bedrooms are elegant and comfortable, the bathrooms well planned, and each has a hairdryer. The bar and small lounge are both pleasant. The beautiful panelled breakfast room doubles as a meeting room. A few dishes can be served in bedrooms. Sauna, jacuzzi • 1 meeting room (capacity up to 20).

Sofitel $\boxed{F}$///
4 pl St-Pierre-le-Jeune ☎ *88 32 99 30*
🆃 *870894 • AE DC MC V • 180 rooms,
5 suites, 1 restaurant (closed Sun and
first half Aug), 1 bar*
The Sofitel, in the heart of
Strasbourg, is within walking
distance of most major sights and
amenities. The rooms are fairly small
but have the usual Sofitel comforts.
The restaurant and bar are
frequently used for business
entertaining. Hairdresser • 5 meeting
rooms (capacity up to 120).

OTHER HOTELS
Hannong $\boxed{F}$/ *15 rue du 22
Novembre* ☎ *88 32 16 22* 🆃 *890551
• AE DC MC V.* A small, central hotel
within walking distance of the
station. It has a popular wine bar.
Two small meeting rooms (capacity
up to 30).
Monopole-Métropole $\boxed{F}$/ *16
rue Kuhn* ☎ *88 32 11 94* 🆃 *890366
• AE DC MC V.* The best of the hotels
near the station with good old-
fashioned service. No restaurant.
1 meeting room (capacity up to 30).
Novotel Centre Halles $\boxed{F}$///
Quai Kléber ☎ *88 22 10 99* 🆃 *880700
• AE DC MC V.* A somewhat
impersonal modern hotel in the
World Trade Center complex.

Hôtel des Rohan $\boxed{F}$/ *17 rue du
Maroquin* ☎ *88 32 85 11* 🆃 *870047
• MC V.* A delightful little hotel near
the cathedral. Few business amenities
but great charm. No restaurant.

Out of town
Altea Pont de l'Europe
☎ 88 61 03 23 🆃 870833 in the
Parc du Rhin is one of France's
few motels. *Le Moulin*
☎ 88 96 27 83 13km/8miles
northeast at La Wantzenau is in a
lovely setting on the banks of the
Ill. There is a delightful restaurant
next door, also called *Le Moulin*. A
number of Alsace's top restaurants
are within easy reach of
Strasbourg by car. At
Marlenheim, 20km/12 miles away,
is *Hostellerie du Cerf*
☎ 88 87 73 73, closed Mon, Tue.
At Landersheim, 5km/3 miles
farther away, is the Adidas
factory's famous staff canteen,
Auberge du Kochersberg
☎ 88 69 91 58, closed Sun D,
Tue, Wed; it is undoubtedly one
of the region's finest restaurants.
Visitors' lunches start at 1 on
weekdays.

Restaurants
The Strasbourgeois love their food and wine, so it is not surprising that
the city offers a wide choice of excellent restaurants. The two top
gourmet restaurants, Buerehiesel and Au Crocodile, have a mixed
clientele of Eurocrats, business people, wealthy tourists and locals. Few
restaurants are geared solely to business meals.

L'Arsenal $\boxed{F}$/
11 rue de l'Abreuvoir ☎ *88 35 03 69
• AE DC MC V • closed Sat, Sun,
2 weeks end Jan, L mid-Jul–
mid-Aug*
Small, attractive and impeccably run,
this restaurant is a favourite of
diplomats, 5min by taxi from the
older part of town. Superb Alsatian
(but delicate) food at reasonable
prices, and an excellent wine list
punctiliously served.

Buerehiesel $\boxed{F}$////
4 parc de l'Orangerie ☎ *88 61 62 24
• closed Tue (except Tue L in summer),
Wed, second half Aug, Christmas, New
Year • AE DC MC V*
An authentic 17thC Alsatian
farmhouse lovingly reconstructed in
the Orangerie park is the setting for
one of Strasbourg's finest restaurants.
The *nouvelle cuisine* comes in generous
portions and the service is pleasantly
relaxed.

Au Crocodile [F]////
10 rue de l'Outre ☎ *88 32 13 02*
• *closed Sun, Mon, mid-Jul–mid-Aug,*
Christmas, New Year • *AE DC MC*
This elegant restaurant is more
formal than the Buerehiesel, but
offers equally accomplished cooking
with some interesting *nouvelle*
versions of filling regional dishes.
Private dining rooms available.

La Maison du Boeuf [F]///
ave Herrenschmidt ☎ *88 37 10 10*
• *closed Aug* • *AE DC MC V*
The Hilton's restaurant is one of the
best in town, offering excellent fish
as well as meat. In summer meals are
served on a pleasant terrace.

Maison Kammerzell [F]////
16 pl de la Cathédrale ☎ *88 32 42 14*
• *closed mid-Jan–mid-Feb* • *AE DC*
MC V
Housed in a picturesque 15th–16thC
building with ornate woodcarvings,
this restaurant offers two types of
cuisine: Alsatian on the ground floor
and *nouvelle* upstairs.

La Maison des Tanneurs [F]/
42 rue du Bain-aux-Plantes
☎ *88 32 79 70* • *closed Sun, Mon*
(*open Sun L in May, Jun and Sep*)
• *AE DC MC V*
This is a charming and very popular
restaurant in a 16thC tannery in
Petite France specializing in
Alsatian dishes. A good place for
business entertaining.

Zimmer-Sengel [F]//
8 rue du Temple-Neuf ☎ *88 32 35 01*
• *closed weekends and most of Aug*
• *AE DC MC V*
An old-established restaurant near the
cathedral. It specializes in *nouvelle*
cuisine and the fixed-price menu is
good value.

Good but casual
The well-run station buffet
L'Argentoratum ☎ *88 32 59 40* is
often used for less formal business
entertaining; private dining rooms
are available. *Le Bec Doré*, 8 quai des

Pêcheurs ☎ 88 35 39 57, overlooks
the river and is popular for both
business and more casual dining. Also
overlooking the river is *A l'Ancienne*
Douane, 6 rue Douane ☎ 88 32 42 19,
a large and busy brasserie.

The food, wine and beer are all
Alsatian at *L'Ami Schutz*, 1 Ponts-
Couverts ☎ 88 32 76 98, where there
is a convivial atmosphere in the
evening.

Winstubs
Somewhere between a German
Bierkeller and an English pub in
atmosphere, but very much an
Alsatian institution, the *Winstub* is a
congenial place to meet friends after
work over a jug of wine and a filling
local dish; most open from late
afternoon until the early hours.
Among the best is *Le Clou*, 3 rue
Chaudron ☎ 88 32 11 67, but
traditionalists swear by *s'Burjerstuewel*
(also known, less tongue-twistingly,
as *Chez Yvonne*), 10 rue du Sanglier
☎ 88 32 84 15. *Strissel*, 5 pl de la
Grande-Boucherie ☎ 88 32 14 73, is
particularly atmospheric with its
rustic decor.

Bars
The bar in the World Trade Center
is useful for meeting business
contacts, though it closes at 6.30. The
Sofitel's bar is central, and the
Hilton's *Bugatti* piano-bar is handy
for those attending conferences.
Local businessmen are fond of the
beer in the bar of the Hôtel de
France, 20 rue Jeu-des-Enfants. *Le*
Wyn Bar in the Hannong hotel is
among the best for food.

Entertainment
Strasbourg offers fine musical
entertainment, particularly during
the June music festival. There is little
nightlife other than discos, but Kehl,
just across the German border, has a
varied nightlife, much of it rather
sleazy.
Theatre, dance, opera The *Théâtre*
Municipal, pl Broglie ☎ 88 36 43 41,
stages plays and has lively opera and

operetta seasons by the Opéra du Rhin company. The *Théâtre National de Strasbourg*, 1 rue du Général-Gouraud ☎ 88 35 63 60, has a complicated season-ticket system that often makes it difficult for visitors to obtain tickets. The *Théâtre Alsacien de Strasbourg*, pl Broglie ☎ 88 36 43 41, specializes in plays in dialect. *Le Maillon*, pl André Malraux ☎ 88 26 16 17 or 88 26 12 66, is a lively arts complex offering theatre, jazz, modern dance and film.
Music The *Orchestre Philharmonique de Strasbourg* ☎ 88 22 15 60 performs in the municipal theatre or in the *Palais de la Musique et des Congrès*, ave Schutzenberger ☎ 88 35 03 00. Concerts are also held in the *Pavillon Joséphine* in the Orangerie park and, in summer, in the courtyard of the *Château des Rohan* (see *Sightseeing*).

Shopping

The narrow old streets near the cathedral – Rue du Dôme, Rue des Hallebardes, Rue des Orfèvres – are full of chic boutiques; Place de la Cathédrale itself is more touristy, with the accent on local wares. The Place Kléber area has the city's department stores – *Magmod*, *Printemps* and the *Fnac*. The *Centre Halles*, in the same complex as the World Trade Center, is a useful place for one-stop shopping.

The city is famous for its fruit brandies (*alcools blancs*) and its excellent *foie gras*.

Sightseeing

Strasbourg has many picturesque buildings, including one of the country's finest cathedrals, as well as several good museums. All keep to the same opening hours: Jun–Sep, 10–12, 2–6; Oct–May, afternoons only, but open Sun morning (closed Tue).
Cathédrale Notre-Dame Gothic cathedral in pinkish sandstone, with elaborate carvings, lofty spire and famous astronomical clock. *Son-et-lumière* (in French and German) is staged in the cathedral from about Easter to September.

Château des Rohan Beautiful 18thC château (also known as Palais Rohan), now housing three museums: the *Musée Archéologique*, the *Musée des Beaux-Arts* and the *Musée des Arts Décoratifs*. Also worth seeing in the château are the *Cabinet des Estampes*, with over 20,000 prints and drawings, and the *grands appartements*. 2 pl du Château ☎ 88 32 31 54.
Musée Historique A local history collection. *3 pl de la Grande-Boucherie* ☎ 88 32 25 63.
Musée de l'Oeuvre Notre-Dame Alsatian art from the Middle Ages to the Renaissance. *3 pl du Château* ☎ 88 32 06 39.
Orangerie Attractive public gardens designed by Le Nôtre.
Palais de l'Europe The Council of Europe and the European Parliament can be seen from sightseeing boats, or visited by appointment. *Bd de la Dordogne* ☎ 88 37 40 01.
Petite France Picturesque area of half-timbered houses and quiet canals; attractive old streets are linked by three bridges, the *Ponts Couverts*; beyond them the *Barrage Vauban*, part of the old fortifications, affords a striking view of the old town. There is an enjoyable boat trip, starting with a tour of Petite France and then going right up to the Palais de l'Europe, which is worth fitting into even a busy schedule.

Out of town

The beautiful countryside around Strasbourg is well worth exploring. The imposing castle of Haut-Koenigsbourg, 60km/37 miles southwest of the city, is an extraordinary folly built for Kaiser Wilhelm II in 1901 on the site of a medieval ruin; and all along the *Route de Vin de l'Alsace* (Wine Road), which starts at Marlenheim and meanders through 100km/62 miles of vineyards, are picturesque villages such as Obernai, Ottrott, Ribeauvillé and Riquewihr, where the local wines can be tasted.

Spectator sports

Horse-racing The nearest racecourse is 16km/10 miles north of the city at *Hoerdt* ☎ 88 51 32 44; open Mar–Jun, Sep–Oct.

Soccer Extremely popular, even though the local team has not done well in recent years. The *Racing-Club de Strasbourg* stadium is at *Meinau* ☎ 88 34 08 47; the *Association Sportive de Strasbourg* has another soccer stadium at *Tivoli-Wacken* ☎ 88 36 60 78.

Keeping fit

Fitness centres Two in the city centre are *L'Eau Vive*, 29 rue du Vieux-Marché-aux-Vins ☎ 88 22 36 55, which also offers aerobics and modern dance; and *Energy Centre*, 2 rue Moll ☎ 88 22 12 44, which also has martial arts and aerobics. *Le Maintien*, in the suburbs at Neudorf ☎ 88 34 26 44, is open until 10 every evening. (See also *Hotels*.)

Golf The top local club is *Golf-Club de Strasbourg*, rte du Rhin, Illkirch ☎ 88 66 17 22.

Riding *Centre Equestre*, rue de l'Hippodrôme in the Parc du Rhin ☎ 88 61 67 35; *L'Etrier de Strasbourg*, 13km/8 miles northeast at Le Wantzenau ☎ 88 96 60 57.

Squash and tennis There are courts near the exhibition grounds run by the *Association Sportive de Strasbourg* ☎ 88 35 29 23; *Centre Halles* (2nd floor) ☎ 88 23 00 55 also has courts, sauna, bar and restaurant.

Swimming There is an olympic-size pool in the suburban *Centre Nautique de Schiltigheim* ☎ 88 33 24 40; an indoor municipal pool quite close to the city centre, bd de la Victoire ☎ 88 35 51 56; outdoor pools in Wacken ☎ 88 31 49 10 and close to the Pont de l'Europe ☎ 88 61 92 30.

Local resources

Business services

France's first World Trade Center, the *Maison du Commerce International de Strasbourg* (MCIS), 4 quai Kléber ☎ 88 32 48 90 ▨ 890673, was opened in 1979. It covers 5,000 sq metres on eight floors and offers a good range of business services; with shops, parking areas and hotels nearby.

Fully equipped office space can be rented from one day to three months, and meeting rooms are available. Services offered free to World Trade Center members, for a fee to others, include a well-stocked information library; legal, accounting and tax advice; telex and fax; photocopying. The centre has a restaurant and a bar, and companies in the same building can supply translating, interpreting and messenger services.

Photocopying and printing *Eclair Print* 5–7 rue Jacques-Peirotes ☎ 88 35 22 96; *SAID*, 36 fbg de Saverne ☎ 88 32 02 25 and 1 pl du Foin ☎ 88 35 34 84.

Secretarial services *Allo Secrétariat*, 9 pl Kléber ☎ 88 32 68 32; *Secrétariat no. 1*, 58 ave des Vosges ☎ 88 36 56 16.

Translating and interpreting *Interpretations Traductions Alsace* ☎ 88 22 20 22 ▨ 890673 is in the MCIS.

Communications

Long-distance delivery DHL (international) ☎ 05 11 95 31 (toll free); *Chronopost* ☎ 05 30 05 30 (toll free) or at main post office; *SERNAM* ☎ 88 28 00 12 (international), 88 28 46 10 (national).

Post office Main office: 5 ave de la Marseillaise ☎ 88 23 44 00; others are at the station and Centre Halles.

Telex and fax At main post office; *International Telex Assistance* ☎ 88 22 20 22 ▨ 890673.

Conference/exhibition centres

The attractive *Palais de la Musique et des Congrès*, ave Schutzenberger ☎ 88 35 03 00 ▨ 890666 is the third largest conference centre in France. Its current facilities include the 2,000-seat Salle Erasme auditorium, the 500-seat Salle Robert Schuman, and five other rooms (capacity up to 350). Most rooms are air-conditioned and equipped with a wide range of facilities, including simultaneous interpreting equipment. The centre has bars, cafeteria, telex and telephone, a bank, travel agency, gift shop, infirmary and a photo lab. The 1,700 sq metre *Galerie de Marbre* (Marble Gallery) can be rented for exhibitions or banquets (capacity up to 1,000).

An extension due to open in spring 1989 will include a 1,000-seat auditorium and 2,000 sq metres of exhibition space, plus a banqueting hall seating up to 1,400.

Close by is an exhibition centre, the *Parc des Expositions Strasbourg-Wacken* ☎ 88 36 11 90 ☎ 870096.

Emergencies
Bureaux de change The exchange counter at the station is open 9–8 (sometimes later in summer); *CMDP*, 26 rue du Vieux-Marché-aux-Poissons ☎ 88 32 12 08, is open Sun to about 5.
Medical emergencies SAMU ☎ 88 33 33 33; *Médecins de Garde* ☎ 88 36 09 93; *Hôpital Civil* ☎ 88 36 71 11; *Centre Hospitalier Régional*, ave Molière, Hautepierre ☎ 88 28 90 00.
Pharmacies The main police station has a list of pharmacies open outside usual business hours.
Police Main station: 11 rue de la Nuée-Bleue ☎ 88 32 99 08. Emergencies ☎ 17.

Government offices
Hôtel de Ville, 9 rue Brûlée ☎ 88 32 99 03; *Préfecture*, 5 pl de la République ☎ 88 32 99 00; *Douane* (regional customs office), 11 ave de la Liberté ☎ 88 35 48 40; *Centre Régional de Promotion Economique et Sociale*, 1 pl Gutenberg ☎ 88 32 99 08.
EC offices Parlement Européen, ave de l'Europe ☎ 88 37 40 01; *Conseil de l'Europe*, ave de l'Europe ☎ 88 61 49 61.

Information sources
Business information The best source of information is the *MCIS* (see *Business services*), with its large information library. Local economic data can be supplied by *Chambre de Commerce du Bas-Rhin*, 10 pl Gutenberg ☎ 88 32 12 55; and INSEE's *Observatoire Economique de l'Alsace* ☎ 88 32 03 18.
Local media The main regional daily is *Les Dernières Nouvelles d'Alsace*. The chamber of commerce publishes *Le Point Economique* every two months, with articles on local business topics; and a monthly *Bulletin d'Opportunités Commerciales* which aims to match those seeking and offering business opportunities. *FR3 Alsace* is the regional station of the third television channel.
Tourist information Office de Tourisme de Strasbourg et sa Région, Palais des Congrès has two "welcome offices" opposite the station ☎ 88 32 51 49 and at the Pont de l'Europe ☎ 88 61 39 23. Open winter Mon–Fri, 9–12.30, 1.45–6; summer 8–7 daily.

Thank-yous
Cakes Kohler-Rehm, pl Kléber ☎ 88 32 15 93, has an "*Intergâteaux*" dispatch service.
Confectionery Catalin, 4 pl de l'Homme-de-Fer ☎ 88 32 62 45; *Gross*, Centre Halles ☎ 88 22 22 77; *Léonidas*, pl de la Cathédrale ☎ 88 32 19 81.
Florists Fuchs, 19 rue des Orfèvres ☎ 88 32 19 57, and *Fleurs pour Ma Dame*, 8 rue Friesé ☎ 88 32 10 03, both take telephone credit card orders.

TOULOUSE
Zip code 31000

The ancient city of Toulouse has expanded and been modernized spectacularly since the war, becoming France's leading centre of high-tech research and the de facto capital of Europe's aerospace industries. It all began during World War I when the government transferred armament and aircraft industries here from the north in order to keep them as far from the Germans as possible. Then in the 1950s the government made it the main focus for its policy of developing the backward southwest, and many key state enterprises, public services and colleges were transferred from Paris. Private firms have followed in their wake.

Today the state-owned Aérospatiale employs 7,500 people; Airbus Industrie's head office is here, and so are the main Air France workshops. The Centre National des Etudes Spatiales (CNES) has 2,000 staff, working on the Hermès spacecraft and other projects. Other firms which have followed include Zodiac-Espace, Matra Espace and Alcatel Espace. Foreign investors in the aerospace field include Sperry Flight Systems, Rohr-Industrie and Rockwell Collins. The growing electronics industry has attracted Motorola, Bendix, ITT Cannon and Materials Research. France's three aeronautic *grandes écoles* have all been based in Toulouse since the 1960s, and the city now has some 300 research laboratories and 5,000 full-time researchers.

While "old-style" local civic leaders are rather wary of newcomers, the city's business people are dynamic and international in their approach. However, amid all the high-tech activity, Toulouse still retains something of the charm of an ancient southern city.

Arriving
Toulouse is well provided with transport links. The A61 autoroute from Bordeaux continues southeast to Narbonne, connecting with Montpellier and Paris, and Barcelona to the south. Rail links are adequate, and air services excellent.

Toulouse-Blagnac airport
This modern airport has direct scheduled flights to 29 French and foreign cities. The terminal has an information office, photocopy service, post office, showers, shops, bars, a restaurant of average quality (L'Horizon ☎ 61 30 02 75), a bank and bureau de change (open till 6.45 weekdays, 5.30 Sat, Sun). There are four meeting rooms for up to 120 people, with secretarial help if needed. All airport inquiries ☎ 61 71 11 14.

Nearby hotels Sofitel, 31700 Blagnac ☎ 61 71 11 25 ⊤⊠ 520178 • AE DC MC V. Sizable modern hotel (free bus shuttle); attractive soundproofed bedrooms; useful restaurant, Le Caouec; heated pool, sauna, tennis, 6 meeting rooms (capacity up to 125). *Campanile*, 31700 Blagnac ☎ 61 30 03 40 • DC MC V. Modern, motel style, with simple, reliable restaurant. Free shuttle from airport.
City link The airport is at Blagnac, 7km/4 miles northwest of town. A bus shuttle leaves every 15min from the Gare Matabiau, 6am–8.15pm; the journey takes 15–30min.
Taxis Airport cabs ☎ 61 30 02 54. Those arriving late in the evening are strongly advised to reserve a taxi in advance, for the bus shuttle often stops before the last flights.
Car rental Major firms have desks.

Railway station
Gare Matabiau is quite central. There are six trains a day to Paris, taking 6–7hr (no TGV). The station has a taxi rank and a bureau de change. Passenger inquiries ☎ 61 62 50 50; reservations ☎ 61 62 85 44.

Getting around
The city is circular shaped, with three concentric ring roads. The historic central area is compact and can be tackled on foot, but the new industrial and research zones are in the suburbs, best reached by taxi.

Taxis These are plentiful and easy to spot. *Taxis Bleus* ☎ 61 80 36 36 has a 24hr service. There are several ranks in town.

Driving This presents few problems, except at rush hours. Avoid the narrow streets of the centre. There are several big underground garages.

Walking Pleasant and safe in the old streets, tedious elsewhere.

Bus A good network extends into the suburbs, but buses are few after 9pm. Inquiries ☎ 61 41 70 70. A Métro line will open in 1992.

Area by area
Toulouse lies astride the river Garonne, with its business area on the right (east) bank. Here the lovely medieval core is still the main focus of activity. The heart of town is Place du Capitole, next to the stately 18thC town hall: not far away are the Préfecture and chamber of

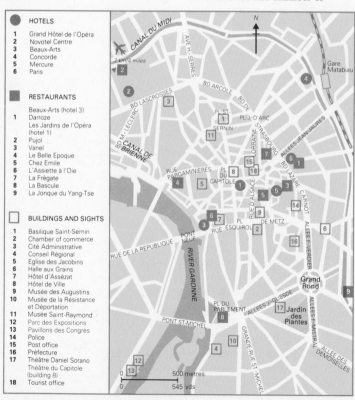

HOTELS

1 Grand Hôtel de l'Opéra
2 Novotel Centre
3 Beaux-Arts
4 Concorde
5 Mercure
6 Paris

RESTAURANTS

   Beaux-Arts (hotel 3)
1 Darroze
   Les Jardins de l'Opéra
   (hotel 1)
2 Pujol
3 Vanel
4 Le Belle Epoque
5 Chez Emile
6 L'Assiette à l'Oie
7 La Frégate
8 La Bascule
9 La Jonque du Yang-Tse

BUILDINGS AND SIGHTS

1 Basilique Saint-Sernin
2 Chamber of commerce
3 Cité Administrative
4 Conseil Régional
5 Eglise des Jacobins
6 Halle aux Grains
7 Hôtel d'Assézat
8 Hôtel de Ville
9 Musée des Augustins
10 Musée de la Résistance
   et Déportation
11 Musée Saint-Raymond
12 Parc des Expositions
13 Pavillons des Congrès
14 Police
15 Post office
16 Préfecture
17 Théâtre Daniel Sorano
   Théâtre du Capitole
   (building 8)
18 Tourist office

commerce, many fine old churches and the university faculties of law and social sciences.

The 19thC residential districts and the modern town stretch beyond. Les Minimes and Lalandre are districts of mixed housing with some older light industry. The Côte Pavée and Montplaisir, to the east of the centre, are pleasant middle-class areas. Farther south is the huge university and scientific complex of Rangeuil, with elite aeronautical colleges, many key research centres and the workshops of Air France. The island of Ramier holds the main sports and exhibition centres. To the west, Le Mirail is a sprawling dormitory suburb. Just south lies the big new industrial estate of Thibaud. To the north is the huge Purpan teaching hospital and beyond it, at Saint-Martin du Touch, the main Aérospatiale factories where Airbuses are assembled.

The outer suburbs Just north of Saint-Martin du Touch, the separate commune of Blagnac contains more Aérospatiale factories, more industrial estates and the airport. Many of the employees live in the thriving new town of Colomiers, to the west. South of the city, the hilly country east of the Garonne is a fashionable area where many senior executives live.

Hotels

The city's main hotels are nearly all central. Although much used by business people, few have exceptional facilities for them. Parking is not usually a problem. Currency exchange is generally available.

Grand Hôtel de l'Opéra F///
1 pl du Capitole ☎ *61 21 82 66*
TX *521998 • AE DC MC V • 46 rooms, 4 suites, 2 restaurants, 1 bar*
Recently converted from a 17thC convent, this lovely central hotel is a haven of peace. All rooms have air conditioning and double glazing. Les Jardins de l'Opéra restaurant is excellent (see *Restaurants*), and the intimate *salons* and alcoves off the foyer are ideal for a business chat. 24hr room service • gym, sauna, jacuzzi, pool • fax, 2 meeting rooms (capacity up to 100).

Novotel Centre F//
5 pl Alfonse-Jourdain ☎ *61 21 74 74*
TX *532400 • AE DC MC V • 125 rooms, 6 suites, 1 restaurant, 1 bar/lounge*
This impressive new hotel is beside a big public park, yet is also fairly central. Drinks and meals are served on the terrace in fine weather. Facilities include 17-channel satellite TV in all bedrooms and Minitels and mini-computers in a few. The service is excellent, public rooms are big and bright, and the food in Le Grill is appetizing. 6 meeting rooms (capacity up to 250).

OTHER HOTELS
Beaux-Arts F// *1 pl du Pont-Neuf* ☎ *61 23 40 50* TX *532451 • AE DC MC V.* An unusual modern hotel. Some rooms are small; those on the top floor have views over the river. 24hr room service.

Concorde F// *16 bd de Bon Repos* ☎ *61 62 48 60* TX *531686 • AE DC MC V.* Close to the station and well geared to business needs. Sizable bedrooms, some suited for daytime use as offices; well-equipped meeting rooms.

Mercure F// *rue St-Jérome* ☎ *61 23 11 77* TX *520760 • Mercure • AE DC MC V* A pleasant, functional chain hotel situated beside a shopping centre. Rooms are small but well-equipped. 11 meeting rooms (capacity up to 250).

Paris F// *18 allées Jean-Jaurès* ☎ *61 62 98 30* TX *521950 • AE DC MC V.* A small, central hotel much used by middle-rank business people. 24hr room service. No restaurant.

Restaurants

Toulouse and its suburbs have many excellent eating places. Their accent is usually on local cuisine: the famous *cassoulet* of Toulouse, a rich stew of preserved goose, spicy sausage and beans, is a little heavy for lunchtime, but the southwest has other notable dishes, many featuring fish, duck and *foie gras*.

Beaux-Arts *F/*
1 quai de la Daurade ☎ *61 21 12 12*
• *AE DC MC V*
Opened recently by the Alsatian owners of the famous "Flo" in Paris, this brasserie offers classic cuisine with a southwestern bias and very good fish. The tables outside, facing the river, are airy but a bit noisy.

Darroze *F///*
19 rue Castellane ☎ *61 62 34 70*
• *closed Sat L, Sun, 3 weeks Jul/Aug, 1 week Feb* • *AE DC MC V*
This family-run restaurant offers cooking from the Landes and Toulouse regions, including *foie gras*, duck and *cassoulet*. The desserts, wines and armagnacs are superb. Good value set menus available.

Les Jardins de l'Opéra *F///*
1 pl du Capitole ☎ *61 23 07 76*
• *closed Sun, Aug 15–22* • *AE DC MC V*
The city's best hotel also has its best restaurant in an enchanting courtyard across the street from the Opéra. On fine days you eat on the flowery patio; on colder days, in snug little *salons* with well-spaced tables. Dominique Toulousy, chef and co-owner, offers inventive regional-based cuisine and two very good value set menus.

Pujol *F///*
21 ave du Général-Compans, Blagnac ☎ *61 71 13 58* • *closed Sun D, Sat, 1 week Feb, 3 weeks Aug* • *DC MC V*
This suburban restaurant has long been a favourite with senior business people who come for the excellent regional cooking (the *cassoulet* is the best in Toulouse, and the game dishes in season are unbeatable). Pleasant terrace and garden.

Vanel *F///*
22 rue Maurice-Fonvieille
☎ *61 21 51 82* • *closed Sun, Mon L, nat hols, Aug* • *AE MC V*
Many of the locals would declare Louis Vanel's restaurant the best in town. He specializes in pigeon and lamb, but also offers such novelties as scrambled eggs with leeks and blood-sausage. A remarkable selection of liqueurs and armagnacs is also available.

Other good restaurants
La Belle Epoque, 3 rue Pargaminières ☎ 61 23 22 12 offers good regional cooking, and *Chez Emile*, 13 pl St-Georges ☎ 61 21 05 56, serves unusual fish dishes and local classics. *L'Assiette à l'Oie*, 28 rue Peyrolières ☎ 61 21 50 91, and *La Frégate*, 1 rue d'Austerlitz ☎ 61 21 59 61, are two good choices in the middle-price range, while *La Bascule*, 14 ave Maurice-Hauriou ☎ 61 52 09 51, is a lively and inexpensive bistro. *La Jonque du Yang-Tse*, bd Griffoul-Dorval ☎ 61 20 74 74, is actually a barge moored on a canal, serving Pekinese food.

Out of town
Two small but select hotels about 8km/5 miles out of town, neither with a restaurant, are: *Les Chanterelles* ☎ 61 86 21 86, at Tournefeuille to the west, and *La Flânerie* ☎ 61 73 39 12, outside Vieille-Toulouse to the south. *L'Auberge de Tournebride* ☎ 61 73 34 49, 12km/7 miles south of town, is an excellent restaurant in a rural setting.

Bars

The city has a wide selection. The best of the hotel bars is at the Opéra.

Also very suitable are *Le Bibent* and *Le Florida*, both in Place du Capitole. *Le Père Léon*, in Place Esquirol, is a Toulouse institution. The best terrace-cafés are in Place Wilson, notably *Le Capoul* and *La Frégate*. *Le London Pub* in Rue d'Austerlitz is fun, but not at all British.

Entertainment

Listings appear in the weekly magazine *Flash.*

Theatre, dance, opera The municipal *Théâtre Daniel Serano*, 35 allées Jules-Guesde ☎ 61 25 66 87, is used by the state-backed Grenier de Toulouse company, which also performs at 3 rue de la Digue ☎ 61 42 97 79. Popular productions on tour go to *Théâtre du Capitole* ☎ 61 22 80 22, the home of the resident opera and ballet companies.

Cinema The best place for foreign sub-titled films is *ABC*, 13 rue St-Bernard ☎ 61 21 20 46.

Music Classical concerts, notably those of the famous Orchestre de Toulouse under Michel Plasson, are given in the big *Halle aux Grains*, pl Dupuy ☎ 61 62 02 70; operas are staged here too. The city's chamber orchestra is excellent. In July and August frequent concerts are held in the cloister of the Jacobins church and other lovely old courtyards.

Nightclubs Ubu, 16 rue St-Rome ☎ 61 23 26 75, is smart and has a good restaurant. *New-Privé*, 23 rue St-Rome ☎ 61 21 70 51, is for the fashionable young.

Shopping

Big department stores are in Avenue Alsace-Lorraine and supermarkets are in the St-Georges shopping centre. Best luxury boutiques are in Rue Croix-Baragnon, Rue de la Pomme (good antiques market at 28). Best for local products: *Munt*, marché Victor-Hugo (Toulouse sausages); *Comtesse du Barry*, 8 pl St-Etienne (*foie gras*); *Xavier*, 6 pl Victor-Hugo (cheeses).

Sightseeing

This historic city has many fine museums and churches.

Hôtel d'Assézat The city's most beautiful Renaissance mansion. *Rue de Metz. Open 9–12, 2.30–6.30.*

Basilique Saint-Sernin Dating from the 11thC, the most famous Romanesque church in southern France. *Place St-Sernin.*

Eglise des Jacobins A 14thC Gothic masterpiece. *Rue Lakanal. Open 10–12, 2.30–6.*

Musée des Augustins Paintings by Toulouse-Lautrec, Delacroix; fine sculptures. *Rue de Metz. Open Thu–Mon, 10–12, 2–6; Wed 2–10.*

Musée de la Résistance et Déportation Souvenirs of the Occupation, 1940–44. *Rue Achille-Viadieu. Open Mon–Fri, 2–5.*

Musée Saint-Raymond Roman mosaics, sculpture and pottery. *Place St-Sernin. Open Wed–Mon, 10–12, 2–6.*

Guided tours Organized daily, Jul–Sep: apply at tourist office.

Spectator sports

Rugby A very popular sport with a prestigious team, playing at *Le Stade Toulousain*, 114 rue Troënes ☎ 61 47 05 05.

Soccer FC Toulouse is based at *Stade Municipal*, allée Gabriel-Biénès ☎ 61 55 11 11.

Keeping fit

The hotels have few facilities, but there are numerous public and private centres. The *Parc Municipal des Sports* on the Ile du Ramier ☎ 61 22 29 22 offers many activities.

Fitness centres Diapason, 10 bd de la Gare ☎ 61 34 92 10; *Le Gymnase*, 45 rue Alfred-Duméril ☎ 61 53 89 21.

Golf Clubs with 18-hole courses close to town are *Vieille-Toulouse*, at Castanet Tolesan ☎ 61 73 45 48, and *Palmola* at Buzet ☎ 61 84 20 50.

Squash Try *Capitole*, 43 rue Gambetta ☎ 61 22 83 00, which also has a sauna, jacuzzi and solarium.

Swimming There are 13 public pools around town, notably at the

Parc Municipal des Sports
☎ 61 52 86 30, *Alban-Minville*
(*Mirail*), allée Belfontaine
☎ 61 40 18 08 and *Bellevue*, 86
chemin de la Salade Ponsan
☎ 61 52 93 53.
Tennis *Stade Toulousain* (see
above); *Parc Municipal des Sports*
☎ 61 55 13 38.

Local resources
Business services
Advice on finding the best business
services can be obtained from the
Bureau Régional d'Industrialisation, 14
rue de Tivoli ☎ 61 33 50 50. Private
companies include *Acte*
☎ 61 22 92 60 and *Interpac*
☎ 61 41 11 81. (See also *Hotels*.)
Photocopying and printing *Canon*
☎ 61 47 22 77, *Copy 2000*
☎ 61 63 93 93, *Dactilocopie*
☎ 61 23 55 51.
Secretarial *Permanence Secrétariat*
☎ 61 21 60 66, *Manpower*
☎ 61 53 30 49.
Translation *Eclair Services*
☎ 61 23 81 12, *Barbara Schantz*
☎ 61 44 81 75, *Huw Ap Thomas*
☎ 61 42 98 73.

Communications
Local delivery *Toulouse Courses*
☎ 61 52 07 79.
Long-distance delivery DHL
☎ 61 30 07 07, MSAS ☎ 71 61 00 23.
Post office Main office: 9 rue
Lafayette ☎ 61 22 33 11.
Telex and fax PTT ☎ 61 23 30 00
(telex), ☎ 61 23 77 32 (fax); SMH-
Alcatel ☎ 61 40 39 59.

Conference/exhibition centres
Promo-Toulouse ☎ 61 21 92 32,
located in the tourist office, gives
advice and help with setting up
conferences. The *Pavillons des
Congrès*, Parc des Expositions
☎ 61 52 51 01 is the best centre and
has rooms with up to 650 seats. The
Université de Rangueil ☎ 61 55 66 11
ext. 033 has rooms that seat up to
700. Both these centres have
simultaneous translation equipment.
Other venues include *Le Belvédère*,

bd des Récollets ☎ 61 53 34 23, and
the *Théâtre du Taur*, rue du Taur
☎ 61 21 77 13.

Emergencies
Bureaux de change Gare
Matabiau, 6am–8pm daily; tourist
office, 11–1, 2–4.30, daily May–Sep.
Hospitals Largest are *Rangueil*,
chemin du Vallon ☎ 61 53 11 33, and
Purpan ☎ 61 49 11 33. Urgent 24hr
medical service: SAMU ☎ 61 49 33 33.
Pharmacies Open all night: 17 rue
de Rémusat ☎ 61 21 81 20.
Police Main station: rue du
Rempart-St-Etienne ☎ 61 29 70 00.

Government offices
Hôtel de Ville, pl du Capitole
☎ 61 22 29 22; *Préfecture d'Haute-
Garonne*, pl St-Etienne
☎ 61 33 40 00; *Conseil Régional de
Midi-Pyrénées*, bd Maréchal-Juin
☎ 61 33 50 50. The *Cité
Administrative*, housing state and
local authority services, is at bd
Armand-Duportal ☎ 61 58 58 58.

Information sources
Business help and advice are offered
by the *Chambre de Commerce et
d'Industrie*, 2 rue Alsace-Lorraine
☎ 61 33 65 00, and the *Bureau
Régional d'Industrialisation*, 14 rue de
Tivoli ☎ 61 33 50 50. The best local
business directories are *Toulouse
Business* and *Toulouse Pratique*.
Local media The only local daily
paper is *Dépêche du Midi*, politically
left-of-centre. Much more interesting
and lively is the new centre-right
weekly *Courrier Sud*. *Toulouse-
Actualités* is a Catholic weekly. The
state TV channel FR3 has a nightly
local news magazine. *Sud-Radio* gives
detailed local news coverage.
Tourist information *Office du
Tourisme*, Donjon du Capitole
☎ 61 23 32 00. Open 9–7; 9–6 winter.

Thank-yous
Confectionery *Chiche*, 3 rue St-
Pantaléon ☎ 61 21 80 80.
Florist *Bocarnéa*, 6 rue Rivals
☎ 61 21 28 14.

MONACO
Zip code 98000

The sovereign principality of Monaco is a tiny 190ha/468-acre strip of land squeezed between sea and mountains. Only 27,000 people live there, but under the rule of Prince Rainier III, assisted by an elected council, it has become one of the world's most glamorous, dynamic and efficient centres for business and tourism.

When the Nice area became part of France in 1860 the Grimaldi dynasty retained its independence and kept the economy afloat by building a casino on the headland of Monte Carlo. Although decline had set in by the time Rainier III took the throne in 1949, the astute prince has since diversified to build up a very wealthy state.

Today gambling accounts for only 4% of state revenue, and tourism for 25%. Tourists are mostly upmarket, and the nightlife is the smartest on the Riviera. The Société des Bains de Mer (SBM), 69% state-owned, controls all the casinos, several leading hotels, many office blocks and most of the best sporting and leisure amenities.

Prince Rainier has built big new centres for the thriving convention trade and created a favourable tax climate which has attracted much banking and business. Monaco today is rather Americanized, and English is spoken widely in business circles. While the whole principality is a highly organized business machine, it has also retained a good deal of diamond-studded glamour. This successful mixture is due above all to Rainier, to his wife Grace Kelly who died so tragically in 1982, and to their three much publicized children.

Arriving
Just behind Monaco is the A8 autoroute which leads west to Nice and Paris, east into Italy; three other coast roads also go to Nice. Monaco is within easy reach of Nice airport and has good international rail links.

Airport
The Nice-Côte d'Azur Airport (see Nice) is 25km/16 miles away. By car or taxi the journey takes about 40min. The regular helicopter service, which is actually cheaper than a taxi, connects with main flights, takes 7min and runs 14 times a day: a bus shuttle runs between Monaco Heliport ☎ 93 30 80 88 and the main hotels. The minibus service to Nice is cheaper still and takes about 50min ☎ 93 85 61 81.

Railway station
Express trains run to Paris (journey time about 7hr 30min) and to other major cities. In summer a fast service every 30min links all the Côte d'Azur towns. Taxi rank ☎ 93 50 92 27. Passenger inquiries ☎ 93 87 50 50.

Getting around
Monte Carlo is best tackled on foot, but it is worth taking a cab or bus to go to Fontvieille or Monaco Vieille Ville.

Taxis can be hailed, but it is best to phone or visit a rank at the Casino ☎ 93 50 56 28, the beach ☎ 93 50 47 26, or the station ☎ 93 50 92 27.

Driving Traffic is seldom jammed, thanks to an ingenious road system and 14 covered parking areas. All major car rental firms have offices.

Walking is safe and easy, but some find the steps up the hillsides rather steep.

Bus The network is good, with five lines running every 11min, 7am–9pm. Information ☎ 93 50 62 41.

Area by area

The principality is divided into roughly four parts: Vieille Ville, the old part of Monaco, with the Palais du Prince and museums; to its southwest, the industrial and sports zone of Fontvieille, recently reclaimed from the sea; to its northeast, the commercial area of La Condamine; farther along the coast, Monte Carlo, where the Casino is encircled by the new convention centre, huge hotels and skyscrapers.

Hotels

The range of excellent hotels includes two sumptuous "palaces" dating from the *belle époque*, two large modern ones and several smaller places. Reservations are advisable in summer. All the hotels listed have 24hr room service and can meet at least basic business needs.

Beach Plaza [F]||||

22 ave Princesse-Grace ☎ *93 30 98 80*
℡ *479 617* • *THF* • *AE DC MC V* • *313 rooms, 9 suites, 3 restaurants, 1 bar*
This excellent, British-run, modern hotel would be just right for a working holiday. Rooms are spacious and pleasantly furnished: many have sea-facing balconies. There is a good restaurant indoors, and several others outside. Travel agency, boutiques
• outdoor heated pool, private beach, access to club next door offering subaqua diving and waterskiing • 7 meeting rooms (capacity up to 480).

Hermitage [F]|||||

sq Beaumarchais ☎ *93 50 67 31*
℡ *479432* • *AE DC MC V* • *220 rooms, 20 suites, 1 restaurant, 1 bar*
Built in 1906 and once used by English and Russian royalty, the beautiful Hermitage is as much a

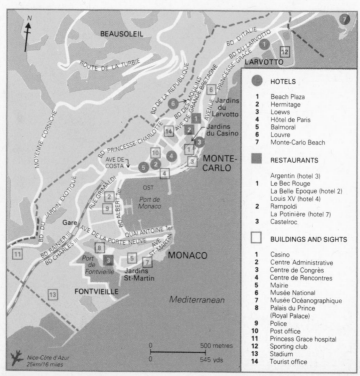

HOTELS
1 Beach Plaza
2 Hermitage
3 Loews
4 Hôtel de Paris
5 Balmoral
6 Louvre
7 Monte-Carlo Beach

RESTAURANTS

Argentin (hotel 3)
1 Le Bec Rouge
La Belle Époque (hotel 2)
Louis XV (hotel 4)
2 Rampoldi
La Potinière (hotel 7)
3 Castelroc

BUILDINGS AND SIGHTS

1 Casino
2 Centre Administrative
3 Centre de Congrès
4 Centre de Rencontres
5 Mairie
6 Musée National
7 Musée Océanographique
8 Palais du Prince (Royal Palace)
9 Police
10 Post office
11 Princess Grace hospital
12 Sporting club
13 Stadium
14 Tourist office

historical monument as a hotel, and now it has been lovingly restored. The large and exquisite bedrooms have all modern comforts. Its top restaurant, *La Belle Epoque*, is first-class and used by senior executives (see *Restaurants*). For a drink, there is no better place in town than the wide terrace with its view of sea and palace, or the bar. Health and beauty centre • 6 meeting rooms (capacity up to 80).

Loews *F*/////
ave des Spélugues ☎ 93 50 65 00
☎ *479435* • *AE DC MC V* • *573 rooms, 68 suites, 5 restaurants, 4 bars*
This ultra-modern American hotel is the Côte's largest by far, even having its own casino and cabaret. The bedrooms, although not large, have cheerful decor. The Argentin restaurant is one of the best features of this breezily brash hotel (see *Restaurants*). Travel agency, hairdresser, bank, 14 boutiques • heated rooftop pool, fitness centre • fax, 9 meeting rooms (capacity up to 1,900).

Hôtel de Paris *F*//////
pl du Casino ☎ 93 50 80 80 ☎ *469925* • *AE DC MC V* • *231 rooms, 40 suites, 3 restaurants, 2 bars*
Opened in 1865, and much favoured by Europe's royalty, the Paris now caters to less elevated guests, but the staff are still in white tie and tails. The pretty and spacious bedrooms have been well modernized and service is outstanding. The three restaurants offer variety and high quality (see *Restaurants*). Travel agency, boutiques, florist • fax, 4 meeting rooms (capacity up to 150).

Credit card abbreviations

AE	American Express
DC	Diners Club
MC	Access/MasterCard
V	Visa

OTHER HOTELS
Balmoral *F*/ *12 ave de la Costa*
☎ *93 50 62 37* ☎ *479436* • *AE DC MC V*. A classic medium-sized hotel, modestly priced but comfortable, with friendly, unpretentious service. Snack bar.
Louvre *F*/// *16 bd des Moulins*
☎ *93 50 65 25* ☎ *479645* • *DC V*.
A small, well-run alternative to the exotic palaces.
Monte-Carlo Beach *F*/////
06190 Roquebrune ☎ *93 78 21 40*
☎ *462010* • *SBM* • *AE DC MC V*.
Enchanting little luxury hotel, with pretty rooms; well away from the downtown hubbub, it is just inside France and adjoins a bathing club. (See *Restaurants*.)

Restaurants
Several of the best restaurants are in the big hotels, but there are other good places for business meals, and a range of lively cheaper ones; it is always best to reserve.

Argentin *F*///
ave des Spélugues ☎ *93 50 65 00* •
D only • *AE DC MC V* • *jacket*
The attractive Loews restaurant specializes in South American dishes, such as *ceviche* and spiced beef. Deft service by young staff.

Le Bec Rouge *F*///
11 ave de Grande-Bretagne
☎ *93 30 74 91* • *closed Jan* •
AE DC MC V
This is the best place to eat in town, apart from the big hotels. Roger Roux offers top-flight classic cuisine in an elegant setting. In summer you can eat outside.

La Belle Epoque *F*///
sq Beaumarchais ☎ *93 50 67 31* • *AE DC MC V* • *dress smart but informal*
The restaurant of the Hermitage is an obvious choice for important business meals. You can eat outdoors on the terrace, or in the rococo banqueting room. The cuisine is classic, and as deftly executed as the very superior service.

Le Louis XV Alain Ducasse [F]////
pl du Casino ☎ *93 50 80 80* • *closed
Tue, Wed, mid-Nov–Dec 20* • *AE DC
MC V* • *jacket and tie*
At the restaurant of the Hôtel de
Paris, Alain Ducasse, one of the
Côte's most celebrated chefs, serves
very personal Italo-Provençal cuisine.
All is supremely high class, but in
summer it can be more fun to eat in
the grandly ornate Salle Empire with
its lively open terrace facing the
Casino: here the cooking is more
classical. The hotel's third restaurant,
the handsome rooftop grill (closed
June, and lunch all summer), is a
little cheaper but equally suitable for
business meals.

OTHER RESTAURANTS

The rather expensive *Rampoldi*, 3 ave
des Spélugues ☎ 93 30 70 65, is
fashionable and has a nice terrace. *La
Potinière*, attached to the Monte-
Carlo Beach hotel, is a delightful
place for summer meals (closed
winter), with very good buffet.
Rather cheaper is *Castelroc*, pl du
Palais ☎ 93 30 36 68, where you can
lunch on a terrace opposite the Palace
(closed Sat).

Out of town
Most of the best places are to the
west (see *Nice*). To the northeast,
the *Vista Palace* ☎ 93 35 01 50 is a
luxurious hotel perched giddily
on the Grande Corniche outside
Roquebrune. Up in the hills there
are several pleasant smaller hotels
on the edge of ancient hill
villages, notably the *Auberge de la
Madone* ☎ 93 79 91 53 at Peillon,
a friendly place with good food.

Bars

The outstanding hotel bars are
those of the Hermitage and Hôtel de
Paris, but all the other big hotels also
have smart ones. The informal *Café
de Paris* is right opposite the
Casino.

Relaxation

Entertainment Cultural activity is
the best on the Côte. The elegant
Salle Garnier (opera house) in the
Casino ☎ 93 50 76 54 is used by the
resident opera company and by the
Monte Carlo Ballet. The *Rainier III
Auditorium* in the Centre de Congrès
☎ 93 50 93 00 hosts regular concerts
by the Monte Carlo Philharmonic
Orchestra, which also performs in the
courtyard of the Royal Palace in July
and August. The *Princess Grace
Theatre* is used for visiting and local
drama productions and for concerts
during the Spring Arts Festival.
There is a baroque music festival in
early September.

Nightlife activity is intense. The
state *Casino*, pl du Casino
☎ 93 50 69 31, is open nightly 4pm–
4am; its Cabaret ☎ 93 50 80 80 has a
dinner-dance and floor show. *Loews*
also has a casino open nightly 5pm–
4am, and La Folie Russe dinner-
dance and floor show. The
misleadingly named *Monte Carlo
Sporting Club*, 26 ave Princesse-Grace
☎ 93 30 71 71, open Jun–Sep, is a
huge complex of four nightspots, of
which Jimmy'z is the most
fashionable disco on the Côte. In
winter Jimmy'z moves to simpler
premises ☎ 93 50 80 80 near the
Casino.
Shopping Monte Carlo has plenty of
boutiques, but for big stores and local
wares you should go to Nice.
Sightseeing The world-famous
Musée Océanographique, ave St-
Martin, open daily, is noted for its
aquarium and whale skeletons. The
Musée National, 17 ave Princesse-
Grace, open daily, has a fine
collection of mechanical toys and
dolls. The *Palais du Prince* is open
only in July, when the state rooms
can be visited.
Spectator sports Monaco's fine
soccer team plays at the *Louis II
stadium*, Fontvieille ☎ 93 25 40 00.
Top annual events include the Monte
Carlo Rally (Jan), international
tennis championships (Apr) and the
Monaco Grand Prix (May).

Keeping fit Sports and health amenities are extensive. The best fitness centres are *California Terrace*, 2 ave Monte-Carlo ☎ 93 25 57 58, and *Columbia*, 7 ave Princesse-Grace ☎ 93 25 03 27. The *Monte Carlo Golf Club* ☎ 93 41 09 11, at La Turbie, is one of Europe's best. The *Yacht Club de Monaco*, quai Antoine 1er ☎ 93 30 63 63, runs sailing lessons and deep-sea fishing trips in summer. For tennis and squash the best place is the *Monte Carlo Country Club* ☎ 93 78 20 45 on the road to Menton. There are no free beaches in Monaco and the sand is imported and rough. The well-equipped *Monte Carlo Beach* ☎ 93 78 21 40 (open May–Sep) offers most watersports, and the best all-year heated indoor pool is in the *California Terrace*.

Local resources
Business services
Like everything in Monaco, services are highly efficient. *Conference International*, 31 bd Moulins ☎ 93 25 53 07, is an agency that can help with most arrangements, including office rental. The *Direction du Tourisme et des Congrès* (see below) will provide advice, while the big hotels can meet many business needs.
Photocopying and printing *Centre de Congrès Auditorium* ☎ 93 50 93 00.
Secretarial and translation *Business Aids* ☎ 93 50 82 28, *V.I.P.* ☎ 93 25 55 99.

Communications
Local delivery *Business Aids*.
Long-distance delivery *DHL* (near Nice) ☎ 93 07 75 28.
Post office *Main office*: sq Beaumarchais ☎ 93 25 11 11.
Telex and fax *Business Aids*, *V.I.P.* or at main post office.

Conference/exhibition centres
The *Direction du Tourisme et des Congrès*, 2a bd des Moulins ☎ 93 30 87 01 ▥ 469760, will give advice on organizing a conference. The best venue is the ultra-modern

Centre de Congrès ☎ 93 50 93 00. It has a main auditorium seating 1,100, four smaller rooms seating up to 100, and 1,800 sq metres of exhibition space. Nearby is the smaller *International Conference Centre* (Centre de Rencontres Internationales) ☎ 93 50 34 44 with three meeting rooms. The larger hotels also have rooms for conferences.

Emergencies
Bureau de change *Crédit Foncier de Monaco*, at Casino, daily noon–11pm.
Hospital *Centre Hospitalier Princesse Grace*, ave Pasteur ☎ 93 25 99 00. For doctors on duty ☎ 141.
Pharmacies For those open outside normal shopping hours ☎ 141.
Police Main station: rue Suffren-Reymond ☎ 93 15 30 15.

Government offices
The principality's administrative centre is *Centre Administrative*, 8 rue Louis-Notan ☎ 93 30 19 21. *Mairie*, pl de la Mairie ☎ 93 30 28 63.

Information sources
Business information Advice is available from the *Direction du Commerce et de l'Industrie*, 8 rue Louis-Notari ☎ 93 30 19 21 at the Administrative Centre, or from the *Jeune Chambre Economique*, 2 ave Prince Héréditaire Albert ☎ 93 15 04 22.
Local media The daily *Nice Matin* has two pages on Monaco. The *Journal de Monaco* is a weekly official paper. *Radio Monte Carlo* and *Télé Monte Carlo* have local news programmes but little business coverage: better is the local English-language radio station *Riviera 104*.
Tourist information *Office du Tourisme*, 2a bd des Moulins ☎ 93 30 87 01.

Thank-yous
Confectionery *Les Fruits du Palais*, 7 rue Comte Félix Gastaldi ☎ 93 50 07 16.
Florist *Fleurisia* ☎ 93 50 05 62.

Planning and Reference

Entry details

The following requirements and regulations apply to visitors regardless of place of entry.

Documentation

Visas Nationals of *all* non-EC countries except Switzerland must (since September 1986) have a visa. Application is made by post or in person to a French embassy or consulate.

Passports or national identity cards Required of all foreign visitors except residents of the UK and Ireland who are entitled to an excursion pass (see below). A visitor's passport, also available to UK and Irish residents, is obtainable through main post offices or a passport office and lasts for one year.

Excursion pass Available to visitors from the UK and Ireland, allowing a stay of up to 60 hours; obtainable from main post offices on production of photograph and identification, or issued at the point of departure.

Carte de séjour (resident's permit) Officially required by EC nationals wishing to stay longer than 3 months. Apply to the police or local prefecture well before the end of the 3-month period, or to the French consulate before you leave for France. Proof of financial resources will be required.

Visa d'établissement Required by non-EC nationals intending to stay longer than 3 months. Apply to the French consulate before you leave for France.

Driving licence Required if you take a car into France or intend to rent one there. An international driving licence is not necessary.

Customs regulations

Personal possessions are not normally liable to duty or tax if you enter France as a visitor, provided you intend to take them out again. There is no limit on the amount of foreign currency taken into the country but travellers intending to bring out more than Fr50,000 or the equivalent in foreign notes should complete the appropriate form provided by customs when entering France. The import and export of gold, in bars, ingots or coins, is prohibited unless prior authorization is obtained from the Bank of France. Import allowances vary according to where you live and whether you buy the goods in duty- and tax-paid shops in EC countries or duty- and tax-free shops on ships and aircraft. Allowances of duty-free and non-duty-free goods cannot be mixed: for instance you are not permitted to import 1 litre of duty-free gin and 5 litres of duty-paid table wine. The entire alcohol allowance may be used on wine, enabling you to take out 8 litres or 11 72cl bottles duty-free.

Group A Goods bought duty-free or in non-EC countries.

Group B Goods bought in EC countries.

	Group A	Group B
cigarettes	200	300
or cigarillos	100	150
or cigars	50	75
or tobacco	250g	400g
wine	2l	5l
and either:		
drinks over 38.8°	1l	1.5l
or drinks 38.8°		
or under	2l	3l
perfume	50g	75g
toilet water	250ml	375ml
coffee	500g	1,000g
tea	100g	200g
other items (gifts, foodstuffs etc)		
up to	300Fr	2,400Fr

The EC countries are Belgium, Denmark, Ireland, France, West Germany, Greece, Italy, Luxembourg, the Netherlands,

Portugal, Spain (excluding the Canary Islands) and the UK (excluding the Channel Islands).

Climate

The farther south you go in France the hotter the climate. The north, which is not unlike the UK in climate, is temperate and prone to rain, while the south has long hot summers and sunny winters. But the geographical diversity of the country produces marked local variations. The west, which is tempered by the Atlantic, tends to have rain in spring and autumn; the centre and upland areas have an extreme continental climate; and the south is typically Mediterranean.

Even in winter Nice has about 150 hours of sunshine a month and temperatures rising to 35°C during the day. Not so pleasant is the *mistral*, a bitterly cold north wind which blows down the Rhône valley and hits Provence. Inland mountainous areas are notorious for their climatic variations: the surprisingly mild winters in the western Pyrenees, stormy summers in the Massif Central, and long periods of thick snow in the Alps. If you are travelling in France in summer, take lightweight clothing, especially for the south and interior; for winter take medium weights and topcoats.

Holidays

The worst time to arrange a trip to France is July/August when almost the entire population departs in pursuit of the sun, and business and industrial activity comes to a virtual standstill. If possible avoid planning a visit any time between mid-July and early September, unless you have made prior arrangements. Listed below are the main national public holidays:

Jan 1 New Year's Day
Late Mar/Apr Easter Monday
May 1 Labour Day
May 8 VE Day
Sixth Thu after Easter Ascension Day

Second Mon after Ascension Pentecost
Jul 14 Bastille Day
Aug 15 Feast of the Assumption
Nov 1 All Saints' Day
Nov 11 Remembrance Day
Dec 25 Christmas Day
Dec 26 (Alsace Lorraine only) St Stephen's Day

Banks, businesses and most shops shut on public holidays. If the holiday falls on a Sunday it will be taken on the following day instead. When official holidays fall towards the end or near the beginning of a week many people extend them in order to enjoy a long weekend.

Money

Local currency

The basic French monetary unit is the franc, which is divided into 100 centimes. Denominations of bank notes are 20, 50, 100, 200 and 500 francs. Coins come in units of 1, 2, 5 and 10 francs and 5, 10, 20 and 50 centimes. A few die-hards in the provinces, and even some Parisians, still refer to old francs despite the fact that the new system came into operation nearly 30 years ago. Old francs are usually cited to boast about the price of something, like an apartment. If a price strikes you as absurdly high (eg Fr1,000 for a cup of coffee), take off the last two noughts.

Taking money

Traveller's cheques are the safest way of taking large sums of money around with you. The cheques can be in either your own currency or a major international currency. French franc traveller's cheques are the most convenient, though not all hotels, restaurants and shops, especially outside Paris, will accept them as if they were cash. If you change them at a bank, there should be no commission charge.

Eurocheques, used in conjunction with a guarantee card, are accepted throughout France, though not as widely as many travellers assume.

The system is operated by a network of European banks and cheques can be cashed at any bank in France displaying the blue and red EC sign.

Although most hotels, restaurants and filling stations will take Eurocheques, some smaller establishments will insist on cash. Others may charge you a supplement for paying through the Eurocheque system. The bank charges for using Eurocheques are also quite high. With a Eurocheque guarantee card you can also change foreign currency in 780 post offices, indicated by a CHANGE sticker. For UK nationals a special cheque card is available from National Girobank, to be used in conjunction with Postcheques at post offices in France.

Credit and charge cards By far the most useful card is Visa (Carte Bleue in-France). It is accepted by many hotels, restaurants and shops, and frequently at filling stations, but do not count on it. Eurocard/Access/MasterCard is less useful than Visa, though more widely accepted than any other card. Visa and Eurocard can be used to draw cash from branches of banks displaying the relevant sign. With Visa you can also withdraw money at one of 780 post offices, indicated by a Carte Bleue/Visa sign.

Changing money

A few francs in cash are always useful on arrival. Your local bank will probably give you a better rate of exchange than currency exchange offices at points of departure or arrival. Once in France, banks give the best rate of exchange, though their commission charges vary widely; on traveller's cheques denominated in foreign currencies, the differences can be as large as 4-5% from bank to bank. Currency exchange facilities are also available at railway stations, airports and major tourist offices, all of which will give a better rate than hotels, shops or restaurants. Automatic cash distributors, for use with a credit

card and PIN number, are available at railway stations, airports and outside banks, though cash tends to run out at weekends and some machines seem to swallow cards for no apparent reason.

Banks

Standard banking hours are 9 to 4 or 4.30, Monday to Friday, but the hours have become more and more flexible with some banks opening until 6.30 or 7. While most Paris banks stay open during the lunch hour others may close from 12 or 12.30 to 2. In towns with a Saturday market banks usually stay open then, and close on Monday instead. All banks are closed on the half day before a national holiday and all day on Monday when a national holiday falls on a Tuesday.

The Société Générale has offices at Charles-de-Gaulle/Roissy and Orly airports open day and night for foreign exchange transactions.

Tipping

Hotels A service charge is normally included in the price of the hotel or a fixed percentage (10–15%) is added to the bill; anything extra is a matter for your own discretion. Hall porters will expect a few francs.

Restaurants, cafés and bars In restaurants service is either built into the prices or a fixed percentage (10–15%) is added to the bill; nevertheless it is common French practice to leave a few francs if you are happy with the service. In cafés the price of a drink if you sit at a table usually includes service. If you are not sure, look at the bill where service will be marked.

Taxis A tip of 10–15% of the fare is expected.

Other Always give cinema usherettes two or three francs. Toilet attendants will either charge you or expect at least a few centimes. Filling station attendants (who normally clean the windscreen) will not usually expect a tip, but are happy to accept one. Tip barbers and hairdressers 10–15%.

Getting there

Most international airlines fly into one of Paris's two airports and scheduled international services also operate to a number of provincial airports. In some instances, it may be more convenient to fly to an international airport just outside France's borders. For instance, Luxembourg's airport is useful for destinations in northeastern France, and Basle's (which in fact it shares with the French town of Mulhouse) for eastern France. Many of the country's large stations receive trains from all over Europe, including overnight services equipped with couchettes and sleepers. Visitors from Britain may prefer to cross the Channel by ferry or hovercraft which connect with France's excellent train service.

Gateway airports
Paris Charles-de-Gaulle/Roissy
France's busiest airport is served by most international carriers and has a number of flights to regional airports in the rest of the country.
Paris Orly Orly has fewer international flights than Charles-de-Gaulle, though some carriers do still fly there. It does, however, receive the majority of domestic services.
Lyon-Satolas airport receives a fairly large number of international flights.
Nice-Côte-d'Azur airport has scheduled services to and from some 80 cities worldwide.
Marseille Provence airport has flights to and from some 70 cities worldwide.
Others Many of France's regional airports have flights to one or two European destinations, particularly London. Many also have flights to North Africa, designed mainly for immigrant workers returning home for visits.

Major train services
Direct trains link Paris with Liège, Cologne, Düsseldorf, Dortmund, Berlin and Hamburg, with connections to Copenhagen; Brussels, Antwerp, Rotterdam and Amsterdam; Karlsruhe, Stuttgart, Munich and Vienna; Luxembourg, Saarbrücken and Frankfurt; Basle and Zürich; Madrid; Barcelona; Geneva; Turin, Milan, Genoa, Florence and Rome; Berne, Lausanne, Milan and Venice. Some of these direct services are available only on night trains; daytime services involve a change of train. The Brussels–Basle service stops at Metz, Strasbourg and Mulhouse; there are through trains Calais–Basle; frequent services run between Lyon Perrache and Geneva; Bordeaux has a direct overnight service to Rome via Toulouse and the Mediterranean coast and the Barcelona–Rome line stops at various places in southern France.

Channel ports
There is a frequent service between Britain and France via both ferries and hovercrafts to the ports of Calais, Boulogne and Dunkerque, and rather less frequent ferry services to Dieppe, Caen, Cherbourg, Le Havre, St Malo and Roscoff. Sailings are also possible from Roscoff to Ireland.

Road routes
France has land frontiers with six other countries and all are very easy to cross by car. Border crossings are numerous, save that in some cases they are limited by the terrain (the Pyrenees on the border with Spain, the Alps on that with Italy and, partly, Switzerland, the Rhine on much of the border with Germany). Customs and police formalities are almost the same everywhere and today extremely simple: all the six countries except Switzerland are fellow members of the EC. In high summer, or at weekends and public holidays, there can be long lines at the Italian border on the coast at Menton, at the Mont Blanc tunnel, and the Spanish border by the Basque coast at Hendaye.

Getting around

Thanks to one of the best rail services in the world, much business travel in France can now be done by train. The symbol of French rail supremacy is the TGV, *train à grande vitesse*, the fastest train in the world. The journey from Paris to Lyon takes 2 hours, which from city centre to city centre is faster than travelling by air and a good deal cheaper. Over 50% of the Air Inter Paris-to-Lyon service has consequently been wiped out, though the airlines are now fighting back for business with more and more special offers on domestic flights. It is quicker to travel by air on very long journeys, and particularly those not covered by high-speed trains. Driving in France, despite good roads and fast motorways, is rarely the most relaxing way to get around, though it can be the most convenient means of travel over short or medium distances. To the uninitiated, Paris, its *péripherique* (ring road) and its drivers are best avoided.

Air

The domestic network covers all the major cities and brings all of them within a 90min flight from Paris. Air Inter is the main domestic airline. Air France operates services between major cities such as Paris, Lyon, Bordeaux, Marseille, Nice, Strasbourg and Toulouse.

Fares fall into three categories: *vols rouges* (red flights) open only to full fare-paying passengers or those with a commuter card, *vols blancs* (white flights) and *vols bleus* (blue flights), both open to anyone and offering very substantial discounts for certain categories of passengers such as children, families, students and groups who are travelling on Air Inter, Air France and UTA domestic flights. Most blue or white flights operate from 9am to 4pm and from 9 pm to 7am the next day. Special cheap flights from Paris to Nice, Bordeaux, Lyon, Toulouse and Marseille are available if you are going for 7–35 days. There are also various "frequent flier" schemes, valid for 3 months, 6 months or one year. Check-in times for domestic flights are 15 to 25 minutes before departure.

Reservations may be made through any Air France office or travel agent. Central telephone numbers: *Air France* ☎ 45 35 61 61 or 45 35 66 00, *Air Inter* ☎ 45 39 25 25. Other companies offering scheduled domestic flights are TAT (Touraine Air Transport), Aigle Azur, Air Littoral, Air Vendee, Brit Air, Europe Aero Service and UTA. Reservations for flights on all these airlines can be made through Air France.

Train

The state-owned SNCF (Société Nationale des Chemins de Fer) provides the most extensive rail network of western Europe. The high-speed trains and notably the TGVs and Corail trains are super-smooth, stable and comfortable, even in second class, and the prices are reasonable. The TGV now extends to 36 cities, including Lille, Rouen and Nice, and two new lines are under construction: west through Brittany as far as Brest (due for completion in September 1989) and southwest to Bordeaux and Biarritz. Paris to Bordeaux will take just under three hours, a service which will seriously compete with domestic air travel.

The French Motorail service provides some 130 routes, enabling you to travel with the car and save a day's driving.

Reservations Tickets can usually be reserved outside France from overseas offices of SNCF, some travel agents and railway booking offices. In France reservations are made at all main railway stations or by telephone. Advance reservations are required for the TGV but these can be made up to a few minutes before departure by using computerized machines at stations. Alternatively you can make a reservation through the Minitel telecommunications system, available in offices and many private homes. Advance reservations should also be made for the TEE (Trans Europ Express) though these high-speed first-class trains are gradually being superseded by ordinary (but equally fast) intercity trains. All tickets bought in France must be validated in the automatic orange machines at the entrance to station platforms. Failure to do so will incur a supplementary charge.

Fares SNCF offers a range of discounted fares, according to the time of travel. Leaflets available at stations illustrate the red, white and blue periods of travel: red is the most expensive peak period, blue is the cheapest time to travel (usually noon to 3pm, Mon–Sat, and all day Sun). But currently the best offer to foreigners is the France Vacances Pass, which gives unlimited 1st or 2nd class rail travel throughout France on any 4 days during a period of 15 days or on any 9 or 16 days during a period of a month. This could mean a saving even if you only intend to do one long return journey. Various bonus offers are thrown in with the card; among them are reductions on car rental at 200 stations and free rail fares from Paris airports to the city centre. The pass is available from SNCF offices, travel agents or main rail centres in your own country. A whole range of other discounted passes are available, including the *billet séjour*, offering a reduction of 25% for return or circular journeys of more than 1,000km provided the journey covers a Sunday; and the Eurailpass, available to non-EC residents only, covering 18 European networks.

The TGV is no more expensive than conventional rail travel though peak hour journeys are subject to a supplementary fee. The TEE trains, which are first class, require a supplement whatever the time of day.

Standards The standards of Corail and TGV trains are particularly impressive, and the speed,

cleanliness, comfort and punctuality put British and many other European railways to shame. Standards of catering, however, rarely live up to expectations, particularly the snacks, which are expensive and dreary. TEEs are the only trains that still retain a proper restaurant car. In the first class of other intercity trains full meals are served at your seat, in second class a trolley service provides snacks. Some of the Corail services offer a Grill Express self-service restaurant where the standard and choice of food are quite good. Rural lines are served by the older, noisier rolling stock, and food and drink services are rarely available. Stations often provide excellent restaurants or brasseries, especially in Paris, but business facilities are limited except for passengers using TEE trains. Following a year's experimentation on the Paris Est–Nancy–Strasbourg service, a new luxury first-class service (*la nouvelle première*), with well-equipped waiting rooms and revamped rolling stock, is scheduled to be operating by late 1988/early 1989.

Car

France has a comprehensive system of autoroutes, most of which radiate from Paris and reach out into the different corners of the country. Tolls make them expensive to use: from Paris to Lyon, for example, will cost over 150Fr. The alternative *routes nationales* (N) or main trunk roads are straight and well-maintained but often slowed down by heavy traffic. Over the last few years many of these N roads have been changed to D roads or *routes départementales* and some signposts and maps are still out of date. Travelling by car is best avoided during high summer weekends. Horrendous jams build up, particularly around Paris and the autoroute going south. Figures of fatal accidents are frighteningly high, particularly at the end of July and beginning of August. If you are obliged to travel during peak periods, it is worth using the government-inspired *Bison Futé* system which suggests alternative routes to avoid traffic jams. Free maps are available at autoroute toll booths and information centres at service stations. A useful system for pinpointing traffic jams (and often combined with *Bison Futé*) is the telephone-based Minitel service found on many autoroute service areas. The system can also advise on the cost of road tolls and help find hotels and restaurants.

The French autoroutes are privately owned but government subsidized and controlled. All but a few are subject to tolls. The ticket you take when you join the autoroute will determine the amount you pay when you exit. Some toll booths take Eurocheques and/or Visa, others take only cash.

There are twice as many fatal road accidents in France as there are in Britain, alcohol being the main cause. The drink-drive laws (similar to those of the UK) are now quite rigorously enforced and random testing (with steep on-the-spot fines) is commonplace.

Legal requirements Visitors to France must carry with them a valid driving licence and, if taking their own car, have proof of third-party insurance.

The following speed limits apply: 130kmph/80mph on toll highways, 110kmph/68mph on other divided highways, 90kmph/56mph on other roads, 60kmph/37mph in towns. There is a minimum speed of 80kmph/50mph for outside lanes on autoroutes in daylight. If you are caught failing to observe speed limits you may incur on-the-spot fines of up to Fr1,300.

Seat belts are compulsory for drivers and, if safety belts are fitted to the rear, passengers in the back must use them. Red triangles for use after breakdowns are compulsory. Cars drive on the right and the key rule to remember in France is *priorité*

à droite: give way to any traffic coming from the right unless otherwise indicated.

Parking Main towns have parking meters and expensive underground garages. Towing away illegally parked cars is becoming increasingly common. In Paris few hotels have private garages.

Emergencies On autoroutes there are free emergency telephones every 2km. On other roads telephone a local garage (look in the yellow pages) or call the police ☎ 17. There is no nationwide road assistance service in France. In the case of an accident, ring for an ambulance ☎ 17 (police) or ☎ 18 (fire). Calls from a public telephone box require a franc, which will be returned when you get through, but emergency calls are free from private telephones. Both parties involved should fill in their version of the accident in a *constat à l'amiable* or European accident statement form. If one party refuses to complete the form, a bailiff known as a *constat d'huissier* is called along to make a written report.

Most autoroute filling stations and some in city centres are open 24hr, others are open 8–6, except on Sundays and public holidays. In August many garages close down completely.

Car rental in France is expensive compared with most other EC countries, but it can be a useful way of getting around if you intend to make several short or medium journeys, particularly in areas not well served by the SNCF. A passport or identity papers and a driving licence are essential, and a credit card is useful if you want to avoid paying large deposits of cash. Cars can be rented at airports, air terminals and railways stations and through large hotels. Making a reservation through one of the main international companies before you go usually works out slightly cheaper than renting the car from the same company in France. The SNCF "train + auto" service, where a car awaits you at your rail destination, is available at 200 towns and you can leave the car at any one of them. Central reservations in Paris: *Avis* ☏ 46 09 92 12, *Budget* ☏ 43 87 55 55, *Europcar* ☏ 30 43 82 82, *Hertz* ☏ 47 88 51 51.

Limousines are usually available from the big international car rental companies and from various specialist companies in Paris with multilingual chauffeurs.

Bus

Outstripped in number, efficiency and speed by SNCF, buses are rarely used by business people for long-distance travel. Their main use is connecting rural areas; some complete the SNCF rail service, putting even the tiniest places on the map, others are geared to schoolchildren and market days. Long-distance services cannot compare with rail for comfort or convenience, but SNCF offers over 1,000 bus tours starting from all over the country. In cities, the bus can be a useful way to get around – if you know the routes.

Taxi

Taxis will pick up fares anywhere on the street, but mainly they pick up from ranks (*stations de taxi* or *têtes de taxi*), which are located on main streets of towns and at stations and airports. For numbers of radio-taxis and taxis at ranks see *City by City*, or ask your hotel to call you a cab. Unofficial, meterless cabs tend to hover outside train stations, large hotels and nightclubs to pick up unsuspecting foreigners and charge whatever price they like. Official cabs have a taxi sign on the roof, a list of charges and a meter. Charges vary from town to province. Paris has three fare zones and fares are slightly more expensive than those of the provinces. Rates are always more expensive at night and on Sundays. There are also extra charges for pick-ups at stations and air terminals, and for each piece of baggage.

Hotels

Most of the larger French industrial and commercial cities are also historic places of great character, sometimes set amid beautiful scenery, and so their better hotels cater to tourists as well as business people. The modern business hotel does of course exist. Usually it belongs to one of the major French chains and, though its decor may be bright and cheerful, it lacks individual charm; and it does not generally offer any wide range of business facilities.

In the provinces, a business visitor can often gain more kudos – and certainly more pleasure – by staying at one of the smaller, more traditional hotels, many of which are privately owned. The better ones today have been well modernized, while also offering the stylish "period" furnishings and decor that the French prize; and they tend to provide a more personal service. Some have been recently converted from lovely old buildings; reservations should be made well ahead. They do not always have restaurants, but there are usually good ones close by. Conversely, others are primarily luxury restaurants with a few rooms attached; some of these are old *auberges*, in villages just outside the city but within easy reach of its new business areas.

Facilities and service Only a tiny handful of large luxury hotels, nearly all of them in Paris or on the Côte d'Azur, have a modern "business centre" providing such services as secretarial help and translation. Many other hotels claim to be able to hire secretaries or interpreters from outside, but in practice they are seldom used to such demands being made on them. On the other hand, in most business-class French hotels, bedrooms have local or international direct dial telephones and there is access to the hotel's telex and photocopier, both of which a guest can use in moderation.

Bedrooms in business-class hotels

are well equipped. Almost all have colour TV and a private bathroom or shower-room (often the bath has a shower attached); most have a minibar, and many have hairdryers (though trouser-presses are rare). Laundry and valet services are often available. Some grander hotels will offer bathrobes, luxury toiletries and maybe bowls of fruit. Room service is usually available until about 11pm, but full 24hr service is rare. Air conditioning is generally found in the large modern hotels, especially in the south where it is certainly needed in summer. Bedroom windows facing a main street are usually double-glazed, but it is wise to check this when making a reservation and to ask for a quiet room. Very few hotels in Paris have a swimming pool, but in the south these are now becoming more common; lock-up garages are infrequent in city-centre hotels. Service is generally helpful and efficient in the older traditional hotels; in the newer ones it can be variable.

Grading The tourist ministry formally grades hotels, from ★★★★ luxe down to ★: but these ratings are based on facilities and are little guide to quality. The grades given in hotel guides such as *Michelin* are much more useful.

Making reservations Advance reservations are advisable at any time, and especially for visits coinciding with major trade fairs, conventions or cultural festivals: these are periods when even the biggest hotels become full. Reservations can be made by letter or telex, or via another hotel in the same chain. *Accueil de France* tourist offices can help personal callers to reserve accommodation in the same town or in other towns belonging to the network. A charge is made to cover telephone or telex costs and reservations can be made up to eight days in advance. Apart from Monaco, Montpellier and Rennes, all the cities covered in this guide belong to this network. Other tourist offices are usually able to indicate which hotels might have rooms available.

Prices In a modern hotel, especially those of the big chains, all the rooms are usually very similar (except for suites) and the price range is minimal. But in many older hotels, where the rooms can vary enormously in size and comfort (some may be without baths), room rates can vary by as much as 300%, suites excluded. It is therefore wise when reserving to specify the kind of room required. Single rooms tend to be only 15–20% cheaper than double ones, and in many hotels you pay a flat rate for the room irrespective of number of occupants (double beds are much commoner than twin ones, except in the newer hotels).

Prices are far higher in Paris, and on the Côte d'Azur in summer, than elsewhere. Many hotels offer cheaper rates for business groups, but weekend discounts are rare. All prices are inclusive of taxes and service, but breakfast is usually extra.

Breakfast Hotels traditionally serve just a Continental breakfast of coffee with croissants or rolls at a modest charge. But extras such as fruit juices and cooked eggs are usually available. And some hotels now also offer a copious German-style help-yourself buffet breakfast.

Hotel groups

Fewer hotels belong to chains than in the USA. But the larger French groups have been expanding fast, notably by building new utility hotels in the medium and lower ranges, mostly on the edge of towns.

Accor ☎ 60 77 27 27 ℡ 600644 This large and dynamic group has hotels in five categories four of which are represented in this guide: Sofitel, Mercure, Novotel and Ibis.

Sofitel These are spread around France with five in Paris and 19 elsewhere. Some are in the city centres, others out in suburbs or close to airports. Some are classic hotels converted, but most are very modern, and their standards of comfort, service and amenities are high; many have excellent restaurants.

Mercure Cheaper and less prestigious than Sofitels, with 13 hotels in the Paris area, 45 around the rest of France. Some are central but more are on the edge of towns, and all are modern and purpose-built; they have smallish but comfortable rooms, cheerful decor and simple grill-type restaurants. Many also have a swimming pool and other leisure facilities.

Novotel There are 16 Novotels in Paris, 70 elsewhere, often close to airports or autoroute exits. They are comfortable but functional.

Ibis The cheapest hotels in the Accor group.

Concorde ☎ 47 58 12 25 ⊤ₓ 650990 Not the biggest, but the best of the French groups, with 6 hotels in Paris, 14 elsewhere. Most of them are traditional rather than new hotels; all are individual and, while some are famous luxury palaces, such as the Crillon in Paris and the Martinez in Cannes, others are in the middle range. Service is always excellent. Standards of comfort vary with price.

Meridien ☎ 42 56 01 01 ⊤ₓ 642749 This international chain owned by Air France has only four hotels inside France, all but one of them large and expensive. They are efficiently run, but a little dull.

Pullman ☎ 42 68 22 88 ⊤ₓ 640709 Of the 90 hotels of this nationwide chain, most are modern, though some are classic hotels that have been nicely modernized. With a recent change of group ownership, their names have been changed from Frantel and PLM. Today the best are called Pullman, and they can be excellent; the slightly cheaper Altea hotels are well-equipped, but they tend to lack style or charm.

Associations

Many smaller hotels in France group together for joint marketing, publicity and reservations, while remaining individually owned and run. The following are best-known.

Logis de France ☎ 43 59 86 67 ⊤ₓ 643562 Mostly rural inns, quite cheap, but of fair quality.

Mapotel ☎ 43 41 22 44 ⊤ₓ 214267 Medium-priced town hotels, linked to the Best Western system.

Relais et Châteaux (no central reservation number) Small luxury hotels, nearly all rural, many of them converted manor houses or châteaux.

Our recommended hotels

The hotels given full entries have been selected as those most likely to suit and please a business visitor. Listed under "Other hotels" are establishments which may not have the same charm, quality or facilities as the full entries, but which are perfectly adequate. In contrast, the establishments listed under "Out of town" are often of considerable character and elegance.

The price symbols denote the following:

F up to 250Fr
F/ 250–400Fr
F// 400–600Fr
F/// 600–900Fr
F//// 900–1,200Fr
F///// over 1,200Fr

These reflect the cost in francs at the time of going to press for one person occupying a typical room.

Restaurants

The tradition of good eating in France has not been imposed from above by an elite class but springs from local rural origins; and today the most enjoyable food is very often found in simple country places with farm connections. Value for money is far better than in most parts of Europe, especially the fixed-price menus in middle-range family-run restaurants. And the range and diversity of regional cooking, with the many thousands of subtly varied dishes, is staggering. So it is of little surprise that foreign restaurants, apart from some Sino-Vietnamese and a few Italian, should be so sparsely represented, at least in the provinces.

Some of the best cooking is to be found in those smart hotels that have taken the trouble to hire a star chef: here the atmosphere is elegant and formal, and the prices high. Another good choice is the small luxury restaurant where the owner is also chef.

Farther down the scale, for more casual or routine meals, there are various kinds of establishment. The *brasserie*, formerly a beer-house but today also serving wines and other drinks, is a traditional no-nonsense middle-price restaurant with fairly closely spaced tables, swift service and a short menu of simple classic dishes. These places are today much in vogue with the French, who enjoy the bustle and chatter, and the mirrors-and-brass decor. The *auberge* (inn), commonest in the country but found in cities too, is usually an old building with rustic decor and regional cuisine, and it varies from the simple to the smartly fashionable. A *bistro* in France is properly a simple café, but it has also come to mean a small restaurant, often candelit, and popular with young people.

At the lower end of the market, many cafés in cities will serve a light lunch of sandwiches, salads or a cooked *plat du jour* (dish of the day), popular with office workers; the numerous pizzerias have deft, cheerful service and are excellent value for a quick meal; the self-service cafeteria has real French dishes, albeit roughly cooked and presented, and is better than its equivalents in many countries; but the "fast-food" burger-bars, recently imported, are even more unappetizing than elsewhere in Europe.

Many good restaurants are owned and run by dedicated families working long hours. Usually the wife acts as front-of-house and takes the guests' orders, while her husband does the cooking; in the smarter places he may emerge at the end of

the meal, in his white garb, to discuss his dishes with his visitors. Service in these restaurants is often by waitresses, but waiters are commoner in the big hotels. Only a few very grand places have sommeliers: but generally all staff are highly knowledgeable about the wines and dishes on offer.

Meal times Lunch is usually not before 1pm in Paris, earlier in the provinces. Restaurants, but not snack-bars and some brasseries, close all afternoon and until early evening, so that to obtain a full meal at 5pm or 6pm is not easy. The French like to dine late. Many smart restaurants do not open their doors until 8pm and do not get busy till 9pm or so, especially in the south and in summer.

In larger towns, there are always several good places taking orders up to midnight or 1am.

Reservations It is advisable to make reservations in advance, especially if the restaurant is well-known or your party numbers more than four or if you need a quiet table, or a small private room. To get a table in a top restaurant it may be necessary to reserve weeks ahead. If you are going to arrive more than about 15 minutes late, it is wise to warn the restaurant or you may lose the table. Cancellations are always accepted graciously.

Dress Restaurants are extremely wary of imposing rules on their guests, against either smoking or informal dress. Only a tiny number of restaurants, mostly in Paris, insist on jacket and tie.

Prix fixe and à la carte In Paris it is more usual to eat *à la carte*, but most restaurants at all levels will also offer one or two fixed-price menus with dishes of the day. These can be good value, and you can suggest them to your guests without appearing mean, in particular the *menu dégustation* which is a range of small helpings of the chef's special dishes. In the provinces, especially in middle-priced or cheaper restaurants, the French generally prefer the set menus, for these offer the best value: a three-course meal will cost little more than one main dish *à la carte*.

Menu prices today are legally required to be inclusive of both tax and service, though in practice some restaurants will still add on the 15% service charge afterwards. It is usual to leave a small further sum, perhaps 2% or 3%, if service has been good. Cloakroom attendants should also be tipped a few francs for looking after coats and briefcases.

French cuisine

Traditional French cooking can be roughly divided into *paysanne, bourgeoise* and *haute. Cuisine paysanne* consists of the hearty but inexpensive dishes that you will find in many simple country places, such as *boeuf en daube* (beef stewed in wine) or *pot-au-feu* (boiled beef and vegetables). *Cuisine bourgeoise* features these dishes too, but in a more refined style, and it covers the whole range of classic French dishes such as *coq au vin* (chicken stewed in wine) or *petit salé aux lentilles* (salted pork with lentils). *Haute cuisine* was a 19thC invention for the sophisticated end of the market: it uses expensive ingredients such as *foie gras* and truffles, and makes lavish use of cognac, cream and butter for its rich and complex sauces. This style of cooking is still found in some older luxury restaurants; but today's more calorie-conscious age tends to find it too heavy, and since the 1960s it has been losing ground to what is called *nouvelle cuisine*. Also known loosely as *la cuisine moderne* or *la cuisine innovative*, this new style was pioneered by a number of star chefs such as Paul Bocuse, Pierre Troisgros and Michel Guérard. High-quality expensive ingredients are used, but cooked much more lightly and rapidly, without heavy sauces. This style of cooking also encourages the chef to invent new dishes and to experiment with new taste blends, such as cooked oysters with leeks or

foie gras with apple. Helpings tend to be small, and very decoratively arranged on the plate. In the hands of a master the results can be brilliant, but the vogue has caught on so widely that many less talented chefs have been creating absurdities.

Today most of the smarter restaurants in France serve food that is more *nouvelle* than *haute*. The dishes bear long and unusual names, and no menu is like another, for each chef likes to invent his own repertoire; but the sillier extravagances are on the wane. Portions have become less absurdly tiny than 10 years ago, and many of the better chefs are moving back to a mode that unites classical with modern, and in many cases offers light, exciting variations on old regional dishes.

Regional cuisines

Each region of France has its own style of cooking. Some dishes regional in origin are common all over France, such as the *choucroute* of Alsace. Paris has no special cuisine of its own, but restaurants from all regions are to be found there. These are the main styles (and cities they relate to in this guide).

Alsace (Strasbourg) The commonest dish is a copious platter of pork and sausage with sour cabbage (*choucroute* or *sauerkraut*) cooked in white wine. The local wines are also used in the cooking of chicken (*coq au riesling*) and snails.

Aquitaine and Gascony (Bordeaux, Toulouse) The rich cuisine of the southwest features *foie gras* of goose or duck, sometimes served hot with small grapes; steak of duck (*magret de canard*); and preserved goose and duck. In the Toulouse area, the most famous dish is *cassoulet*, a complex goose-and-bean stew. Bordeaux is noted for its red wine sauce that accompanies *entrecôte*. Mussels and monkfish are cooked in elaborate ways.

Auvergne A hearty peasant cuisine, with tripe, stuffed cabbage, thick soups and *pot-au-feu*.

Brittany (Rennes, Nantes) The
accent is on local fish, notably
shellfish, eaten either uncooked
(oysters and shrimps), or cooked in
wine (mussels) or a pungent sauce
(lobster and monkfish). Local lamb is
served with white beans. Thin
buckwheat pancakes (*crêpes*) are
popular as snacks or dessert.

Burgundy Its fruity red wines are
used in such culinary classics as *coq
au vin* and *boeuf bourguignon*.
Parsleyed ham (*jambon persillé*) and
snails cooked in white wine and garlic
are other typical dishes.

Languedoc (Montpellier) Often
similar to that of Provence plus its
own fish dishes.

Lyon area This is often regarded as
the heartland of French cuisine,
where the humble pig's trotter, or a
hot garlic sausage, becomes a major
delicacy. *Quenelles de brochet* (pike
mousse), *poularde demi-deuil* (chicken
with truffles) and *ragoût d'écrevisses*
(crayfish stew) are other well-known
dishes.

Normandy (Rouen) The rich
Norman cuisine makes plentiful use
of cream and butter, and sometimes
of local cider or calvados too, for
preparing veal, chicken and fish in
many subtle ways. Caen is famous for
its tripe, and Rouen for its duck with
cherries.

Provence/Côte d'Azur (Marseille,
Nice, Cannes) The cream and butter
used in so much northern cooking is
replaced by olive oil in the south,
where the accent is on garlic and
fresh local herbs. This is true notably
of the spicy cuisine of Provence, with
its rich, garlicky fish stews
(*bouillabaisse* and *bourride*) and the
more everyday *soupe de poissons* (fish
soup). Popular meat dishes are
agneau de Sisteron (mountain lamb
with herbs), rabbit in a mustard
sauce, and chicken or frogs' legs
à la provençale (with a garlic-
and-tomato sauce). The Nice area
has its own special dishes, such as
ravioli, anchovy tart and *salade
niçoise*.

Our recommended restaurants
Full entries have been given to those
places judged most suitable for
business entertaining. The first
priority has been put on the quality
of the food, for that is where the
French put it: but well-spaced tables,
comfort, good service and smart
decor have also been taken into
account.

Under "Good but casual" are
listed some further choices suitable
for less formal business meals, plus a
few simpler but attractive places.
The price symbols denote the
following:

- F up to 180Fr
- F/ 180–230Fr
- F// 230–300Fr
- F/// 300–400Fr
- F//// 400–500Fr
- F///// over 500Fr

These reflect the price at the time of
going to press of a typical *à la carte*
meal, including coffee, service, and
half a bottle of one of the more
modest wines on the list. Most
restaurants will offer at least one and
sometimes several fixed-price menus,
which will be much cheaper than the
à la carte.

Bars and cafés
Cocktail bars are largely confined to
the better hotels, and are usually
comfortable and elegant. Individual
bars, smaller, darker and more
crowded, are found in bigger towns:
often they are the trendy rendezvous
of young people.

The usual French social meeting-
place, for other than a meal, is not
the bar but the café: these are
ubiquitous, and are of all kinds from
the smart to the squalid. Usually they
have tiny tables and upright chairs
and are not very comfortable, but
their pavement terraces make them
pleasant on a fine day, even if traffic
noise can be tiresome. There is waiter
service at the tables, but the same
drinks will be a little cheaper if
ordered standing up at the counter.
Cafés serve every kind of drink –
coffee, tea, wine by the glass, beer,

aperitifs, juices, mineral water – and sometimes light lunches too. There are no laws regulating hours and they can be open any time: most close at 1am or midnight, though in city centres some stay open till 1am or later. Children are admitted and are frequently seen sitting with their parents, even late in the evening; but minors cannot be served alcoholic drinks.

A few wine bars and so-called "pubs" have appeared in recent years. The latter are more like brasseries, for they usually serve light meals, along with beers, whiskies and other drinks.

Vintage chart

A chart which dictates good and bad years for wine is inevitably inexact because it denies the possibility of exceptions: a talented producer can sometimes make better wine in a so-called "bad" year than his less able neighbour in a "good" one. However, a vintage chart does provide some guidelines.

Very good years are indicated by *
Years to avoid are given in *italics* at the end of each list
Too young (n) indicates those wines which are not yet ready for drinking; (w) indicates those wines which are ready for drinking but which will improve. Remember that in France the tendency is to drink red Bordeaux and red Burgundy when it is comparatively young, and the French seem to neglect older vintages of Alsace, which can be tremendous.

Red
Bordeaux
Médoc, Graves 87(n) 86*(n) 85*(n) 83*(n) 82*(n) 81(w) 80 79 78*(w) 76 75 71 70* 66* 62* 61* 59* 55* 53* 52* 49* 47* 45* 28*; *77 74 72*
St-Emilion, Pomerol 87(n) 86*(n) 85*(n) 83(n) 82(n) 81 80 79 78* 76 75 71 70* 66* 64* 62* 61* 59* 55* 53* 52* 49* 47* 45* 28*; *77 74 72*
Lesser châteaux 87(n) 86(n) 85(n) 83(w) 82(w) 81 80 79 78; *84 80*
Burgundy
Côte d'Or 87(n) 86(n) 85*(n) 83(w) 82 80 79 78* 76 72 71* 70 69* 66* 64* 62* 61* 59* 53* 49* 47* 45*; *84 81 77 75 74*
Beaujolais 87(w) 85 83 81 78; *84*
Rhône
Côte Rôtie, Hermitage 87(n)

86(n) 85*(n) 83*(n) 82(w) 80 79 78* 76 72 71* 70* 64* 61*; *84 77*
Châteauneuf-du-Pape 87(n) 86(n) 85(n) 83 81 78*; *77*
Southwest (eg *Cahors*) 86(n) 85(w) 83(w) 82 80 79 78; *84*
Provence (eg *Bandol*) 86(n) 85(n) 83(w) 82*(w) 81 80 79 78
Loire (eg *Chinon*) 86 85 83 82 78

White
Bordeaux
Top dry Graves 87(n) 86*(n) 85*(n) 83*(n) 82* 81 80 78* 76* 75* 71* 70*
Sauternes 86(n) 85(n) 83*(n) 81 80* 78 76* 75 71 70 67* 62* 59*; *84 77 74 72*
Burgundy
Côte d'Or 87(n) 86(n) 85*(w) 83 82 79 78* 75 73* 71* 70 69* 67* 66* 64* 62* 61*; *77 74 72*
Chablis 87(n) 86*(w) 85 84 83 82 81* 80 79 78* 75* 71* 70; *77 74 72*
Mâcon 87 86 85 83 82; *84*
Rhône
North 87(n) 86(w) 85* 83* 82 81 80 78* 71* 70*
Loire
Dry 87 86 85 83; *84*
Sweet (eg Coteaux du Layon) 85* 83* 82 79 78 76* 69* 64*; *84 80*
Alsace 87 86 85* 83* 81 79 76* 71* 67*
Champagne 83(n) 82*(w) 81(w) 79* 78 76 75* 73 71 70*

Information sources

In your own country

The overseas section of your own country's Department of Trade should be able to provide information and advice on doing business in France. The French embassy in your country may have a commercial section and there may be a branch of the French chamber of commerce. The *French Chamber of Commerce in Great Britain* is at Knightsbridge House, 197 Knightsbridge, London SW7 1RB ☎ (01) 225 5250 ⓉⓍ 269132. Among the eleven chambers of commerce in the USA are: *French American Chamber of Commerce*, 509 Madison Ave, Suite 1900, NY 10022 ☎ (212) 371-4466 ⓉⓍ 6720504 and the *Los Angeles Chapter*, 6399A Wilshire Blvd, Suite 1018, CA 90048 ☎ (213) 651-4741

If you want to set up business in France, useful contacts can be made with the overseas representatives of *DATAR*, the French government development agency (see below). They can provide information on appropriate locations in France, financial incentives, and joint-venture partners in both the industrial and service sectors. There are offices in London, New York, Chicago, Los Angeles and other financial centres.

For general information about travelling to and within France, contact the *French National Tourist Office*, which has offices in over 34 countries.

Local information

Chambers of commerce There are over 150 chambers of commerce in France, at least one for every *département*. They represent and promote member companies, as well as providing information.
Main reference libraries usually have a copy of business directories such as the French edition of *Kompass*.
Other organizations The following organizations are also useful sources

of information.
DATAR (*Délégation à l'Aménagement du Territoire et à l'Action Régionale*), 1 ave Charles-Floquet, 75007 Paris ☎ 47 83 61 20 ⓉⓍ 200970. Monitors the development of France and coordinates the work of various government bodies at national and local level. DATAR can provide grants and advice on obtaining corporate and business tax exemption. A network of associate offices (*commissariats à l'industrialisation*) exists among which are those with responsibility for the West, Normandy, the North, the Lorraine and South Central respectively. These are based in Nantes, Rouen, Lille, Metz and Clermont Ferrand. They work closely with regional development authorities.
CNPF (*Conseil National du Patronat Français*) (National Council of French Employers), 31 ave Pierre-1er-de-Serbie, 75116 Paris ☎ 47 23 61 58. Produces a biennial directory (*annuaire*) (Editions Techniques Professionelles). Present cost is 450Fr. The library may be used on prior request.
Ministére du Commerce et l'Artisanat et des Services, 41 quai Branly, 75007 ☎ 45 50 71 11. Can provide free copies of the trade fairs handbook *Foires et Salons agrés et autorisés* to nonresident foreign business executives. Present *Imprimerie Nationale* price is 42Fr.
Conseils régionaux (regional governments) offer grants, low interest loans and help with the acquisition of land or buildings.
Tourist information There are some 500 tourist information centres in France. Larger towns have an *Office de Tourisme*, usually with a salaried director. *Syndicats d'Initiative* are generally found in smaller places and are staffed by volunteers. *Accueil de France* tourist offices can assist personal callers with hotel reservations in the same town or in other towns belonging to the network, which include all the cities

covered in this guide except for
Monaco, Montpellier and Rennes.
Other tourist offices can usually
indicate which hotels might have
rooms available.

The international "i" symbol is
used; alternatively there may be signs
for *Information, Office du Tourisme* or
Syndicat d'Initiative.

Shopping

Non-food shops are open from 9 or
9.30 to 6 or later from Monday or
Tuesday to Saturday. The smaller
shops tend to shut for lunch from 12
to 2, or from 12 to 4 in the south.
Food shops may open as early as
7 and stay open on Sunday mornings,
closing on Monday instead. Large
department stores open from 9.30 to
6.30, Tuesday to Saturday, but most
in Paris open all day on Monday.
Hypermarkets stay open until 10 at
night, as do some department stores
on certain days of the week.

The big names of the Paris
department stores are *Galeries
Lafayette* and *Au Printemps*, both in
the boulevard Haussmann, 9e.
Fashion is their forte but both stores
have a wide-ranging selection of
other goods and excellent *parfumeries.*
Monoprix and *Prisunic*, found
throughout France, are their cheaper
(and more downmarket) subsidiaries.
Hypermarkets are now well
established all over France, usually
on the edge of towns.

On substantial purchases visitors
may be able to claim exemption from
TVA, the French value-added tax.
The minimum purchase price to
qualify for an exemption is 2,400Fr
for EC residents, 1,200Fr for other
nationals. The discounts, which
range from 13% to 23%, are granted
by certain shops only. The best bets
are department stores or large shops
catering to foreigners. Usually you
pay the full amount and the discount
is sent to you (or your bank) in due
course. Non-EC nationals should
present the relevant forms and show
the purchases to the customs official
on leaving France. If you live inside

the EC, the papers are dealt with by
customs when you arrive in your
home country. In some cases the tax
you have to pay at customs will
cancel out the saving you made on
the TVA.

Crime

The highest incidence of crime in
France is in and around the large
cities and along the Côte d'Azur.
Marseille is notorious as the city of
heroin, thieves and prostitutes, and
the south coast has been the scene of
a number of violent crimes and
numerous petty thefts.

In Paris, mugging and theft are on
the increase, and many of the
offenders are groups of children too
young to be prosecuted. But as a
traveller in France you are unlikely to
encounter crime if you take the usual
precautions. Avoid deserted city
districts and red-light areas after
dark. Keep valuables in your hotel
safe and wallets well hidden from
potential pickpockets, especially in
public areas like the Paris Métro.
Women should keep an eagle eye on
handbags, particularly in Paris.
Cheques, cash and cards should be
kept separate. Car break-ins are
common and valuables should never
be left inside. In rural France you
have little to worry about though it is
still wise to keep the car locked and
take out valuables.

If you are robbed ring the police
(☎ 17) immediately or go to the
nearest police station, either the
commissariat de police or, in the
country, *la gendarmerie.* The
telephone numbers are listed at the
beginning of local directories. Failing
that, you can always try the
mairie/hôtel de ville (town hall) where
you can get general assistance. Loss
of a passport should be reported first
to the police, then to the nearest
consulate. Lost credit cards or
traveller's cheques should be reported
to the issuer or its local
representative. See *Paris: Local
resources* for the telephone numbers
to call for AE, DC, MC, and V.

The police

The average French policeman (colloquially known as a *flic*) is a serious and unsmiling individual. His powers are somewhat arbitrary and he can hold you in custody for 48 hours without charge. There are three main types of police: the *Police Nationale* and *Gendarmerie Nationale* who make up the large part of the police force and the *Compagnies Republicaines de Sécurité* or riot police, also responsible for duties such as motorway patrols and mountain rescue.

As a business traveller you are unlikely to experience a brush with the law, except possibly over a driving offence. On-the-spot fines for drinking and driving or speeding are steep and must be paid in cash.

If you are arrested

Your rights as a detainee are not as clearly defined or as easily enforceable as, say, in Britain. Unless your French is perfect it is best to explain that you do not understand or speak the language. If you are arrested, ask to telephone the nearest consulate and request one of the staff to come to the police station, who can advise you about your rights and provide a list of lawyers. If you are accused of a serious offence it may prove difficult or impossible to get bail. Penalties for the possession of narcotics, even small quantities of soft drugs, can be very severe. The same is true of small offences of fraud such as cheque and credit card crimes.

Embassies

All the embassies listed below are in Paris. Many countries also maintain consulates in Paris or other major French cities, among them Britain, Canada, Denmark, Ireland, the Netherlands, Sweden and the USA.
Australia 4 rue Jean-Rey, 75015 ☎ 45 75 62 00.
Austria 12 rue Edmond Valentin, 75007 ☎ 47 05 27 17
Belgium 9 rue Tilsitt, 75017

☎ 43 80 61 00
Canada 35 ave Montaigne, 75008 ☎ 47 23 01 01
Denmark 77 ave Marceau, 75116 ☎ 47 23 54 20
Finland 39 Quai d'Orsay, 75007 ☎ 47 05 35 45
Greece 17 rue Auguste Vacquerie, 75016 ☎ 47 23 72 28
Ireland 4 rue Rude, 75116 ☎ 45 00 20 87
Italy 47 rue de Varenne, 75007 ☎ 45 44 38 90
Japan 7 ave Hoche, 75008 ☎ 47 66 02 22
Netherlands 7 rue Eblé, 75007 ☎ 43 06 61 88
New Zealand 9 rue Léonardo de Vinci, 75116 ☎ 45 00 24 11
Norway 28 rue Bayard, 75008 ☎ 47 23 72 78
Portugal 9 rue Noisiel, 75016 ☎ 47 27 35 29
Spain 13 ave George V, 75008 ☎ 47 23 61 83
Sweden 17 rue Barbet-de-Jouy, 75007 ☎ 45 55 92 15
Switzerland 142 rue de Grenelle, 75007 ☎ 45 50 34 46
UK 35 rue du Faubourg-St-Honoré, 75008 ☎ 42 66 91 42
USA 2 ave Gabriel, 75008 ☎ 42 96 12 02
West Germany 13 ave Franklin Roosevelt, 75008 ☎ 43 59 33 51
Yugoslavia 54 rue de la Faisanderie, 75016 ☎ 45 04 05 05

Health care

The level of health care available in France is in general as good of that of the UK or the USA though the difference between the standard in cities (which is usually excellent) and that in the provinces (which is comparatively poor) is more pronounced. More of the national budget is spent on health than on either education or defence and the number of doctors has increased dramatically over the last 20 years. Technical expertise and equipment are as modern as you will find anywhere in the world and the quality of the state-run hospitals is as good as that of many of the private establishments. Many people opt for private treatment in hospitals and clinics since, under the social security system, 80–100% of the costs are reimbursed.

Like many other countries France has seen a fitness boom in the last few years. Jogging and work-outs in gymnasiums are becoming as popular as *le cyclisme*, though since this is France, the clothes are just as crucial as the actual sport or activity. Spa treatment is widely available (much of it is paid for by the state) and acupuncture and homeopathy are increasingly popular. Smoking is on the decline although it is still more widespread than in most other European counties; tobacco is a state monopoly and the warnings against it are less apparent than in other countries.

If you fall ill

Visitors taking drugs or medicines or suffering from a long-standing complaint or disease should take a prescription or validating letter from a doctor giving treatment details, preferably in French. If you fall ill you can seek treatment from a pharmacist, doctor, specialist or hospital.

Pharmacies, identified by a green cross, are a useful source of first aid and medical advice. In addition to apothecary-like skills of homoeopathy and mushroom identification, French pharmacists are well qualified to advise on ailments. They will take your blood pressure or a urine sample (usually for a small fee) and supply a far wider range of medicines over the counter than are available without prescription in Britain or the USA. They may also be willing to recommend a doctor. In main cities there are 24hr pharmacies; elsewhere they stay open on a rotating schedule which is usually displayed on the pharmacy doors. Do not confuse the *pharmacie* with the *droguerie* which supplies only household goods.

Seeing a doctor Medical practitioner standards are as high as those in the UK or the USA. Most doctors are specialists rather than general practitioners, and there is nothing preventing you going to a specialist direct. If you need a doctor consult your hotel or the local pharmacy, or look in the yellow pages under *Médecins*. A consulate will be able to give you telephone numbers of English-speaking doctors. Foreigners not accustomed to French habits may be surprised by the standard rectal thermometers and the fact that many medicines come in suppository form, even for headaches and sore throats.

Emergency treatment In emergencies, dial ☎ 17 (police) or ☎ 18 (fire brigade) for an ambulance. Every city (or large town) has a *Service d'Aide Médicale d'Urgence* or SAMU, whose number is listed in the front of the local telephone directory. The Paris SAMU number is ☎ 45 67 50 50 and the city's 24hr visiting doctor service (SOS médicins) is ☎ 47 07 77 77. Unless your French is good ask someone else to make the call, or call the English-speaking operator ☎ 19, wait for the tone then dial ☎ 3313 and ask for the *bureau anglais*. At large hotels doctors on call usually speak English.

Dental treatment The French dental service works in exactly the same way as medical treatment. Emergency dental care is available throughout France – see the front page of the local telephone directory. The Paris number for SOS emergency dental service is ☎ 43 37 51 00.

Paying for treatment

Members of the EC who are permanently resident outside France are entitled to French social security medical treatment on the same basis as French nationals. The cover provided is not fully comprehensive and the bureaucratic procedures at both ends (although recently simplified) are tedious. Most business travellers will prefer to take out

insurance, which should cover the cost of emergency repatriation.
Costs A very brief doctor's consultation costs 80Fr at the very least. Specialists charge what they like and their fees vary widely. The cost of hospital and medical care is around 1,000Fr a day.

Communications

The postal and telephone services in France are both run by the state-controlled *Postes, Télégraphes-Téléphones* or PTT (pronounced "pay tay tay"). Massive investment and political commitment have revolutionized telecommunications, and the system is now one of the most advanced in the world. The mail service, though very regular, is less impressive. Letters can take several days to arrive within France and often well over a week to arrive in the USA or UK. There are, however, express services which can guarantee speedier delivery.

Telephones

The improvement in the French telephone system since the late 1960s is quite dramatic. The network is now almost completely automated and internationally linked. Over 90% of householders now have a telephone and 9 out of 10 applicants have a new one installed in less than a fortnight. In 1985 every telephone number in France was changed overnight to give greater access and more numbers. From 70 zones, the country was divided into two: Paris and the rest of the country. The only codes you need now are 16-1 if telephoning Paris and 16 if telephoning out of Paris. All telephone numbers throughout the country are now eight digits. The Minitel system, used by businesses, post offices and an increasing number of private homes acts as a directory inquiry system. The number of public telephones has increased substantially and most are equipped for international calls. A few of the old-fashioned *taxiphones*, particularly in bars, only take *jetons*,

or tokens (bought at the counter). The cost of calls depends on the time of day. Reduced rates for USA and Canada apply between 8pm and 10am and all day Sundays and public holidays. To the rest of the EC, reduced rates apply between 9.30pm and 8am, Monday to Friday, 2pm to 8am Saturday and all day on Sundays and holidays. Public telephones take coins of 50 centimes, 1, 5 and occasionally 10 francs. Unused coins are returned at the end of a call.

To make a call, lift the receiver, wait for the continuous high-pitched dialling tone and insert the money before you dial. If you are calling within France you will hear long bleeps for the ringing tone, or fast short ones if the telephone is engaged. International calls can be made from any of the grey metallic boxes, all of which give instructions and list international dialling codes: dial ☎ 19, wait for the continuous tone, then dial the country code, followed by the area code (minus the prefix 0), then the local number. A simpler and no more costly method is to make the call from a post office where you are allocated a booth and put straight through to the number required. Payment is made after the call is finished. If you are making a number of long-distance calls it is worth buying a telephone card, to be used in call boxes displaying the *Télécarte* sign. You can buy these at post offices, railway stations, and some tobacconists (tabacs) and cafés. Hotels levy high surcharges on calls made from rooms. Restaurants and cafés can also charge what they like. There are no reversed charge/collect calls in France.

The French cite numbers two by two rather than in individual units; for example 23 13 44 30 will be given as *vingt-trois, treize, quarante-quatre, trente* unless you ask for the numbers to be cited *chiffre par chiffre* (digit by digit).

Useful numbers are *operator services* ☎ 13, *directory inquiries* ☎ 12 *international code* ☎ 19 33 plus country code, *talking clock* ☎ 3699, *morning call* ☎ 3688. Other numbers for, say, information on local weather are listed in the telephone directories. **Telegrams** can be sent from a post office or by telephone (24hr).

Telex and fax

Telex facilities are available in the central post offices of most major towns and are very common in offices and big hotels. The public telex offices at 7 pl de la Bourse and 7 rue Feydeau, 75002 Paris are open 24 hours a day. Fax is fast on the increase. The electronic Minitel system, with news and other services, is widely used in offices, homes and post offices.

Mail

Letters and parcels sent via the PTT nearly always arrive safely but prompt delivery can be guaranteed only by the use of one of the special express services (see below). Stamps are available at any post office, but it is normally quicker and more convenient to buy them from either your hotel, a *tabac*, or the yellow coin-operated vending machines outside some post offices. Letters up to 20g cost 2.40Fr within France or to any EC country except Britain, Ireland and Denmark, which are 2.50Fr. Letters to European countries automatically go by air mail; they will go surface mail to other countries unless you specify otherwise. Air-mail letters up to 5g to the USA cost 4.05Fr.

Mail can be posted from hotels, post offices or from the yellow letter boxes outside *tabacs*. Parcels addressed abroad and weighing up to 1kg (or 2kg at letter-post rate) must bear a green customs label to be accepted by the post office. Large parcels are accepted at the main post office in each town, air mail up to 10kg or 20kg depending on destination, surface mail up to 5kg and up to a certain size, beyond which they may be sent via French Railways.

Main post offices are usually open on weekdays from 8 to 7 (smaller offices close between 12 and 2) and from 8 to 12 on Saturdays. The main Paris post office at 52 rue du Louvre 75001 is open 24 hours.

The fastest way to send letters or parcels in France or abroad is through the *Chronopost* system. Within France packages up to 25kg are guaranteed to arrive at their destination within 24 hours and mail sent at the end of the day will arrive the following morning. Mail sent to EC countries may arrive within 24 hours, depending on the country. The maximum time for delivery to any country is supposed to be 72 hours. The costs (which are high) cover standard insurance for theft, loss or damage. Registered mail, within France and abroad, guarantees evidence of posting and compensation for loss or damage. The cost is 15.20Fr within France, 17.10Fr for EC countries. SNCF operates an express package and parcel service (SERNAM) within France and to European countries. The Special Express service operates from door to door, the Direct Express from station to station. Charges are made according to speed of delivery, distance and whether the package is collected and delivered at either end. Air Inter also provides an express freight service, guaranteeing airport to airport delivery within 4 hours, plus optional delivery (at extra cost) at the other end.

Some international dialling codes

Before dialling the country's code dial 19. The figures in brackets indicate how many hours the country is ahead or behind Central European Time (one hour ahead of Greenwich Mean Time). In Mar–Sep, clocks are put forward one hour.

Australia	61	(+7–9hr)
Austria	43	
Belgium	32	
Canada	1	(-4hr 30min–9hr)

Denmark	45		New Zealand	64 (+11hr)
Germany West	49		Norway	47
Greece	30 (+1hr)		Pakistan	92 (+4hr)
Hong Kong	852 (+7hr)		Portugal	351 (-1hr)
India	91 (+4hr 30min)		Singapore	65 (+7hr)
Ireland	353 (-1hr)		Spain	34
Israel	972 (+1hr)		Sweden	46
Italy	39		Switzerland	41
Japan	81 (+8hr)		UK	44 (-1hr)
Netherlands	31		USA	1 (-6–11hr)

Conversion charts

France uses the metric system of measurement. In this guide, metric measurements are always used except in the case of distances, which are given in both miles and kilometres.

Length

centimeters (cm)	cm or in	inches (in)
2.54	= in 1 cm =	0.394
5.08	2	0.787
7.62	3	1.181
10.16	4	1.575
12.70	5	1.969
15.24	6	2.362
17.70	7	2.756
20.32	8	3.150
22.86	9	3.543
25.40	10	3.937
50.80	20	7.874
76.20	30	11.811
101.60	40	15.748
127.00	50	19.685

Mass (weight)

kilograms (kg)	kg or lb	pounds (lb)
0.454	= lb 1 kg =	2.205
0.907	2	4.409
1.361	3	6.614
1.814	4	8.819
2.268	5	11.023
2.722	6	13.228
3.175	7	15.432
3.629	8	17.637
4.082	9	19.842
4.536	10	22.046
9.072	20	44.092
13.608	30	66.139
18.144	40	88.185
22.680	50	110.231

Distance

kilometers (km)	km or miles	miles
1.609	= mi 1 km =	0.621
3.219	2	1.243
4.828	3	1.864
6.437	4	2.485
8.047	5	3.107
9.656	6	3.728
11.265	7	4.350
12.875	8	4.971
14.484	9	5.592
16.093	10	6.214
32.187	20	12.427
48.280	30	18.641
64.374	40	24.855
80.467	50	31.069

Volume

liters	liters or US galls	US galls
3.79	= l 1 gall =	0.26
7.58	2	0.52
11.37	3	0.78
15.16	4	1.04
18.95	5	1.30
22.74	6	1.56
26.53	7	1.82
30.32	8	2.08
34.11	9	2.34
37.90	10	2.60
75.80	20	5.20
113.70	30	7.80
151.60	40	10.40
189.50	50	13.00

Temperature

°F: 32 40 50 60 70 75 85 95 105 140 175 212
°C: 0 5 10 15 20 25 30 35 40 60 80 100

Index

INDEX